McCartney

THE BIOGRAPHY

McCartney

THE BIOGRAPHY

CHET FLIPPO

SIDGWICK & JACKSON
LONDON

ACKNOWLEDGMENTS

Special thanks go to many people, especially Jim Fitzgerald, my editor at Doubleday, and a number of present and past employees of MPL, EMI, Capitol, CBS, and Rogers and Cowan, who asked to remain anonymous. Others who greatly helped include Timothy White, Charles M. Young, John Wiener, Eliot Mintz, Yoko Ono, Mark Hurst, Marianne Velmans, Michael Ochs, Ben Fong-Torres, Bill Carter, Roberg Sabbag, Kinky Friedman, Vivien Sheldon, Peter Jenner, Andy Kershaw, Laura Sanderson-Healy, Mark Ellen, David Hepworth, the staff of Q *Magazine* of London, Mick Brown, Neil McAleer, John Fielding, Roland W. McIntosh, Wilfred M. Mercer, Joseph Angier, The Liverpool Irregulars, Winston X. Huxtable, Clive Darlington, Twiggs Havisham, Tom Miller, Nancy Milford, the Writers Room in New York City, the BBC, and the staff of the British Library, especially the British Newspaper Library at Colindale.

First published in Great Britain in 1988
by Sidgwick and Jackson Limited
1 Tavistock Chambers, Bloomsbury Way
London WC1A 2SG

First published in the United States of America
in 1988 by Doubleday and Company Inc

ISBN 0 283 99768 0

Printed in Great Britain by
Butler & Tanner Ltd, Frome, Somerset

For Dr. Winston O'Boogie
and Paul Ramon

Contents

Introduction

IN the hallowed British Museum there is an exhibit these days that is dedicated to Lennon and McCartney. In reality it's not all that much of an exhibit: a double-coffin-sized wooden display glass holding boyhood pictures of the Fab Twosome and the original handwritten lyrics to "Help!", "Yesterday," "I Want to Hold Your Hand," "Ticket to Ride," and "Michelle." Boyish handwriting on ruled notepads. A letter from John to Stu Sutcliffe. Little scrawled messages from a bygone era.

It may not be an elaborate display, but what is astonishing is people's reactions to it. Stand nearby and eavesdrop as the museumgoers happen upon the little unheralded display case. Fully half of them start singing or at least humming one of their fave Beatle songs as they glimpse for the first time the humble origins of a phenomenon that truly shook the world. Now and then a tear wells up in the corner of an eye of someone who is remembering too much too suddenly in a wellspring of memories that are triggered by these little evocations of a happier day. It's truly a shock to suddenly turn away from Chaucer and Shakespeare and encounter icons from your adolescence.

I had gone with a London editor to the museum. He had known the Beatles, although—as he was wisely quick to admit—no one *really* knows them well. The Lennon–McCartney display at the museum had oddly moved him, though, stirring up memories and associations that he thought were long forgotten. After drinks that evening (and the inevitable playing of *Sgt. Pepper* and *Abbey Road),* he decided to take me on a driving tour of "The Beatles' London."

There isn't too much left of their presence. The scandalously psychedelic Apple Boutique on Baker Street is now a travel firm. Apple Corps no longer inhabits the elegant townhouse at 3 Savile Row. There is, of course, the most famous remaining landmark, the zebra crossing at EMI's Abbey Road Studios at 3 Abbey Road. And not far away is what was the Beatle headquarters when they were still functioning. We turn off Circus Road onto the quiet block-long Cavendish Avenue. The CAVENDISH AVE-NUE NW8 sign at the corner is covered with handwritten messages: MCCARTNEY RULES! PRESS ON, MATE! PAUL IS GOOD, BUT CLAPTON IS GOD! We slow down at midblock, outside Paul's house at number 7. The house is a three-story Georgian, hidden behind a brick wall and tall trees. There is no number on the large iron gate. A Paul fan is aiming her Instamatic at a graffito on the gate that reads: CLAPTON IS GOD!

My friend brings his car to a halt and points to the house with its darkened windows. *"Lord* McCartney lives there," he says, with no little sarcasm in his voice. "Oh yes. He'll be a *sir.* That one's locked in. But the *Lord* is the one that he wants. And you know what? He'll get it." Knighthood, he means, of course.

> The singers with the greatest sales of any group has been the Beatles . . . The all-time Beatles sales by May 1984 have been estimated by EMI at over 1,000 million discs and tapes . . . In terms of sales of single records, the most successful of all song writers has been Paul McCartney, formerly of the Beatles and Wings. Between 1962 and Jan. 1, 1978, he wrote jointly or solo 43 songs which sold one million or more records.
>
> —*Guinness Book of World Records,*
> 1986

Paul McCartney may be the most successful songwriter in history and one of the richest men in the world, but he has his certain priorities. One such priority was learned by a senior executive of Paul's company, McCartney Productions Limited. This MPL executive was summoned to Paul's farm in Scotland to deal with an emergency. It is not an easy trip to get to Paul's

High Park Farm (next to Paul's Low Park Farm, purchased to discourage sight-seers from gaining any access to the McCartney acreage). But the MPL executive got there by four-wheel drive across the rocky scrubland. And he asked what the emergency was.

It was this. The "senior sheep" at High Park Farm had begun to present a bit of a problem. A flock of the gentle creatures had come with the farm, since the land was so rough that only sheep could survive on it. But one afternoon, as Linda McCartney was serving up a sizzling platter of mutton to Paul and their little ones, Linda happened to look out the window upon a Biblical scene of little lambs gamboling about and nuzzling their mothers and her heart was touched. So the McCartney brood decided to eschew eating their brothers and sisters of the animal world. That is, they became vegetarians.

The only problem was that they had all these sheep. And they kept on tending them and raising them and then these sheep kept having lambs and the lambs grew up. Then they became middle-aged sheep and then downright geriatric sheep. And the biggest problem that Paul discovered was that these senior sheep had ground their teeth down to the very nubs. They were having a terrible time trying to gum their alfalfa and oats. They were going to starve to death.

So Paul summoned his MPL man up from London to deal with the crisis. The MPL man ended up going out to the barn with an ordinary household blender and blending up a mixture of oats and alfalfa for the toothless old sheep.

No matter that the executive had to temporarily abandon MPL, which administers Paul's extensive publishing copyrights—fifty thousand songs, by one estimate, encompassing Broadway, pop, and rock—which have made him one of the richest men in the world. The senior sheep were all that mattered to him.

Paul McCartney does not live like one of the richest men in the world—other than to make his employees feed his sheep. He and Linda have raised their four children—Heather, Mary, Stella, and James—completely out of the public eye. They live mostly on their rambling farm in Sussex, although there is the large farm in Scotland, the Cavendish Avenue house in London, and other reported properties on Long Island, in Arizona, and elsewhere. Housekeeping in the various McCartney homes has been described as "casual" at best. Paul is a concerned parent, who voiced sympathy with the PMRC's campaign in the United States for essentially censoring rock 'n' roll. Paul said he thought a watchdog group was not a bad idea.

One day in 1985 Paul got into an argument with a striking teacher at East Sussex School, where he had just delivered his son James. Paul tore up the leaflet that teacher Brian Moses handed him and lectured him about teachers going on strike.

There are no superstar trappings in the McCartney country homes: all of the gold and platinum records and awards are up on the walls of MPL Communications, an elegant five-story Georgian townhouse at number 1 Soho Square in London (and, remember, Paul owns the only "Rhodium Disc" ever awarded: It was given to Paul by the *Guinness Book of World Records* because rhodium is the rarest metal there is).

In the soft twilight, if you stand in just the right position outside MPL, you can almost hear some of the musical copyrights that Paul holds prisoner inside the building. A faint bit of ragtime, a scrap of showtime, a shout of early rock 'n' roll. Scott Joplin is paying for this building and so is Ira Gershwin and so is Buddy Holly. They're working for Paul, night and day: He owns them in death. Just as Michael Jackson owns Paul McCartney in life.

Paul, these days (early 1988), has finally started collaborating with someone other than his wife, with someone whose songwriting ability might match his own. His brief songwriting dalliance with Michael Jackson and his 1986 work with Eric Stewart on the album *Press to Play* notwithstanding, Paul has really trusted no one in a true musical partnership since he and John split up. He's finally started to come to grips with the fact that his Beatle years actually might have amounted to a great deal. He started writing with Elvis Costello, who would certainly qualify as a Beatle child in musical terms. And Paul actually said that writing with Costello reminded him of working with John in the old days. And, in a radical departure for Paul, he said that he would like to record some of John's earlier stuff because everyone else has recorded those songs "except me."

A word about this book: It was actually suggested by John Lennon in the early 1970s. I met John when he was freshly arrived in New York City and we knew each other only as ex-Beatle and reporter. After John became separated from Yoko, he spent a bit of time pursuing my editorial assistant and we subsequently started to socialize. After John mentioned his difficulties in legally staying in the United States, I started to investigate his legal status in this country. The Nixon administration was trying to have him deported and it became a very ugly case.

After I was able to obtain and publish (in *Rolling Stone)* a confidential memorandum from Senator Strom Thurmond to Attorney General John Mitchell that graphically spelled out the political reasons for Nixon's vendetta against Lennon, John opened up to me as a friend and we shared many conversations about his case, about himself, about the Beatles, about whatever.

I also went to court to sit with him about an unrelated matter, a lawsuit for many millions of dollars against him for an album he had supposedly agreed to make. By that time John, like all the Beatles, was so accustomed to lawsuits that he liked to hold his own little open court. During recesses and at lunch John loved to talk and to be listened to. At that time there was so little public or press interest in the Beatles that I was often the only reporter in the courtroom and the only one to invite John to lunch in nearby Chinatown.

At one point at lunch one day, I proposed to him the idea of doing a book about him and Paul. I was rhapsodizing about them being the new Rodgers and Hammerstein and all that and John just threw up his hands in disgust. "Shurrup!" he said, reverting to Liverpool scouse. "Paul's the one wants the book. Not me!"

John was actually charitable about Paul, praising some of the things he had written for the Beatles, admitting that Paul was the one who held the Beatles together until it was too late. All the press interest back then was in John, but John told me—How modest is this?—that Paul was worth a book first. (Since John garnered all the press then as the "hip" Beatle, who would have guessed that Paul actually had run the Beatles from *Sgt. Pepper* on?)

When John was murdered in 1980, I spent that night, the night of December 8, in the emergency room at Roosevelt Hospital, listening to John's fans and Beatles' fans express their grief. After that I packed away all my Lennon tapes and notebooks and rejected offers to write about him and the Beatles.

Later, for a book whose royalties were to go to an anti-handgun foundation, I wrote a remembrance of John that appeared as a chapter called "1976–80: The Private Years" in the book *The Ballad of John and Yoko.*

Years later, when all the Beatle stuff seemed to have simmered down, it was a good time to unpack some of those memories. Portions of this book are based on John's recollections. As he was the first to admit, Beatle history is a most inexact science. Almost everyone who was involved in the Beatle Project was at one time or another coasting on illegal drugs. As they will tell you—if they are still alive and can remember. Oral history is great until the people supplying it simply can't remember what went on.

The Beatles must remain unique in the fact that they were the most undocumented social phenomenon in recent history. Not after they became the Fab Four. But what went on before that is mostly uncharted. Only the odd newspaper ad took note of the Silver Beetles appearing somewhere.

No one kept journals (no one knew they would become what they became, after all). Even after the Beatles became what they became, no one kept a journal. Even after they all broke up and all became ex-Beatles, no one kept a journal. Business records were spotty and haphazard or lost entirely. Everything along the way was more or less inexact. And personal recollection, as welcome as it has been, is not necessarily a final arbiter of fact. On the other hand, every Beatle book that I have run across carries an invisible proprietary stamp of Beatle exactness. And no two sources agree for long about anything.

Accordingly, I have tried to sift the Beatle "facts" as best as possible, balancing a recent interview against the written account of an old one, weighing a yellowed newspaper clipping against a biased memory. For years, believe it or not, there raged a controversy in Beatle scholar circles over the date that John and Paul met for the first time. Not the day of the week, nor of the month: It was the *year* that no two people could decide upon. I don't pretend to be a Beatle scholar, but I found plenty of mistakes that had been accepted as gospel. Anyway, my aim was to tell the story of one of the most important and influential men in the history of rock 'n' roll, of pop music, and of all of the popular culture, for that matter.

—Chet Flippo
New York City
February 1988

Up on the Roof

THIS, after all they had been through together, was their mountaintop. This antenna-riddled and chimney-stacked asphalt and tar roof atop the elegant five-story Georgian mansion in London's patrician Savile Row that was Apple Corps was as far and as high as the Beatles would go. No farther and no higher. They had conquered the world—true. What they had wrought in popular culture could never be equaled—without a doubt.

But on this cold gray high noon of January 30, 1969, as the other three Beatles found themselves being prodded, cajoled, and coerced by Paul up onto this rooftop in London's bespoken tailor district for what would become their final performance together, the Beatles found themselves lacking any taste of triumph or of the glories that should have been theirs. There were only ashes in their mouths and the bitter residues of the bile that had been building up for a long time.

It was between Paul and John, of course, the two geniuses, the yin and the yang of the peculiar four-headed creature that the Beatles became. Many factors had contributed to their ever-widening split. It wasn't, as many had charged, just the intense-looking little Oriental woman who seemed to have became a permanent appendage on John's left side as they started threading their way through all the cables and lines that the movie and sound crews had snaked across the roof. Nor was it the straw-haired American woman with the Nikon attached to her face who was always half a step behind Paul.

It was many things. Both of them had had immense fame, of the most blinding intensity, thrust upon them before they had had a chance to really grow up. Whatever maturing either one of them managed to achieve was done in a weird goldfish bowl sort of life and now the both of them resented that. Also, the Beatles as an entity represented different things to them both. For Paul, it amounted to his whole life. His identity was wrapped up in being a Beatle. Now that the Beatles were turning into a rotting corpse, he refused to believe it, wouldn't allow it to happen.

He had been after the others for months to regroup and go back and tour together—or at the very least perform together. Performing music was his whole life. After approximately one thousand and four hundred live performances as the Beatles, the others were sick of it. Their last concert had been on August 29, 1966, at San Francisco's Candlestick Park. On the plane back to London, George had been the first to speak up. "Well, that's it. I'm not a Beatle anymore," he had said flatly.

Though no one knew it at the time, John was already thinking the same thing. For John, the Beatles had just been a horse to ride. One hell of a horse, for all that, but it had been his creation, a tribute to his genius. Once it ceased to be that and became a monster, an all-devouring freak beyond his control, he wanted no more of it. John had also, as he would do, over-excessed with his excesses. He had always been their leader in every way and had led the way in abusing alcohol, amphetamines, marijuana, and finally LSD. He later estimated that he had taken a thousand trips on LSD and finally it took him over and literally destroyed his ego. Throughout 1968 and into 1969 he was slowly trying to put himself back together: his two methods of choice being, first, the Maharishi Mahesh Yogi and second, Yoko Ono.

As John increasingly withdrew and ceased to be the Beatles' leader and simply lost interest, it was Paul of course who hurried to fill the vacuum. It was Paul who took charge of the various Beatle projects, of *Sgt. Pepper,* of the Magical Mystery Tour, of Apple Corps, of the *White Album (The Beatles),* and now of his current rooftop project.

Paul wanted literally to "Get Back," to go back to the way things had been before, when they were still just a little boys' club—albeit the most exclusive one in the world—and were having fun with music and wowing everybody.

Paul was sure that performing together again could cure all the ills of the group. The others resisted, accurately pointing out the fact that it was literally too dangerous for the four of them to get up on a stage together. Beatlemania had been a fearsome phenomenon and no one knew just how far it could run, just what the Beatle public might actually end up doing. Public safety would not allow the Beatles to appear in public.

As a reply to that, Paul actually had the loopy idea that the four of them could rename themselves Ricky and the Red Streaks and go out unannounced and play small college dates and dances and so on.

The others weren't having any of that. Paul did not realize that what was gone and could not be recaptured was the relationship that they had had, which had created the magic that was the Beatles. It wasn't just what he and John accomplished when they had still written together. It was what the four of them together came to represent that had been magical. That was lost. They had all fragmented and things had soured and disintegrated. A lot of things had happened since the days when the four of them had shared the small stages of the crowded cellar clubs of Liverpool and Hamburg and created a musical excitement that unbelievably, even after being diluted and tamed, captured the imagination of the world.

Now John and George groused privately that they were tired of being "Paul's sidemen." Only days before the ascension to the roof, George had angrily quit the group after a set-to with Paul and that had been kept a secret. He had been persuaded to return and here he was, plugging in his Fender yet again to back up Paul. George was wearing his Keds black high-top sneakers, baggy jeans, and a ratty thigh-length fur jacket.

To his right, John took the central microphone. Yoko finally disengaged herself from John's side and sat down a few feet away, next to the roof's low overhang. John, in granny glasses, his long hair and bushy sideburns buffeted by the wind, also wore a fur jacket. He was not terribly interested in the day's proceedings as things got under way.

Ringo hoisted himself down behind his drums just a few feet behind John, hefted his sticks, and beat out a tattoo on his toms.

Ringo, as ever, was pretty much removed from day-to-day Beatle politics. To his right was Billy Preston, the black American journeyman keyboard player who was signed to Apple Records.

The ringmaster saw that all was in readiness and then strapped on his beloved old violin-shaped Hofner bass and strode over to the microphone just to John's right. Paul looked bristling, with his bushy beard, thick long hair, dark suit, and black dress loafers. He jumped up and down to test the flooring. He hit the first notes and started singing, that sweet familiar voice already alerting passersby five stories down on Savile Row and in Regent Street that those wacky Beatles were up to something again.

Paul started singing the words to "Get Back," as John's and George's guitars and Ringo's drums and Preston's keyboard slid in under his voice. The cameras whirred and tape machines silently captured everything. They weren't just doing it for fun, the Beatles. No, what Paul had finally talked them all into was a combination film and recording session. Paul's philosophy about what would cure all that ailed the Beatles was if they could just "get back" to where they once belonged, all would again be well and the sun would shine once more. For him, getting back included a sort of mock documentary movie of the Beatles putting together a session and talking and bantering and eating and drinking together and rehearsing for a performance just like they used to do. The problem was, they didn't do that anymore and the cameras captured that. It captured more of the bickering than the bantering.

Paul wanted to believe that the final healing process would be a Beatle performance somewhere and that it would be captured on camera and would complete the film. Accordingly, he had actually planned shows, reserving the Roundhouse Theatre in Chalk Farm on two dates in December 1968 and on January 18, 1969. The others wouldn't do it.

As the days wore on, as did the rehearsing and the filming, tempers and patience wore down also. Paul wanted to know—dammit—just where would the others agree to play, then? Some serious and not-so-serious recommendations were made. The film's director, Michael Lindsay-Hogg, envisioned all of Africa as a suitable screen, with the Beatles "singing 'Hey Jude' nine thousand times all over Africa." Other ideas were a Roman amphitheater in Tunisia, in the middle of the Sahara desert, on a cruise liner, or in an asylum for the mentally ill. John favored the latter, he said slyly.

Finally Paul talked them into as safe a place as possible: their own Apple. At first they were going to rehearse in their basement studio, which Magic Alex, an Apple magician they had hired at great expense, had supposedly transformed into the world's state-of-the-art 72-track recording studio. Of course, as with all Apple projects, the studio sat unfinished as just another half-assed if well-intentioned mess. So they got EMI to send over mobile recording equipment and Paul pushed them up onto the roof. This would have to serve as the performance.

Even as he sang "Get Back," the song simply wasn't having the palliative results Paul had hoped for. Even though the song generally was coming across as a "get back" Beatles sermon, John and Yoko thought it was more of Paul's vicious sniping at Yoko. Get back to where Yoko belonged, they thought the message was.

The song, in fact, began as political satire, directed at England's immigration policies, particularly those restrictive to immigrants from Pakistan. Paul originally called the song "Don't Dig No Pakistanis."

At least he was in fine voice and despite the cold and the animosities lingering in the air, the Beatles' innate musicianship took over. They sounded simply great.

Down in the street heads turned as knots of people gathered and traffic ground to an impatient standstill. They could hear the Beatles, knew they were up there somewhere, but they couldn't see a blessed thing. Still, there were a great many Beatle-starved people in London, as there were all over the world. Even Savile Row had its share of the Beatle-hungry. After all, the group had not performed in England since May 1, 1966, and that had been a brief unannounced five-song appearance at the music newspaper *New Musical Express*'s Annual Poll Winners' Concert at the Empire Pool in Wembley and before that, the last London proper show had been on December 11, 1965, at the Astoria Cinema in Finsbury Park. There were a lot of people who missed their Beatles. And, all of a blessed sudden, here they were, raining that wonderful music down on them from somewhere in heaven, it seemed.

The workaday world, at least that portion of the workaday world within the sound of 100-decibel rock 'n' roll, stopped. There were smiles breaking out all over Savile Row. This wasn't exactly Swinging London again, but it was much like a visit from some very, very old friends who had been away for far too long.

There were grinches, to be sure. Those who could actually see the Beatles were people who had access to adjoining rooftops and those were, in the main, men in well-tailored suits who stood calmly with their arms folded, looking as bored as possible.

John, becoming a little more animated as things went on, next took the lead on his own "Don't Let Me Down" and there were puffs of frost popping from his mouth as he bit down on the words.

Then he and Paul got together, exchanging glances, on one of the few songs that they had truly written together, that they had sat down and traded lines on: "I've Got a Feeling." This was the first time in years, since before Beatlemania had set in, that one could actually watch and hear the Beatles at the same time and the combination was powerful. As in pre-hysteria days, pre-screaming days, Paul and John once again proved—as if they had a need to—that they possessed two of the most distinctive sets of pipes in all of music, in addition to their singular songwriting talents.

Down in the street the film crew they were paying for was taping a Slightly Annoyed Businessman, who was tightly saying, "This kind of music is very good in its place, but it's a bit of an imposition when it disrupts all the business in the area." Had he but known it, that Annoyed Businessman had brilliantly and succinctly summed up the whole of the history of the Beatles in one sour sentence. And on that cold gray day of January 30, everything finally came together for them and for the last time it still presented a smiling face to the public. The public squabbles and the bloodletting and the dirty laundry and the hair shirts and the name-calling, all of that was still behind Apple's closed doors.

Paul and John, singing together for the last time, next joined voices on John's first rock 'n' roll composition and the first one to bear their bound-in-blood imprimateur of Lennon–McCartney. "The One After 909" was pre-Beatles and it took John and Paul back to their early days together when both were still schoolboys.

Downstairs the film crews were setting up to film the arriving bobbies. Apple publicists would later claim that businessmen in the neighborhood filed so many complaints that the police were forced to move in and shut down the Beatles for a last time, just like in the good old days when the Establishment sought to crush the life out of rebellious rock 'n' rollers. Before rock 'n' rollers became the Establishment and were quite capable of crushing out their own lives, thank you, without any outside help. A chief complainant, they said, was the chief accountant at the Royal Bank of Scotland, one Stephen King, but Mr. King was not located in subsequent days to corroborate the publicity handouts.

Meanwhile the film crews were busy setting up reverse shots— that is, cops coming into Apple were being filmed from both sides of the door as they entered and so on. These are the sort of shots that require premeditation and are hardly the sort of flying filming associated with a sudden police bust. It was, after all, just a movie.

George then knelt at John's feet during "Dig a Pony."

Beatle assistant Mal Evans led the police up the stairs to the roof. More reverse setup shots going on. The cops came out onto the roof as John ended the song and sort of hung back, as if they were waiting for a signal.

Paul and John took the Beatles out forever, in their final seconds together as a live group, with a reprise of "Get Back." They were laughing together for the last time as the bobbies politely moved in and invited them to terminate the noise, please, sirs.

Paul improvised a few words: "Loretta, you been singin' on the roof again and that's bad. It'll get you arrested!" John delivered the tag line: "Thank you on behalf of the group and myself. I hope we passed the audition."

And that was it.

Down the stairwell they disappeared, each to his own private demons. And to his own private desires. Ringo just wanted to get along. George wanted some peace and quiet and to be left alone to pursue music the way he wanted to. John wanted to be John and to let his genius take its course. Paul wanted to keep the Beatles together, but only on his own terms and in his own image.

They got what they wanted, but they lost what they had.

Mother Mary

THE British council houses were always cold—bone-chilling cold. Living in one, in government-subsidized housing, was supposed to be a privilege because not everybody could have that luxury. Even so, these prefab, synth-construct, row house cubicles were but a poor excuse for a real substantial British brick house. But the council houses were the temporary answer to the post-World War II population increase.

Getting out of bed in the morning was only the second-coldest part of the day for Paul and his kid brother Mike. Putting those bare feet on the icy floor, rushing to get dressed and bundled off to school, that was bad. Especially since the McCartneys didn't have an indoor facility—or "loo," as they called it—until they moved to 20 Forthlin Road. No more frosty moons once they got to number 20.

But what was colder was the house after their mother died. The worst part was coming home from school in the afternoon. Before she was gone, Mother would have the house warm and toasty and cheerful and they would be greeted by warm hugs and the lovely kitchen with its spreading aromas of hot tea brewing and a warm little sweet something to go with it.

Then, abruptly, nothing. Coming home in the afternoon to a cold and silent and dark house was like death. That was why, after little Paul became Beatle Paul and could afford to buy a house for his father, the most important thing about the house was that it have central heat and wall-to-wall carpeting. They helped drive out the memories of those frigid mornings when he was left alone without his mother and also those dreadful afternoons without her. Even so, there wasn't enough central heat and wall-to-wall in the world to make up for Mother Mary's loss. After she was gone, nothing could or would ever warm the house again.

Paul's father was born on July 7, 1902, at number 8 Fishguard Street in the poor Everton district of Liverpool. He was christened into the Church of England simply as James McCartney. His parents were Joseph and Florence McCartney. Joseph was a tobacco cutter who had been born in Everton in 1866. His father was James McCartney II, a journeyman painter and plumber who was born in either Liverpool or Ireland. His father, in turn, was one James McCartney, upholsterer, whose origins disappear in the mists of Ireland.

James McCartney was one of nine children. The others were Joe (who died as an infant), a second Joe, Jack, Edie, Ann Alice (who also died as a child), Mill, a second Ann, and Jin.

As a child, growing up in Everton's rough streets, James learned the lessons and acquired the traits that would largely inform his son Paul later on: distrust of the church (James became a lifelong agnostic) and reliance on the self, the importance of close family ties and an attendant suspicion of strangers, keen appreciation of the value of a penny if not of a farthing, the joy and worth of a nice tune or melody as a little escape from life's everyday miseries.

Jim McCartney was attracted to music early on, even though at age ten he suffered a broken right eardrum in a street fall. He taught himself rudimentary piano on a secondhand NEMS (for North End Music Stores) piano the McCartneys got during World War I. Jim worked after school selling programs at the Theatre Royal. Ever-enterprising, he would pick up discarded programs at the end of a performance, take them home, and clean and iron them to be sold on the morrow.

Jim went to work with a "job for life" in Liverpool's thriving Cotton Exchange when he was fourteen. Even though he would later have his own little band, he knew better than to challenge life's realities by risking the known (hard work for a steady little income) for the unknown (the unknown vagaries of a musical life). The cotton firm of A. Hannay & Co. took him on as a sample boy for six shillings a week.

Over the next few years Jim applied himself to his job, eventually being promoted to salesman at the salary of five pounds a week. He also toyed with music on the side and became proficient at ragtime piano. He formed a group known as the Masked Melody Makers. Their trademark was the black masks they wore, but as they quickly discovered that perspiration caused the masks to bleed black dye, they switched to the more conventional dress of tuxedos. As Jim Mac's Jazz Band, they played background music for silent movies at the local cinemas and for dances at St. Catherine's Hall or Oak Hall. Their repertoire included "The Birth of the Blues," "Stairway to Paradise," and such McCartney originals as "Eloise."

Jim also enjoyed betting the horses—until his hobby caught up with him. He was in debt to the bookies and was brought up before Mr. Hannay at work to explain himself. He said—truthfully—that he was trying to get enough money together to send his mother on a vacation. Mr. Hannay paid Jim's debts, but insisted on a strict payback schedule. But he also advanced enough money for Jim's mother, Florence, to go away to Devon for a few days. For the next year, until he paid back the money, Jim walked to work and back every day to save money. That was a scary lesson in finances that Jim would later tell his children about.

James McCartney met Mary Patricia Mohin during World War II at his sister Jin's house. Mary, a nursing sister at Walton Hospital, was visiting Jin and her new husband, Harry Harris, at number 11 Scargreen Avenue when Jim happened by. An air raid brought on a blackout and both Mary and Jim were forced to stay overnight at Jin's and love blossomed.

Mary was born September 29, 1909, at number 2 Third Avenue, Fazakerley, in Liverpool. Her parents were Owen Mohin and Mary Teresa Danher Mohin. She was christened a Catholic and kept the faith until her death. After her mother died in childbirth in 1919, her father remarried and Mary and her new stepmother, Rose, disliked each other on sight, to the extent that thirteen-year-old Mary left home to live with Danher relatives in Litherland and shortly thereafter entered nursing.

She was thirty-one when she and Jim, thirty-nine, were married at St. Swithens Roman Catholic Chapel in Gill Moss, Liverpool, on April 15, 1941. They first lived in rooms on Sunbury Road in Anfield. During the war Jim, who was too old to be drafted, went to work for the war effort as a lathe turner at Napiers, an aircraft factory. He qualified for Air Force housing and they moved, shortly after their first son was born, to a house at 92 Broadway in Wallasey, across the Mersey River from Liverpool.

James Paul McCartney was born in Walton Hospital at 107 Rice Lane in Liverpool on June 18, 1942. Since Mary had been a sister there, she was in a private ward—quite a privilege. Their second son, Peter Michael McCartney, was born on January 7, 1944, also in Walton Hospital. Both boys were baptized Catholic, but both were circumcised. The McCartneys moved to a new prefab house on Roach Avenue, Knowsley Estate, in Liverpool. Mary was soon back in the hospital with mastitis. After returning home, she gave up nursing to first become a health visitor and then became a district midwife. That position entitled the family to subsidized housing, first in Sir Thomas White Gardens in Liverpool City Centre, then to 72 Western Avenue in Speke. She was regarded with respect in the neighborhood and people looked to her as a sort of substitute doctor. One favorite family story was about the neighborhood woman who showed up, distraught, on the doorstep at 72 Western. She had a screaming baby in her arms and could only say, "I've done something terrible, nurse!"

Mary unwrapped the child and found that the mother had stuck a diaper pin through his little penis. Mary coolly dealt with the crisis.

Always trying to better the family, Mary secured a bigger house in a new section on the edge of Speke at number 12 Ardwick Road.

Shortly after the move, young Paul and Mike almost drowned in an adventure in a vacant area across the street. The lot contained a lime pit that rapidly filled after a rain. Jim told Paul and Mike to stay away from that pit. After a rain, Paul and Mike headed straight there and decided to walk across a plank over the pit. They fell in. Neither could swim and they couldn't climb up the slick lime walls of the pit. No one heard their cries. Finally

Mike secured a hold on a part of a tree stump and held them both up until a passerby heard their wailing. The two boys were spanked and sent to bed without their supper. Then Jim happened to overhear a weeping Paul telling Mike how he was going to dig a big hole and fill it full of water and then take their dad up in an airplane and then push him out into the big hole: So there, Dad! Jim had a word with Mary and she took a tray of food up to the boys, admonishing them to "not let Dad hear."

Paul and Mike had, by all accounts, an early childhood that was both typical and unremarkable. They played marbles ("ollies" in local slang) and collected cigarette cards and bus tickets. Jim ran earphones up to the bedroom they shared from the wireless downstairs, so they could lie in bed and shiver to the thrills provided by their favorite radio programs, such as "Dick Barton, Special Agent."

Paul and Mike went off to Stockton Wood Road Infants School, where they saw their first movie. It was Dick Barton, their favorite crime fighter, who had graduated to the silver screen. It scared Paul and he jumped up and ran out. Mike later remembered, though, how Paul would always stand up for him if any bully accosted him. Paul would be there to whomp anyone who dared to attack his little brother.

They played hooky from school ("sagging from school," they called it), skipped through Speke down to the banks of the Mersey River, and ill-advisedly went skinny-dipping in the river's murky waters. They would, on a Saturday, set off with their part-sheep dog named Prince through Bluebell Woods to Tabletop Bridge. This was a large concrete air raid shelter constructed during the war over the train tracks for the London-to-Liverpool railway line. Paul and Mike started their train experiments by placing various denominations of coins on the tracks, just to see what a train's passage over them would do to them. Then they moved on to twigs, pebbles, tree branches, and bricks. Finally, since they were next to a field full of turnips, they started what they came to call "turnip time." Basically, they stood on the bridge, with turnips lined up in a row, and dropped their cargo in an attempt to hit the train's engineer on the head as the train steamed by underneath them. Mike remembered their relatives characterizing himself and Paul as "two right little swine."

Another afternoon Paul and Mike were nosing around in back of Aunt Jin's house in Huyton and found a can of gasoline. Paul and Mike wondered whether or not it would burn up the wall behind the garage. They made bets against each other and poured gasoline down the side of the garage. Then Mike positioned himself on the roof as a sort of scientific observer. Once Paul set fire to the wall, Mike was trapped on the roof. Fortunately, a policeman on patrol happened along and nipped the experiment in the bud.

Another adventure occurred one day when they decided to pilfer apples from a farmer's orchard near the Bluebell Woods. Farm workers caught them at it and Mike and their dog Prince got away. Paul, who was chubby then, was apprehended as he tried to hoist himself over a gate. Mike came back to help him and the two of them were held in the barn until Jim, summoned by the farmer, arrived to collect his two apple thieves.

There were the usual childhood crises. Paul was in the habit of picking Mike up by his ankles and swinging him around, until one day his grip slipped and Mike took a dive, headfirst, onto the cement, thus eliminating the worry of when his baby front teeth were going to fall out.

After another physical roughing up by Paul, young Mike decided to try to get even and his form of extracting revenge was pretty mild, actually. He waited until Paul was asleep one night, then plucked a fat feather from his pillow and tried to tickle Paul to death. First, though, he got the fright of his life: Mike had never noticed that Paul slept with his eyes kept partly open and he thought that Paul was lying in wait for him. Once he verified that he was asleep, though, Mike sat up most of the night, tickling Paul until he tossed and turned miserably, but never quite awakened.

Stockton Wood school became overloaded with baby-boom children in Speke, fifteen hundred of them by early 1950. Consequently, Mike and Paul were transferred to Joseph Williams Primary School in the Gateacre (which they called "Getaca") section, a half-hour bus ride each way. They initially loved the novelty of the bus ride, where they could clamber to the second deck of the bus and create all manner of mischief. At the time, Williams school was virtually out in the country, so the headmaster, John Gore, who was informally called "Pop," took the children on frequent nature walks.

This was the only period in Paul's life that people around him noticed that he seemed to be acutely unhappy: He had gotten fat and, as a result, became uncommonly sensitive to any slight. Mike recalled that that was the only time that "anything outwardly affected him." He was quite vain and Mike soon learned that nothing would make him angrier than the sobriquet of "Fatty!" This was the only period of his life—with rare exceptions to come much later—when he let others know what he actually felt and thought. Usually, he strove for such self-control that he seemed unusually mature for his years.

He also learned, early on, a sort of lifelong philosophy of avoiding arguments, of a duplicitous diplomacy in which he would never admit to anything. If caught, he would deny all knowledge of the misdeed and find someone else to lay the blame onto. He was the diamond in Mary's eye and she was loath to blame her Paulie for anything. The few times he was out-and-out guilty, he would get even with his parents by stealing into their bedroom and ripping the lace curtains on the windows. Not badly, not enough for the damage to be immediately noticeable. Just enough for him to feel a sense of revenge.

Once, when Mary found some dirty drawings in his pockets—crude sketches of a nude woman with explicitly detailed pubic hair—he denied ownership for days, blaming a classmate. Paul was sexually precocious and was more or less educating his schoolmates. These particular drawings were thought to be especially clever, being foldouts. He finally broke down and admitted that he had drawn the filthy things. "The shame was terrible," he said many years later.

Mary's final triumph was to see both of her boys placed in a good school and to get her family into the best house they had ever had.

Paul had always done well in school, a combination of his upbringing, his nimble mind, and his innate diplomacy and ability to be what others seemed to want. In 1953 he had won a Coronation Prize for an essay on potholing. The prize was the book *Seven Queens of England*. Paul later admitted that all he knew about potholing he had learned from lying in bed at night and listening to the radio on his headset.

Mary was proud of him when he passed his "eleven-plus" examination and was admitted to the Liverpool Institute on

Mount Street. The eleven-plus determined whether a student could go into a grammar (high) school and prepare for university or be delegated to secondary modern schools (lower schools) and prepare for a trade as a metalworker or a woodworker.

The Institute was begun in 1825 as a Mechanics Institute. Charles Dickens once taught there and Charles Lamb had been a student. In 1890 half the physical plant was converted into the Liverpool College of Art. In 1944 the Institute—or "Inny," as its pupils liked to call it—was turned into a grammar school and fees were removed.

When Mike finally scraped by his exams and got into the Inny, Mary wept with joy. It was a proud mother who outfitted her two boys in their school uniforms of blazers, shorts, and matching caps and knee socks. She would not have long to enjoy her pride, though.

She also managed to get the McCartney family into their best house yet, an attached row house at 20 Forthlin Road. It had a little garden in back that faced onto an open field, but, best of all, it had the first McCartney indoor bathroom. What a revelation that was for the boys on those cold mornings.

They had been in the house less than a year when Mary fell ill. The first inkling the boys had that anything might be wrong came one day when Mike surprised Mary crying alone in her bedroom. She was holding a crucifix and a picture of a relative who was a priest. She denied that anything was wrong, but in the days to come her chest pains grew worse. She took Bisodol for the pain, but obviously knew that something was very wrong. Mary finally went to see a doctor. He found extensive cancer of the breast.

When Paul learned she was ill, the first thing he said was: "What are we going to do without her money?" He was to regret that later and to spend many nights in weeping and in prayer.

Within a month of the diagnosis of cancer, Mary was dead, on October 31, 1956. She was given last rites and died in Northern Hospital with rosary beads tied around her wrists. She told her brother Bill's wife, Dill, "I would have liked to have seen the boys growing up." Paul was fourteen; Mike was just twelve.

During the week of the funeral, Paul and Mike moved in with their Aunt Jin in Huyton, with Paul complaining because they had to sleep in the same bed.

Paul later said that he had soured on religion because of Mary's death. He had prayed devoutly and intensely for Mary's recovery. But, he said, "the prayers didn't work, when I really needed them to. . . ."

Mary was buried in Yew Tree Cemetery on November 3, 1956. Mike McCartney decided to finally visit the grave in 1978. Mike had to call his aunts Jin and Mill to learn the exact location of the gravesite: section 3A, grave number 276, Yew Tree Cemetery, on Finch Lane in Huyton. It took Mike and the chief gravedigger quite some time to find the gravesite. She was listed in cemetery records as Mary McCarthey. The gravesite, when Mike had finally located it, had no headstone and was heavily overgrown with weeds and brush.

Things could never be the same after Mary's death. Paul's regrettable concern about the family's finances turned out to be well founded. In 1956 Jim McCartney was earning only about eight pounds a week at the Cotton Exchange. He had not exactly been a barn burner as a cotton salesman. After the war, he had first worked as an inspector for the Sanitation Department in Liverpool before being taken back by A. Hannay & Co. His "job for life" with the cotton company was just that, but it wasn't making him a wealthy man.

He also had the burden of being both mother and father to two teenaged boys, when Mary had done most of the parenting before. His sisters Jin and Mill helped as they could, coming to 20 Forthlin Road at least once a week to clean the house. Still, it was up to Paul and Mike to try to warm up the cold house. Jim tried his best, as both Paul and Mike later agreed. He in turn tried to instill responsibility in his sons; responsibility to get up and get to school on time and do their homework and tend house and take care of their clothing and not have their worthless schoolmates in the house unless one of their aunts was there to supervise and to not raid the icebox. And he tried to teach them what Paul and Mike came to mockingly term his two "ations." He tried to teach toleration and moderation in all things. He was partly successful.

Paul showed no real musical interest until after Mary's death. Then music became an obsession for him, the outlet for his pent-up emotions.

As a child, though, he was not terribly interested in music. Jim had tried to get him into the Liverpool Cathedral choir, but Paul failed the audition and Jim thought he had cracked his voice on purpose, just out of perversity and laziness. He later sang with St. Chad's choir, but dropped out. Jim sent Paul and Mike to piano lessons, but they didn't take. Paul later took up the trumpet. They were at Auntie Jin's one day when their cousin Ian Harris was trying to play his trumpet and handed it over to Paul as a challenge to see if he could coax a tune out of it. He was successful enough that Jim got Paul a trumpet for his birthday. But, Paul said, he quickly got a sore lip trying to play it and he also realized that if he played trumpet, then he couldn't sing, and if he couldn't sing, then he wouldn't be the center of attention. Paul later said, "As many people already know, the very first musical instrument I played was a trumpet, a rather battered old thing which was given to me when I was fourteen years old. My father says he gave it to me because I'd always seemed interested in music from the time I was a 'tiddler' and he thought it would be a suitable instrument for me to learn to play. Course, I immediately fancied myself as Louis Armstrong, but I only got as far as learning 'The Saints Go Marching In' before I got fed up with it. It used to hurt my lip and I didn't fancy the thought of walking around like a beat-up boxer, so I decided to buy myself a guitar."

Paul said that he went out and bought a Zenith guitar for fifteen pounds, but where he could get what amounted to almost two weeks of his father's salary is hard to imagine. "It's funny, but every one remembers his first string-box," Paul later said. "Mine was a Zenith. I'd no idea where it was all going to lead at the time—the main reason I chose to play a guitar was because it wouldn't hurt my lip. I started bashing away and pretty soon I had the basic chords well and truly learnt. Then I got a bit more ambitious and bought a solid Rosetti [a "Lucky Seven"]. It only had two strings and when I played it it didn't produce a very melodic sound. But I kept the volume right down and it seemed okay to me."

Once Paul had his first guitar, he seemed to withdraw into himself. His brother Mike said that once Paul discovered the guitar, he was "lost in another world, particularly after Mum died. It was useless talking to him. In fact, I had better conversations with brick walls around this period." Paul even, Mike said, took the guitar with him to the bathroom and often sat, music-absorbed as it were, for hours.

As Mike said, "You lose a mother and you find a guitar?" The guitar was obviously Paul's escape valve. He had first listened to the skiffle of Lonnie Donegan, and at age fourteen, went to see Donegan perform. He listened to American rock 'n' roll, especially Bill Haley, Elvis Presley, and Little Richard. He started trying impersonations in his bedroom and soon had Little Richard down by rote. He had already made friends with another rock 'n' roll nut on the number 86 bus to school, a fellow guitar player named George Harrison. He and George went together to see the movie *Blackboard Jungle* when Paul was sixteen and George, who was only fifteen, was too young to get into the theater. George's mother laughed at them as they set out and told them that they would never be allowed in. So Paul and George went out into the yard and picked up mud and rubbed it on what few hairs of a mustache George had on his callow face. They got into the show. They had gone to the movie, Paul said, only because he had heard about a powerful song called "Rock Around the Clock" that was in it.

Paul and Ian James, a classmate, went around with their guitars together, playing at fairs and wearing matching white sports jackets and doing Marty Robbins's hit song "A White Sport Coat and a Pink Carnation."

Even as Paul listened to and loved and lusted after rock 'n' roll hits by Elvis and Little Richard and Buddy Holly and the Everly Brothers, he still kept a certain distance from rock 'n' roll by dint of his love for the music hall tradition that his dad had brought to him. Even as Paul listened to Elvis, he still admired the likes of Fred Astaire and went around the house singing "White Christmas" because "I like a good tune." He would add "Over the Rainbow" to his repertoire later, but he claimed it was because the American rocker Gene Vincent was doing it, not because he had seen Judy Garland singing it in *The Wizard of Oz*. He was also absorbing such pop and show tunes as "The Honeymoon Song," "A Taste of Honey," "Till There Was You" from *The Music Man,* and "Besame Mucho" that would always stay with him.

Many years later, in 1987, Paul would tell radio interviewer Timothy White that his dad's music hall tradition had been very important to him as a child. "When people of my generation—who would have been born in the 1940s and obviously be around forty now—when they were growing up, rock 'n' roll hadn't been invented yet. Blues had started, but that was nowhere near as popular; you had to be a real folkie to be into blues. Anything up to the 1950s was the old traditions and in Britain that was music hall—or vaudeville, as you call it.

"My dad, sitting around the house tapping things like 'Chicago' on the ivories, he used to get told off by his dad for playing what his dad called 'tin can music.' To me, it's the great old standards now. It's silly to realize, but the waltz was once a scandalous dance and 'Chicago' was once considered raucous pop. If anyone wanted to go into show business before the mid-1950s, you were looking at a Sinatra-type person as the most rocking you were gonna get. Then suddenly Elvis arrived and Chuck Berry, Fats Domino, Little Richard, Jerry Lee, and all the guys. From then on, that was the whole direction.

"Anyway, as a result, my father was very sympathetic when I was getting into music and consequently there was a lot of that music hall music around our house on the radio and the telly. Later, occasionally, you began to hear little pieces of that influence in songs I had begun writing. 'When I'm Sixty-Four' was one of mine that I wrote in that vein. I was about sixteen when I wrote that—and my dad would have been fifty-six or fifty-eight. Retirement age over here is sixty-five, so maybe I thought sixty-four was a good prelude. But probably sixty-four just worked good as a number; you don't always think these things out. I don't—certainly. So that's where I get all my music hall stuff from. And when I used to introduce 'You Gave Me the Answer,' I always used to dedicate it to Fred Astaire. He's one of my favorite dancers and singers. I love his voice on things like 'Cheek to Cheek.' His style and delivery were real neat and he was a great athlete. A combination of all that has led me in that slightly fruity direction, but I like it."

As Paul discovered music, he began more and more to leave school behind him. There were no other Inny kids in his neighborhood and the other kids started calling him a "college pudding, fucking college pudding." He also sat in the little McCartney garden and looked across at the open field and saw the other boys playing and he would ditch his homework and run out the door to play also. He later called up reasons for hating school, saying that the masters would hit him for no good reason and would drone on and on endlessly about what they did in the last war and that no one could explain to Paul just what the hell good all these certificates were to him if he studied and got them. All he wanted, he said later, was "women, money, and clothes." He started shoplifting cigarettes and lay in bed fantasizing endlessly: If only he could assemble one hundred pounds, he thought, he would be set for life.

He also, as he bragged to everyone in school, lost his virginity at age fifteen. He said that "she was older and bigger than me. It was at her house. She was supposed to be baby-sitting while her mum was out. I told everybody at school next day, of course. I was a real squealer."

The Quarry Men

3

$JOHN$ was drunk at a church dance the day he met Paul. The date was July 6, 1957, and the affair was the summer garden fete held at St. Peter's Parish Church in Woolton. John's skiffle group, the Quarry Men, had been booked for the afternoon show. Quarry Man member Pete Shotton's mother was responsible for the booking, as the group's performance record—a set at Quarry Bank's Sixth Form dance and a few unsuccessful auditions—was not impressive thus far.

John had been jolted into a love for music and rebellion by American movies he saw as a teenager: *Rock Around the Clock* and *Rebel Without a Cause* and *Blackboard Jungle*. They effectively launched what would become the teddy boy movement in England: moody rebels with DA haircuts, T-shirts, tight jeans, and engineer boots. The music that propelled the movement was what was quickly becoming known as rock 'n' roll, a violent reaction to the cool jazz and smooth pop music that reigned in England. John was further rallied to the cause by Elvis, of course, especially after "Heartbreak Hotel." Elvis had the look and the sound and the sneer. Closer to home, though, the big influence on John and on many young English musicians was skiffle music, as exemplified by the musician Lonnie Donegan. In 1956, when John was sixteen, Donegan was—unlike the distant

Elvis—nearby and accessible and also fairly easy to emulate. Skiffle was basically jazzed-up folk music, performed with guitar, bass, drums, and optional banjo. The first record John Lennon bought was Donegan's revved-up version of the American folk standard "Rock Island Line."

John, as a natural leader, decided to form a skiffle group at Quarry Bank High School, where he was a well-noticed if not studious student. He was encouraged by both his teachers and his Aunt Mimi and his mother, Julia. Julia actually knew the banjo and taught John how to play. When he started playing guitar, all he knew was banjo tuning, so he tuned the top four strings on his guitar like a banjo and paid no attention to the bottom two.

John and his best friend Pete Shotton were walking on the high school grounds one day when John suggested forming a skiffle band. Shotton was aghast at the idea. John persisted with the notion, saying, "Well, look at Lonnie Donegan. Now that I've got me guitar, all we really need is a skiffle board and a tea chest—and even *you* could play one of those." Shotton, who suffered from what would turn out to be an incurable case of stage fright, agreed and they launched the group with John playing guitar, Shotton strumming a washboard liberated from his mother's garden shed, and classmate Bill Smith trying to play the bass that had been jury-rigged from a tea chest and broom handle. The thus-far-unnamed group's first rehearsals were held in an iron air raid shelter in Shotton's backyard. The repertoire consisted mainly of "Rock Island Line," "Cumberland Gap," and "Wabash Cannonball." Smith was deemed to be insincere in his efforts and was more or less sacked, thus establishing a firm precedent for future groups stemming from this one. Len Garry took his place on tea chest bass, Eric Griffiths was added on guitar, Rod Davis on banjo, and Colin Hanton on drums. John first called the group the Black Jacks. John subsequently changed the name to the Quarry Men, after the school. The group lineup was not fixed: Nigel Whalley from Bluecoat Grammar School and Ivan Vaughan, who went to Liverpool Institute, also joined, alternating on the tea chest bass. Whalley became the de facto manager and started carrying business cards that read:

The group would later do increasingly well with small engagements, although there were disagreements from the first within the group as Lennon more and more tried to force rock 'n' roll songs into the lineup. Even though the group was booed lustily by jazz fans at a rare club date at the Cavern in Liverpool, John, as the strong-willed lead singer, still had his way. Even when he did have his way with performing rock songs, John seldom knew all the words to the songs—he couldn't afford the records and had to rely on what he heard on radio or at other shows—so he made them up. That was the least of his worries. He was not doing well in school; Aunt Mimi was getting sick and tired of his adolescent tremors both in school and at home; if a Quarry Men gig did do well, it would probably lead to a fistfight with the local toughs in Garston or the like. John had limited options but, still, he was only sixteen, pushing seventeen, on that mild afternoon in Woolton. The Quarry Men were the opening act for the Band of the Cheshire Yeomanry.

That morning John had had a row with Aunt Mimi over his lack of progress at school. And over his teddy boy clothes. And his Tony Curtis hairdo, with its elephant trunk hanging over the front. As was becoming his practice, he got ahold of a couple of bottles of ale and had a mild buzz on before the Quarry Men took the stage. He had no way of knowing and indeed would not have cared a damn if he had known that his sometime bandmate Ivan Vaughan had brought a mate of his, Paul McCartney, to the fete, solely to see the Quarry Men. Vaughan had attended Dovedale Primary School with John, then had gone on to the tonier Liverpool Institute while John had to settle for Quarry Bank. Vaughan was very taken with John, though, and he decided to bring his friend Paul to see this skiffle group, once he learned that Paul was interested in music.

There were no bolts of lightning that day, no Signals That Great Forces Are Unleashed. Neither Paul nor John recognized that anything untoward had happened, although each was impressed with the other. Aunt Mimi was also greatly impressed that day, not having any idea that John would be performing there and then having the shock of not only seeing him onstage but of seeing him in his full teddy boy regalia: padded shoulders, greasy DA hair, drainies, and all.

Paul was struck by John's stage presence, especially since John was singing the Del-Vikings' "Come Go with Me" and didn't know all the words so he made them up. John came across as a take-charge guy onstage, for all his tender years.

Paul later wrote in his foreword to John's book *In His Own Write,* "At Woolton village fete I met him. I was a fat schoolboy and, as he leaned an arm on my shoulder, I realized that he was drunk. We were twelve then but in spite of his sideboards we went on to become teenage pals. Aunt Mimi, who had looked after him since he was so high, used to tell me he was much cleverer than he pretended."

Between the Quarry Men's two sets, Vaughan took Paul to meet John in the church hall and they struck it off immediately, Paul showing John how to tune his guitar like a guitar rather than a banjo, Paul writing out from memory all the words to Eddie Cochran's "Twenty Flight Rock," as well as Gene Vincent's "Be-Bop-A-Lula." Paul played and sang for John and the latter was greatly impressed by what he saw and heard. Even so, the ever-glacial Lennon would not admit to being impressed. (In fact, for several years, he deliberately misspelled Paul's last name as McArtrey). That evening, though, John asked Shotton, "Well, what did you think of him?" Shotton said he thought Paul was okay. "So what would you think," John asked, almost as an afterthought, "about having Paul in the group, then?" "Fine," said Shotton, "as long as you want him." John wouldn't say anything himself directly to Paul; he got his friend Pete Shotton to ask Paul to join the Quarry Men. Pete passed on the invitation one day a week later as he and Paul rode their bikes on the golf course in Allerton. Paul was grateful, but had to ask for a postponement. He had to go to scout camp for two months first.

A curious note about St. Peter's Parish Church, where John and Paul first met: Even though Paul would later claim that the song "Eleanor Rigby" was about no one in particular and that, in fact, he had started the song as being about first Daisy Hawkins and then Daisy McKenzie and then yet later to Daisy Rigby, there is an Eleanor Rigby buried in the St. Peter's Parish Church Cemetery. Her name is on a large stone marker devoted to the John Rigby family. Eleanor died on October 10, 1939.

So, before Paul could join his first band, he and brother Mike were packed off to camp for a week beginning July 29, 1957, as loyal members of the Nineteenth City School Scouts. For the sum of two pounds and fifteen shillings each, including the bus ride, they went off to Callow Farm at Hathersage in Derbyshire. Things went swimmingly until Paul got the idea to streamline the camp's method of hauling firewood up and down a cliffside. He decided that a scout could just as easily be hoisted up and down on the rope-and-pulley device. Younger brother Mike was decided upon as the guinea pig. Halfway down the cliffside, the device—or the nerve of its handlers—broke and Mike sailed into an oak tree with sufficient force to break his left arm in several places. He was hospitalized for a month in Sheffield.

So Paul's membership in the Quarry Men had to wait yet a while longer. As soon as Mike was able to travel in August, Jim took him and Paul off to Butlin's Holiday Camp at Filey in Yorkshire. It was here that Paul actually made his first public performance. A McCartney cousin, Bett, worked at the camp and her husband, Mike Robbins, was a McCartney hero as host of "The People" national talent contest. Auditions for that contest were being held at Butlin's and Paul, who had brought his ever-present guitar with him, decided to enter. "Cash prizes of over 5,000 pounds must be won" was the contest's slogan. Paul had almost perfected his "Long Tall Sally" and he and Mike had worked at home on an adequate version of the Everly Brothers' "Bye Bye Love." Jim himself was proud of that Everly version.

Paul told Mike that he was going to enter the contest and enlisted his little brother's support. When they got to the Gaiety Theatre and hero Mike Robbins introduced Paul from the stage, Paul stopped the show and whispered into Robbins's ear. "Ladies and gentlemen," boomed Robbins, "for the first time on any stage, a really warm welcome for . . . the McCartney Brothers!"

Mike, all of thirteen years old with his arm in a sling, swore at his big brother, but he had to get up onstage, nonetheless, for a spirited "Bye Bye Love." Then Paul got into his "Long Tall Sally." Big applause for the little lads, but no prize. The first McCartney public performance did, however, produce the first McCartney female fan, a girl named Angela.

While Paul was away at camp, enjoying his newfound celebrity-hood, the Quarry Men shouldered on without him. The group actually managed one booking while Paul was gone and it is one that has not been generally acknowledged in the past. (The Beatles themselves, after playing thousands of dates, long ago admitted that their memories are less than precise on when and where they played and what transpired. Additionally, there remain few, if any, written records of most small rock 'n' roll performances.) British researcher Mark Lewisohn found that, despite the usually ballyhooed date of March 21, 1961, as the day the Beatles—or any of them—first played the Cavern Club in Liverpool, the Quarry Men actually played there on August 7, 1957, while Paul was off at Butlin's.

The Cavern had opened on January 16, 1957, at number 10a Mathew Street, as Liverpool's premiere jazz showcase. The Quarry Men got booked onto a skiffle night bill because the Cavern's owner, Alan Sytner, happened to have as father a man who golfed with occasional Quarry Men manager Nigel Whalley. Those who were there that night recalled that Lennon immediately led the Quarry Men over the line from skiffle to rock. After his usual garbling of the Del-Vikings' "Come Go with Me," John launched into "Hound Dog" and "Blue Suede Shoes." Sytner, the owner, himself sent a note to the stage, reading: CUT OUT THE BLOODY ROCK.

Paul came back from Butlin's and joined the Quarry Men. He and John began to practice together and they also began to write songs—separately at first, then together. Through 1957, 1958, and 1959 they would compose a body of songs that was impressive: "The One After 909," "When I'm Sixty-Four," "Hot as Sun," "Hello Little Girl," "I Lost My Little Girl," "That's My Woman," "Like Dreamers Do," "Winston's Walk," "Thinking of Linking," "Years Roll Along," "Too Bad About Sorrows," "Catswalk," "Keep Looking That Way," "Love Me Do," "Just Fun," and "Looking Glass."

In September 1957 John started classes at the Liverpool College of Art, just around the corner from the Liverpool Institute, where Paul was a student. Paul and John began to fall into a musical camaraderie as they played and sang together more often. One problem with practicing was that John's Aunt Mimi disapproved of Paul and would close the door in his face and Paul's father Jim didn't like the cut of John's jib either. Each was certain that it was the other who was the bad influence and the cause of the drainies and the Tony Curtis hairdos.

Paul began talking up a young guitar player named George. He said George was even better than he was. Finally Paul got John and the others to troop over to George's house in Speke to check out this budding guitar wizard. John was visibly unimpressed to find a nervous fourteen-year-old. George silenced him, though, with a note-perfect performance of the Bill Justis guitar instrumental song "Raunchy."

John was impressed, but not enough to make George a band member immediately. So George just sort of tagged along, like everyone's kid brother.

Shotton began to notice, even before George was allowed into the group, that John was shaping the band after his own likeness. Paul would stay: That was obvious. John respected Paul and he was the first musician to practically treat and regard John as an equal. But as John became increasingly serious about the music, the less-talented members of the group began to receive a definite freeze-out treatment. Shotton himself, although he would remain close friends with John for the remainder of the latter's life, found himself getting a very abrupt bum's rush from the Quarry Men and, oddly enough, being grateful to John for it. The Quarry Men had performed in the Toxteth section of Liverpool and, afterward, drummer Colin Hanton's aunt had a party for the group. Shotton and Lennon got drunk on beer and John picked up Shotton's washboard and broke it over his head. "Well," John said, "that takes care of that problem, doesn't it, Pete?" Exit Pete Shotton as Quarry Man.

Paul was also quickly leaving his mark on the others, complaining about Nigel Whalley's taking a commission as "manager" of the group, sniping at drummer Colin Hanton and telling—and offering to show—him how to play on one song or another, although, as far as anyone knew, Paul had never yet so much as touched a drum. Shotton, who remained a friend, observed that what John was essentially instigating and approving was a set of standards to ensure that he would have a band that was not so much musically compatible with him as personally compatible. The worst sin was to be boring. And that was something that Paul immediately sensed and that he and John agreed upon, although it was and always would remain an unspoken topic. They began to silently understand each other on such subjects. Even though Paul and John did talk as teenagers about having both lost their mothers, they came to adopt a common expression within the group: "Don't get real on me, man."

On October 18, the Quarry Men landed another gig, Paul's first with the band. It was with South Liverpool promoter Charlie McBain and it was at the Conservative Club's New Clubmoor Hall on Back Broadway. The Quarry Men had gotten matching outfits of a sort: white long-sleeved cowboy shirts, black string ties, black trousers. Paul and John wore matching white sport coats. The other three Quarry Men—drummer Colin Hanton, tea chest bassist Len Garry, and guitarist Eric Griffiths—did not. Already John and Paul were more equal than their colleagues in the band. As the new hotshot guitarist in the group, Paul was playing lead guitar that night (for the first and only time in his career). He blew a guitar solo on Arthur Smith's "Guitar Boogie." To his credit, he was playing his guitar upside down and backward because he still didn't know how to restring a guitar for a left-hander.

The Quarry Men were to play four more public performances in 1957. Two were at Charlie McBain's "rhythm nights" at Wilson Hall in Garston, a true rock 'em and sock 'em tough joint. Another was a return engagement to the Conservative Club, but the fourth was a true curiosity. On November 16 the group played a Saturday night dance for the Stanley Abattoir Social Club in Old Swan for a group of butchers and their wives.

Bookings continued to be scarce throughout 1958. George joined the group early in the year, more or less as Paul's protégé. They had known each other since the time the McCartneys lived near the Harrisons in Speke before Jim moved the Macs to Forthlin Road in Allerton. George and Paul rode the same bus every day—it took them an hour each way—and they became well acquainted after they discovered a mutual love for rock 'n' roll. When Eric Griffiths was finally eased out of the band by Paul and John, their method was typical. Griffiths was simply not told of the next rehearsal at Paul's house and George took his place. When Griffiths learned of the rehearsal and telephoned, John and Paul made Griffith's close friend Hanton break the news to him. John and Paul wanted to keep Hanton because he owned a drum kit, which was rare among boys of their age, but Hanton soon exited on his own in early 1959 after a performance. They were all drunk and began arguing and Hanton took himself and his drum kit and left and that was that for him.

Another reason George was welcomed into the group was that everyone also loved George's mother, Louise, who—unlike most parents of the day—supported George and the band whole-heartedly. The group could always count on a welcome from Louise if they had no place else to rehearse. She was also very tolerant of George's drainies, his foppish pink shirts, and his yellow vests.

Although the Quarry Men had few bookings that year, one of the more pleasant was on December 20 at the Harrisons', where they played for the wedding reception of George's brother Harry. George's father (Harry Sr.) also booked them for the Christmas party, held on New Year's Day, of the Speke Bus Depot Social Club, of which he was chairman.

Sometime during the summer of 1958, the Quarry Men—then John, Paul, George, pianist John Lowe, and drummer Colin Hanton—pooled their money to make their first record. For seventeen shillings and sixpence, they cut a two-sided record at the home of a man named Percy Phillips in Liverpool. John sang lead on the Buddy Holly song "That'll Be the Day." Paul sang lead on the flip side, a song called "In Spite of All the Danger," the first recorded Lennon–McCartney collaboration. (Paul has the only copy of the record.) Paul started carrying a school exercise book in which he wrote down all of his compositions and those that he and John wrote together. This was also when he and John solemnly shook hands one day on an unwritten agreement that everything they were to write—together or apart—would be credited to the partnership of Lennon–McCartney.

Also during the summer of 1958, Paul wrote to Mike Robbins, asking for work for the group at Butlin's. Work was not forthcoming.

In early 1959, after Griffiths and Hanton were gone, the three-guitar lineup of the Quarry Men was not in great demand. This was also when John had fallen in lust and love with Cynthia Powell. He also began to hang out with Stu Sutcliffe and then moved in with him on Gambier Terrace. Paul and—to a lesser degree—George would hang out with John at school and come over for lunch.

For a while, George, bored with the musical inactivity, started playing with another group, the Les Stewart Quartet. It was because of that group that the Quarry Men would be resurrected later in the year.

It was also indirectly due to Mrs. Mona Best. She had been born in New Delhi of English parentage, married British soldier John Best, and went to England after the war with him, where they eventually settled in a rambling fifteen-room Victorian house at number 8 Hayman's Green in the quiet Liverpool suburb of West Derby. Mona—nicknamed "Mo" by everyone—had two sons, Rory and Peter, fifteen and eighteen, respectively, in 1959. As Peter especially began to bring friends home from school to listen to rock 'n' roll records, Mo sent them to the basement, which in her house was enormous. Seven huge adjacent cellar rooms full of teenagers playing loud music. Then Mo had a brainstorm. She had heard about the cellar coffee bars in London's Soho that were havens for young people. Why didn't she just start one in her cellar? So she did. After six months of refurbishing and painting by enthusiastic teenaged volunteers, she was ready to open a club that would soon have two thousand members. It still had no name and no band for the opening, however. For the name, Mo finally decided on Casbah Coffee Club—after the hoary line "Come with me to the . . ." For talent, the Les Stewart Quartet was considered, but Ken Brown, a friend of George's and the bassist in the group, had left the Quartet in a snit. Brown had done volunteer work on the Casbah and was prevailed upon to furnish an opening night band, so he talked to George, who talked to Paul, who talked to John, and so the Quarry Men were reborn, with fourth guitarist Ken Brown added. Several days before the opening in August, Brown brought the others around, with Cynthia Powell in tow.

Peter Best remembered meeting them then and recognizing immediately that John was the leader and that Paul and George "hovered in the background, silently agreeing" with everything that he decided. John picked out a spot in front of the jukebox and declared that to be the group's bandstand. "We'll play here," he announced. Paul and George nodded assent. Mo then put them all to work, with the end result costing her fifty pounds in repairs because nearsighted John selected the wrong paint for the wrong finish. Nonplussed, John forged ahead and decorated part of the ceiling with some of his patented deformed cartoon characters: pot-bellied, three-toed, grotesquely malformed men and women.

For opening night at the Casbah, on Saturday, August 29, the Quarry Men were there at four-thirty in the afternoon, set up and ready to roll. And the place didn't open until seven-thirty. Peter Best remembered that there were already a thousand members signed up and a large portion of them arrived early and lined up in the backyard. Memberships cost half a crown annually (twelve and a half pence), plus one shilling at the door, where Mo sold tickets. Hundreds crowded into the cellar to hear John, Paul, George, and Ken working out with "Long Tall Sally," "Maggie May," "Sweet Little Sixteen," "Whole Lotta Shakin' Goin' On," and the like. By then the boys had worked up more than five dozen songs in their repertoire. More than a dozen were Lennon–McCartney originals. Otherwise they relied heavily on songs from Buddy Holly, Little Richard, Chuck Berry, the Coasters, Jerry Lee Lewis, Elvis, Carl Perkins, and Eddie Cochran. Paul and John had begun to divide the lead vocals up between them to conserve their voices during a long night of playing. Paul did the Little Richard screams; John handled Chuck Berry. John sang "Blue Suede Shoes"; Paul did "Blue Moon of Kentucky." George even got to sing: He did lead vocals on Coasters' songs "Youngblood" and "Three Cool Cats" and Carl Perkins's "Your True Love" and he and Paul sang a duet on "In Spite of All the Danger." (It would, of course, be a long time before George was allowed to contribute much to the group's body of songs.) The Quarry Men still had a few holdover skiffle songs, such as "Railroad Bill," "Freight Train," "Midnight Special," and "Rock Island Line," but they were moving increasingly toward an all-rock 'n' roll lineup.

The Casbah thrived and became a virtual teenage heaven, especially since it was essentially the only rock 'n' roll hangout in

Liverpool. The Cavern Club downtown was still a jazz joint and, as skiffle gave way to rock 'n' roll, there was noplace else regularly presenting what would soon be known as the Mersey Beat. During the week, teenagers flocked to the Casbah to sip Cokes or coffee, eat hot dogs and potato chips, and dance to the jukebox. Amazingly, there were few complaints by neighbors. For one thing, few of the teenagers had cars or even motorbikes. No alcohol was allowed and Mo had a stern bouncer at the door to keep an eye on things. Other such venues were not so lucky or so well run: Earlier, in 1958, on March 13, the Quarry Men had played the opening night of a new cellar club called the Morgue Skiffle Club, located underneath a Victorian house in Broadgreen, Liverpool. It was started by Alan Caldwell, eighteen, who had a group called Al Caldwell's Texans, which Ringo Starr joined as the drummer in 1959 when the group became the Raving Texans. The band soon turned into Rory Storm and the Hurricanes, the most flamboyant and popular of the early Mersey Beat bands. Al Caldwell, who had a terrible stammer, turned into glam-rocker Rory Storm (first he was Jett Storm for a while) onstage. He had no luck with the Morgue Skiffle Club, though, which had a short-lived life. The cellar held only about a hundred people and had no plumbing or ventilation or emergency exits. The police regularly swooped down on the place and shut it down for good on April 22, 1959.

At the (by comparison) bucolic Casbah, the Quarry Men were booked for every Saturday night and for six weeks all was wonderful. Then trouble erupted. On the night of October 10, Ken Brown showed up with a terrible cold and was too ill to play. Mo insisted that he go upstairs and sit with her bedridden mother. After the show that night when it came time to pay the band, Mo included Ken in the payment of fifteen shillings (seventy-five pence) each. Paul blew up. "He didn't play, so he shouldn't get paid!" he said and John and George backed him up. Paul was notoriously tight with a coin even then and Mo later recalled that the three of them "would fight over sixpence in those days and always insisted on being given the exact amount—and no leaving it to the next time if there was no change available." Mo wouldn't back down, though, and insisted that the sick Brown be paid. John, Paul, and George, tight-lipped and furious, walked out, vowing to never again darken Mo's stage—and they didn't, not until December of 1960 when they had become the Beatles and Mo's son Pete was their drummer.

Ironically, their leaving led to Pete Best's initiation into music. At the time he had a mild interest in drumming but no experience beyond watching Gene Krupa on the silver screen and thumping away on tabletops down in the Casbah. Ken Brown, of course, had quit the Quarry Men over the fifteen-shilling misunderstanding. He didn't want to give up the music, though. He had grown friendly with Pete and one night he decided to try to form a group with him. "Why don't we form a group of our own, Pete?" he asked. "Come on! You on drums."

Well, they did. It of course helped that Mo could front the money for a drum kit, drum kits being the most valued ingredients of groups then. So Pete started trying to learn drums on his own. He and Ken formed a group called the Blackjacks (no relation to John's old group the Black Jacks) and of course had a standing venue with the Casbah being there. The Blackjacks, with Chas Newby added on bass and guitarist Bill Barlow, became a very popular Casbah attraction. Pete even won a one-pound bet with Rory Storm that the Blackjacks would outdraw Rory and his Hurricanes (with Ringo Starr, then unheralded, on drums). Pete won the bet when the Blackjacks drew 1,350 paying customers to the Casbah, compared to the 1,335 that Rory got the following Saturday. It was purely nepotism, Rory joked. Rory, at six feet two inches, golden-maned and fiery-eyed, was the exuberant uncrowned king of the early Mersey Beat. He was then the forerunner of what Rod Stewart later became and the comparison is not made lightly: Stewart literally took over the mannerisms and the stage act that Rory had. (After a series of career setbacks, Rory later took his own life in a bizarre suicide pact with his mother.)

After John, Paul, and George walked angrily out of the Casbah, their next gig was a defiant run at a national talent contest. It was the same one that John had lost and failed to make any impact on two years earlier, when his Quarry Men had auditioned for the Carroll Levis show "TV Star Search" at the Empire Theatre in Liverpool on June 9, 1957.

This time John renamed his group, which after all had no more Quarry Men in it besides himself, Johnny and the Moondogs. They went off to the Empire Theatre in Liverpool for the preliminary rounds. They qualified for that, along with Jett Storm and the Hurricanes, and went on to the finals in late October at the Empire Theatre. They lost out on this round to the group the Connaughts, who were—despite the new name—the same group that had sunk the Quarry Men in this same contest in 1957, when they were called the Sunnyside Skiffle Group, with the same midget, Nicky Cuff, whom John detested so heartily.

Johnny and the Moondogs did, though, qualify for the absolute final auditions in Manchester on November 15. If the boys just made that, they might qualify for Levis's TV show. So on November 15 John, Paul, and George were off to Manchester for the finals at the Hippodrome Theatre. They did not realize that the judging was to be based on the audience applause for each participating group. John, Paul, and George did not have the price of a hotel room in Manchester between them and when they realized that they needed to be around onstage for the audience's response very late in the night—after the last train back to Liverpool, they knew they couldn't stick around. Johnny and the Moondogs took the last train home instead.

The Silver Beetles

4

JOHN began studying at the Liverpool College of Art when he was eighteen and Paul and George—then seventeen and sixteen, respectively—tried their best to look manly when they came around the college. Paul would wear an overcoat or macintosh buttoned up to the top to hide his school uniform. He brushed his hair down to make it look longer. He managed to evade his father's rule against wearing drainies by having a neighborhood tailor taper his trousers gradually. A nip and a tuck a week and, even as they got tighter, Paul could still protest to Jim that those were the very trousers Jim had bought for him.

George had so transmogrified his school uniform that the authorities were more amused than horrified by him. He was the very image of an archrebel. He had as much of a duck's ass hairdo as one could have and stay in school. His school cap sat on the very back of the DA like a little toy boat. His drainies were tight all the way down to his fluorescent socks. He sported a lime green vest under his school blazer and he was the first person that anyone thereabouts could recall wearing blue suede winkle-picker shoes. He worked very hard at being accepted by the older guys.

When John first started dating Cynthia Powell, he and Cynthia often found themselves transformed into a threesome by George, who wanted to tag along, not knowing he was queering the romance. They wanted to run off to bed and there was George attaching himself to them. "Hi, where you goin'? Can I come too?" George and Paul and John also grew more serious in their music and rehearsed more often. They often cut classes and made an afternoon of it. John knew a friend of his mother, a head-waiter named Twitchy, so named for a facial tic. John found out Twitchy's work habits and he led the others through a window into Twitchy's house at Spring Wood, where they could rehearse the day away and raid the refrigerator. Cynthia asked him, the first time, how they would possibly get into the house. John said casually, "Oh, don't worry about a simple thing like that. He usually leaves his larder window open." What John didn't tell the others was that Twitchy, whose real name was John Dykins, had been his mother's common-law husband and she had lived in that house. John didn't like to advertise that fact or the fact that he had two half-sisters, Julia and Jacqueline Dykins. John's mother Julia had been killed earlier that year when she was struck by a car on July 15, 1958. John had lived with his Aunt Mimi (Mary Elizabeth Smith), his mother's older sister, at Mendips, her house on Melove Avenue in Woolton. Julia had essentially given John to Mimi as an infant after his father, Freddy, a ship's waiter, went back to sea and she took up with another man.

Aunt Mimi noticed that John was greatly impressed by certain items of clothing that Paul and George wore on their first visits to Mendips: Paul had buckled shoes and George wore his ever-present winkle-pickers, plus a pink shirt. John made the mistake of asking Aunt Mimi if he could get the same sorts of things. "Certainly not" was the short reply.

Paul and George met John's best friend Stu Sutcliffe, generally regarded as the most gifted of the art students at the Liverpool College of Art. He was, in a sense, the first true Bohemian that Paul and John knew. At the time, he lived alone in an almost unbelievably cluttered studio on Gambier Terrace, which he would not leave to attend classes. His art professors came to his studio, which consisted of one large room adorned with a double mattress on the floor in one corner and dozens of large canvases in various states of completion. Sutcliffe and John had been attracted to each other immediately. For Stu, John was almost a blank canvas that he could transform into the bold and even dashing figure that this slight studious artist felt that he could not otherwise ever become. To John, Stu was the ultrasensitive, truly talented artist that he felt he was and could be, given the right opportunity. Paul and George weren't really part of the bargain, except insofar as they were the only remaining members of John's band. John came up with the idea that Stu would be the ideal bass player for the group. Stu couldn't play any instruments, but he was ecstatic at the thought of joining the band. He also had little or no money. That problem was solved in 1959 when Stu entered a painting in the John Moores Exhibition in the Walker Art Gallery. Stu's painting was not only chosen to hang in the elite exhibition, but the great John Moores himself bought it for sixty-five pounds. Stu raced off to buy himself a bass with his prize money and thus did this true aesthete join what would soon become the Beatles.

As Stu's influence grew on John, he stopped paying any attention to his lettering course and threw his energies into becoming a painter. If John had continued on that course, there probably would never have been any Beatles. But, as John grew more interested in painting, Stu became more and more fascinated by music. He was in a such a hurry to learn that he never really allowed calluses to develop on his fingers and they were usually raw and sliced up from the piano strings he used on his bass to save money. Ironically, it was Stu who was responsible for the club break that ultimately led to the Beatles' rapid ascent to Beatledom.

John and Cynthia, along with many other students, spent a lot of time in the Jacaranda—or the "Jac," as they called it—a tiny coffee bar on Slater Street on the edge of Chinatown. John and Cynthia would often hold hands—gazing "moonstruck" into each other's eyes—over a cuppa for two hours. If Cynthia was flush (and had already bought John's cigarettes), she would spring for a couple of the Jac's famous bacon butties (sandwiches).

The Jac's proprietor was a short, bearded, outspoken Welshman named Allan Williams, the type of swaggering small-time entrepreneur and jack of all trades, master of none, common to such a relatively open and tolerant port city as Liverpool. He was the type even more common to the entertainment or, in his case at the time, the nightclub field. Downstairs at the Jac, in the dank brick-floored basement, he presented live entertainment. At the time, going directly against the grain of what was popular in England—cool jazz and smooth synthetic pop music—he presented groups that the global flow of influences in and out of the port told him were the sounds favored by the gritty world he inhabited. At the time he was presenting the Royal Caribbean Steel Band, the first time anyone could recall seeing an authentic black steel band in the United Kingdom.

Williams knew, if only by sight, the art students who littered up the seats in his Jac and, even though he sneeringly referred to John, Stu, Paul, and George as "layabouts and dreamers, the advance guard of the Hippie movement," he was tolerant of them. And, although he would sometimes allow John to put the bite on him for the odd meal or bit of pocket change, he always kept a soft spot in his self-described hard heart for Stuart. He perhaps saw in Stu the artist that he would never be or he saw the fragile being that Stu was and knew that he didn't belong in the knockdown piss-alley yobbo-gobbo world of the Liverpool basement beat club. That's why, Cynthia Powell was certain, when John finally went to Allan and asked for a chance for his group to play the Jac, that Allan gave in. It was for Stu's sake only.

It was not because of Stu's musicianship. Paul and John regularly berated him onstage, made fun of his playing to audiences, and ragged him unmercifully. Even Williams admitted Stu couldn't play bass guitar worth a plugged fart. But his boho sincerity lent the group an ethereal beauty it could never have achieved otherwise, which is why John knew what he was doing when he courted Stu. If Rimbaud could have been a rock star, he would have been Stu Sutcliffe. That was Stu's appeal and it was certainly not a lesson lost on the generations of budding rock poets and artistes who have since gotten off the boat.

John himself would not have been so emboldened as to ask Williams for a chance on the Jac's stage had it not been for Art—or art, as Allan Williams perceived it.

Paul celebrated his eighteenth birthday watching fights from the stage as he played on June 18 at one of the toughest venues around, the Grosvenor Ballroom on Grosvenor Road, across the Mersey in Liscard, Wallasey. The dances turned the venerable ballroom into a real bucket of blood joint, where the gang fights were bad to start with and only became worse and worse. The

Silver Beetles, as they briefly called themselves, were quickly learning as much about violence as about music.

They first played the Grosvenor on Saturday, June 4, 1960, as part of promoter Les Dodd's "big beat" nights at the sprawling ballroom. A notice in the Wallasey *News* announced: "The Grosvenor Ballroom tonight introduces a new series of summer Saturday evening dances for youthful patrons, when the all-star outfit The Silver Beetles will be playing." Two days earlier they had played their first date for old-time promoter Dodd at the Neston Institute in Cheshire, near North Wales. Dodd had run "strict tempo" dance nights at both places since 1936, but shrewdly glimpsed a potential in the new "jive" or "rock 'n' roll" groups and their young fans. For the Neston show, the group billed itself as the Beatles, but throughout 1960 they would continue to experiment with the band's name, going from Beatals to Silver Beetles to Silver Beatles to Silver Beats to Beatles and back again. Even as they continued playing Thursday nights at the Neston Institute as the Beatles, they would be the Silver Beetles on Saturday nights at the Grosvenor Ballroom. Some of that had to do, of course, with promoters, who didn't always know how to bill them or which name they were flying under that week. As recently as that April, Paul and John had billed themselves as the Nerk Twins. These were still boys, remember, who were having fun with music. Even after they later returned from Hamburg as the Beatles, they were billed at a Christmas Eve show at the Grosvenor Ballroom as the Silver Beetles.

That first Neston show earned them their first ever newspaper review in the local paper, the Heswall and Neston *News and Advertiser*:

A Liverpool rhythm group, "The Beatles," made their debut at Neston Institute on Thursday night when north-west promoter, Mr. Les Dodd, presented three and a half hours of rock 'n' roll. The five strong group, which has been pulling in capacity houses on Merseyside, comprises three guitars, bass and drums. John Lennon, the leader, plays one of the three rhythm guitars, the other guitarists being Paul Ramon [McCartney's stage name] and Carl [George] Harrison. Stuart Da Stael [Sutcliffe] plays the bass, and the drummer is Thomas Moore. They all sing, either together, or as soloists. Recently they returned from a Scottish tour, starring Johnny Gentle, and are looking forward to a return visit in a months time.

The boys, except for Tommy Moore, were overjoyed. They had been written up, Dodd wanted them for more shows, and they had gotten paid the sum of ten pounds for the whole group—minus a one-pound agent's fee to Allan Williams.

Two nights later they went on at the Grosvenor, with Williams magnanimously providing his van and one of his bouncers as driver. They were glad they had both the van and bouncer, for it was a tough crowd at the Grosvenor. The patrons included gangs who fought each other and the bands, hormone-crazed teddy boys who became enraged when their girlfriends made it painfully obvious that they were sexually excited by the boys in the band, dead-end kids with no future and nothing to lose, and mean drunks whose every Saturday night was a sullen crawl through Liverpool's night haunts in search of trouble. Almost without exception, every one of the several hundred dance shows at which the Beetles played in their early career possessed a very real potential for violence. All it took was the wrong word or the wrong look and the tinderbox would ignite. Fortunately for the band, the violence was usually between members of the crowd. Also—and this was to prove very fortunate indeed for the Beetles— they were a group that from the very first attracted male as well as female fans and fanatics in almost equal numbers. Much of that appeal, of course, had to do with John, rather than Paul or George, or later with Pete Best or Ringo Starr. John's "I don't give a damn" tough-guy stance, his unquenchable exuberance, his cheerful nihilism, and above all the sheer talent with which he pulled it all off earned him instant respect from boys in the crowd who could very easily identify with him.

From the very first, Paul, with those doelike eyes and angelic countenance, drew the girls. George, at the time, was not much of a factor either way, what with his kid-brother look and attitude. Stuart unfortunately possessed the limited appeal of the aesthete and attracted a limited number of arty girls who wanted to mother him and, also unfortunately for Stuart in his short life, a few tough guys who always like to stomp such an obviously vulnerable person.

There were no casualties that night at the Grosvenor and the Beatles or Silver Beetles assembled back at the Jacaranda afterward to divide up their booty. Out of their ten-pound payment, Williams and the bouncer each took one pound. That left eight pounds divvied up five ways. Still, it was money. Williams later remembered that it was that night that the formerly freeloading John and Paul ordered—and paid for—jam with their usual order of toast. For the first time, he thought, but they would never go without jam again. They still cadged coffee off him.

Les Dodd had them back to the Grosvenor two nights later for a special Monday night show on Whitsun Bank Holiday. He paired them with another up-and-coming group that would for a time rival the Beatles in Mersey popularity: Gerry and the Pace-Makers. Dodd promoted them both as: TWO BIG BEAT BANDS. JIVE AND ROCK SPECIALISTS! The newspaper announcement had read:

> Paramount Enterprises, in complete contrast to their Tuesday "Plus 21" Night, are presenting two of the star "Rock" groups in the North West, at the Grosvenor Ballroom on Whit Monday. Pride of place goes to the Silver Beetles, who are returning to Merseyside after a successful tour with Johnny Gentle. Supporting them on the same programme will be another new group to Wallasey—Gerry and the Pace-Makers. Both these groups are jive and rock specialists.

"Plus 21" referred to the generation gap. On Tuesdays oldsters—over twenty-one years of age—were allowed in for "strict tempo" dances, with groups on the order of the Nignett Quartet. The ads trumpeted the "adult" qualities of the evening: NO JIVING! NO ROCK 'N' ROLL! NO TEENAGERS!

As summer of 1960 unfurled before them, the boys in the Silver Beetles had every reason to be optimistic that their fledgling musical careers might bear fruit. They were developing a local following; they were starting to be pretty good onstage, even though Stu was fairly hopeless on his new Hofner bass; they had bookings; they were making a little money; and in general they were feeling a little bit vindicated for pursuing a hopeless teenaged dream.

Then trouble struck. Drummer trouble. Even though Tommy Moore, at thirty-six, was much older than the others were, he was a very solid drummer and good drummers—and drum kits—

were not that easy to find in Liverpool. Being younger than he was and having different values, they didn't fully appreciate the fact that Tommy Moore came back from the brief Scottish tour with Johnny Gentle hating the Silver Beetles and jive and rock 'n' roll. He had hated the tour, hated the travel, hated the abysmal and cheap living conditions on the tour, hated the adolescent condescension and taunts he got from the Beetles. Hated too what happened in the aftermath of the van wreck on May 23.

They were traveling from Inverness to Fraserburgh when their van rammed into the rear of a stopped car. No one was hurt but Tommy, who was hit in the face by a guitar case. He suffered a concussion, in addition to facial contusions and several lost teeth. That night while he was lying in the hospital, the Beetles and the show manager came and pulled him out of bed, propped him up onstage, and made him play. The Beetles also joked onstage about his ravaged face. So he was pretty hot about the whole business when he got back. He had a perfectly good job out at the Garston Bottle Works, as the woman he was living with constantly reminded him.

Tommy didn't hang out with the others, so they didn't realize that he had quit until he failed to show up at the Jac on June 11, where they had agreed to meet before heading out to Grosvenor Ballroom for the night's dance. His drum kit was at the Jac, but no Tommy. The dances started at eight o'clock sharp and time was awasting. John finally called Allan Williams at home. "There's no fucking drummer, Allan!" Williams hit the panic button and raced down to the Jac in his car. The others crowded in and Williams floored it, in his usual driving fashion, out to Tommy's flat in Liverpool 8, a district of whorehouses and shebeens and seedy rooming houses.

When they knocked on the door at Tommy's, a window up above flew open and a woman stuck her head out, demanding to know what their business was. "We want Tommy Moore!" Allan shouted back.

"Well, yez can't bloody 'ave him!" she screamed.

They bantered back and forth for a while, Williams nervously consulting his watch. "You know these are the Beetles, don't you?"

That only increased her fury and she told them what they could do with their bloody Beetles when all they did was lead her Tommy off down the garden path when he ought to be off at the works, which was, by the way, where he was now. "You can piss off," she added. "The lot of yez."

With a few more invectives hurled at her, Williams decided to try another tack. He and the others jumped back into the car and peeled out, heading for the Garston Bottle Works. Once at the works they finally located Tommy, who was working a forklift. He refused to come down. "It's no go. I just can't do it any-more," he told them.

Paul spoke up. "Come on, Tommy. How can we get by without a drummer? You're too good for this lot."

The foreman took exception with that sentiment, so Williams and the others tried gentler persuasion. But Tommy wasn't having any of it. He had decided he was a working man. He preferred a solid job to all that larking about with flighty kid musicians. They left him hunkered down up there on his forklift, his pale pinched face peering down with an uncertain mixture of relief and regret.

Drummerless again, they nonetheless made it onstage for their eight o'clock Grosvenor start that night, just the four of them. Allan's bouncer had brought their equipment on ahead, including Tommy's drum kit. At the start of the dance, John made what was to be considered an ill-advised announcement. "Ladies and gentlemen, boys and girls, women and children, no doubt some of you have noticed that because of circumstances quite beyond our control, as they say in government circles, we have arrived here with no drummer. Now, we can play with no drummer. But it would be a better sound if we had one. If there is anyone among you lot who fancies himself on the skins, let's be having yer."

Unfortunately, Lennon had reckoned without one of the local gang leaders, a strapping giant named Ronnie. "Hey, skin," Ronnie called to John, "I can play the drums." His fellow goons cheered as the Beetles paled onstage. If they weren't very careful, they could all get stomped very easily for their trouble on this night. John's usual wise-ass attitude might cost them, although you never saw the others acting all that brave. When Stu had been stomped so badly, back on May 14 at the dance at Lathom Hall in Seaforth, only John had gone to his aid. Stu had been knocked down and savagely kicked in the head by the sharp toe of a winkle-picker boot. John had leapt onto his assailant, severely spraining his own wrist in the rescue operation. Mainly what they all wanted was to avoid trouble at any costs.

But this night at the Grosvenor it looked as if they were stuck with big Ronnie. He climbed up onstage to more raucous cheers from his pals. Lennon compounded his gaffe by attempting to ask Ronnie if he had ever played drums before. Ronnie stopped and glowered. Lennon backed down and Ronnie heavily lowered himself behind Tommy's fairly elegant blue pearl drum kit. With a slack-jawed grin, he kicked the bass drum and said, "Let's go, fellers!"

They had no choice but to try to play behind his crashing and banging. As the night wore on, Ronnie liked what he was doing more and more. The Beetles started to get really worried. Not only about that evening, where the place could fly apart in a minute if they said or did anything to upset Ronnie or his pals. No, it was what Ronnie told John and Paul during a break. He said that he liked being in the group and if that drummer feller that didn't show up tonight didn't show up anymore, then Ronnie would just join the group. "How would that be, fellers?" Ronnie concluded.

Lennon ran to phone Allan Williams back at the Jac. For the first time since he had known him, Williams detected genuine fear in John's voice. He had no idea of how to handle the situation, any more than did the other Beetles. So Williams got back into his Jaguar and roared back out to the Grosvenor, where he encountered just what he had feared. The Beetles were loading up their equipment, surrounded by a sullen pack of Ronnie's boys, fingering their barely concealed chains, coshes, brass knuckles, knives, and God knew what else. Ronnie pounced on Allan: "You their fuckin' manager?"

"Yes," Allan allowed, while trying to hurry up the equipment loading and to get everyone the hell out. Ronnie told Allan how well he had played that night and he turned on the Beetles to demand their rating of his performance that night. "Fuckin' great, Ronnie!"

They rushed to load their guitar cases and poor Tommy's drums into a van driven by Allan's bouncer, Big Mac. Big Mac himself was hanging back: He and the diminutive Beetles and the five-foot-plus Allan would only be matchsticks against a gang such as this.

"What about it, then?" Ronnie demanded when even he finally figured out that the Beetles and company were trying to flee. Ronnie grabbed Allan with a viselike grip. "Wh-what about what, Ronnie?"

"You know, about taking me on!"

Williams began babbling while the others piled into the van. He remembered thanking Ronnie profusely for filling in so ably in the group's time of great need. "And if we ever need a drummer again at Grosvenor Ballroom, because we aren't at all sure, you see, my good man, whether or not our regular drummer, Tommy, a workingman like yourself, Ronnie, would be there for the next show or not, but if he weren't, well, then, sir, you would be only too welcome. In fact," Williams helplessly heard himself gibbering, "the Beetles are booked here next Saturday night and if old Tommy doesn't show then we'll certainly look forward to greeting you, Ronnie, pal."

They finally made their escape. The threat of Ronnie joining them as drummer made such an impression on them all that Allan was able to convince them to take a run with him back out to the Garston Bottle Works that very night to make one last pitch to Tommy. All of a sudden they all—even John—appreciated Tommy a great deal. Tommy was so touched that, leaning down from his forklift, he agreed to maybe give it another try. He played with the boys once more on the following Monday, June 13, at the Jac, but then disappeared again and that was the last they heard of him. The Beetles were drummerless yet again. Although Tommy's drum kit disappeared after his final date at the Jac and he didn't take it with him, no one seemed to know what had become of it. It was along about that time that Paul's brother Mike noticed that a nice-looking bluish drum kit appeared at the McCartney home and that Paul started teaching himself how to play drums on it. Allan Williams later claimed that George Harrison swore to him—in front of Ringo Starr—that Tommy Moore was the "best, by God" drummer that the Beatles ever had.

They went back to playing the Neston Institute on Thursdays, the Jac on Monday nights when the Royal Caribbean Steel Band had their regular night off, and the Grosvenor Ballroom on Saturday nights. Ronnie—the Beetles thanked their lucky stars—lost interest in being a Beetle or else had a very short memory. He never made another appearance.

The Beetles, meanwhile, were so desperate to find a drummer that they literally tracked one down on the streets. One night Williams left the Jac to catch a breath of air on Slater Street and, after a moment, noticed the unmistakable rumble of a drummer running through his drums, getting ready to practice. Then the mystery drummer got down to it, really rattling his traps, and Williams ran inside to fetch the Beetles from the basement to come and hear. They did and agreed with Williams that whoever and wherever the drummer was, he was pretty good. They actually fanned out, ears cocked, up and down Slater Street to try to direction-find the sound. It was coming from somewhere above, but they couldn't locate it.

They started knocking on doors at random, with no luck. They tried again the next night and finally pinpointed the sound as coming from a window above the National Cash Register office across the street. When the Beetles knocked on the door and shouted up at the window, the drumming stopped and the light went out. They persisted, shouting up, "Hey, Mr. Drummer, please come down! We're musicians. We want to talk to you." Down came one Norman Chapman, picture-frame maker. He worked above the National Cash Register office. He liked to use his little workshop to practice playing the drums after everyone had gone home for the evening. He was only an amateur, he told them, but he loved to play the drums.

He was good, they agreed on that, so Norman Chapman sat in with the Beetles for part of that summer of 1960 until he was conscripted for national service and went off to serve in Kenya and Kuwait with the Army. He was good, but at six feet two inches Norman Chapman was much too tall to ever be considered a permanent Beatle.

John and Paul and George and Stu blundered on drummerless through the summer of 1960, meeting at the Jac and hanging out there, cadging coffee and cigarettes and toast. For a while Stu worked as a garbageman in Huyton, on Liverpool's edge, the only job he would ever hold other than as the Beatles' bass player. He told Allan he did not so much for the few bob he was making—although he could use those—as for the "real" people he got to meet as he went from door to door picking up their garbage. He made paintings of some of them, done in a truly grotesque style. A major influence on John's style, as well.

Naturally Paul and John made fun of Stu's new job, holding their noses when they saw him or jumping into an empty garbage can at the Jac. Bad as they thought the garbage business was, though, their next job took them down as far as they could go. "You're broke," Allan told them. "Right?" "Right," they answered. "You need work, right?" "Right." "Well," he said, "I have just the job for you." When they found out what it was, they were stupefied, shell-shocked, and truly amazed by the sheer breathtaking crassness of it. They thought that the time he had them paint the ladies' loo in the Jac was bad enough—and now this? But Allan wore them down and browbeat them into taking the job.

He had recently branched out into a new line of work with a friend and associate of his named Lord Woodbine, who was really neither. The "Lord" was manufactured and the "Woodbine" monicker came from the brand of cheap cigarette that was always stuck to his lower lip. Lord Woodbine was a West Indian who was a colorful character in the seedy Liverpool 8 section. He worked as barman and bouncer in the shebeens and was well known for the large cutlass he kept under the bar in case of trouble.

Allan Williams, ever alert for business possibilities, noticed that there were no strip joints in Liverpool. Brothels, yes, and shebeens, plenty of those. But Manchester was getting strip clubs and it looked as if they would spread across the country, so Williams decided to open, in partnership with Lord Woodbine, Liverpool's first. It was in the dim cramped cellar of a terraced house at 174a Upper Parliament. They gave it a grand name: the New Cabaret Artistes Club. It had a little seven-foot-square stage, a tiny bar, and a few ramshackle tables and rickety chairs. The coatrack was seldom used, the clientele mainly preferring to keep their raincoats on. A little phonograph with some standard strip records completed the tableau. And the place was a success from the first.

Williams's main problem was in finding—and keeping, since he was not well known for paying large salaries to anyone—good-looking strippers. Liverpool 8 had plenty of hookers, but the area was not overrun with buff-shop bait. Williams turned to a stripmeister he knew in Manchester who sent over a candidate for an audition. Her name was Shirley and she descended into the dingy basement and removed her gear in order to display herself to Allan for his approval. He was suitably goggle-eyed, but when they got down to negotiations, she demanded a live band to back her up—or else no Shirley at the New Cabaret Artistes Club. He was furious and argued. "Look at the size of this club. There's noplace to put a fucking band." She was adamant. He took another look at her. (Her "tits stuck out like train buffers . . . no spaniel ears there" was his cogent assessment.) He realized he was in no position to argue. "I'll get you a band," he said. "You see if I don't."

He drove back to the Jac, wheels turning in his mind. The Beetles were barely working as long as they couldn't get a drummer, he thought. And—hmmm—they're sitting around nicking bacon butties from my kitchen and getting fat and sassy. It would do the lads good to get a spot of work. Be doing them a favor, actually. They shouldn't mind. After all, with a set of knockers like Shirley is carrying around, no one will notice who the scruffy lot of musicians is anyway.

He walked into the Jac and announced, "Coffee all round on the house for the Beetles."

They walked right into his trap after Williams's brilliant display of logic. "You lot have got almost no work anyway right now, so what could it hurt? All you have to do is play twice a night, twenty minutes a pop, and there's ten bob a night in it— ten bob a man."

They argued. "Do we have to do this thing?" Paul asked.

Williams kept after them until they finally admitted they were crazy to be turning down a paying job. Stu finally asked that the ante be raised up to a quid each.

"Balls to that," Williams said. "Why that much?"

"For the bloody indignity," Paul said.

Williams said he would talk to Lord Woodbine about a raise and that he, personally, felt they should get more money but naturally they ended up going on for ten bob each.

Williams took them over to the New Cabaret Artistes Club. They were horrified at what they beheld: a dank urine-smelling basement, cigarette butts littering the sticky floor, some discarded panties under the little awning that served as "dressing room" for the strippers, a mangy curtain behind the tiny stage. They swore under their breath, then they swore at Williams.

"We've come a long fucking way, Allan," Paul said.

He tried to mollify them, but they knew they had definitely come to some sort of bottoming-out moment, careerwise.

"The one time we had to play for a fuckin' stripper is when I really started thinkin'," John later told me. "That did us a favor in a lot of ways. I knew then I couldn't sit around on my fuckin' ass and wait for lightnin' to strike us. Time to get serious about a few things. I had to ask myself: How serious was I? Was I content to play the bleedin' piss cellars the rest of my life?"

Things couldn't change overnight, though. First, they were committed to backing Shirley up for a week.

She actually handed them sheet music for *Sabre Dance* and the odd Beethoven medley. They had to laugh. She had to settle for what strip-suitable songs they had in their repertoire: "Moonglow (The Theme from *Picnic)*," "September Song," "The Harry Lime Theme," "Ramrod," and so on.

So they got along tolerably well for a week. The Beetles, in their matching lilac jackets, were barely noticed by the patrons, just as Williams had predicted. A couple of them complained that the music seemed to destroy their rhythm, their stroke.

Paul later wrote a short article about the strip episode for *Mersey Beat* and recalled that he thought Shirley's name was Janice. He also, in typical boyish Paul fashion, claimed that the four of them had virtually been blushing throughout their sets whenever they had to look at Janice/Shirley. "We were all young lads, we'd never seen anything like it and all blushed . . . four blushing red-faced lads."

George was the one Shirley fancied anyway.

The strip business ultimately proved to be a little more than Williams and the Lord had envisioned. On Shirley's and the Beetles' last night, Shirley put on an unrestrained performance in which she simulated a sexual act with the floor. One of the raincoat brigade tried to trade places with the section of the floor Shirley had selected. Williams was no match for the wild man and Lord Woodbine had to chase him out at cutlass point.

The troublemaker returned two days later, forced his way in, and shot the place up. If that weren't enough to shake the entrepreneurs' resolve, they heard that the police were starting to develop an unhealthy interest in the joint.

So Williams and Woodbine sold out their interests to the local pornography lord. Williams went back to the Jac. Lord Woodbine bought a Cadillac and a shebeen in the very heart of Liverpool's vice district on Berkley Street. It was called the New Colony Club and its main function was as an afternoon and early evening bar where businessmen and others could meet hookers. A "booze and birds" bar: No sex on the premises. Consenting adults could meet there and agree to go elsewhere to consummate whatever they wanted to consummate, whether it was a "knee trembler" standing up in an alleyway or a more formal assignation in a cheap by-the-hour hotel.

Lord Woodbine and the Beetles had hit it off during the Shirley week. Their senses of humor meshed nicely and he enjoyed their music. He invited them to the New Colony to play when they had nothing better to do in the afternoon. They could drink free, banter with the girls, joke with the Lord, and poke fun at the boozing businessmen, which they loved doing. For their trouble, they would split four pounds among the four of them for a couple of hours' work. Sometimes, on nights when they were working late at the Jac, rather than take the bus home, they would repair to the New Colony. After Lord Woodbine finally closed his door for the morning, he and the Beetles would talk into the early hours while they drank Scotch and Coke, which quickly became the Beetles' favorite drink when they could get it (especially free). Often they would stretch out with the Lord's blankets on the dance floor of the cellar and sleep there. Sometimes it would occur to them that they spent most of their time in cellars.

They got so hard-up for work that Paul wrote once again to Butlin's, the holiday camp where he and Mike had debuted as the McCartney Brothers and where his cousin Bett and her husband Mike used to work. Paul wrote an ink-stained—with cross-outs—handwritten letter beginning: "I should like to apply on behalf of the group," which he then spelled as Beatals. Paul went on to say that the group had much experience and had acquired three vital things: "competence, confidence, & continuity." He signed the letter: "Yours Sincerely, J. P. McCartney."

They didn't get the gig.

And in early August they lost their only regular bookings that counted (playing at the Jac was hardly a way of life). Because of serious recurring gang violence, promoter Les Dodd had given up his "big beat" nights at Neston Institute. Gang fights became so serious and so identified with rock 'n' roll that dances at many venues were canceled. At other ballrooms and halls the promoters, unwilling to give up the increased revenues that jive and rock 'n' roll audiences brought in, simply stepped up the number and ferocity of the bouncers—"stewards"—they employed. At one performance by Jerry Lee Lewis at the Tower Ballroom in New Brighton, across the Mersey, Lewis had to go on entirely surrounded by stewards jamming the stage to protect him. The Garston Baths, where the Beetles sometimes performed, was in a very tough section and was known thereabouts as the Blood Baths. Unless there were specific citizen complaints, police regularly left the dances alone. It was not their duty to stop one teenaged lout from jumping on another one.

At such places as the Blood Baths, often the whole purpose of the evening for many was The Fight. The gangs went ready to take each other on or to do battle with the stewards. Those stewards became sorts of gangs on their own, since everyone was their enemy. They each carried a heavy wooden billy club and swung it liberally at the first sign of trouble. Those wooden batons bloodied many a skull, albeit the skulls of fourteen-year-old boys. Neither side gave quarter. The bands found themselves treading a very thin line. The fans supposedly came to see the bands, but many of these same fans just wanted to kick the crap out of them, along with everyone else they wanted to put the boot to. The bouncers were supposed to protect the bands, but often just regarded them as a bunch of faggot poufs who were causing and getting in the way of their nightly joust with the enemy. The bands were clearly in a no-win situation.

After their July 30 dance, the Silver Beetles were abruptly canceled out of their regular Saturday nights at the Grosvenor Ballroom in the first week of August. The article in the Wallasey *News* was headlined: DANCE OFF AT GROSVENOR TO-NIGHT: BID TO STOP TEENAGE GANGS' "DISGRACEFUL BEHAVIOR." The articcle itself said:

> Rock 'n' roll rows, hooliganism and complaints from residents living nearby have caused the cancellation of tonight's swing-session dance at the Corporation's Grosvenor Ball-

room, Liscard. The decision has been taken after reports of fights and rowdyism among groups of teenagers. "The trouble makers are small gangs determined to spoil the enjoyment of others," Mr. A. W. Micklewright, Wallasey's Publicity and Entertainments Manager, told the *News* yesterday. "Their behavior during the past two or three weeks has been disgraceful. Members of the staff have been threatened by them. We are determined to stamp out the menace and maintain the good reputation of the ballroom." Residents of Grosvenor Street and other roads in the area have forwarded to the Council a 21-signature petition complaining about "hooliganism and unreasonable noise at Saturday rock 'n' roll sessions."

Stuart Ferguson Victor Sutcliffe was the one who would introduce the group to its first influential impresario and who would, in fact, come up with the lasting group name (which began as Beatals). Under John Lennon's feverish influence, Stu had virtually quit painting. John, who was truly becoming a fanatic without a cause, had yet to have a clue that the music he loved could actually turn into his lifeblood and life's work. But as he soured on the art school, which he felt failed to recognize or acknowledge his genius, his life became his art. Or his statement. He would sit in Ye Cracke, the college pub, and act the Angry Young Man, the misunderstood poet. He was, in fact, drunk much of the time, but he had been doing that—sedating himself with lager—for so long since Julia had been killed that he could usually function under the influence. He and Paul were growing closer, in many ways because both of them had lost their mothers at a critical age. They spoke of the shared experience only in a sort of John–Paul code indecipherable to anyone else, but it was an essential bond. It would become obvious only after many years that John was externalizing Julia's death very noisily and messily, acting it out, while Paul internalized his mother's death and buttoned his emotions up tighter than a drum. Everyone around them knew of Julia's horrific death, but few were aware that Paul's mother Mary had died tragically around the same time. (The two mothers would, of course, later become immortalized in Beatles' songs: Julia in "Julia" and Mother Mary in "Let It Be.")

It was very important to John that he have his disciples around him. Paul was the rock upon which he built his group. Ever since their chance meeting at the Woolton fete, John and Paul had gradually become close-knit and John depended on Paul as a sort of second banana, as a loyal kid brother who would take up the slack wherever it was needed, as the unswerving loyalist who was there no matter what. And John had Cynthia Powell, who had fallen in love with him and would do anything that he asked or even suggested. And he had Stu Sutcliffe, the quiet aesthete who worshipped him. And there was Rod Murray, who moved into the Gambier Terrace flat with Stu and later shared it with John as well. And Rod's girlfriend Dizzy and Bill Harry, who would later start the influential Liverpool music newspaper known as *Mersey Beat*.

John also still had his sometime musical group. They were worshippers as well. John later talked about how he hand-picked his group: first laying his hand on Paul, then letting Paul bring George into the group. Paul and George came as often as they could to be with John at the art college and try to act like their hero. Bill Harry later remembered noticing Paul for the first time when Paul came to a college Panto Day, or Pantomime Day, an annual carnival. He especially noticed John's friend Paul because Paul came in drag, as did John. John and Rod Murray wrote a skit called "Cinderella," in which John was an ugly sister and Stu was Fairy Snow. At the previous Panto Day, John and Paul and George dressed up as vicars and paraded through Liverpool's department stores, leaping atop tables in the stores' cafés and demanding money for charity.

Those who came under John's spell would do whatever it took to please him or impress him. When John finally decided to tap Stu to join his group, he actually made it a sort of cruel competition between Stu and Rod Murray. He told them both that he needed another musician in the group and would prefer him (Rod/Stu), but it had to be someone who owned an instrument, preferably a bass guitar, which the Quarry Men needed. Neither Murray nor Sutcliffe could afford a guitar, of course. Murray began building a bass guitar, hand-carving the wooden body, and hoped John would select him. Then Stu was ecstatic when his painting at the John Moores Exhibition was bought for the staggering sum of sixty-five pounds. Now Stu could buy a bass and please John. In the third week of January in 1960, he spent the entire sixty-five pounds on a Hofner President bass guitar. He proudly told his parents that he was joining John's group. Neither Paul nor George was consulted about Stu's joining the band. It was John's decision and it was becoming obvious that John was not so much seeking talented musicians—indeed sheer musical talent never held any appeal for him—as he was searching for kindred spirits. Even though Stu had no feel for the music at all, he filled a vacant slot and he also bought an instrument the group needed. Plus he looked right and he was a friend of John.

Stu was also a member of the student union committee and, while he was being courted as a potential Quarry Man, he was able to book John's group into frequent dances at the art college's canteen. Additionally, Stu persuaded the student union committee that, since the Quarry Men had no amplifier, the committee should buy one. Strictly for use in the canteen, of course, and not to be removed from the building. Agreed. A new Tru-voice amp soon appeared and would just as soon disappear.

Musically, the group was not yet good at all. John and Paul were improving on their guitars, thanks to constant practice together, but they were no match even for George, who really provided what musicianship they boasted. Stu attempted to play bass, but really just noodled around on the strings. He had already started wearing his Ray-Ban sunglasses onstage and begun his trademark stance of turning his back on the audience. It was not, as some thought, an act of Bohemian defiance. He was merely trying to hide the fact that he couldn't play. The four of them had a definite presence, though: four whip-thin handsome sneering adolescents, with their greased-up Tony Curtis hairdos. And, although they had not yet developed the frantic stage show that would come in Hamburg, they nonetheless had gone beyond the wooden stage movements expected of a British music hall performer. The most a pop group, such as Cliff Richard and the Shadows, would do in the past was to essay a corny little step or two in unison or sway a little bit together. Very mannered. In March, though, they had seen Gene Vincent and Eddie Cochran at the Liverpool Empire and their rawness impressed them greatly.

It was also unheard of for performers to look the way the Beatals did. They were scruffy and they played in their street clothes because that's all they had. The closest they came to matching outfits in those days were dirty jeans, black T-shirts, and scuffed tennis shoes, or plimsolls. Cynthia Powell spoke for their female following when she said she found them "young, rough, and sexy."

And, even though Paul found initial audience hesitation—if not outright laughter—when he did the softer numbers, such as "Over the Rainbow," the girls soon started screaming for such numbers. Especially when he proved he could go from a crooning song to a full-bore screamer with "Long Tall Sally." His and John's singing improved markedly as they worked on their repertoire. They eventually let the others have a few numbers, of course. Stu would get his one song, when they let him croon Elvis's "Love Me Tender," and George could do Buddy Holly's "Crying, Waiting, Hoping," Elvis's "I Forgot to Remember to Forget," and a couple of others. But it was mostly a John and Paul show. They found that their styles complemented each other onstage, as did their writing styles together. And they were writing more together, even though they still performed only a handful of Lennon–McCartney originals: John's "The One After 909," Paul's "Like Dreamers Do," John's "Hello Little Girl," Paul's "Love of the Loved," and Paul's instrumental called "Catswalk."

John and Paul were also becoming fast friends. In April, during school holidays, the two of them took off together for the south of England. They hitchhiked, with guitars and packs on their backs. They spent part of their time visiting Paul's cousin Bett Robbins and her husband Mike. They had left Butlin's and were running the Fox and Hounds pub on Gosbrook Road in Caversham, Berkshire. While they were there Uncle Mike got them to perform twice at the pub, Saturday night and Sunday afternoon, April 23 and 24. He hand-lettered posters for their little show, nicknaming them the Nerk Twins, a name that they never used again.

Back at school they continued to hang around the Jacaranda on the fringes of the popular big groups such as Rory Storm and his Hurricanes and Cass and his Cassanovas, who would come in at night after their gigs around town and sit around and incite envy by being able to order—and pay for—whatever they wanted to eat.

Stu had attracted the attention of Allan Williams when he had helped Allan with his Mersey Arts Ball, a gala affair at the imposing St. George's Hall in the center of town. Stu, with John's assistance, had designed and built the elaborate floats, which were to be destroyed at the end of the evening—as at the Chelsea Arts Ball in London, which Williams was copying. In true Williams style, though, the crowd did not stop with the floats and almost wrecked the venerable hall when the fights started with fire extinguishers and flour bombs.

Williams respected Stu, which was the only reason he was to pay any attention at all to Paul, George, and John. He hired them to paint the ladies' lavatory at the Jac. (After the health authorities ordered him to. There was no men's room at the Jac—men went out back.) Stu and Rod Murray went on to paint elaborate murals on the walls downstairs (although Williams would later claim that John and Stu had painted them).

Williams, meanwhile, was plotting a huge career move for himself. Back in early March he had gone to the pop show at the Liverpool Empire that was headlined by the American rock 'n' rollers Gene Vincent and Eddie Cochran. Williams couldn't believe what he was witnessing. Not what he saw on the stage or what he heard coming from the musicians. Williams was never accused of having a golden ear. It was rather the audience reaction that astounded him. Allan Williams, at twenty-nine, was watching teenage girls actually caress their intimate private parts as they screamed at unkempt scruffy performers. He had never been in the midst of such a turned-on crowd, let alone been a close witness to such a sexual reaction to music or to musicians. He wasn't yet sure which it was or whether it was both. Naturally, though, given Williams's nature, whatever it was that he was caught up in there would be translated in his mind into profit. As an operator, he could smell the crisp aroma of new money in the air intermingled with the thick odor of teenage musk.

Right after the show he buttonholed Larry Parnes, the promoter, to see how he, Williams, could hitch a ride on this money machine. Parnes was England's big-time pop impresario. He had started by discovering Tommy Steele at the Two I's Coffee Bar in Soho and making him a star. That had been in 1956 and Parnes then assembled a collection of almost interchangeable young singers, whom he invariably renamed with new "power" show business names: Johnny Gentle, Billy Fury, Vince Eager, Dickie Pride, Lance Fortune, and so on. He also quickly became the Dick Clark of England, as the chief supplier of talent to the enormously influential music show called "Oh Boy!", which was avidly followed on television every Saturday night by every young aspiring musician in the country, including John and Paul. Parnes was also known in the business as "Mister Parnes Shillings and Pence," for reasons apparently connected with payment policies.

Williams met with Parnes and persuaded him to copromote another Liverpool show, with Cochran and Vincent returning to headline over a list of British and Liverpool groups. Williams scheduled it for May 3 at Liverpool Stadium, a 6,000-seat boxing and wrestling venue. Tickets sold well and Williams—"trembling with excitement"—was poised to enter the upper reaches of the entertainment business. It would make his name as a big-time promoter, as well as establish him as controlling all the Liverpool groups. Besides the headliners and Parnes's other performers, Williams had added the two biggest local acts, Rory Storm and the Hurricanes and Cass and the Cassanovas. He was modestly billing the night as "the greatest beat show ever to be staged in Britain."

Then the worst that could happen did so. Williams turned on his radio on April 17 to hear that Cochran and Vincent, on their way from Bristol to London, had been in a horrible car wreck near Chippenham. Cochran had been killed and Vincent, who was crippled anyway, was seriously injured. Williams, naturally, was filled with shock and regret. But he telephoned Larry Parnes straightaway, of course, to see what could be done to salvage his ailing show. Parnes told him that Vincent was not hurt badly and could still perform, but he advised Williams to cancel the show because he felt the Liverpool kids would feel sufficiently cheated by Cochran's absence and that there would be big trouble.

Williams felt the show should go on. To beef up the bill he added more local groups: Gerry and the Pacemakers, Bob Evans and his Five Shillings, Derry Wilkie and the Seniors, Mal Perry, and the Connaughts, who were still featuring Nicky Cuff, the midget singer.

John, Paul, George, and Stu came along as paying customers, since Williams didn't feel that they were ready for the big time yet. He was right, as it turned out. The four were students that evening and from their cheap seats they studied what went on, analyzed the stage movements, and made note of what worked musically and what did not.

By all accounts, the night was a great success. This was the first time that the Liverpudlian beat groups had been presented on a large scale—their first time out of the cellars—and the audience reaction to them had been overwhelming. It was the first indication that the local groups had that what they were doing was not an isolated thing, that there was some kind of massive demand out there for them. And, when the place turned into a riot after Gene Vincent came on and the gangs started ripping up the seats and hurling them and Williams and Parnes ran around the boxing ring that was the stage and were stomping on kids' fingers to encourage them to fall back into the crowd, it had been Liverpool's own Rory Storm who quelled the riot. Storm, who had a bad stutter except when he sang, leapt onto the stage during the worst of it and started a stern lecture: "S-s-s-s, s-s-s-s, s-stop it, you k-k-kids!" They listened to him and stopped it.

Afterward Williams was flushed with excitement. Obviously, the local beat groups and—coincidentally—Allan Williams had an incredible future ahead. He took Larry Parnes back to the Jac for late-night sandwiches and to talk about his future. Parnes told Williams he was quite impressed by the reception the local groups had gotten and he felt he might be able to use some in the future to back his singers on tour. He had two stars, Duffy Power and Johnny Gentle, about to tour Scotland and he might call on Williams to supply backing groups. Williams knew Parnes did not pay all that well, but he agreed it could be a big break for the local bands. As the night wound down, Williams noticed, off in a corner, John, Paul, George, and Stu listening intently to what was being said.

A couple of days later John came to Allan as he stood in the doorway of the kitchen of the Jac and asked the now-famous question, "Hey there, Al, why don't you do something for us?"

"Like what?" Williams sneered. "Like use us as one of the groups Parnes wants," John said. "You've got no fucking drummer," Williams told him. "How can you do anything without a drummer?"

Lennon was crestfallen for once. "Christ," he said, "we don't know any fucking drummers." Williams continued to rag him about having no drummer, but finally said he would try to help.

It was Brian Casser, the Cass of the Cassanovas, at Williams's suggestion, who finally found the Beatals their first drummer: Tommy Moore. He came in and met the Beatals. They had absolutely nothing in common, but they needed him. Williams let them set up in the basement and practice during slow afternoons. As they improved, he would let them play on Monday nights, when the Royal Caribbean Steel Band had the night off. They had no mike stands, so George hit upon the idea of fastening the microphones to the ends of some broomsticks that Allan had lying around the Jac. Female friends of the band were easily persuaded to squat in front of them and hold the broomsticks up as if they were microphone stands. They actually preferred that. Williams's usual payment for the group was Cokes and beans on toast.

Cass also let the group sit in one afternoon at the Cassanova Club on Temple Street. It was Casser who also suggested that they add Silver to their name. They were fooling around with the name Beetles as a change from Beatals because John liked the idea of an insect name in the style of Buddy Holly's Crickets. Casser suggested—since it was obviously John's band—the name of Long John Silver and the Beetles. John wasn't having any of that, but he and the others liked Silver Beetles or Silver Beats as an alternative.

Meanwhile, in London, Larry Parnes had not forgotten about the Liverpool groups. He wrote to Williams, telling him that he would like to bring singer Billy Fury to Liverpool to audition groups there for Fury's upcoming tour. Would Williams, Parnes's letter continued, care to assemble his best local bands? Williams would and did and there was a palpable sweat on in Liverpool. Even though the groups didn't give a damn about Billy Fury, Larry Parnes could still be the magician to pluck them from the dank cellars of Liverpool and into the bright lights of "Oh Boy!" and beyond into the cosmos.

Williams, too, was a nervous wreck. His budding career as promoter and manager was on the line. He decided to hold the auditions in the basement of the Wyvern Social Club, around the corner from the Jac, on Seel Street. He was in the process of acquiring it and turning it into the Blue Angel. For groups, he decided on the obvious big two: Rory Storm and the Hurricanes, who were just coming off a big tour of Butlin's holiday camps, and Cass and the Cassanovas. Also Derry and the Seniors. And, after intensive lobbying by Stu and John, he included the Silver Beetles.

On the big day, May 10, the groups assembled at the Wyvern. Paul and John, for whom this audition was a very big deal indeed, had decided to spruce up the band's image. They all wore clean jeans, semi-matching dark shirts, and sporty black-and-white canvas shoes. Cynthia Powell came along for inspiration and sat in the darkness in a corner, with her legs and her fingers crossed to try to bring good luck to her boys.

Williams posted one of his employees at the door to signal him when Parnes and Fury got there. He walked around telling everyone to be cool, that Parnes and Fury were ordinary men who put their pants on one leg at a time just as they did. Just as everyone was calming down a bit, Williams was abruptly seized by a spell of the dry heaves and ran out back to try to bring up whatever was there. The bands eyed each other warily. They knew each other, but not well, mainly on sight. Rory Storm, the six-foot-two golden boy of the local scene, was known to all of them. Despite his stutter, he was the most self-assured of the local stars. He had the biggest local following and he had assembled what was well and away the best of the local bands. He also had one of the two best local drummers in Richard Starkey, a sad-eyed, big-nosed, bearded lad from Dingle. His fondness for rings was already earning him the nickname of Ringo. He was not terribly outgoing and not known outside of the Hurricanes.

The other powerhouse local drummer was a Maltese, a brawny shirt-sleeved dynamo named Johnny Hutchinson. His sobriquet was Johnny Hutch and he kept the beat for Cass and the Cassanovas. Johnny Hutch had been derisive toward the Beatals/ Beetles as soon as he saw them. As a workingman, he pegged them correctly as a bunch of artsy-fartsy students playing at rock 'n' roll. As he observed, they could neither attract nor hold a drummer. With that he rested his case.

So imagine Johnny Hutch's irritation later on when the Beetles' drummer, Tommy Moore, was nowhere to be seen when Mr. Parnes and Mr. Fury signaled for the next group to play. Parnes and Fury, in their decidedly non-Liverpool silk suits, had arrived at the Wyvern's cellar in a wave of strong after-shave lotion, then had plonked themselves down and waited to be impressed.

Without Moore in sight, the Beetles were frantic when it came time for their ten-minute spot. Lennon pleaded with Williams, who called on Johnny Hutch to fill in for Tommy. Hutch was furious, but did so until Moore dragged in a few minutes later, trailing feeble apologies all the way. By then the damage had been done.

Oddly, to this day no one who was there recalls what songs the Beetles did in their brief audition. Given their repertoire at the time, it is likely that John did an Elvis or a Buddy Holly or Chuck Berry song—probably "Jailhouse Rock" or "That'll Be the Day" or "Rock and Roll Music"—and Paul did Little Richard, as he was starting to do so well, with "Long Tall Sally" or "Tutti Frutti." The remaining snapshots of that audition show a supremely uninterested Johnny Hutch in the background, Stu typically turning away to hide his face and his talent (or lack of it) at stage right, George trying to look professional on guitar at stage left, and at stage center—at stage center, ladies and gentlemen, we have John and Paul doing their best to rock out and look as cool as can be, bent over at the waist, flexing that pelvis, turning those ankles over, moving and grooving. Two obvious stars-to-be.

Fury was terrifically impressed and turned to Parnes. "This is it, Larry," he said. Parnes, the old-timer, held back. When the Beetles had finished, he pulled Williams aside and asked if he could hear the group do another number without the bass player. Fury protested, but Parnes persisted. Williams, since Stu was his friend and the only reason he had met and gotten to know the Beetles, was more than reluctant to ask "his group" to play without Stu. He did, of course, pass on Parnes's request to the Beetles to have Stu sit out for a number. Apparently even Parnes had glommed onto Stu's lack of musicianship and he wanted to hear if the Beetles sounded better without Stu.

There was a sudden silence in the cellar. Lennon said, "We're a group. All or none." There was much shuffling of feet and more awkward silence. John made it plain that they would play with Stu or they would not play at all. Paul looked to John to see what he should do. Even though Paul did not like Stu and resented John's bringing him into the group, Paul appreciated and fully understood the economic realities of bringing in someone who could actually buy a bass for the band, not to mention the Tru-voice amplifier Stu had "provided." John wanted results and Paul learned that fairly quickly from him. So Paul looked to John for his lead. Paul also knew that he served in the band at John's whim, even though they were writing songs together. They were pals and partners, but it was always obvious that John was the senior partner. If John mentioned that he wanted something, it always seemed that Paul greatly desired the exact same thing about ten seconds later. So when John flared up about Parnes's resistance to Stu, so did Paul, even if as an echo: the "me too, me too" became almost a rote John/Paul response in any situation. Once John spoke on any subject, Paul could be counted on for the "amen corner."

Everyone at the audition thought that was that. Cynthia Powell and Allan Williams, as two fierce Beetles fans, were sure that their chances were forever pissed away. Loyalty to the inferior bass player had apparently cost the Beetles their ticket to the big time. The Beetles were acting like prima donnas, though, once John and Paul saw that they had leapfrogged past the hottest Liverpool groups of Rory and Cass in the emotional reactions of Parnes and Fury. John knew that they had it locked (or at least he claimed many years later that he knew they had some kind of a lock when Parnes asked for a number without Stu and his pitiful bass playing) and sensed, rightly, that he and Paul were the group's appeal.

Allan Williams took Stu aside and apologized profusely. Then he prevailed upon Stu to take out his sketch pad, which he always carried with him, and—as a kind of last-ditch suck-ass appeal to Parnes—to make and present to Parnes a sketch of him and Fury at this audition. Well, the sensitive Stu finally broke down and did that. He autographed the drawing and gave it to Parnes. "No hard feelings," Stu said. It may well have made a bigger impression than the audition did. (In later years, Parnes would claim that he thought the Beetles, even with Stu, were absolutely fab and gear and that it was only their middle-aged drummer, Tommy Moore, who arrived for the audition late and crabby, who initially put him off the Beetles.

(Many, many years later, in 1982, Paul talked on a BBC show about his first exposure to Parnes at that awkward audition and the fact that he and the Beetles subsequently did a tour for Parnes. Obviously joking, Paul said that he had never been paid for that tour. He was shortly thereafter sued for slander by Parnes in a lawsuit that was finally settled in 1984 with Paul apologizing to Parnes on the air. Ironically, the original talk show that Paul had allegedly slandered Parnes on was called "Desert Island Discs" and dealt with what records or sounds Paul would take with him if he were stranded on a desert isle. Paul obviously wanted to hear the sound of a cash register ringing on his desert isle.)

Paul was still sending out handwritten letters to promoters and journalists and anyone else whose ear or address he could attract. A sample letter found him introducing the lineup of himself (first), John, Stu, and then George. He admitted that this "line-up may at first seem dull but it must be appreciated that as the boys have above average instrumental ability they achieve surprisingly varied effects. Their basic beat is off-beat, but this has recently tended to be accompanied by a faint on-beat; thus the overall sound is rather reminiscent of the four in the bar of traditional jazz. This could possibly be put down to the influence of Mr. McCartney who led one of the top local jazz bands (Jim Mac's Jazz Band) in the 1920s."

Paul went on and on about the marvels of his little four-piece band. He said that modern music was the "group's delight, and, as if to prove the point, John and Paul have written over fifty tunes, ballads and faster numbers, during the last three years."

Paul went on to list the titles of some of their original songs and, he said, the boys liked to rearrange such golden chestnuts as "Moonglow," "You Are My Sunshine," "Ain't She Sweet," and "You Were Meant for Me."

As for biographical material, Paul wrote that John was a student at the Liverpool College of Art, nineteen years old, and a veteran musician and poet. And guitarist Paul McCartney, he wrote, was eighteen years old and was "reading English Literature at Liverpool University." The letters would have been more convincing had they not arrived scribbled on lined composition paper, with ink splotches and cross-outs.

*   *   *

The Parnes audition did a lot for the Silver Beetles. Cynthia Powell had never seen John and Paul so puffed up. It was all they could talk about for days. Mr. Parnes, Mr. Big-Time London Music Man, had liked them. And Billy Fury too, even if they didn't give two damns about his taste. All that mattered was that he had been impressed. But they were actually starting to think the unthinkable: that they were good enough to be professionals, to actually make a living at the one thing that they loved. There were no precedents for what they were doing and they really had no one to learn from. British pop music was mostly a disaster area as far as they were concerned. They were not pretty boys that Larry Parnes could discover, rename as Paul Pride and Johnny Justice, dress up in silk suits, and present to the world as smiling, polished, domesticated—read: castrated—music hall gents, swaying gently onstage to a safe-as-milk melody. They had absolutely nothing to do with that. But what they did have to do with, they weren't sure.

But the Parnes business gave the guys some swagger. It gave John a little more gumption the next time his Aunt Mimi was on his back about him wasting his time fooling around with that silly guitar. And Paul started to feel a certain vindication in his zealous pursuit of music. Jim encouraged him, although Jim didn't really understand the music scene that Paul was part of. Still, the notion of this rock 'n' roll turning into a serious career was just man-in-the-moon talk. Kids could play around with this rock 'n' roll all they wanted to, but when they got out of school, they found a job and that was that. That was Liverpool reality.

Another thing the Parnes audition got them was another audition, one that could lead to bigger things locally. A promoter named Brian Kelly had started presenting jive sessions in North Liverpool in mid-1959 and had been the promoter most aware of what was becoming the beat sound. On May 14, just four days after the Parnes audition, the Silver Beetles, known as the Silver Beats that night, auditioned onstage for Kelly in the middle of a jive night at Lathom Hall in Seaforth. Kelly was presenting Ted "Kingsize" Taylor and the Dominoes, Cliff Roberts and the Rockers, and the Deltones that night. Although that was the night that Stu was attacked and kicked in the head by teds who didn't like the Silver Beats' looks, Kelly liked them well enough to book them for the next Saturday night, on May 21. And a local newspaper, the Bootle *Times,* trumpeted the Silver Beats as having made a "sensational appearance."

They never made the May 21 show, though, and didn't even bother to let Kelly know they wouldn't be there, even though he had advertised their scheduled appearance. He was obviously not happy about such cavalier treatment from a group that, at that time, needed him more than he needed them.

The reason the Silver Beats missed their May 21 show at Lathom Hall and the reason it never entered their excited brains to let Kelly know they wouldn't be there was that the Big Larry Parnes Break had finally come, although it was not exactly the lightning bolt of stardom they had half-expected. Parnes called Allan Williams up on the eighteenth and booked the Silver Beats to back up a singer known as Johnny Gentle on his tour of Scotland, beginning two days later, on Friday the twentieth, in Alloa. Johnny Gentle (real name: John Askew) was not the Silver Beats' idea of a star to hitch a ride on, but he was all they had. It was not much of a tour, either: nine days in towns in northern Scotland, hardly the entertainment capitals of the world. And the pay was only eighteen pounds a week each, with the matter of expenses too vaguely unsettled and unstated to work in their favor. But the Silver Beetles were ecstatic. They were going on the road and being professional.

That was when the nom de plume jag hit them. Lennon was above such childish excitement and for Tommy Moore the concept was simply inconceivable, but Paul, George, and Stu all decided to adopt stage names for the tour. After much discussion, George decided to become Carl Harrison (in honor of American rocker Carl Perkins), Stu snagged onto Stuart de Staël (from a Russian painter), and Paul, after considering and rejecting the Valentino name, came close to it by becoming Paul Ramon, a name that many years later the pivotal American punk rock group the Ramones would take from Paul.

There was also the matter of responsibilities in Liverpool. George was working for an electrical company and had to figure out an excuse to be gone from work for more than a week. Tommy Moore had to do the same thing at the Garston Bottle Works. John could simply keep doing what he had been doing, which was not going to class. Stu could start doing the same.

And Paul. Paul has always maintained that he was able to persuade Jim that he, Paul, would be in much better shape to tackle his upcoming exams at school if he traveled in Scotland for a while. Jim, as bachelor father and sole wage earner after his Mary's death, was not able to be both father and mother and to be as close to his boys as he would like to be. Paul could get his way if he wanted.

So John, Paul, George, Stu, and Tommy set off from Lime Street Station to conquer the world. Or at least part of Scotland. The tour was mostly a disaster. Allan Williams got a call early on from a furious Larry Parnes, who had just heard from his Scottish promoter Duncan McKenna, who was outraged when he first got a glimpse of the scruffy backup group that piled off the train. These Silver Beetles, with their greasy DA hairdos, tight jeans, black T-shirts and sweaters, and scuffed tennis shoes, were not the model of fashion for Scottish dance halls. They were also not really matched for the Johnny Gentle sound. Johnny would go on in his best white sport coat and behind him were five scruffy louts in jeans and whatever.

The tour was also logistically a disaster, zigzagging from Alloa to Inverness to Fraserburgh to Keith to Forres to Nairn to Peterhead. And the Silver Beetles' money did not seem to cover their expenses. John and Paul called up Allan Williams at the Jac to plead with him to wire money to them and they called Parnes collect to try to get money out of him.

Tommy Moore quickly began to hate the Beetles. John and Paul made fun of him, even onstage. He was always relegated to the worst bed, when they would have to crowd in together to one or two cramped hotel rooms for the whole band. The others, especially John, also ate everything in sight immediately, a catastrophe for other band members on a shoestring tour.

Then there was the van accident, when Moore lost his front teeth and also his temper and his patience.

The road to Hamburg had started very indirectly, back in late June, when Everett, Pecan, Bones, and Slim—the members of the Royal Caribbean Steel Band—jumped ship from the Jac. One night they were there and the next evening, when Williams tooled his Jaguar down from Huskisson Street in Princes Park, they were gone. The rumor on the street was that they had been lured away to Hamburg, of all places, by a German club owner. Williams was mystified. First of all, he didn't understand what the possible appeal of a Caribbean steel band could be for a club in Germany. Second, he couldn't comprehend why Everett, Pecan, Bones, and Slim could be such ingrates as to abandon such a swell place as the Jac, where they had such a cushy gig. Sure, he didn't pay them that much, but they were drawing side money on the dole, weren't they? Williams was at a loss to figure it. Meanwhile, without a nightly music draw, he let the Beetles play now and again down in the stifling unventilated cellar. Mostly, they were paid in the form of whatever they could eat, drink, and smoke in the Jac.

The members of the Royal Caribbean Steel Band still possessed enough warm feelings for Allan Williams that they wrote him a "Having a good time, wish you were here" letter from Hamburg, detailing for him the golden allure of the nightlife on the Reeperbahn. The music clubs, they wrote, amounted to picking up found money on the street. What's more, the clubs were desperate for good groups. Allan should come on over, they wrote, and check it out. If ever there were a man for whom "check it out" was a way of life, Williams was it. He started thinking about Hamburg, hatching little ideas, mulling things over.

Williams tried, with no success, to borrow money from his bank to finance a trip to Hamburg. He intended, he said later, to take the Beetles over with him. He had similar lack of luck in trying to borrow money from his friends. Then he hit upon a scheme: a charter planeload of Liverpool businessmen bound for Amsterdam. He couldn't take the Beetles along, but there was room for himself and his sidekick Lord Woodbine. They would hitch along to Amsterdam and then take the train on to Hamburg, visit Everett and the others, and check out the Reeperbahn for themselves.

First, though, Williams decided to make a sort of sampler tape of some of the Liverpool groups to take along as a sort of Liverpudlian showcase to play for the Hamburg big shots he was certain he would meet.

So, in the cellar of the Jac, he assembled the Beetles, Cass and the Cassanovas, and Noel Walker and the Stompers. He set up a tape recorder in the cellar and said, "There you are, boys.

Play your numbers and I'll take this tape over to Hamburg."
None of them were terribly eager to do so and they had no
idea what he meant with his Hamburg venture, but they agreed
to make a tape. Williams had a pressing engagement with his
accountant, so he left John Lennon in charge of the recording
session. Lennon agreed only after delivering a number of his
Kraut jokes.

When it came time to enplane for Amsterdam, Williams packed
up the Jac cellar tapes, along with a change of underwear and a
clean shirt, and he and Lord Woodbine set off—top hats firmly in
place—to conquer the Continent. After drinking their way through
Amsterdam, they finally took a train to Hamburg and started
hitting the clubs. They found no sign of Everett, Pecan, Bones,
and Slim where they had heard they might be ensconced, but a
club owner directed them on to the red-light district. After a
round of club crawling, Williams left Lord Woodbine with a
stripper and ended up in a giant basement club called the
Kaiserkeller. He had never seen anything like it: a giant subterra-
nean dance hall where a thousand people could be packed in.
Liverpool certainly had nothing like it.

Williams was quite impressed with the tasteful nautical
decorating motif: fishing nets and glass floats hanging everywhere and a ship-shaped bar and brass portholes lining the
walls. What impressed him even more was that, in a place
this huge, there was not a single empty table. There were
patrons as far as the eye could see. The cash register in his
soul started ka-chinging away. What bothered him though was
the sort of malaise hanging in the air. There was a German
band onstage, woodenly trying to play rock 'n' roll and sound-
ing like a military ensemble rendering a leaden version of "Tutti
Frutti."

The patrons, Williams noticed, were not responsive to the
band at all and seemed to be just sitting around drinking and
waiting for something to happen. For Williams's part, he made a
quick mental comparison of the sounds coming from this German Death March Quartet with the quicksilver, explosive young
bands back in Liverpool's cellars. There was no contest, he
knew. Then, to confirm his feelings, the Death March Quartet
finally stopped and people started moving around expectantly.
When a song by Elvis jumped out of the jukebox, the place

figuratively exploded with rock 'n' roll fever and Williams knew that he was really on to something. He had never seen such a social experiment carried out.

In the one brilliant inspiration of his life, Williams knew instantly that the Mersey bands back busking in the Liverpool 8 cellars for cigarette and coffee money could come to Hamburg and be transformed into something . . . big. He had some kind of instinctual feeling that the young Liverpool bands were the key and that the Hamburg crowd represented the giant lock and that all he had to do was combine the two. Each had what the other sought, in a very sensuous, sweaty, and urgent sort of way. Rumbustious and lusty, he thought. A coupling was definitely in order.

Williams had his Jacaranda tapes with him, but of course spoke no German and had no idea of what to do next. Then his inbred nightclub instincts took over and told him: He was in a club that could use those groups he had on tape there in his pocket. All he had to do was find the boss man of the joint, give him an earful, and there he'd be. So Williams started in through the chain of command of the club. When he let a waiter know he wanted the boss, the waiter sent over a suspicious bouncer. In his best pidgin German, Williams told the bouncer that he came in peace and needed to jaw with Mr. Big about music: "You know, 'Tutti Frutti' and all that."

That got him to the floor manager, who finally took him in to see the owner. He was ushered in to see an unprepossessing figure named Bruno Koschmider. He was a bulbous-nosed, crippled former circus clown who spoke no English. Koschmider summoned an English-speaking waiter to translate, but just as talks got under way, there was an interruption. Bruno got word that a customer was causing trouble on the dance floor. Bruno reached for his personal cosh—a long ebony truncheon—and rushed out and waded through the crowd of bouncers who already had the hapless troublemaker down and were kicking him. With evident relish that turned even Williams's stomach, Bruno set to with his cosh until it was covered with blood.

Back in his office he wiped the blood off as if nothing untoward had happened, sat down, and resumed talking. Williams gave the German the spiel of his life. "I represent," Allan said, "the greatest fucking rock 'n' roll groups in the world back in Liverpool—the very home of rock 'n' roll—and they are the very ticket that you need to liven up this place."

"Are they as good as Elvis?" Bruno wanted to know.

Williams acted incredulous. "Elvis fucking Presley? Any one of these groups would shut down poor old Elvis in a Hamburg minute. The Beetles are destined," he said, "to be the biggest thing since the zipper."

Bruno was intrigued. Williams tapped his finger on the tape lying on Bruno's desk and told Bruno that those bands would make him "a fucking fortune."

Bruno was even more intrigued. He asked how much it would cost him. Williams said, "Oh, about a hundred pounds a week, plus travel money to come over from Liverpool."

Bruno nodded assent and asked to hear the tape. He hauled out his Grundig, spooled the tape up, and sat back expectantly to hear the best fucking music in the history of the world or, at least, of Hamburg nightclubs.

Silence from the Grundig. Then the most ear-splitting, atonal piece of noise imaginable rent the air. Nothing even close to music. Bruno looked puzzled and Williams was livid, already cursing under his breath: "Goddamn Beetles." It was too obvious what had happened. The Beetles were not yet studio wizards and had thoroughly botched the recording.

Strangely Bruno wasn't offended. "Make another tape and send it," he instructed Williams. If the groups were as good as the spiel had been, he was still interested.

Williams dragged home to Liverpool, very dejected. Not only had his big scheme fallen through, but his pal Lord Woodbine had been so taken by the intrigue and the pleasures of Hamburg that he had decided to stay on. So Williams went home alone.

Back in Liverpool nothing was shaking but the leaves on the trees. The Silver Beetles or Silver Beatles, as they were known from one day to the next, were severely chastised by Williams for wrecking his big Hamburg chance. "The tapes were okay when they left *our* hands," they protested. Williams, whose life included such defeats on a depressingly regular basis, shrugged it off stoically. Life went back to a semblance of normalcy.

The Beetles, still drummerless and rudderless, hung out at the Jac or practiced at George's house or at Twitchy's or—not so often—at Paul's when Jim was sure not to be there. John failed his lettering examinations at college. Cynthia actually did the test. Even though Arthur Ballard, the one teacher there who saw artistic potential in John, succeeded in getting probation for John, he started skipping classes and it was obvious that his school days were numbered. The wreck of a room that he shared for a while with Stu on Gambier Terrace ended up in, of all places, *The People* newspaper one Sunday. Under a headline reading: THIS IS THE BEATNIK HORROR was the untidy studio, with the empty coffin that John sometimes slept in prominently featured.

Once John was out of Aunt Mimi's house and out on his own on Gambier Terrace, his girlfriend Cynthia Powell started sleeping over with him. To say the place was never cleaned is an understatement. Often the electricity was off and they had to make do with cold water and candlelight. Cynthia later remembered that everything was covered with dirt and that they would often emerge in the morning looking "like a couple of chimney sweeps."

John was very taken by Brigitte Bardot and began trying to shape Cynthia in BB's image. She went from brunette to blonde and shocked her parents when she started sporting black net stockings, a tight miniskirt, a tight black sweater, and high heels. As the only identifiable Beetle girl, Cynthia soon found herself very uncomfortable. Even this early in their career, the Beatles were acquiring hard-core fans who felt no sympathy or liking for her. Just as many of the teddy boys hated John, the teds' birds detested Cynthia on sight. "The most dangerous place for me in those days was the ladies' loo. I honestly thought that once I entered, I wouldn't get out again in one piece, or worse still that I would never be seen alive again."

Paul had been dating a friend of Cynthia's named Dorothy Rhone, whom everyone called "Dot." She was just seventeen when they met. Dot had short naturally blond hair, a vivacious personality, and she had, everyone agreed, a pixie face. She was from Childwall, very near Woolton. She worked in a pharmacy and still lived at home with her parents, who were strict with her. She was very soft-spoken, blushed easily, and, Cynthia said, "idolized Paul." He often wrote to her and for her eighteenth birthday, hand-lettered a card to her that read:

THE WOMAN OF ALLERTON. FROM THE LATE SIR JAMES CROW, TO DOT, HAPPY BIRTHDAY, HIGHNESS, O GREAT SILVER BUBBLE OF THE SILVER SEAS, HANDSPUN.

Another card he sent to her from Hamburg read:

TO DOT OF ENGLISH FAME AND GREAT RENOWN. THIS ONE'S A QUICK & HAPPY. HE HASN'T SHAVED, BUT HE LOOKS GOOD ALL TIME SAME. ALL MY LOVE PAUL.

As the summer of 1960 wound on and the Beetles began running out of bookings, there was still the off-chance that Larry Parnes would pluck them to back yet another of his oddly renamed singers, such as Georgie Fame, on tour.

Then Parnes struck—although indirectly and again it was one of the improbable events of Allan Williams's life that led the Beetles to Hamburg. During that summer, as musical fortunes waxed and waned for the beat groups, not all of them stayed together. Band members went back to their day jobs as the reality of the beat economy came home to them. One such group, which Williams represented occasionally, was Derry and the Seniors, featuring Derry Wilkie, a West Indian singer. They had gotten bookings from Parnes and had regrouped and were buying new stage outfits and equipment and so on. Then disaster struck.

The first Williams heard about it was a hammering at the door of the Wyvern Club. The door flew open and in came the Seniors' large sax player, Howie Casey, trailed by Derry. Casey, a large man, was enraged and he grabbed Williams by his lapels and threatened to knock him into next week. Williams had no idea what he was talking about and he tried to mollify Casey as the story slowly came out. Casey was apoplectic because he had given up his day job to go back out on the road with the Seniors and now here out of the blue came a letter from the eminent Mr. Parnes, canceling their Blackpool date. "So," Casey said, "first you get bounced around and then I'll go find the great Larry Parnes and tear him apart as well."

Williams, naturally, wanted to preserve his own skin as well as his profitable and prestigious working relationship with Parnes, so he racked his inventive brain for a solution to the problem at hand. What he came up with is implausible as ever, although it worked. Even though Williams had never thought of taking "his groups" to London to try to make it and the groups themselves had never thought of trying to go to London for the Big Break, a vision of London came to him. London had not been a really viable option for the Mersey groups. That was mainly because of the snobbery of the London musical establishment toward the provinces (that would, of course, be the main reason why it took the Beatles so long to get recorded), as well of the almost complete disdain of rock 'n' roll on the part of Official England, from the BBC to the local promoter to the police. The groups, responding to and even anticipating that rejection, never made the effort.

But Allan Williams suddenly got it into his head to take Derry and the Seniors to London to find them immediate work. Williams knew that the famous Two I's Coffee Bar in Soho was auditioning groups. The Two I's had been the jumping off spot for singer Tommy Steele. Williams knew Tommy Littlewood, the owner of the Two I's, and Tommy suddenly became his best friend. So he had an immediate mental picture of Derry and the Seniors taking all of London by storm.

Williams, while Howie still was holding him up by the lapels and shaking him, managed to present this glowing scenario to Howie and Derry and they bought it immediately. Excited, they rushed outside to tell the other Seniors, who were just idling out in the car while Howie put the boot to Allan Williams. Even as Williams mopped his brow in relief, the Seniors ran back in, ready to set sail for London and success. Williams packed them and their gear all up in his van and off they went to London, two hundred miles away.

At the Two I's, not only did Tommy Littlewood recognize Allan Williams, he let him put Derry and the Seniors on his stage immediately. Amazing, the Seniors thought.

While Williams was savoring his triumph, a strange man wearing eyeglasses and an eye patch came up to tell him that a German man in the corner wanted to talk about the group onstage. Williams went over and . . . he gasped. There was Bruno Koschmider, whom he had last glimpsed puzzling about the garbled Beetles tape in the Kaiserkeller in Hamburg. Bruno and Allan fell over each other like long-lost brothers. Through a local interpreter, Herr Steiner, that Bruno had fetched from a spot called the Heaven and Hell, Williams learned that Bruno, seemingly despairing after receiving no tapes from Allan, had set off for England to find some of the fabulous fucking rock 'n' roll groups that Allan had rhapsodized about. Not knowing the difference between Liverpool and London, Bruno had ended up in London, asked to see the hot club, and was directed to the Two I's, where he had plucked singer Tony Sheridan and had taken him back to the Kaiserkeller, where he was a smash. Sheridan's real name was Anthony Esmond Sheridan McGinnity and he had been a staple on the Saturday night TV show "Oh Boy!" Sheridan had been fired from the show and was on his way down the ladder when Bruno happened upon him at the Two I's and thought him a rising rock 'n' roll star.

Sheridan, a gifted singer and guitar player, had done well at the Kaiserkeller. Too well, in fact. He had been lured away by the owner of a soon-to-open club. So Bruno was back at the Two I's, looking for more British stars to bolster his nightclub. Williams gave him Derry and the Seniors and executed a verbal contract on the spot. Derry and the Seniors were in Hamburg and onstage performing before the week was out. "I trusted Bruno and Bruno trusted me," Williams later wrote. He was happy to find them work, but just as happy to get them off his back and out of the country. Not that the Seniors had no difficulty, though, in getting there. Neither Williams nor Bruno bothered with getting work permits for the band (and, in fact, told them to present themselves as students at the border), so when the members of the group headed for Hamburg immediately, they were taken off the train by German border guards and held until they pooled their money to make a panicked phone call to Williams, who did the same to Bruno, who seemed to have enough influence to get them into the country. Once they got to the Kaiserkeller, though, tired and broke, they were forced onto the stage immediately by Bruno and they exceeded his expectations. They were great. He was back in business in a big way. Bruno got his crowds back and he started thinking expansion. He decided to open another beat club on the Reeperbahn and he wrote to Allan to tell him to get him another great beat group.

Williams wrote back, suggesting the Beetles. He also wrote to Derry and the Seniors, telling them to expect the Beetles. He did not expect the vitriolic reply he received from Howie Casey, who informed Williams that they had "a great fucking scene going here in Hamburg. Now you want to fuck it up by sending over that bum group, the Beatles." (Ironically, Casey would many years later play sax with Paul McCartney and Wings.) Casey went on to punctuate his expletives by reminding Williams several times that the Beetles were no fucking good and that if another Mersey group had to come, it should be Rory Storm and the Hurricanes.

Williams actually checked, but Rory and the Hurricanes were playing up at a Butlin's holiday camp in North Wales and were completely unavailable. He also offered the gig to Gerry and the Pacemakers, but they declined.

Williams didn't have much of a choice of groups left to him. Although he claimed to be managing a number of groups, technically speaking, he was acting as their agent. In those days, given the youth of the groups and the newness of the whole rock 'n' roll scene, anyone with a telephone could be an agent. Someone such as Williams, with a telephone and a car, was a manager. In that sense, he managed the Beetles.

So he dangled the tantalizing plum of Hamburg before the Beetles, reminding them again that they would have to have a drummer before they could go.

George Harrison and his brother Peter regularly would hang out at the Casbah, where his friend Ken Brown was playing. The matter of Brown's exit from the Quarry Men at the Casbah many months before had been forgotten. Brown had gone on to form the Blackjacks, with Mo's son Pete Best on drums, along with Chas Newby and Bill Barlow.

The first week of August, when the Beetles learned that they had lost their only remaining paying gig—at the Grosvenor Ballroom—they went out to the Casbah, at number 8 Hayman's Green. They knew that they had a chance for the Hamburg gig, but only if they had a drummer. And there were no surplus drummers or drum kits around. And they knew that Pete Best, although he had been drumming only a few months, had a spanking new drum kit of blue mother-of-pearl, with real calf-skin skins instead of the usual cheap plastic. They gave Pete a big hello that night and admired his drum kit.

A couple of days later, Pete got a call at home. It was Paul McCartney. "How'd you like to come to Hamburg with the Beetles?" Paul asked. Pete was excited. Paul cautioned him that there were auditions going on and that it was by no means a sure gig for Pete. Tommy Moore, for instance, Pete was told, might or might not be able to go, but was Pete up for auditioning? (Pete, of course, did not know that Tommy Moore had forever gone back to the Garston Bottle Works). "Sure!" Pete said. He always wondered later why the call had come from Paul, when he had always had the impression that John was the leader of the group.

That very week, on Friday, August 12, the Beetles had Pete Best come down to Williams's Wyvern Club on Seel Street for his audition. It was a sham, a preordained matter that he and his drum kit would propel the group to Hamburg. He didn't know that, of course.

He was a little surprised, though, at how casual the audition was. Only John was there when Pete arrived and set up his kit. John noodled around on "Ramrod" for a while, none too concerned. Stu and George dragged in after a while. Much later Paul, who had been the one to give Pete the exciting news, came in and they all played for a bit. Then Pete got the news: "Yeah! You're in, Pete!" Allan Williams arrived after the fact, none too interested in the proceedings. And Pete Best was thrilled at becoming a Beetle.

Hamburg was the litmus test, the trial by fire for Paul, the place where he grew up in a big hurry. Had Jim McCartney known what was in store for his firstborn, he would never have assented to Paul's German adventure. Even though Jim had been a musician and still had those wild stray Jim Mac's Jazz Band memories shooting around in his brain, he wanted only for Paul to escape the uncertainty that he had known and to find and hold on to the best—i.e., most lasting—form of job security that he could.

After all, Paul had demonstrated not a single iota of musical inspiration. He had, it was true, taken to the guitar with an intensity, but thus far not that much had come of it. True, he wouldn't even seat himself on the toilet without his ever-loving guitar, but what did that count for? Even though Jim had that old stand-up NEMS piano in the parlor, neither Paul nor Mike went near it. Once Paul discovered skiffle and then jive and rock 'n' roll, the guitar was the only instrument that mattered. Even though he would forever hold on to and treasure and be influenced by and even record some of those old music hall standards taught to him by Jim, Paul was captivated by the new guitar-centered sound.

Jim was after Paul to strive for Teachers Training College and probably would have gotten him there if Paul's mother had still been living. She would never have put up with the drainies and the late hours and the drinking and the John Lennon whom Jim would not tolerate at all. She had dreamed that her boys could have escaped what she had known of life and would have gone on to become professionals: doctors or barristers.

Paul, though, was always very sly about getting what he wanted. His teachers saw one side of him, his mom and dad glimpsed yet another, and his rock 'n' roll mates experienced a totally different Paul. He projected the image that would get him what he wanted.

With the Hamburg thing, he first recruited his little brother Mike to work on Jim. That was a pattern consistent with Paul and he soon recognized a kindred pattern in John. Neither of them would ever do the dirty work—the convincing or the talking-to—themselves, as long as they could charm or browbeat or threaten a loved one or an underling into undertaking that function for them. Once Paul and John discovered that, they flourished, because they had found the great secret of powerful people who use others. They were rewarded and glorified for whatever they did that was wonderful, but if they did anything that was less than wonderful, they had any number of scapegoats to look to. Many were the shoulders to bear the blame; few were the hands to receive the gold.

Paul went to Mike. "I've had some amazing news, but I don't know whether I can tell you," he teased. Of course, in a few minutes he had spilled the beans to Mike that he had the chance to go to Hamburg and become rich and famous and also along the way he would buy little brother lots of great presents—

unless, of course, Dad stands in the way. Only little brother could help persuade Dad.

Even that didn't fully persuade Jim, so Paul called in Allan Williams, who visited Jim at 20 Forthlin Road. Allan, who could be very persuasive, talked of the cultural advantages to be gained by becoming a musician in Germany, of the, uhm, high cultural standards and the, ahm, interaction with German counterparts and the fresh input and so on. And the culture. And the travel. Allan made it sound like a well-chaperoned combination of summer camp and study abroad. So Jim finally gave Paul his blessings.

Hamburg

THE good ship Beatles—they finally settled on this spelling of the group's name—set sail from Liverpool early on the cool morning of Tuesday, August 16, 1960. Allan Williams got to the Jac just after dawn and parked his shabby old green Austin van on Slater Street. The bulbous vehicle was actually closer to being a minibus, with four windows on either side and low wooden benches running down either side of the interior, from just behind the front seat to the rear door. The rest of it was just bare metal. Williams had no idea of whether or not the old Austin could actually make it all the way to Hamburg, but with his ever-present optimism he was ready to force it all the way there by sheer willpower.

He unlocked the Jac and started bustling around the kitchen. While he was occupied, the Beatles started arriving. Untypically, Paul was the first. He had come in on the bus from home, where his father, in giving him his final blessings for the big adventure, also gave Paul vague advice on keeping healthy and clean in the foreign land to which he was bound. Mike was actually more excited than Paul was and made his big brother promise to write often and get him lots of presents in Germany.

Paul got to the Jac with his guitar and a kit bag with clean underwear, extra jeans and tennis shoes, and a couple of black Marks and Spencer sweaters. To get ready for the big trip, Paul and Stu had nicked fifteen pounds in an advance from Allan for extra clothing and toiletries and so on. (Allan made Stu and Paul sign an official IOU, of course.) Even so, they were traveling light. Paul, anticipating chilly Hamburg evenings even in August, wore a waist-length heavy jacket with a thick fur collar that he kept turned up.

John and Stu arrived together, with their guitars and the Tru-voice amp. Stu wore his ever-present Ray-Ban shades, which were just beginning to get under Paul's skin. This morning, though, they were all too excited about the trip to let anything bother them.

Pete pulled up in a taxi with his precious drum kit. As they waited for George, the other four were too keyed up to do anything but mill around and speculate about the trip. They were caught up in a genuine holiday spirit. "Almost like going away to scout camp," Paul joked. Since he was the only one of them who had actually been away to scout camp, the others ragged him about that.

Williams started loading bags and equipment into the Austin, barking directions and generally taking charge. He instructed his wife Beryl to go inside the Jac and have the girls in the kitchen make up a hamperload of bacon butties for the long trip.

Meanwhile, who else should show up but Lord Woodbine? Back from Hamburg on a brief visit, he was hitching a ride back to Germany with them. Allan sent Lord Woodbine off to rustle up a little propane stove to brew tea during roadside stops. It was to be a very low-budget excursion. Beryl's brother, Barry Chang, had decided to go along for the ride, as had Beryl, so they already had a passenger manifest of nine persons, plus the drum set, four guitars, bags, and so on.

As Williams piled the luggage higher and higher on the roof rack of the old Austin, the Beatles got into the spirit of adventure more and more. They had wanted Allan to paint their names on the sides of the van, so they would look like—so they thought—a professional touring troupe. Williams, perhaps wisely, had neglected to get that done.

After George arrived, the Beatles decided to put their names on the van themselves. They were art students, after all, some of them. So, while they got one of the girls in the kitchen to mix them up a big bowl of flour and water, they sat down with a stack of newspapers from Allan's office and painstakingly cut out the word "Beatles" and their own names. These they very carefully slathered with paste and stuck on both sides of the van. People would know who they were now, that was for sure. It looked like hell, they cheerfully admitted as they stood back to admire their handiwork, but it was certainly in keeping with the quality of their recent career.

Finally Allan got everything stowed away to his satisfaction and they all piled in, three on the front seat and six on the little benches in back. And away they went down Slater Street, off for the Continent and God only knew what else. John and Stu were nineteen years old, Paul and Pete were eighteen, and George was just seventeen. He was too young to even be legally admitted to the roaring nightclubs of Hamburg's notorious red-light district, much less play in a band in them. In point of fact, the whole band was on somewhat shaky ground for even entering Germany.

To save time and money, Allan—just as he had done with Derry and the Seniors when he sent them off to Hamburg— planned to have the Beatles enter Germany in the guise of "vacationing students." They could explain the presence of all the musical gear as being necessary to serenade any fellow students they might encounter during their travels. Thus, the Beatles carried no work permits at all. John himself barely had a passport. He and Allan had had a frantic last-minute bit of scrambling around to get him one; the main problem being that his mother was dead, his father was missing, and his guardian, Aunt Mimi, had not legally adopted him. But they finally made him legal.

It was still early as the Austin van edged out onto the A5 and Williams goosed it up to almost fifty as they headed for London, singing and joking. Even though they hadn't known it, they had had one solitary person representing a farewell committee back in Liverpool. Stu's mother, Millie Sutcliffe, even after her painful good-bye from Stu, had stolen down to Slater Street and stood, unseen, in a doorway, from which she bade Stu a tearful silent farewell.

As he maneuvered the Austin down the A5, Williams delivered a travelogue to the others on what they might expect in Hamburg's notorious St. Pauli district. Although Lord Woodbine was technically more of a Hamburg expert, Williams was after all the foreman of this little expedition.

With his bushy bristling beard, intense manner, his vest and tie, and garters puffing out his shirt sleeves just above the elbows, Williams looked rather like a slightly shabby schoolmaster. His motives were anything but educational and charitable. In return for his chauffeuring them to Hamburg, the Beatles were expected to pay him ten pounds apiece (a sum he later claimed he never received, along with the fifteen pounds he had advanced Paul and Stu. The IOU for the latter sum, however, specified that it was to be deducted from earnings). He was also going to Hamburg because he smelled money. If he could become Bruno Koschmider's British agent, he could perhaps then grow to control what he saw as the lucrative shipment of British bands to Germany.

Williams also stood, of course, to collect a percentage from the Beatles' earnings in Hamburg. Though he had yet to spell out to them all the minute details of his contract with Bruno, he was to collect—via bank deposit from the Bruno Koschmider Betriebe (agency)—an initial ten pounds a week commission from their total salary. For their part, the Beatles would be paid thirty DM, German marks, a day from August 17 to October 16. In exchange for that salary, they were expected to play every night at the Indra Club from eight to nine-thirty, ten to eleven, eleven-thirty to twelve-thirty, and one to two. On Saturdays they would start at seven and end at three in the morning, with half-hour breaks, and on Sundays they would begin at five and end at one-thirty in the morning. They ended up often playing longer hours and their breaks, called "pauses" and pronounced "powzers" in German, seemed to shrink. There were other contractual restrictions they didn't know about yet.

All that, though, was far in the future as they sailed down the A5, eating bacon butties and singing snatches of "Maggie May," the bawdy anthem of Liverpool's seedy Lime Street.

For their part, though, the Beatles really had no illusions about Williams. The nature of their relationship has been open to dispute by both sides over the years, but there can be little doubt in retrospect that it was strictly a matter of mutual exploitation. As the Beatles began to have their little successes and to gradually become more knowledgeable about the business of the music business, they didn't and wouldn't hesitate to exploit and use anyone that they could to advance themselves. That had been obvious on John's part—and then on Paul's—as soon as they caught on to the name of the game. Quick as they found out that they had something unique—a musical persona unlike any other— that other people wanted a piece of or merely to bask in the reflected light of, they were just as quick to extract an admission fee from anyone who wanted in. Whether it was members of the Quarry Men who were used up and discarded, or girlfriends being curried because they had money or useful friends, or musicians who had drum kits they needed, or even John's friend Stu being pitted against his friend Rod Murray to see which one of them could first win the Beatles' favor by getting a bass guitar for the band, or a promoter with some useful club dates they needed, or anyone else to come (Pete and his drum kit were acquired pretty quickly), there came to be a pretty price that was extracted for access to the Godhead.

For his part, Williams was smart in recognizing their talent first. He wanted to get a huge return for that. He was no different from them in that each sought what they could get from the other.

Their personal relationship was tenuous. John and Allan saw each other immediately for what they were and gave each other a grudging respect for that. Allan always claimed that he and Stu were close. Since Sutcliffe is long dead, there is no method or even a reason to prove otherwise. Paul disliked Allan from the start. Even back then Paul was visibly offended by people who came across as plain hustlers and who pretended to no gentility whatsoever. He was social climbing even then. It was obvious that Paul felt that Allan was beneath him. It was strictly a matter of the class that Paul pretended to.

As for the others, George was still the silent kid brother who went along with what John and Paul wanted. Pete and Allan did not get along at all, although Pete was so quiet and moody it was hard to tell who did get along with him.

As far as their business relationship went, Williams maintained then—as he still does—that he was their first manager, although the contracts that he did have with them were only for engagements he secured. That was something he was doing with other groups and he said he managed them too. Semantics aside, they found each other useful.

On August 16, 1960, though, the future seemed nothing but rosy for all concerned as the Beatle express rolled into London.

They had to make a stop, Allan explained to the complaining Beatles, to take on yet another passenger. He was George Steiner, who had been Bruno's translator and man-on-the-scene at the Two I's. Herr Steiner was on his way to Hamburg to work for Bruno. He was waiting for them outside the Heaven and Hell and squeezed into the back.

Then on to the North Sea crossing to the Netherlands. The dockworkers at Harwich at first refused to handle the scruffy old Austin. They said they were afraid that, with its unwieldy load on top, it was too unstable to survive the lift by the crane's sling onto the ferry. Williams talked them into giving it a try. Today there is a very famous picture, taken by Allan's Chinese brother-in-law Barry Chang, of that Austin—license number VKF 961—hanging in midair, dangling from the ropes like some helpless fat green beetle. They got everything stowed on board the ferry, had a few beers, and then bedded down on the benches and the floor of the ferry's bar.

The next morning, when they got off the ferry in the Netherlands, the Dutch authorities weren't buying the happy students abroad story and wanted to question this merry band made up of five greasy-haired Scouse louts with a lot of guitars and drums, a Chinese brother and sister, a German national who was acting a little nervous and edging away from the others, a black Lord from Liverpool with a Caribbean accent, and a fast-talking bearded little dynamo of a man who admitted nothing. They finally sailed on through Customs. Williams claimed it was Paul's baby-faced charm and John's cockney cheekiness that got them through. It may well have been just due to the impossible implausibility of that strange gang of ten traveling together in the worn-out old Austin van with the odd markings on the sides.

There was a war memorial to British soldiers at Arnhem that Allan wanted to see, whether anyone else wanted to or not, so that was the first stop after clearing Customs. They had sandwiches and tea and a pleasant enough time, except for John, who refused to get out of the van and made some pointed remarks about glorifying war that excited Allan's ire. Even so, they were all still having a lovely time and posed for pictures (except for John and Herr Steiner, whose absence remains unexplained) that Barry Chang took of them in front of a memorial inscribed with the words: THEIR NAME LIVETH FOR EVERMORE. That was, of course, later to be judged highly prophetic. At the time it was just another memorial and they were just some generally unremarkable travelers who happened to stop there.

After the stop at the memorial, Allan and John soon exchanged harsh words over another matter. The Beatles went off to look for souvenirs in a shop and John went on a shoplifting jag. It horrified Allan when John emptied his pockets of a harmonica, guitar strings, jewelry, and some handkerchiefs. For the group, it was just survival as usual. When they needed something badly enough and didn't have the ready cash for it, there was only one thing to do, they reasoned. This shoplifting habit was to follow one or two members of the group long after he or they became extremely rich and he or they continued to nick things for the thrill of it and because he or they liked to save a few pennies by doing so. At the time, though, Allan was right to advise John and the group that if they wanted to be deported or arrested as soon as possible, shoplifting was the fastest ticket going. As soon as Allan started lecturing him, though, John put on his arrogant face, his silent face, that would become in self-defense the Beatle face that all of them would present to the world when the world came after them. At the time it was just John telling Allan, "Too fucking bad. I did it. So what?" The other Beatles backed John up.

They drove on toward the German border in a stony silence. At the border the authorities didn't question the cock-and-bull story of the happy students on holiday and their spirits all went back up. Especially after they picked up some German beer and started singing again and wondering aloud about Hamburg and how wonderful it would all be. They had hardly gained Hamburg proper when near-disaster struck. Lord Woodbine had spelled Allan at the wheel and he promptly ran the van aground on some tram tracks. Got the wheels stuck firmly and then through the large van windows they could see a tram bearing down on them and they all yelled for Lord Woodbine to get the fuck moving. Wheels smoking and spinning, he did so just in time. "Jesus Christ! That was close," Allan said as he regained the wheel and reassumed command of the ship. And then—shit!—he promptly rear-ended a woman driver and there they were. Fortunately, the damage was minimal and they were off again, searching for the neon lights. They finally pulled into the St. Pauli district just at nightfall.

The bright garish inviting lights that make up the hot neon façade of the St. Pauli were just winking on as the Beatles cruised down the Reeperbahn in search of the Grosse Freiheit, which held Bruno Koschmider's two clubs, the Kaiserkeller and the Indra. The Beatles were literally open-mouthed. Allan had told them it was a wide-open district, but nobody had imagined just how wide-open it really was. Forget poor old Lime Street in Liverpool. This was perversion on the grand scale. Prostitutes and pimps as far as the eye could see, strip dives nestled cheek to cheek on the pulsating street, the hot white lights pushing the flesh for sale, the raucous bark of the touts as they stood out on the grimy sidewalks and tried to lure the suckers to just come in and check it out, sailors and hoodlums and just plain good-time Charlies all out on the night's stroll and jostling each other as the desperate search for the night's good times—and the night's profits—began. Everything and everybody seemed to be for sale. Transvestites, dope pushers, dope fiends, hookers beyond all imagination, flaming homosexuals, cross-dressing lesbians—just imagine it and it was there. All manner of the residents of society's dark underbelly could find a home in the St. Pauli. The very air was electric with the smell of perversion. This was truly a city without limits.

Allan pulled the van up outside number 36 Grosse Freiheit, Bruno's Kaiserkeller. The Beatles jumped out, stretched, looked around, and took in all the bright lights. They liked what they saw. "A bit of all right, lads," said John, the captain. "We're gonna like it here," seconded the first mate, Paul. Their eyes were shiny bright as they made their way through the noisy crowd downstairs into the Kaiserkeller to meet their great bene-factor, Bruno Koschmider.

They were not exactly made welcome by their Mersey mates. Howie Casey of Derry and the Seniors, who were on a brief break between sets on the Kaiserkeller's stage, walked up to inform them loudly: "You're not playing here. You're on at the Indra, a fucking strip club." He smiled with disdain.

Allan rushed in to try to reassure his boys that the Indra was only a former strip club and that Bruno thought so much of their capabilities that he had transformed the Indra into a musical showcase just to hold the fragile genius that was theirs and that they would be the very first band in the whole world to set foot on the stage of the Indra and that they would, in fact, do that very soon, that very evening. Just a few moments away.

Bruno came limping up to check out his new charges. He proclaimed himself charmed by them. They didn't know what to make of this gimpy-legged, bullet-necked, grim-faced, stove-up old ex-circus clown who was giving them the eye the way a butcher would size up a fat cow.

With his newly arrived translator, Herr Steiner, in tow, Bruno led them out of the Kaiserkeller and down the Grosse Freiheit to the Indra Club. They were dismayed to see that, as they proceeded down the strip, the lights grew dimmer, the action slower, the fleshpots less fleshy. If there was a wrong end of the Grosse Freiheit, the Indra was it.

Outside number 34, there were no blinking, winking lights, no screaming touts, no action, no marquee screaming: BEATLES! "There are no lights whatever," an astonished John remarked. He stepped into the dimness of the little foyer and struck a match. "Amazing," he said, as the other Beatles crowded around him to decipher, in the faltering light of the match, a tiny poster that read: THE FABULOUS BEATLES FROM LIVERPOOL, ENGLAND.

Bruno brushed by and motioned for them to go inside and have a look around. The place was so dead they might as well have been back in Scotland with Johnny Gentle at one of those fucking "beat ballad shows." There were two bored-looking patrons knocking back glasses of schnapps. They looked like they had raincoats on. A silent jukebox. A funereal bartender. Gloom, nothing but gloom. "Is early yet," Bruno said in his pidgin English, which was sometimes translated by Herr Steiner, sometimes not.

"Okay, boys?" Bruno asked on his own. The boys grumbled one or two okays. Bruno gave them a little pep talk, translated here and there. He told them that the Indra may have been just a strip club, but it had been transformed for the arrival of the Fabulous Beatles and once the Fabulous Beatles took over, people would come from far and wide just to watch them "mak show." That was the closest he could come to saying "make show" and those were two words the Beatles would soon dread the very sound of. As of yet, though, they hadn't any idea what he was talking about.

Bruno clapped his hand Teutonically and led his lads outside and down the street and into a decrepit-looking movie theater that he owned called the Bambi-Filmkunsttheater at number 33 Paul-Roosen Strasse. No one had yet dared ask where they would be staying. In all the excitement that issue had just never come up. They were about to find out.

The theater was better known as the Bambi Kino. As Bruno took them around to the stage door, they each had a sinking feeling in their gut that they were about to see their billets. They were all too right. The Bambi was a crumbling old hulk of a theater that had been converted into a cinema and its old dressing rooms lay in acute disrepair. It was to these that Bruno led the Beatles.

It was completely dark inside. They went down an old stone corridor, past the back of the cinema's screen. They could hear muffled gunshots and horses' hooves pounding and more gunshots. Just past the cinema's toilets they came to a "dressing room." As soon as they saw a light ahead, the Beatles began running to claim the best spot. They drew up short at what they found: a tiny windowless room crammed full with two camp beds and a suspicious-looking couch.

John won the footrace to the room and claimed the best bed. Stu took the second one and George was third, so he got the couch. Paul and Pete brightened up when Bruno announced that there were two more "bedrooms." They were about twenty-five feet farther down the stone hallway. There were no more lights and each "bedroom"—as Paul and Pete discovered when they lit a match and held it up for illumination—was just about five feet by six feet and held a camp bed. There was no room for anything else. That was their home. As they stood there, matches burning down, Paul tried to joke to Pete that they could swing a cat in there—"providing it's got no tail!" The walls were grimy with years of accumulated grease and dust, although Paul and Pete would never actually see those walls. No daylight ever penetrated those chambers and the only illumination that those dungeons ever had were the tiny beams from the pocket flashlights Pete and Paul carried to get dressed with or the glow from the embers of cigarettes smoked late in the night.

Allan and his sister and her brother and Lord Woodbine left to try to find a cheap hotel.

One of Bruno's bouncers came along directly to knock the Beatles out of their trances. He brought some thick blankets and lumpy pillows and he informed them that the cinema's toilets would be their personal bathroom. And he brought greetings from Bruno, who wished to inform them that they were due—by contract—onstage at any moment. If there could be one isolated moment when the Beatles grew up, this was it. As they looked at each other in the pale glow cast by the one bare light bulb in the "master dungeon," they could hear the gunshots popping away from the cheap Western movie on the nearby screen and they could smell the urine and the disinfectant from the toilets only a few feet away. And they could feel how empty their pockets were. And they also knew how far away they were from home. So they shrugged, smiled at each other, picked up their instruments, and went out to play.

The Beatles' debut in Hamburg was not the stuff of which legends are woven—or even whispered about. Not a hint of a legend or even a myth came close to the semideserted Indra Club on the night of August 17, 1960. The five of them were still exhausted from their thirty-six-hour journey from Liverpool, but they were troupers, so they clambered up onto that low cramped stage, plugged in, and hit it. Paul, his Tony Curtis hairdo glistening with pomade applied two days earlier, screamed into "Long Tall Sally" for the few perplexed customers who were settling in and getting ready for the usual evening of tits and ass. No tits and ass, the regulars noticed, as they gripped and then gulped their schnapps as this loud long-haired band assaulted their senses. Even Bruno must have had second thoughts that first evening when he watched his five greasy, skinny scouse teenagers in dirty jeans, sweaters, and tennis shoes bang away on their cheap guitars.

What even these critics couldn't know was that the Beatles still weren't very good musically but would be after a few weeks of this nightly practice by fire for hours on end. What was doubly worse was that the acoustics in the Indra were probably the worst of anyplace the Beatles had ever played. Like most of the strip joints, it was a narrow room, designed to hold as many patrons as possible. Since the place was still decorated (after a fashion) as a strip club, there were heavy drapes and curtains hanging everywhere and a cheap but thick carpet on the floor. As a result, whatever sounds the Beatles could make were immediately enveloped, muffled, and distorted by all that fabric.

That first night all five of them were heartsick as soon as the novelty of being in Hamburg quickly wore off and they realized that they had just started serving the first night of a two-month sentence in the Indra. All they had to look forward to after the long hours onstage was a return to the cold camp beds and the damp darkness of their "dungeons." And in the morning they could go for cold-water shaves in the Bambi's toilets. And then out onto the cold cobblestones to try to rustle up some breakfast in stone-sober daylight in the middle of a red-light district. Fleshpots don't burn well in daylight, the Beatles quickly observed. There was probably nothing as depressing as a strip joint at high noon.

The first few days in Hamburg, the Beatles didn't venture beyond the Bambi and the Indra. They were gaining some fans, but it seemed an odd exercise to play rock 'n' roll for a vacuum. Bruno, of course, was studying them closely, the old profit motive and so on bothering him. On one of the first few Beatles' nights at the Indra, he was impatiently watching while Paul droned through a fairly lazy rendition of "Somewhere Over the Rainbow." Bruno started fuming. This was not what he was paying good money for. He frowned and then stamped on the floor with his good leg and loudly ordered "his" Beatles (as he called them) to "mak show." The exhortation was taken up by some of the drunker members of the sparse crowd. "Mak show, boys, mak show!" "Mak show!"

Mostly out of the anger they had for Bruno and the contempt they felt for the audiences, John and Paul started doing what at first was their idea of a parody of a stage show.

Paul began racing around the stage imitating Little Richard, which he could do very well. He could outscream Little Richard and to that he added more falsetto screams and laughter and leaps and splits and bending over backward and "Ohhh! My soul!" fits. Trembling legs and pelvic seizures and rotating knees and windmill arms: Paul had it all down. He didn't mind because even then he would do whatever it took to draw an audience, to satisfy an audience, and to encourage an audience to come back again.

That was the British music hall tradition that his father Jim had instilled in him. Paul would never shed it. Without an audience, he did not really exist. With one, he became almost superhuman. It was the big difference between him and John. Paul had to have that fix that an audience's attention and applause provided him. John began to shrink from it, as if he wasn't worthy of an audience's approval and applause. And if he wasn't worthy of it, then any scumbag audience that would offer him that was obviously a bunch of dirtbag shitheads beneath even *his* contempt. And that became obvious even then. It was a yin and yang thing. John harangued and abused the audiences, rebuked them and scorned them, and then silver-tongued Paul came along to woo them and wow them, seduce them and bow to them, and to show that the whole Beatle act really was just an act and that the Beatles really did love you.

Even on those days when John was at his most vicious and drunk and spaced out on amphetamines and he really meant what he said, Paul was usually able to gloss over it and the whole thing became an act.

Even the songs* they were writing then and over the next couple of years showed that essential Beatle split: John's songs were invariably first-person songs, lyrics of introspection, of self-absorption, personal songs. Paul wrote mostly third-person songs, where he stepped outside himself and commented on others. No gut-spilling for Paul, unlike John. Paul became a control freak early on and John started going in the other direction almost as a reaction to that. But, again, that's where they would complement each other and were learning to do so in lousy fucking places like a third-rate ex-skin palace on the Grosse Freiheit, where they were expected to make the raincoat brigade get excited when they heard "Shimmy Shimmy" played by five half-drunk scousers with at least two of their guitars unplugged on purpose.

When the "mak show" business first started becoming serious, John as the leader was, of course, the first to react to it. And his typical reaction was to over-react to it. If Bruno wanted movement, well then he could expect fuck-all. John bitterly complained to Paul and George that they had not come all the way

*Even though all Lennon–McCartney songs were attributed to both of them, most were written separately.

over from Liverpool to "leap around like a lot of idiots." But, he reasoned, if they had to do so to ensure their survival, then he by God would be the leapingest around.

John started by resurrecting his favorite moves from Liverpool, where said moves had not been especially well received: his George Vincent cripple imitations. And his spastic impressions. In Hamburg the drunks loved watching John imitate a drunk and reel around the stage while he actually was drunk and reeling around the stage. Life and art sometimes merged in the demimondes of Hamburg and the participants in the action didn't always know or recognize the distinction or the boundary line. When the Beatles got into performing seven hours a night and were popping diet pills and slurping down the crates of beer that the punters were delivering up to them, they were lucky sometimes to crawl back to their dungeons still remembering at least their first names.

As time went on and word of their "mak show" spread, the Beatles began to acquire a considerable Hamburg following, even drawing away fans from the Kaiserkeller to the Indra. And it was for all the wrong reasons, at least as far as the Beatles thought. None of the fans wanted to hear original Beatles songs and, in fact, would not have known one if it bit them. These fans wanted original American rock 'n' roll songs that they already knew, they wanted them played loud, and they wanted them delivered with as much "mak show" as the boys could muster.

That was entirely up to John and Paul to deliver. Anchored as he was to his drums and his surly silence, the most Pete Best could manage was a bit of silly leaping about now and then with a tom-tom under his arm. Stu Sutcliffe was incapable—totally incapable—of doing *anything* onstage. He never learned a note on his bass before he gave it to Paul and he was terrified of being up there onstage at all. If he had not gotten that money for his painting that he immediately spent to buy a bass guitar because John needed a bass guitar, he might today be a live artist rather than a dead fifth Beatle.

Stu hovered as far as he could go at the edge of the Indra's stage and made what could charitably be called puppetlike movements. Paul started unplugging Stu's bass more and more without telling him and Stu didn't even notice. Once it seemed to be okay with John to criticize Stu full-bore, then Paul started doing so. John and Stu were friends, but not onstage. It became pathetically clear early on that John had drafted Stu into the Beatles only because he bought the bass the band needed. But as things wore on and on . . . it was plain that Stu wouldn't last in the group. But it was also plain that John would never say or do anything to hurt his best friend. No, he couldn't. So John put it off on Paul, who would inherit Stu's number one cabinet seat next to Lennon, to dust off Stu. Which Paul did. Slowly, in what became the standard drawn-out Beatle freeze-out, Stu was slowly being turned into a non-Beatle.

During the first Hamburg engagement, they were all still close—all the Beatles—but it didn't take long for things to change. And not for the better.

As for George's "mak show" duties, he was pretty much left alone. There was a good reason for that: As the best musician among them, he often had to carry all the musical weight. Someone had to hold things together onstage while John and Paul ran amok.

Sometimes Paul would unplug his guitar and throw himself at John. Or the two of them would leap from the stage and pretend to be wild bulls rampaging through the dancers. Or John would leap up on Paul's shoulders and the two of them would crash into Stu, knocking him down. Or Paul would butt John from behind while he was singing and the two of them would engage in a mock brawl that would have the lusty Germans cheering.

To their ultimate dismay, the Beatles found that their vituperative "mak show" performances were becoming the hit of Hamburg. The more contempt and anger they displayed—genuine contempt and anger—the more Bruno and the Germans loved it, banging their glasses on the tables and shouting and clapping along. The fans started sending drinks up to the stage for the boys and then began having whole crates of beer and champagne hauled up to them. *"Trinken! Trinken!"* they ordered the boys, who followed orders. Over the course of a long night onstage, they found that the more they drank, the better they felt and the better they felt, the more they drank. They began to feel that they could get away with anything onstage and to a certain extent they were right. Fans started referring to them as the "beknakked Beatles"—the crazy Beatles.

They all taunted the crowds to a certain extent, but John became an expert at it. He would call them "fucking Nazis" or "fucking krauts" or "German spassies" (Liverpool scouse for "spastic"). He would goose-step around the stage, saluting, and daring the crowd to "get up and dance, you lazy bastards!" Sometimes, to taunt the crowd even more, they would cease all movement onstage and play and sing while standing perfectly still, in a sort of "no mak show." It infuriated Bruno, which of course was the whole point. When Bruno's bullying failed to intimidate the Beatles, who were finishing their growing up very quickly in Hamburg's steamy hothouse, Bruno wrote to Allan Williams to try to get him to coerce "his group" into behaving. Good luck.

Allan wrote to them, advising them to heed Mr. Koschmider's words. "I understand," he wrote, "that you only move around the stage when there is no audience [Bruno probably exaggerated that part]—this is stupid and a suicidal attitude for any band to adopt." Allan went on to lecture the boys on what the public expected in a band (one which had superb stage moves, good music, and the correct attitude), to caution them that their entire future with Mr. Koschmider as well as with him was in jeopardy if they continued to behave in such a "casual manner," to warn them that if the rumors Mr. Koschmider had heard of their wanting to take a holiday were in fact true, well, then they could just expect one very long holiday indeed. It seemed to Allan that they were on a right bloody holiday as it was, having fun in Hamburg and getting paid a lot. And so on. In short, they should shape up and obey orders and become good little soldiers. He ended the letter on what he thought was a sarcastic note by thanking them for all the letters they had written to him.

John read the letter to the others in the master dungeon behind the screen of the Bambi Kino. They all had a good laugh at Allan, the little fuck, and then John crumpled the letter into a ball and set fire to it and tossed it in the middle of the floor, along with all the other crap lying there. "Screw Allan, that little pissant. We don't need him anymore."

They were in serious high dudgeon, though, with Bruno Koschmider. They really hated that jack-legged gimp with no reservations. All their illusions about Hamburg (and, by associa- tion, all their illusions about the world out there and their place in it) had been grossly violated by Bruno the first night they got to Hamburg. Between being locked in servitude to Bruno to "mak show" at the Indra every night and living virtually in the toilets at the Bambi Kino, they were in a constant state of seethe. They were further enraged that Bruno's contract with Allan prohibited them from performing at any other club within a radius of forty kilometers of the Indra without Bruno's specific permission. For their servitude they were being paid the equivalent of fifteen pounds a week apiece.

They complained on a daily basis to Bruno or his stooge and translator, Herr Steiner, about their dungeons at the Bambi. At first, Bruno assured them their quarters were only temporary and that practically any day now they would be moving into a luxurious dormitory. As the days went by and it became obvious that Bruno was lying to them, they hated him more and more.

The more they took their frustrations out onstage, though, the more popular they became and the more money they made for Bruno. If they changed the words of "Shimmy Shimmy" to "Shitty Shitty," the crowd cheered even more. So much the better, the drunken punters in the crowd agreed.

As the Indra became more and more of an attraction, though, Bruno began to hear complaints about the noise. Noise was perhaps the only thing that was illegal in Hamburg. Finally, without the Beatles having any advance warning, Bruno told them toward the end of September that he was being forced by the police to close down the Indra as a musical club and reopen it as a strip joint. The Beatles' joy was short-lived. Even though the Indra was shutting down, they were still under contract to Bruno and he had contract renewal rights. They had no rights. They were stuck. Early pictures from the Indra show them as extremely sullen-faced teenagers, glaring defiantly at the camera while wearing their best stage costumes: matching outfits of cheap fake-crocodile winkle-pickers, pegged black slacks, black shirts, and mauve sport coats.

The only good news coming out of the Indra's closing was that Bruno had decided to move the Beatles over to the Kaiserkeller, his flagship club, where Derry and the Seniors were about to be replaced by Rory Storm and the Hurricanes. That was perfectly jake with John and Paul, who were quickly turning into charismatic rock 'n' roll stars.

As their onstage confidence increased, so did their offstage behavior display an increasing self-confidence that was marked with a disdain for all things and people not Beatle-connected. They hadn't yet gotten into pissing on nuns (which would come later), but they were quickly learning that certain social immunities came with being a star.

John later told me during an interview that he actually didn't remember most of what happened during the group's five visits to Hamburg. It was partly, he said, due to the fact that any musician who has played thousands of shows remembers very little about most of those shows. But it was also due to alcohol and pills. "I was drunk most of the time," he said. "We were wild back then. And we pulled the birds like you wouldn't believe. Paul never likes to talk about that, but it was true. Hamburg. What a time. I mean, I can vaguely remember going onstage on all fours and then pulling myself up by the mike stand to sing. And they loved it, God bless the fucking krauts, they loved it. Yeah, I guess you could say Hamburg made us. But we fucking well made Hamburg too!"

Yeah, he said, he did remember sitting in the little dressing room at the Indra and sewing up his pants on many nights. During their powzers, the Beatles went to the bar or mingled with some of the girls and sometimes went for a quickie. John was the only one who exerted himself so much onstage that he often needed a needle and a thread, which were handed to him in the dressing room by a woman lavatory attendant. The Beatles christened her "Mutti" after the German word *Mutter* (for "mother").

Mutti took care of the Beatles when they came offstage and were soaked to the skin with sweat from all that making show and drinking. She dispensed towels while they stripped, toweled off, and changed into dry clothes. She would later move on to the Kaiserkeller with them, as would her large jar of "Prellies," or Preludins, a popular amphetamine tablet that would become standard Beatle fuel for those long nights onstage. (It should be stated that Pete Best said that he never took any Prellies or any other pills while in the Beatles.) Speed, like everything else the Beatles encountered, was regarded as a tool, as a means to an end. A pony to ride, as it were.

Then came sex. Sex was a whole other matter altogether. That's the closed and sealed and locked chapter in the official

Beatles archives. The fact that the Beatles enjoyed to the fullest the natural spoils of the rock 'n' roll game has always been a painful subject for the Beatles and their public relations apologists. Fucking was okay for scouse groups, even scouse groups that got by pretty well over there in Germany. Rock groups on the road fucked girls that they met, but after the Beatles got to a certain public relations plateau, they were not allowed to be viewed as fucking girls anymore.

Especially after Brian Epstein came along and gave them the squeaky-clean Doris Day make-over, the press and TV were quick to accept and dispense as official fact the myth of the mop-tops, the four cute-as-pie Liverpudlians in their matching Pierre Cardin collarless suits and squeaky clean haircuts. Your average American parent thought these were four *castrati*. And then there was the strange, partly sexless, totally unthreatening, partly feminine image that Brian wanted to project of them. In an America where short hair on men was a necessary badge of virility, this was a shocking change. But Epstein successfully sold the myth that they were wholesome lads, high school valedictorians, probably, and Merit Scholars and members of the choir, no doubt. They were nothing but wisecracking teenagers, according to the myth, who wanted nothing more than to hold your daughter's hand and of course do the decent thing by her, once they got past her hand. After the American mass media adopted the Beatles and officially proclaimed them Good Clean Fun, that was pretty much that. The Beatles could and did fuck their brains out while on tour and no one wanted to know or hear about it. Eagle Scouts don't fuck.

But back there in Hamburg in the fall of 1960, the Beatles were largely unknown. They had a modest and growing rock 'n' roll following. But they had never before known the kind of frenetic sexual behavior that was brewing up around them. Back in Liverpool they had had girlfriends and they had drawn a few dolly birds—splotchy-faced unpopular girls in the main—who would do anything for attention. But when you go to and from your gig on the number 86 bus, it's hard to get any romantic action going. Fucking standing up in a tiny dressing room was not an attractive girl's idea of a romantic evening. Any band with a van had an automatic bedroom, but the notion of screwing on a cold steel floorboard strewn with tom-toms and guitar strings and ciggie butts and empty beer bottles didn't attract the fashion models. And in Liverpool the Beatles didn't even have a van. Rock 'n' roll groupiedom had not yet achieved the social status that it would in the years to come. Scrubbers and slags were what the musicians could look forward to. "Last night you said you loved me" was an oft-repeated Liverpool lament.

But Hamburg. Hamburg was another story. In the St. Pauli district everybody was already walking around with their fuses half-lit anyway and it didn't take much to finish off the action. The Beatles were a bunch of randy sods and they suddenly found themselves in a sexual paradise. They came dangerously close to oversexing themselves—if there is such a thing.

What the Beatles never wanted to make public was the fact that they were regularly having sex with Hamburg's prostitutes. Not that that's such a terrible thing. But at first the Beatles didn't know that they were prostitutes. They fell in love with some of them before learning the awful truth and their boyish illusions were shattered all to hell.

It's not surprising that they would attract female followers. They were young, good-looking, playing sexy music in the open sex capital of Europe, and they made no secret of the fact that they were open to sex. Paul and John, especially, and mostly Paul because of his cherubic looks, were objects of terrific sexual desire. Even the transvestites from the queer bars came around for a try on these hot Liverpool lads. Good-looking teenagers in tight clothes singing hot rock 'n' roll and throwing their young bodies all across the stage? Forget it. The demand was there. As Pete Best later said, they didn't realize until they got to Hamburg that there was an infinite number of young women out there who would literally do anything for them. Anything. Just because they were Beatles. And this was before they were really famous.

What quickly happened in Hamburg was that they found that there was an amazing number of girls who wanted to fuck them. When they started meeting these great-looking young girls during their powzers in the Indra, they were frantic to find someplace to take them because they were sure that such great-looking chicks would never drop their panties in such a dump as the little dungeons behind the Bambi's movie screen.

Were they ever wrong. The Beatles soon had their pick of an astonishing number of desirable girls who didn't mind braving the damp dark dungeons behind the Bambi. And unlike the passive Liverpool scrubbers and slags, these girls were aggressive and experienced. They knew what the hell was going on. Not like the coy dolly birds who wanted to get married or some damn thing.

Some of these girls even initiated quickies back in the Indra's dressing room during the powzers. But the Beatles began to become a bit suspicious. Why were so many young, beautiful, available single women coming into a district that pandered to base male desires? The Beatles didn't answer the question and didn't care, as long as they were being regularly serviced. Screw it, Liverpool was never like this. Some nights when they went back to their dungeons, Paul and Pete could hear giggles and could smell the perfume wafting down the hallway. The chicks were laying in wait for them. They had discovered that they could buy a ticket to the shoot-'em-up movie at the Bambi and then sneak back to the Beatles' rooms. Because of the lighting situation, there were many young women with whom they became intimate that they never saw at all. Wham, bam. Take a ticket and wait.

Pete Best later claimed that the all-time record for a Beatle fuckfest in the dungeons was eight girls at once in a giant swap-o-rama between four Beatles (after Stu had moved out). Trading off was a big part of the agenda. Since Pete and Paul were about twenty-five feet down the hall from John and George, they had to yell back and forth: "Ready to switch?" "You finished yet?" "Want this one?"

The Beatles still hadn't ciphered out the puzzle of where all this manna from heaven had come from for such simple boys as they. Then one night at the Indra one of the waiters told them that they could go and visit most of their girlfriends if they wanted to in the daytime in one district. Where? "The Herbertstrasse," the waiter said with a knowing wink and guffaw.

In the few weeks the Beatles had been in Hamburg, they had seen none of it save the Indra and the Bambi. They had had no time for sight-seeing, since most of their waking hours were spent playing at the Indra or getting ready to play or coming down from playing or fucking or drinking. They had discovered a neat place for breakfast. The British Seaman's Mission was a welcome spot of England for them where they could fill up, for only a few pfennig, on cornflakes and milk, with beer on the side, which became their favorite (and their only guaranteed) meal every day. But they really didn't know Hamburg at all.

So one morning just before noon on their way to the Seaman's Mission, they decided to check out this Herbertstrasse the waiter had been spouting off about.

It turned out to be only about a five minutes' walk from the Bambi. What they found was a blocked-off area, a street that was sealed off at both ends by police barriers, with official signs warning that no one under the age of eighteen was allowed in. Naturally, the Beatles gave seventeen-year-old George hell and tried to make him stay outside, but he wasn't having any of that. So they all went through the entrance and started checking out this here Herbertstrasse. After only a few steps they stopped, literally dumbstruck. If the first sight of Hamburg's lit-up St. Pauli district had rendered them speechless, why, then, their first glimpse of the Herbertstrasse struck them deaf, dumb, and blind. "We didn't," John later said, "know whether to shit or go blind." The Beatles were devastated.

At first glance the Herbertstrasse looked as if it was just a quiet little street full of small shops full of things for sale. At second glance—a second glance that induced whiplash in many second-glancers—it was a quiet little street full of small flats full of things for sale. All of them warm and alive and standing in the doorways and windows, showing off just exactly why they were for sale. The Beatles were literally paralyzed. What they saw was window after window and doorway after doorway filled with the choicest prostitutes that Germany had to offer. And they were showing it off in every imaginable way. In every mode of dress and undress and half-dress. No scrubbers or slags or dolly birds here, not a chance. Just the best stuff: spectacular women and girls wearing everything and nothing. Garter belts, black silk stockings, wispy teddies, taut leather bustiers, peek-a-boo nylon nightgowns, tight lace half-bras, satin tap pants, tight leather pants, six-inch spike heels, thongs and restraints, crotchless pant-ies, unmentionable steel appliances. The whole world of sex was on view right there. Luscious breasts and legs peeking out invit-ingly from tight-to-bursting jeans and straining sweaters. Boots and whips and chains, spiked dog collars and leashes, nipple rings, dildos, butt plugs, vibrators, everything in the damn world was there. "If you don't see something you want, you're either dead or a fag," John joked to Paul.

The Herbertstrasse, they learned, was regulated by the Hamburg Police Department, which insisted on stringent and frequent health examinations of all the prostitutes. The police also ran a tight ship on the street: no pimps, no overt rough stuff, no muggings of the johns. Everything was on the up and up.

As the Beatles slowly made their way down the street, stopping every few feet to gape at some new revelation, they were surprised to see how many girls they recognized from the Indra. "These are whores?" the horrified Beatles asked themselves. Obviously they were, these girlfriends of the night who were now selling their flesh out in the open. After the initial shock, after the heartbreak of seeing the love of one's life flashing her tits in a window at eleven o'clock in the morning for the benefit of any potential buyers passing by, after dodging a leather whip administered by a leather-clad lady who last night had been at the Indra cheering the Beatles, the boys learned another lesson of life. Maybe.

During their first walk-through of the Herbertstrasse, the Beatles found that many of the women on display knew them and called out greetings and even invited them inside for a free sample.

On most days after that first one, the Beatles took what they called a shortcut—though it was actually the long way around—through the Herbertstrasse on their way to the Seaman's Mission for their breakfast of cornflakes and milk and beer. The boys became friends with many of the girls of the Herbertstrasse, who came to make up a loyal core of the Beatle following at the Indra and later at the Kaiserkeller and the Top Ten Club. And they sometimes treated their hooker friends to the spectacle of the Beatles making show on the Herbertstrasse, playing leapfrog down the street, pulling long faces at some of the inviting girls curled up in the windows, writhing in mock pain when a leather dominatrix swished her whip at them. They also attended a lot of hookers' parties and spent a bit of time in bedrooms with mirrors on the ceiling.

So that solved the mystery of where all of those sexually experienced and sophisticated women came from. That sort of information was not included in the sporadic letters home to Jim and Mike McCartney, Aunt Mimi, Rona Best, Millie Sutcliffe, and Louise Harrison.

Even though the hookers wore only strategically placed bits of fabric and so on while on duty in the Herbertstrasse, when they came to the club on their nights off they dressed to the nines and made regal appearances. Once they were elegantly seated at a table, they would send glasses of schnapps or champagne to their favorite Beatle onstage and he had better acknowledge her gift with a toast from the stage or else. Some of the other Beatle camp followers, the dolly birds, seemed a bit coarser and closer to the scrubbers and slags of Liverpool. If they saw something they liked onstage, they would just point to the object of their affection and raise a right forearm with the left hand slapped across the right elbow in the international symbol for an erect penis.

The Beatles also quickly learned the difference between real women and the numerous—often glamorous—transvestites from the steamy queer bars of the St. Pauli. Some of them were so gorgeous, with creamy skin and deep cleavage and long shapely legs, that you might not be able to tell the difference until it was too late. Allan Williams later claimed that a very stunning transvestite, who stood about six feet four in spike heels, told him that she (or he) knew the Beatles very well indeed and named two of them that she (or he) stated flatly that she (or he) knew very, very well indeed in the Biblical sense. Williams said that he didn't believe it for a minute, but he couldn't wait to tell the story.

As it was, the five teenagers from Liverpool had all the real women they could handle—and then some. Since the Beatles were always broke, they started encouraging their women friends—who, after all, were earning more than they were—to take them out to eat before they got down to romance. And to pay for the drinks as well. When they weren't onstage, Pete Best claimed, all the Beatles wanted to do was to screw and drink—in that order.

They were also learning the rules of survival in the tough St. Pauli district. Next to the prostitutes, they quickly found that the best friends they could have were the waiters. They were the Reeperbahn's unofficial police force and they kept the order. Each club owner made sure to have a strong force of these short, stocky, tough waiters, whose ability to fight and intimidate was more important than any waiting skills. Besides their muscles, they also carried spring-action coshes, which they wouldn't hesitate to use when customers caused trouble. Any sort of trouble was immediately quashed by the strong-arm method. It was best not to try to argue in the Hamburg clubs because the waiters weren't there to debate matters. They hit first and didn't bother to ask questions later. A troublemaker was a troublemaker and was asking for it, they reasoned. For the really rough fights, they carried, hidden away at their waistbands in back, tear-gas guns. What couldn't be quelled by the cosh or the tear-gas gun was unimaginable. A flying squad of these beefy waiters, with coshes raised, racing headlong toward a corner of the club was usually terrifying enough on its own to stop any disturbance. The Reeperbahn was a tough area, make no mistake about it. The prostitutes and strippers themselves all carried little rhinestone- or pearl-handled tear-gas guns in their purses and weren't reluctant to use them.

Between the waiters and the prostitutes the Beatles had all the protection they needed. And they became practically fearless, as if they had a guardian angel. If they needed proof of their invisible shield, they got it one evening when they were in a club on the Grosse Freiheit with Allan Williams and some German friends. It was a pleasant break between sets for the Beatles. A band was playing Elvis's "It's Now or Never," which Paul really liked, and he was humming along with the song.

Then, without any warning, a man walked up to the table, pulled out a pistol, and fired point-blank into the face of the German seated next to Paul. Blood and brains flew everywhere. The Beatles were severely shaken, but they were back onstage in a few minutes, playing again and making show.

When they were onstage, they felt truly invincible. Half of their stage banter was four-letter words and what wasn't was a string of insults directed at the audience.

John felt so immune on the stage—sometimes so drunk and high on pills—that he would with impunity kick in the face any hapless drunken German who wandered too near the stage and became too much of a pest.

The others, Paul especially, tried to keep up with John, but he felt driven, it seemed, especially in the fucking and fighting departments. Even with all the sex they were having, with the nightly round-robins, John still made a big show of needing to masturbate. Even after sharing five or six girls the night before, John would get up in the morning, fish out a porno magazine from the pile of garbage on the floor, and head for the toilets. He would emerge smiling a few moments later. "That was very good," he would laugh. The others could only groan.

Unfortunately for Paul, he was the one to end up with a messy paternity dispute out of the Hamburg visits (as well as a later one in Liverpool). The woman in question in Hamburg was named Erika Heubers and she claimed that she had an affair with Paul that resulted in the birth of a daughter named Bettina. Erika sued Paul in 1966 and, without admitting paternity, he paid her twenty-seven hundred pounds. Said Paul: "It was 1966 and we were due to do a European tour. I was told that if the maintenance question wasn't settled we couldn't go to Germany. I wasn't going to sign a crazy document like this, so I didn't. Then we were actually on the plane leaving for the tour when they put the paper under my face and said if I didn't sign the whole tour was off. They said the agreement would deny I was the father and it was a small amount anyway. I've actually seen a letter from Brian Epstein saying it would be cheaper to sign it than not to go to Germany, where we could make a lot of money."

Also unfortunately for Paul, this was a case that would not go away. When Bettina came of age in 1983, Erika sued Paul, seeking an official admittance of paternity, maintenance of three hundred and seventy-five pounds a month, and the right to 10 percent of any inheritance, which was enforceable only in Germany.

Paul agreed to blood tests, which he said proved he was not the father. The German court, though, threw out the tests and awarded full maintenance. "I just want to get the whole thing settled," Paul said, adding that he thought the judge was prejudiced against him because the judge happened to be a pregnant woman.

After Bettina lost a further case against Paul, she was legally bound to pay Paul's legal fees, which amounted to sixty thousand pounds. Paul's German lawyer advised him to pay the fees for "psychological reasons." The lawyer said if he forced her to pay, it would "give Miss Heubers another cause to make bad publicity."

Bettina then announced that she would try again. "I think it is very odd," she said, "that Paul paid these costs for us and this will be prominently brought forward in our new case."

Paul apparently has a twenty-five-year-old illegitimate son living in Crosby, near Liverpool. When the boy's mother was pregnant in Liverpool in 1963, Paul paid her three thousand pounds for her silence. Neither the man—Philip Howarth, according to the London *Sun*—nor Paul will discuss the matter. For years Howarth was referred to in the British press as Mark Paul Doyle until his real name was revealed.

Things were going great for the Beatles on October 4, 1960, when Bruno, bowing to police pressure, turned the Indra back into a strip palace and moved his boys over to the Kaiserkeller. They were living in a pigsty, working seven or eight hours a night for starvation wages, they were wedded to an unbreakable contract with Bruno, and they had absolutely no thoughts of what their future might be. Bruno had promised them a raise if they brought crowds into the Indra. They had done so, but no raise was forthcoming. Bruno had promised them better living conditions, but none were forthcoming. They were often reduced to begging cigarette change from their girlfriends after their girlfriends fed them, made love to them, and maybe washed out some Beatle underwear and socks too.

At least working conditions were a little better at the Kaiserkeller. And they were glad that Rory Storm, their old pal from Liverpool, had come in to replace Derry and the Seniors, starting on October 1. The Beatles were soon sharing the long nights onstage with Rory and the Hurricanes. They also became friends with Rory's drummer, the bearded Ringo Starr, whom they quickly discovered had a sense of humor identical to their own. Rory and his boys were quartered in the dressing rooms at the Kaiserkeller, so they were little better off than the Beatles.

Life fell into a routine of playing and drinking all night, maybe having sex, getting up and eating, and then starting the whole thing over again.

From Hamburg Paul wrote infrequently home to Dad and Mike. Just as the Beatles were starting to go around to the Top Ten Club in late October 1960, Paul sent Jim and Mike a letter saying that the Beatles had played with Tony Sheridan and that the Top Ten was "fabulous." Paul said that he was penning the letter at ten-thirty in the morning, after having been up all night playing and that "everything's mad here. People never sleep." He boasted that he had bought a "cheap watch" at the weekly market. He said that he was getting homesick, especially for English food. He complained that German food was like "English food gone wrong." He went on to itemize what he did not like about German food: "potatoes with salad cream, cold tomatoes, lettus [sic] and that grand luxury dish—pottes frites or something, i.e., chips. Sausages are miles long and are made with fish and meat. Ugh! We can buy cornflakes, beefsteak, liver, mashed potatoes, onions, etc. at the local café now." He went on to rhapsodize about buying cold glasses of milk for only thirteen pfennigs ("cheap enough") and closed by saying, "I'd rather be home."

Then there was the matter of breaking the stage at the Kaiserkeller, which was good for many evenings of speculation. The stage there was a ramshackle affair of plywood sheets placed over beer crates. What with all the making show by two athletic young bands, it was becoming very shaky and rickety. Both the Beatles and Rory were after Bruno to replace it, but he refused. Spending money was not why he was in business. So the Beatles and the Hurricanes decided to try to trash the stage and made a wager with each other. The group actually on the stage when it collapsed would get a crate of champagne and piggy-back rides down the Grosse Freiheit on the backs of the losers.

Rory was a champion swimmer and runner and a born leaper onstage, so the Beatles should have bet against themselves. Both groups, though, began outdoing themselves with making show every night. Bruno knew that something was up, but couldn't prove anything.

The Beatles were enjoying a powzer down the street at Willy's Café the night the stage came down. Rory had really worked himself up that night and the crowd was yelling, "Mak show, Rory! Mak show, Hurricanes!" He kicked into "Blue Suede Shoes" and could feel a tremor under his large boots. He yelled to his band, "She's f-f-fucking well going tonight, boys!" He executed a graceful jete and when he landed it was in a cloud of splinters and sawdust. The Hurricanes, laughing, picked their way out of the wreckage and raced over to Willy's to collect on their bet. They were guzzling champagne and heaping verbal abuse on Bruno without noticing that Bruno's spy and stooge, Herr Steiner, had edged into the café and was listening for evidence of willful destruction. When he had heard enough, he scuttled back to the Kaiserkeller to tell Bruno, who lost his considerable temper and decided to dock all the boys five pounds each for destroying his stage. That was really hitting them where they hurt, for they weren't making much anyway. Money was always a problem. They were always searching for some way to pick up some extra cash.

By that time Stu had moved out of the dungeons into the home of a lovely German girl named Astrid Kirchherr, then twenty-two years old. She had met the Beatles through her boyfriend, Klaus Voorman, who was a doctor's son and was working as a magazine illustrator. Voorman was living in a room at Astrid's parents' house in the suburb of Altona when he met the Beatles by accident one night. He and Astrid had quarreled and he had gone off alone to walk off his anger. He strayed into the St. Pauli district and was passing the Kaiserkeller and found himself drawn in by the sound of powerful rock 'n' roll pounding out of the cellar. It was Rory and the Hurricanes onstage. The Beatles were taking a powzer at a table near the stage and Voorman, fascinated by these exotic teddy boys with their greasy DAs and gray fake-crocodile winkle-pickers, sat down near them and struck up a conversation. He showed them some record jackets he had designed. They weren't terribly interested in those, but they found Klaus and his style interesting. He wore black leather and had his hair in a strange style they had never seen—dry and long and sort of combed forward in a kind of fringe.

He returned to the club the next evening with his girlfriend, Astrid. All five Beatles were mesmerized by her. Paul later said that Astrid and Klaus seemed like a "different race of people" and he didn't just mean that they were German. Even though Astrid spoke no English, she won them all over immediately. She too wore black leather and it was obvious that she had exquisite taste and was responsible for Klaus's taste: She picked out his clothes and cut his hair. She had short-cropped blond hair, china white skin with delicate features, and huge liquid eyes.

She and Klaus, it developed, were serious existentialists— "exis"—and they became regulars at the Kaiserkeller, along with some of their fellow exis. They became great friends of the Beatles. She asked Klaus to start teaching her English, so she could talk to them. It soon became obvious that she and Stu were smitten by each other. The two of them started carrying German-English dictionaries so they could increase communication.

Stu soon moved into Astrid's home, where the others became regular visitors. Astrid's mother cooked eggs and chips for them and Astrid undertook to teach some culture to these teds. She was to have an enormous influence on them. Paul loved to play her Stravinsky records and John read her Marquis de Sade books. Astrid was a photographer and had studied art at Hamburg's Meisterschule. She began to show the Beatles her Hamburg and took her camera along to photograph them. The results were stunning. Everything in her life was black-and-white, down to her all-black bedroom with black silk sheets. She was the first to photograph the Beatles with half their faces in shadow. And she took the famous pictures of the adolescent Beatles standing amid the rolling stock in the marshaling yards and in front of the amusement rides at the Dom fairground.

She also very quickly became a profound fashion influence on the Beatles. The hair took a long time for her to change, but the immediate improvements started. First, Stu showed up wearing a short black leather jacket. Then George got one, then the others got theirs. Next it was tight jeans tucked into the tops of wild-looking cowboy boots. John started that with a pair of black-and-gold ones. Finally, even penurious Paul, notorious for holding on to his pennies, sprang for a pair of black-and-blue boots. And they all got pink Gene Vincent caps.

On their budgets buying clothes was difficult. So they schemed and talked about how they could score some extra cash. Meanwhile, they lost more money one Sunday when they were engaging in one of their regular Sunday sprees. Saturday night was payday and was also their late night, when they had to play until three in the morning. So they would often stay up drinking to wind down the week and then roam around town in the morning. A favorite spot was the fish market on the Elbe River, with its outdoor cafés. There was also a small flea market there, with stalls full of cheap jewelry and what-nots and souvenirs and the like.

For some reason the Beatles liked the idea of taking items from one stand and putting them in another, thus causing mild confusion. One Sunday morning they decided to go one step further and seize one of the stalls and give everything in it away. They did so and a large crowd gathered. The stall owner laughed along with everyone else at the joke until people started leaving with all his belongings. When he tried to grab his stuff back, people refused and ran. Other stall owners waded in to help him, as did some ever-helpful club waiters who happened by.

Within moments there was wide-scale shoving and pushing, which escalated into fighting. The police had to be called in to restore order. The Beatles were drinking at a quayside café and hugely enjoying watching the melee when the police strolled over to arrest them. The cops were serious. The frantic Beatles finally escaped arrest only by promising to repay the losses. They of course didn't have anywhere near that much money, but some of the waiters pooled their money and came up with the equivalent of fifty pounds.

But the waiters wanted their money back, so the Beatles were saddled with more money problems. One evening at the Kaiserkeller they finally came up with an idea for raising cash. They had the brilliant idea of mugging one of the customers. It all started innocently enough. A drunken sailor with a fat wallet kept sending drinks up to the Beatles onstage. As the night wore on, he sent them an invitation along with a tray of schnapps and beer: He wanted to take them all out to dinner when they quit playing. They were, of course, always happy to enjoy a free dinner, so off they went, except for Stu, who went home with Astrid.

At dinner the wine flowed and the sailor spent freely. The Beatles encouraged him to drink up. *Trinken!* At one point, when he went off to the men's room, the four Beatles decided to mug him and take away that big fat wallet. Even though he was big, he was drunk and, after all, there were four of them. "A pushover," John assured them. Pete agreed with John. Paul and George argued against it, but finally gave in.

They left the restaurant at about four in the morning. The friendly Beatles offered to escort the drunken sailor to the train station. Their plan was to take him through the first deserted parking lot they came to, trip him, throw him down, grab the wallet, and run.

As they approached a large dark lot, George and Paul began lagging behind, George announcing very loudly that he felt tired.

As the moment of decision approached, Paul and George turned and ran. "Tarrah," Paul called over his shoulder.

John and Pete decided to go through with it. They threw the sailor up against the gate of the parking lot and then quickly discovered they were in some deep trouble. The sailor may have been drunk, but he knew how to defend himself. John hit him while Pete tried to grab the wallet. They had gotten him to his knees when he hit John, knocking him back. Pete was wrestling with him and managed to get his hand on the wallet when the sailor pulled a gun. Pete and John froze. They didn't know if it was a real gun or a tear-gas gun. Finally they unfroze and John charged the sailor and they both tried to knock him down. They were swinging wildly and trying to butt him when he fired. It was only a tear-gas gun, thank God. Blinded, they tried to land more punches, at least enough to disable him so they could make their getaway. Finally the sailor was down and the boys ran, really picking up their heels, heedless of direction. They just wanted to get away. He fired again and they really picked up speed. They ran—miles—all the way back to the Bambi and fled inside, certain that the cops were hot on their trail.

Paul and George had sat up to wait for them and to get their share of the bounty. They laughed heartily when they saw the ripped jeans and bloody faces and the naked fear in John's and Pete's teary eyes.

They were all afraid the next day, sure that the police would be closing in on them or that, at the very least, the sailor would show up with a lot of his tough buddies to give their asses a royal kicking. They flinched every time a sailor came into the Kaiserkeller, but they never saw the man again.

So the Beatles decided to abandon their lives of crime and return to what they knew best: playing music.

Life went on at the Kaiserkeller. Bruno exercised his renewal option and extended the Beatles' contract through the end of the year. Bruno also talked about the possibility of a club date in Berlin for them after the first of the year.

The only problem was that they hated Bruno more than ever. Allan Williams, meanwhile, had come over from Liverpool for his first visit since August and he tried to placate the Beatles. He even took them on what amounted to their first recording session as Beatles. It took place on October 15 and it was actually for one of the Hurricanes, the bassist and singer Wally Eymond, who used Lou Walters as his stage name. Eymond had a fine voice and decided to try to cut a record. Hurricane drummer Ringo Starr went along to play on it, along with all the Beatles except Pete Best. As the Beatles started getting friendly with Ringo, Pete began to receive what would turn into the typical long Beatle freeze-out.

The "recording session" was held at the Akustik Studio at 57 Kirchenallee. It was one of those places where people go in and make little recorded greetings to send to relatives. For ten quid, anyone could make a little 78 rpm disc. For their first recording Wally and Ringo and the Beatles cut "Summertime." Wally sang lead and the Beatles provided background harmony. On the reverse side of the 78 disc was a sales lecture on the marketing of shoes and other leather goods. Apparently nine copies of "Summertime" were pressed and only one survives today. Wally also recorded "Fever" and "September Song" the same day, but with Johnny Guitar and Ty Brian from the Hurricanes, along with Ringo and without the Beatles.

They had to leave, at Williams's urging. He had kept after them to hurry up because they were due onstage at any moment at the Kaiserkeller and Bruno would be furious if they were late. John and Paul and George and Stu wanted to make a record on their own, without Wally and with they themselves singing. But Allan refused. He packed them up in his car and delivered them back to Bruno, which made them furious, of course.

In late October a new club opened in the St. Pauli and it caused a great stir. The Top Ten, a new and modern club holding about two thousand people, was in the Hippodrome at 136 Reeperbahn. The previous tenant had been a topless circus, which turned out to be too tame for the Reeperbahn. The Top Ten's owner, Peter Eckhorn, was only twenty-one years old and, unlike the tough old-timers running the other clubs, was a real rock 'n' roll fan. He loved the music and built a club intended for rock 'n' roll fans.

He also launched an immediate war with Bruno Koschmider. Eckhorn's first hiring was Bruno's chief bouncer, Horst Fascher, a former boxing champ. And his first musical attraction was a former star of Bruno's, Tony Sheridan and the Jets. Compared to the Kaiserkeller, the Top Ten was plush. Tony and his band were living upstairs at the club in a clean and modern dormitory.

The Top Ten was only a short walk from the Kaiserkeller and the Beatles soon started making that short walk during their powzers. They liked Sheridan and they soon became friends with Eckhorn. It was inevitable that at some point the Beatles would get up onstage and jam with Tony and the Jets and they did so. The ever-vigilant Herr Steiner was lurking in the Top Ten that night when they violated their contract with Bruno by setting foot on another stage within a forty-kilometer radius of ground zero at the Kaiserkeller without Bruno's permission. Herr Steiner rushed back to give the news to Bruno, whose blood pressure must have been truly remarkable.

Eckhorn had already made an offer to the Beatles to come over to his Top Ten, where he offered—by comparison—luxurious living accommodations and a salary of at least a pound a day more than Bruno was paying them. They had already decided to take the offer, concluding that in their own minds all they had was a verbal contract with Bruno, since Bruno's written contract was with Allan and they themselves had no contract with Allan. They were discussing the possible ways to tell Bruno all this—for they knew Bruno could be a formidable opponent—when Bruno heard about their unfaithfulness. He summoned them to his office. Surrounded by some of his musclemen, he threatened them. Paul and Pete, who had become the most proficient in German of all the Beatles, told him that he had promised them more money as well as better living quarters and he had reneged on his promises to them, so there.

Stammering in his rage, Bruno warned them that they would "be shot. If you leave me, you won't ever play the Top Ten! You can take that any way you like. My boys know how to create trouble!" At the very least, he said in a calmer moment, they could expect to "end up with broken fingers!"

The Beatles got angry then. John, as the leader, stood up and exploded: "Get stuffed! We're off to the Top Ten!"

Bruno had already—and to this day no one knows how—found out that George was only seventeen. As soon as he learned from Herr Steiner that the Beatles had committed adultery on

him over there at the Top Ten, he had had the following notice
drawn up:

> I the undersigned, hereby give notice to Mr. GEORGE
> HARRISON and to BEATLES' BAND to leave on No-
> vember 30th 1960. The notice is given to the above by order
> of the Public Authorities who have discovered that Mr.
> GEORGE HARRISON is only 17 (seventeen) years of age.

So the die was cast. The Beatles were legally bound, they
finally decided, to play out their final days for Bruno, through
the end of November. But then they would move immediately
to the Top Ten.

Their final days at the Kaiserkeller were tense and unpleasant,
though. Bruno finally got the authorities to have George deported on November 21 and he was deposited at the border to
get home to Liverpool as best he could.

Even before that one of the Beatles finally snapped and went
after Herr Steiner. They didn't know that he had been the in-
former, for he had always tried to pal around with the Beatles
and be friendly. They still had no idea that he had spied on them
at the Top Ten (or that he had blown the whistle on the affair of
the destroyed stage). What finally happened with Herr Steiner
was that the Beatles were rehearsing one afternoon, when the
Kaiserkeller was closed to the public, and they had invited some
girlfriends in to watch. Herr Steiner was there, too, and he sat at
the bar watching them. At one point Pete started dancing with
one of the girls.

"No dancing!" Herr Steiner snapped. The Beatles just looked
at him. Herr Steiner repeated his order and pushed Pete and the
girl apart and slapped the girl. Pete decked him, to the cheers of
the others. Bruno docked five pounds from Pete's check for
assault and nicked the other Beatles five pounds apiece for "bait-
ing" Herr Steiner.

So at the end of the month the Beatles were eager to kite off to
the Top Ten. Stu was living with Astrid, so moving was no
problem for him and George was already long gone. The others,
though, had to get out of the Bambi. John made it safely with his
little kit bag and took a bottom bunk in the Top Ten's dormitory. Then Paul and Pete went to pack up their gear and get out.
There was, of course, no light in their dungeons. In their haste to

get out in a hurry, they took four condoms from their wallets (condoms were certainly something they had plenty of), pinned them to the rotting tapestry on the stone walls just outside their cubicles, and set fire to them for enough light to see by. By the time they left they had forgotten the condoms, for who expects a rubber to be a fire hazard?

Paul and Pete left with sighs of relief and raced over to the Top Ten. They had a laugh with John, who was waiting for them. Paul took the bunk above John's, Pete picked a nearby bottom bunk, and they all agreed that the world was now a better place. Their new dorm even had windows.

That night they trooped downstairs to play their first official Top Ten gig and fully expected Bruno and his flying squad of tough waiters with coshes at the ready to burst through the door at any minute and turn the place into a battlefield. Nothing happened. Eckhorn, of course, had his own private army of waiters, so that was a definite deterrent. Bruno had vowed that the Beatles would never play the Top Ten and had failed, the Beatles agreed, in trying to make good his threat. The remaining Beatles played several full sets, drank their fill, and went to bed secure in the knowledge that they had won a major battle. A new life dawned ahead.

They had also executed a handwritten agreement with Eckhorn to return in April of 1961 to play the Top Ten all that month. They were to be paid thirty-five DM per day. That was signed on November 30.

Bruno allowed them one more night before he lowered the hammer. They had a very harsh awakening that night. In the middle of the night the lights were thrown on and there were hoarse shouts of "Paul McCartney! Pete Best!" Plainclothes police dragged Paul and Pete out of their bunks and ordered them to get dressed. John looked up sleepily for a moment and then turned over and went back to sleep.

"Get dressed!" the cops repeated. Paul and Pete, wearing only their undershorts as pajamas as usual, got up groggily and started to pull on their suddenly ridiculous-looking tight jeans and flashy cowboy boots. They were pushed and shoved downstairs into a police car and whisked off to the nearest police station on the Reeperbahn, where they were roughly deposited on a bench. "Bambi Kino fire!" were the only English words they heard as they waited on their bench.

At their interrogation they were charged with setting fire to the Bambi Kino. They asked to be allowed to call the British consul. "No," they were told.

After a physical examination by a police doctor, they were bundled back into a car and were relieved to be going back home to the Top Ten. Instead, they were delivered to jail. Once deprived of their belts and jackets, into a cell they went. After three hours or so they were walked back to a police car and were taken straight to the airport, handed their passports, and told they were being deported immediately and they would never be allowed on German soil again.

At the airport Paul broke away and lodged himself in a telephone booth and called the British consul, with Pete wedged into the booth with him to try to keep the cops out. The consul could not help them. The cops marched them to their gate. Up on the plane they went and off to London they flew. In London they had to call home to Liverpool to have money wired for the train trip home. Stu hid out at Astrid's house in Altona. John came home alone by train. It looked pretty much like the Beatles' noble experiment had gone a pisser.

The Beatles

6

PAUL put up a brave front when he dragged ass home to 20 Forthlin Road from his expulsion from Germany, but his life and career, as well as those of his fellow Beatles, were in extreme disarray. His brother Mike was shocked at the change in Paul since he had last seen him in August. Paul looked as thin as a skeleton and as white as an eggshell and as Paul sat down in their little living room to relate his adventures, Mike couldn't help but observe that Paul's ankles, where they peeked out above his winkle-pickers, were "as thin and white as Dad's pipe cleaners."

Paul had managed to bring Mike a blue plastic mac with his meager kit bag the police let him leave Hamburg with, but he had left with precious little else. He did carry his guitar over his shoulder on the flight back from Hamburg, but they had had to leave Pete Best's precious drum kit behind. Fortunately, Peter Eckhorn crated up their equipment and personal effects and shipped it all back to Liverpool.

They were out of touch with each other for days. John left Hamburg alone on December 10, with his beloved amp in a backpack and his guitar in hand, and he landed back in Liverpool on the fifteenth. Stu remained in Hamburg at Astrid's house. George wrote to Stu on December 16 to urge him to "come home sooner, as if we get a new bass player for the time being, it will be crumby [sic], as he will have to learn everything . . . it's no good with Paul playing bass, we've decided, that is if he had some kind of bass + amp to play on!"

Pete Best worked on resurrecting the Beatles' career. As the various Beatles straggled back, they decided to try to regroup as best as possible. Pete and Mona went down to the docks and received the Beatles' crate from Hamburg and set up the equipment back at Mona's Casbah Club, which had been thriving.

One of the first things the Beatles discovered upon returning was that Allan Williams's career was literally in ashes. He had decided to open a Top Ten Club in Liverpool after seeing the reactions to such clubs in Hamburg and observing how the Casbah and the Cavern in Liverpool were doing. Allan's Top Ten was on Soho Street, not far from Lime Street, a tough cheap district. Allan would later claim that his Top Ten was intended as a showcase for the Beatles, although at the time he opened the club—on December 1— they were more or less in the Twilight Zone. They also had not been in touch with Williams, especially after they had negotiated their own contract with Peter Eckhorn at Hamburg's Top Ten.

Williams had big plans for his Top Ten, though, and had hired Liverpool's top Mersey Beat DJ and compere, a twenty-eight-year-old slender railway clerk named Bob Wooler. He was an unlikely champion of the beat sound, but that's just what Wooler became. Right after leaving his secure railroad job and moving to Williams's Top Ten, Wooler found himself literally out in the street, jobwise, when Williams's Top Ten burned to the ground on the night of December 6. It was a suspicious fire, although Williams collected only around a thousand pounds in insurance. Wooler and Williams would still figure in the Beatles' future. Pete Best darkly brooded on the fact that the Beatles were supposed to have been the showcase band of the Liverpool Top Ten. Later in life Best was to argue that, had the fire not happened, the Beatles would likely have stayed with Allan Williams; there would have been no Brian Epstein; and Ringo Starr would never have replaced Best in the Beatles. It is likely, though, that John and Paul had already decided to ax Allan and Ringo was starting to figure in their thoughts. Given the extent of John's ambition, especially, it is doubtful that the group would have stayed with someone of Williams's relatively limited professional vision. And Paul hated his guts.

Before anything else happened with the Beatles' career, though,

Paul got himself a real job. Immediately upon Paul's return, Jim was after him, saying that playing in a group was all well and good, but it would never pay the bills. "I've learned that lesson myself," he told Paul. "It's time for you," he said, "to get serious about life, to look for real work, to make some real money, to get off your behind." Paul actually did so. The previous Christmas season he had done temporary work for the Liverpool Post Office, so he thought he might find something like that again. He went to the Labour Exchange to see what they had. They referred him to the Speedy Prompt Delivery Service, where he was hired as a package deliverer. He was laid off after what he claims was a couple of weeks, after he was "so buggered sometimes I fell asleep on the lorry when we went to places like Chester." Unemployed again, although the Beatles were starting to get dates and notices, Paul felt pressured by Jim to again seek legitimate work.

"Dad started moaning again, the usual stuff about the group being all very well, but I'd never make a living at it. I half-agreed with him, but there was always somebody who said we were promising. . . ."

Paul's next job was with the firm of Massey and Coggins, electrical engineers. When he was interviewed he thought it was for a job of sweeping up. When he was hired he was supposed to wind electrical coils and he wasn't any good at it, even at the fabulous weekly salary of seven pounds, which he ascended to. While most of the workers were winding up to fourteen coils a day, the most Paul could manage was one and a half. Paul conceded that he wasn't actually cut out for real work, even though he had had fantasies of becoming an executive while at Massey and Coggins. He always used to talk about the fact that one fellow at Massey and Coggins had called him "Mantovani" because Paul had longish hair.

Paul toughed it out with the job as long as he could, which wasn't long, to mollify his dad and to also bring in a few bob, which were certainly welcome. Paul later said he thought he had stayed with the job for almost two months. Even after the Beatles got going again, Paul later claimed he was initially uncertain as to whether or not he would commit himself to the group for good.

Meanwhile Pete secured a concert date for the regrouping Beatles, courtesy of his mom. Mona was doing well with the Casbah and had revamped it while the Beatles had been gone, knocking some smaller rooms together for a big central band room in the cellar.

Mona presented the reunited Beatles on December 17, 1960, at the Casbah. They had to find a bass player, since Stu was still in Hamburg, although Paul was starting to make noises about taking over the bass spot. Pete first wanted to get Ken Brown from his old group the Blackjacks, but John and Paul didn't like Brown. Besides, he was living in London. Then Pete suggested Chas Newby, who had played rhythm guitar with the Blackjacks. Chas, who was then a chemistry student, agreed to join the group, at least until Stu rejoined the Beatles, and Paul and John approved him. Chas, who was left-handed, had to scramble to find a bass and a leather jacket to match the Beatles' outfits. But he did so and became a Beatle with the December 17 gig at the Casbah. Newby fit in well with the group. "It was just like the movies," he said later of his brief days as a Beatle. The first thing he noticed when he came offstage was that his feet hurt terribly from all the stamping around the group did. The show itself that night was a bit of a revelation for the Liverpool Beatle fans, who had, of course, not seen them perform since their days in Hamburg. When they came onstage and started leaping about and doing the same forceful show they had been doing for hours every night in Hamburg, the fans in Mona's basement were astounded. They had never seen powerhouse rock 'n' roll on this order before. After the show they were set upon by girls who wanted autographs and perhaps even more.

For that date Mona had gotten a friend of Pete's named Neil Aspinall to make up posters heralding THE RETURN OF THE FABU-LOUS BEATLES. Neil had been at the Inny and had left with eight 0-level exam results and was studying to become an accountant. He had taken a room at the Best compound, renting a furnished room from Mona, when he started looking into the world of rock 'n' roll. He was taking correspondence courses and hanging out at the Casbah.

After that successful Casbah date Mo booked them back for New Year's Eve and Frank Garner, her chief steward, offered— for a one-pound fee—to drive the Beatles to dates in his van and to help with their equipment. Since the Casbah was also Pete's home, they kept their equipment there and used the place as a handy rendezvous and rehearsal hall and hangout.

Allan Williams, in one of his last bookings for the Beatles, got them into the Grosvenor Ballroom in Liscard on Christmas Eve with Derry and the Seniors. They were billed—for the last time—as the Silver Beetles.

But what became probably the most important show in their careers came about very casually and almost didn't happen at all. It turned out to be a dance in North Liverpool, an area where they were not really known. They had performed there only once, back in May, at the Lathom Hall in Seaforth, when Stu had been kicked in the head. The promoter there, Brian Kelly, had booked the group for the following week, but they had stiffed him when they got Larry Parnes's offer to leave immediately on Johnny Gentle's tour of Scotland.

What happened was that Bob Wooler was hanging out on Christmas Day at the Jacaranda and talking to the Beatles about their stuttering career. John, who was increasingly not shy about asking others to help the group, asked Wooler if he could help them. Wooler did know of an opening for a group and went to use the phone. He called his friend Brian Kelly, who had an unpleasant recollection of the Beatles but who listened to his friend Wooler. Kelly was one group short of filling a big bill on Boxing Day, December 27, at the huge Litherland Town Hall ballroom.

Said Wooler: "I've found a group for you at the Jacaranda and they're free. They want eight pounds. Will they do?"

"Not at that price they won't," Kelly replied. "A group won't increase my attendance enough to warrant that." Kelly finally agreed to pay them six pounds—for the whole group. It was too late for Kelly to put the Beatles' name in his newspaper ads for his "Big Beat Extra," so he just had paste-on fliers attached to his posters promoting the other groups: the Searchers, the Deltones, and the Del Renas. His fliers read: DIRECT FROM HAMBURG, THE BEATLES!

The Beatles—John, Paul, George, Pete, and Chas—arrived in Frank Garner's van and drew curious stares as they set up. They were wearing their leather bomber jackets, and with their tight jeans tucked into their colorful German cowboy boots and their greasy Tony Curtis DAs, they looked much rougher than the standard 'Pool group, most of whom had adopted the Cliff Richard and the Shadows look and stage act: neat matching suits, trimmed hair, and genteel stage movements.

There were perhaps fifteen hundred dancers on the floor in Litherland that night when the Beatles took the stage and Paul ripped into "Long Tall Sally." All those hours onstage in Hamburg paid off in one hell of a hurry. The musical urgency and authoritative beat these Beatles were laying down, along with their "We don't give a damn" stage presence, was electrifying. The dancers rushed the stage—unheard of at a dance! They swarmed the stage, jumping up and down, yelling, screaming.

Beatlemania struck that night of December 27, 1960. Girls went crazy; guys went nuts. It was a near-riot. The Beatles looked at each other, puzzled, uncomprehending at first. All they were doing was their German "mak show," after all.

Afterward they were mobbed by autograph seekers. Many complimented them on how well they spoke English. What with the exotic look and sound of the group, many of the fans reasoned that the Beatles actually were German.

Brian Kelly, meanwhile, knew that he had stumbled onto a piece of great good fortune. As soon as the Beatles got to the dressing room after their performance, he had his stewards lock the door. Not to protect the Beatles from the fans; Kelly, rather, wanted to make sure no rival promoters got in to see them and steal them away. He went in and booked them immediately to as many future dances as he could get.

Actually, one rival did get through before he sealed them off, but Kelly was pleased with what had been virtually dropped into his lap. Kelly managed to line up the Beatles for thirty-five shows during the first three months of 1961 before they were scheduled to return to Hamburg.

Within two months they were the hottest things going in Liverpool. It all happened that quickly and that simply. During all of 1960, excluding their Johnny Gentle tour (and apart from their strip club shows), they had played not quite two dozen shows in Liverpool. Now, in the wake of their spectacular "debut" at Litherland, they were playing that many shows a month. And, for the first time, their shows were less dances than they were concerts. People came to see them, to watch the band play, rather than to dance and fight and flirt.

The demand for them was so great that before long they were playing twice, then three times a day. And, at fees ranging from five to eight pounds per show, their little private fortunes were increasing greatly. It was not unusual by the end of February for the Beatles to play at lunchtime somewhere and to play two different dances that evening. Pete Best, as de facto business manager, was handling the bookings, along with his mother Mo (who got them their biggest payday yet: twenty pounds at St. John's Hall in Tuebrook). On nights when they had to dash from, say, the Aintree Institute in Aintree to Hambleton Hall in Huyton, they could no longer rely on public transportation or the occasional steward with a van. So, with the money starting to come in, they persuaded Pete's friend Neil Aspinall, who was wearying of his correspondence accounting studies, to buy an old secondhand van for eighty pounds and to become their first unofficial road manager. They were splitting the money only four ways (apart from paying Neil a pittance). Chas Newby decided to go back to college and left the Beatles after the New Year's Eve dance at the Casbah, even though Stu remained in Hamburg and showed no signs of returning anytime soon. In search of a bass player, John first asked George, who refused, knowing that he was easily the best instrumentalist in the group. So the bass lot of the draw fell to Paul. He played his Lucky 7, upside down and backward, with two and sometimes three piano strings on it. Even John noticed that during many of those first shows when Paul was playing bass he had the cord from his bass stuck into his pocket, rather than plugging it into the amp. He was no better on bass—at least initially—than Stu had been.

The Beatles were both benefiting from and contributing to what was becoming a flourishing beat scene in Liverpool. On March 11, a Saturday, they took part in the first Liverpool beat marathon, an all-night nonstop show by twelve groups at the Liverpool Jazz Society on Temple Street. The lineup included Liverpool's best: Gerry and the Pacemakers, the Sensational Beatles, the Fabulous Remo Four, Rory Storm and the Hurricanes, Kingsize Taylor and the Dominoes, the Big Three, Dale Roberts and the Jaywalkers, Derry and the Seniors, Ray and the Del Renas, the Pressmen, Johnny Rocco and the Jets, Faron and the Tempest Tornadoes.

They also, mostly thanks to Bob Wooler, started playing an occasional date at the Cavern Club downtown on Mathew Street. The Cavern had of course long been a jazz club (scene of the Quarry Men's humiliation long ago), but as the jazz scene in Liverpool waned, the Cavern's new owner, Ray McFall, turned to some of the beat groups. He also hired Wooler, who was still out of work, to be his disc jockey and compere. Wooler pressured McFall to give the Beatles a try.

Mo Best had been calling McFall ever since the Beatles returned from Hamburg, but he had dismissed that as a mother's natural inclination to push her son's group. He listened to Wooler, though, and booked the band for a lunchtime session on February 21. The group and McFall and the Cavern crowds were an immediate match. That was also the first time the Beatles played three separate gigs in one day: lunchtime at the Cavern, later at the Cassanova Club, and still later at the Litherland Town Hall.

They started playing frequent lunchtime sessions at the Cavern and made their nighttime debut there on March 21. The Cavern was becoming a regular haunt.

Their scheduled return to Hamburg and their contract with Peter Eckhorn to play his Top Ten Club for the month of April came next. The matter of Paul's and Pete's deportations and of George's too, for that matter, were still pending.

George solved his problem by turning eighteen on February 25. Paul and Pete had more of a difficulty ahead, what with the arson charge hanging over their heads. Stu, who had returned to Liverpool briefly in late February and then went back to Astrid and his art studies in Hamburg, had been in touch with Peter Eckhorn, who wanted the Beatles back and helped them with the authorities. He reimbursed local authorities for the amount of Paul's and Pete's plane fare when they were deported and he put in a good word for them. Paul and Pete, meanwhile, went to see the German consul in Liverpool and appealed to German Immigration officials.

Stu telephoned Paul with the good news. Stu had a P.S., which he put in a letter to Pete:

Don't be surprized [sic] at this funny green letter, everything has worked out fine. Paul will ring you or you ring Paul as soon as you have this . . . One thing I forgot to tell Paul, and that is that you both must pay Peter Eychorn [sic] 79 D.M. (each), his [sic] the cost of sending you home. The lifting of the deportation ban is only valid for 1 year then you can have it reviewed. One thing they made clear, if you have any trouble with the Police, no matter how small then you've had it forever. (Drunkeness [sic], fighting, women etc.).

Paul and Pete wrote that lesson on their foreheads with indelible ink.

One thread lingered from what already seemed to be a dim past (that is, the past year) when they had been but a struggling bunch of ignored and unknown scouse louts. That hangover was named Allan Williams. He maintains to this day that he was their manager this whole time, through the Beatle explosion of early 1961. Even though, during all this time, the only dates he had secured for the group were the Grosvenor Ballroom on December 24, 1960, on February 24, 1961, and on March 10, 1961 (which was another three-gig Beatle day: lunchtime at the Cavern, a stop at the Grosvenor, and then on to St. John's Hall in Tuebrook). The latter was his last booking for the Beatles. He later claimed that he had pressured the German consul in Liverpool to readmit the Beatles to Germany. Williams later wrote:

> I got a favourable reply from the German consul's office in Liverpool and set about the rest of the necessary paperwork. Since the boys were minors, this included getting written consent from their next of kin. After a lot of hard work I signed contracts with Peter Eckhorn, and the boys toddled off happily to Hamburg and the Top Ten Club.

Perhaps it was his constant use of the sobriquet "boys" and such terms as "toddled off" that soured the Beatles on Allan, just as they would sour over the years on men who insisted on patronizing them and favored addressing them as "the boys" or "the lads." Dick James, the song publisher who later came to own so much of them, earned their eternal hatred with his tossed-off references to "the boys." As Paul and John so often talked about later, one of the reasons they were so determined to make it—apart from London's traditional prejudice against "ignorant Northerners"—was the preponderance of rich, stiff-shirted, shallow music-business executives who expected to make lots of money from exploiting "the boys" of the music world. It was a class issue and the Beatles were the first to challenge it. What they faced was a true plantation system. "The boys" were expected to come up with the product, they would be patted on the head, and their product would be harvested and sold by the brilliant executives who owned "the boys." Paul and John were exactly correct in observing that they were originally regarded by the "men in suits" who ran the music business as freaks, as one-shots, as talented idiots who should be milked of whatever quirky gifts they possibly possessed as soon as feasible. "The boys" were not supposed to know what was going on.

"Economic reality" was a term that the Beatles had not yet been lectured on, but even once they heard it, they tended to get their backs up. The "economic reality" lecture told young song-writers and singers that the only way they could make it was to sign away all their rights to the Elders of the Business, who controlled all facets of the Business. It must be remembered that that sort of thing, while looked down upon, was beginning to be grudgingly accepted in the United States. For the first time, Tin Pan Alley was on the run because true peer group writers such as Bob Dylan were beginning to control their own musical output.

In class-ridden Great Britain, for ill-educated, grammar school scouse louts from the North to question anything, that was totally out of the question. "They all thought we were like Tommy Steele and they could just rip us off," John said. "They treated us like niggers; we were their slaves; we were 'the boys'; we would write and grin and sing and do those fuckin' shows and keep our fuckin' mouths shut. And like it. And be grateful and scrape and bow. And kiss their fuckin' ass. And smile while we're kissin' it."

At any rate John and Paul were quickly learning how to react to the "men in suits" whom they thought were trying to rip them off. Allan Williams, who didn't even wear a suit, was dropped as soon as he became less than useful. Once the Beatles were settled in comfortably in Hamburg at the Top Ten Club and doing fairly well, John and Paul did what they were best at, which was to get somebody else to do their dirty work for them. They got Stu, since he was the only one of them that Allan liked and since they had decided to ease Stu out of the Beatles anyway, to write to Allan Williams and to tell him to fuck off forever, that the Beatles had no more commis-sions for him evermore, that they had gotten their own book-ing with Peter Eckhorn at the Top Ten, and that he should just forget whatever idea he had of collecting any money off them.

In one of his last volleys fired at the Beatles, poor Allan Williams wrote them an ill-tempered letter, dated April 20, 1961. As ever, he addressed them as "Dear All."

I am very distressed to hear you are contemplating not paying my commission out of your pay as was agreed in our
contract . . . May I remind you, seeing you are all appearing
to get more than a little swollen-headed, that you would not
even have smelled Hamburg if I had not made the contacts . . .
So you see Lads, I'm very annoyed you should welsh out of
your contract. If you decide not to pay I promise you that
I shall have you out of Germany inside two weeks through
several legal ways and don't you think I'm bluffing.

And so on and so on. Williams went on to say that he could stiff
them out of opening an upcoming Ray Charles United Kingdom
tour if he, Allan, decided to. He concluded:

I don't want to fall out with you but I can't abide anybody
who does not honour their word or bond, and I could have
sworn you were all decent lads, that is why I pushed you
when nobody wanted to hear you.

The Beatles told him to get fucked. Allan Williams has roughly
spent the rest of his life in trying to get recognition for his input
to the Beatle juggernaut. Of all the Beatle people over the years,
he is not alone in ending up alone. At least, as certain Beatle
advisers like to joke, Allan's still alive.

Allan Williams wrote a book about his experiences called *The
Man Who Gave the Beatles Away*. John actually liked it and said it
was "the only book that can give eyewitness insight into the
making of the Beatles." Paul read Allan's book—or at least heard
of it—and said that Williams's book was "slightly exaggerated,
to put it mildly."

At any rate the Beatles were saying good-bye to a large part of
their Liverpool past when they left for Hamburg for the second
time. It had been only seven months earlier that they had crowded
into Allan's beat-up van, with bags of sandwiches and no money,
and set off on their budget trip for Hamburg and the Indra. They
had done a great deal of growing up, musically and personally,
in the past few months. They had already negotiated the final
terms of their contract over the phone with Peter Eckhorn. On
weekdays they were required to play at the Top Ten from seven
at night until two into the morning, with a fifteen-minute break
every hour. On Saturdays and Sundays they were to play until

three in the morning. Their salary was to be thirty-five DM each per day. And they were to be quartered in the little bunk-bed dormitory upstairs at the Top Ten. Hardly luxurious, but far superior to the dungeons they had occupied at Bruno's Bambi.

On the day they left, March 24, 1961, they took care of business. They squeezed in a lunchtime session at the Cavern and then headed for the train station, where they made the journey to Hamburg by train and boat and train in relative comfort. Astrid met them there at the train station, glad to see them. And, truth to tell, they were happy to be back in Hamburg.

Hamburg the second time around was a lot faster. They were not wide-eyed apple-cheeked teenagers this time. And Peter Eckhorn's Top Ten Club was more sophisticated, the clientele more worldly than Bruno's Indra and Kaiserkeller had been. They also had a ready audience, for people in Hamburg remembered them well. Too, they had a circle of friends in Astrid, Klaus, their photographer friend Jurgen Vollmer, and their crowd of exis. Oddly, the scouse louts from Liverpool with their jeans and boots and greasy hair were now being accepted into an avant-garde scene.

There were other defectors from Bruno's Kaiserkeller waiting to greet them at the Top Ten. Tony Sheridan was back at the Top Ten, but so were Mutti, the friendly lavatory attendant, and Horst Fascher, the former boxer who had been Bruno's chief bouncer.

John, Paul, George, and Pete moved into their little dormitory and Stu went back to stay at Astrid's house. Within a few days he showed up wearing leather trousers—emulating Astrid, who had been decked out in a full leather suit when she met them at the train station. The others followed suit. Then Stu came in draped in a long leather jacket, rather than the bomber jackets they had thought were so hip. Pete went out and bought one and then John liked the look of it so much that he got one. Then George got his. Only Paul, who was as usual close and careful with his money, was a holdout. Pete Best said that they finally took him down to the leather shop and told the salesman, "This guy wants a coat like ours, size thirty-eight to forty!" Paul, Pete observed, was always the last one to offer a smoke and had to be coaxed into buying a round of drinks. That surprised Pete, he said, because, of all the Beatles, Paul seemed to love the limelight most of all and was instantly jealous if another Beatle got more attention than he did.

After the leathers Stu's next fashion innovation was his hair. Astrid's innovation, rather. She had cut Klaus Voorman's hair before and now she started cutting Stu's. One night he appeared at the Top Ten with a radical hairdo that was washed clean and combed forward and down over the forehead. No grease at all. The others laughed and ridiculed his haircut, referring to it as a "fringe." The laughter must have hurt because Stu had his hair up and greasy the next night. Then Astrid obviously got to him again because the following night he was back with his dry fringe and he kept it. After a while it didn't look so weird to the Beatles, especially since they were socializing with Astrid's exi friends, who all sported similar hairstyles.

It was still a drastic change for the Beatles, after all those Liverpool years with the greasy Tony Curtis DAs that were so much a part of what they stood for. Only George washed the grease out of his hair and started brushing it forward. It would not be until later that fall, when Paul and John went on vacation in Paris and visited their friend Jurgen Vollmer, that the two head Beatles would adopt the hairstyle that would later bear their name. Vollmer talked them into it. (He also tried to persuade them to adopt the bell-bottom trousers that he and his friends had started wearing, but Paul and John thought they would be considered "too queer back in Liverpool. We didn't want to appear feminine or anything like that because our audience in Liverpool still had a lot of fellows. We were playing rock, dressed in leather, but Paul's ballads were bringing in more and more girls.") Only Pete Best kept his hair combed back and upswept. Years later, long after he was booted out of the Beatles, Best agonized over whether or not his hairdo had been the factor that caused the others to get rid of him: "During my time as a Beatle this style was not considered to be some sort of trademark."

With their second siege of Hamburg, the Beatles soon found that the novelty of playing those long, long nights onstage had long since worn off. Even at their tender ages, fatigue set in after five or six hours. That was when they really discovered the worth of amphetamine pills. Tony Sheridan was the first to offer them the Musician's Best Friend. "Here's something to keep you awake," Sheridan said, opening his fist to proffer some Preludins. Their old friend Mutti kept her ever-ready jar of Prellies handy. Since they were still drinking their share and the fans were sending up trays of free lager, schnapps, and vodka, the combination of pep pills and alcohol often kept them flying all night—and longer.

Paul had a natural governor built in as far as excess went and he and Pete were on probation anyway, so they didn't get too crazy. George was still the serious musician. Stu was in love and wanted to get back to his art studies. So it was mostly left to John to get seriously fucked up and he did so with a vengeance. There are still Hamburg legends about just how fucked up John would get: appearing onstage in his underwear with a toilet seat around his neck, pissing out the window on nuns walking by, mooning the crowd while cursing them as "Nazi bastards," and the like. Paul later went to great pains to say that the pissing on nuns story was mostly made up. Even so, John was not operating in a vacuum. There were photographs taken of the Beatles squatting on the ground and begging pills from a dope dealer standing over them. "Preludin, please, sir? Captogens, may we have some, please?"

When Bill Harry started the Liverpool music publication *Mersey Beat* later in the year and got his hands on some of the Beatle pictures from Hamburg, he said he couldn't publish many of them: "Photos from Hamburg had shown them with flick-knives [switchblade knives], pep pills, looking mean and evil." After Brian Epstein became the Beatles' manager in December of 1961 and quickly started to change their image, Harry said the Beatles took back many of their Hamburg pictures from *Mersey Beat*.

Much of their tomfoolery was just that: letting off steam by high-spirited kids. On a dare from the others one afternoon, Paul rolled up his jeans, put on a pith helmet, shouldered a broom as if it were a rifle, and goose-stepped up and down the Reeperbahn while the others chanted, *"Seig Heil!"*

Since they were ensconsed in the Top Ten's dorm, there was no easy access to their living quarters for female fans and—even if they could get there—little room for any orgies in a tiny room crammed with bunk beds. Visits continued, though, to the Herbertstrasse and their many old friends there.

Paul and John, meanwhile, before they left Liverpool, had invited their girlfriends to come to Hamburg for a visit. The girls took them up on it. Cynthia Powell and John were quite an intense item and Paul and Dot Rhone had become quite inseparable. Cynthia had no trouble persuading her mother to let her go to Germany, but the younger and less sophisticated Dot had quite a hard time getting her parents to let her go. When Cyn and Dot left, it was Cyn's mother and Paul's father who saw them off at the train station. They carried, for the long train, boat, and train journey, only a couple of cheese sandwiches and a thermos of tea. They didn't realize that, once they were on the Continent, the train had no dining car. By the time they got to Hamburg, they were ravenous with hunger and with the romantic expectations of seeing their own true loves. When they alighted from the train in Hamburg in the dingy early morning stillness of the train station, they at first saw nothing but a deserted platform. Then came Paul and John, as described by Cyn: "two . . . bedraggled baggy-eyed creatures, reeking of alcohol, leaping and bounding towards us like a couple of lunatics. But what a reunion! Hugs, kisses and shouts of joy. Paul and John were overjoyed at our safe arrival . . . The pills and booze they had been stuffing into themselves had heightened their senses beyond our reason, and they overwhelmed us with their nonstop chat and frenzied excitement. Neither of us had seen them in this state before, but we were soon to get accustomed to the reasoning behind this need for artificial highs."

Cynthia stayed with Astrid at her folks' house and Dot moved in with Paul on Mutti's houseboat. After the joy of the reunion and being shown around the Hamburg that Paul and John knew, which didn't take long at all, there was little else left for Dot and Cyn to do. John showed the Herbertstrasse to a shocked Cyn. Otherwise, Cyn and Dot and Astrid spent most evenings sitting at the Top Ten, watching the Beatles play all night. At times, Pete Best reported, Cyn and Dot made their way into the Beatles' dorm room, at which times Pete and George were expected to make themselves absent. Cynthia later described sharing John's lower bunk with him while George snored away only a few inches above them in the upper bunk. "It was such a confined space and the smell of sweaty socks was less than sweet and the toilet facilities were virtually nil, so you can imagine I must have loved John a great deal."

Dot bought herself some tight and sleek Hamburg leather outfits, which would later cause her nothing but trouble when she wore them on the streets of Liverpool. Meanwhile trouble started to brew when Astrid, Cyn, and Dot spent most nights at a ringside table watching their Beatles perform at the Top Ten. Some of the drunken yobbos in the crowd started zeroing in on the unaccompanied good-looking fräuleins and started to aggressively try to make time with them—to the point of physically accosting them. Once the Beatles had come down off the stage to try to kick some ass and to tell the yobbos, "Hey, these are our women," then Astrid and Cyn and Dot were left alone (especially after the tough waiters realized they were Beatle women and adopted them). Pete reported later that it was only he and John who stood up for John's and Paul's and Stu's girls.

After the shows every night, before the girls went home with the guys, they usually went down the Reeperbahn to get an early morning breakfast. Cyn later remembered that, although the Beatles had been playing for hours, "the pills and booze would still be having their effect. Spirits were high and they were all full of devilment. They would leap and shriek down the streets as though they had just been let out of prison, joking and fooling amongst themselves and usually ending up in an exhausted heap on the dirty Hamburg pavements, laughing so much that we were all in tears."

The one thing that Cyn and Dot both noticed immediately was the tension between Paul and Stu onstage. Since Stu had rejoined the group Paul had been relegated to playing rhythm guitar again and he was openly resenting Stu's bass playing and Stu's apparent closeness to John. What had seemed in the past to be mere jollities shouted by Paul to Stu now became revealed as downright obscenities. Stu's one solo singing spot, on Elvis's "Love Me Tender," which Stu always directed in a lovesick way to Astrid at her table, now became an object of Paul's derision onstage, night after night.

Paul finally pushed Stu too far one night when the Beatles were backing Tony Sheridan at the Top Ten. Stu was playing bass and Paul was on piano when Paul made—sotto voce—one remark too many about Astrid. Stu was smaller than Paul and had never been known to be physical, but all of a sudden he dropped his bass, ran across the little stage, and knocked Paul off his piano stool. Paul, astonished, began wrestling with Stu on the stage and they started trading punches for five minutes or so, while Tony continued to sing and the Top Ten crowd cheered, loving these Beatles and the show they made.

When the others finally separated Paul and Stu, Stu yelled to

Paul, "Don't you ever say anything about Astrid again or I'll beat the brains out of you!"

Paul raged at Stu: "I'll say what I like!"

They were pulled apart and they never came to blows again, but it was starting to become clear that Stu was rapidly becoming a non-Beatle. Stu's life, it was obvious, was with his art and with Astrid. Paul, on the other hand, was aggressively a Beatle and even more aggressively was becoming John's right-hand man and more belligerently asserting himself as Beatle Number 2.

That assertion became even more aggressive when the Beatles were tapped to back up Tony Sheridan on a recording session. Paul named himself immediately as the bass player for the session and the others agreed that he would be a better choice. This was in early May. Stu was pretty much presented with a fait accompli, but by that stage in his life he realized that he was not really cut out to be a rock musician. He and Astrid planned to marry. And he had returned to his art studies with a vengeance. Stu had attracted the attention of Eduardo Paolozzi, the teacher and sculptor and artist, who invited Stu to join his master class at the State High School of Hamburg. Stu was also beginning to experience severe, unexplained, debilitating headaches.

Stu decided to be the diplomat and went to the others first. "I've been thinking of leaving for a long time," he said. "It's up to you, Stu," he was told. "No one wants you to leave. You know that." But there was palpable relief on everyone's part. Stu and Astrid continued to come to see the Beatles. Oddly, John and Stu became closer friends once the tension of Stu's position in the band was resolved. John wrote him voluminous letters, pouring out his heart and soul to Stu. (Ironically, later when Stu visited the Cavern wearing a collarless Pierre Cardin suit, long before the Beatles adopted the style, the group mocked his sense of fashion. Stu's sister Pauline told her mother, "Those Beatles hate Stuart, especially Paul McCartney. They were saying, 'Oh, you're wearing your sister's suit, Stuart.' ") Paul later said of Stu that he was a "great fellow, a very good painter who used to get picked on by us generally." Paul denied that there was anything personal involved and that the issue all along had been that Stu simply couldn't play bass. "So what you had to do, if you were having a photo taken, was tell Stu to turn away, do a mean moody thing looking over his shoulder, 'cos you didn't want anyone to see what he was actually playing. 'Cos anyone who knew would realize he couldn't play it. He just used to turn his amp down and sort of make a bass noise. It was quite good. But he didn't know what key we were in half the time."

At any rate Paul got what he wanted and Stu was out. The other four Beatles signed their first recording and publishing contract a few days later, on May 12, 1961, with Bert Kaempfert and his production company. Kaempfert was best known as an orchestra leader and composer of such songs as "Wonderland by Night." He was also a record producer and talent scout for Polydor Records and, as such, had scouted the talent at the Top Ten. He was not greatly impressed by the Beatles, later commenting that it was "obvious that they were enormously talented, but nobody—including the boys themselves—knew how to use it or where that talent would lead them."

Instead he wanted to record Tony Sheridan. But since the Beatles frequently backed Tony onstage and since Tony wanted them on his records, the Beatles were signed to back him up on his Polydor recording session. They were to be paid a flat fee of three hundred DM (about twenty-six pounds) and would not be eligible to receive any royalties.

On the day of the session, June 22, the Beatles found themselves awakened at the un-Beatle hour of 8 A.M. They descended on the impressive-sounding studio, Harburg Friedrich Ebert Halle, only to discover that it was an infants' school. Mobile recording equipment was set up on the stage of the school auditorium and that's where they were to play. They were carrying bottles of Coke—their breakfast—and launched into Tony's first number, "My Bonnie [Lies Over the Ocean]." Things went fine until George knocked over a bottle of Coke and Kaempfert was furious. "All Coke bottles off the stage!"

They went on to record Tony singing "The Saints [When the Saints Go Marching In]," "Why (Can't You Love Me Again)," and "Nobody's Child."

They also recorded John singing lead on "Ain't She Sweet," a number he regularly did at the Top Ten, and a Beatle instrumental that Bert liked. George had written it during their previous Hamburg visit as a send-up to a Cliff Richard and the Shadows song. Rory Storm had asked George if he knew the Shadows' song "Frightened City." George started playing around the melody of that song—he and the other Beatles hated Cliff Richard and the Shadows—and named the result "Cry for a Shadow" (after considering the name "Beatle Bop"). The sessions took three days in all, with one song being cut the third day: Tony singing "If You Love Me, Baby (Take Out Some Insurance on Me, Baby)."

It was not really their own recording session, but it was better than nothing. The Beatles drank up their money and that was that, they thought. Polydor released a single from the session: "My Bonnie" backed with "The Saints." Credits on the record were Tony Sheridan and the Beat Brothers (mostly because Kaempfert feared that Germans would misunderstand the word "Beatles." It sounded like "peedles," the German slang for "penis"). Polydor claimed the record sold upward of one hundred thousand copies in Germany. And the "Peedles" went back to Liverpool on July 2, after Peter Eckhorn had twice extended their engagement. This leave-taking was quite a contrast to the previous December, when three of them had been deported. This time they were sporting new suede overcoats. They were crying when they finally left the Top Ten, waving good-bye to a weeping Horst Fascher and a delegation of crying girl fans.

Liverpool was a big letdown after Hamburg. By midsummer of 1961 the Beatles had become a powerhouse group onstage, they had known enough fan adulation to become blase about it, Paul and John were honing their songwriting skills together, and basically they knew—as John would later say with characteristic lack of modesty—"that we were the greatest." All they lacked was a real recording contract on their own, a star-making manager, recognition outside of Liverpool, and lots of money. John, in a letter to Stu in Hamburg, lamented, "It's all a shitty deal. Something is going to happen, but where is it?"

In Liverpool they had all the work they could handle. Pete was still handling the bookings and was trying to up their prices. As a result, he bragged, they were sharing over a hundred pounds a week, as well as keeping Neil Aspinall and his aged van on the payroll. "Let's get the cash in!" Best said the band's motto became. Even so, they had run out of challenges as far as Liverpool went. After two tours of Hamburg and literally hundreds of hours onstage there playing for and dealing with audiences that could be incredibly difficult, they had become worldly beyond their years. And—just as valuable in light of what they would later face—their musical chops had been honed to perfection and they had developed incredible stage stamina. Three little shows a day in Liverpool—that was nothing. They had already done it all.

Especially as they became regulars at the Cavern's lunchtime sessions, they built up a fanatical following. Or followings— because even that early on each Beatle was establishing his own identity and attracting his own devoted fans. That was very unusual for a group, but the Beatles emerged with strong and distinctly separate personalities. John and Paul, of course, as the focal points, were dominant and that's the way they wanted it. During the Beatles' 274 or so performances at the Cavern, they came to own the stage, in their own peculiar ways. After compere Bob Wooler would introduce the Beatles as the "rock 'n' dole group" or as the "boys with the Benzedrine beat," John occupied stage right, his legs spread defiantly apart, his guitar raised up high on his chest, his eyes apparently unseeing as he stared straight ahead (because he couldn't see without his glasses and vainly wouldn't wear them onstage), his head thrown back as he spat out the words to a Chuck Berry song. (Which he would introduce, typically, by saying, "This is a record by Chuck Berry, a Liverpool-born white singer with bandy legs and no hair!") Paul's brother Mike would "mainly watch Lennon. He's like a caged animal, never mind a Beatle. Not that I've got anything against my brother, but he's just a brother (you know, the one who picks his nose and won't come off the toilet 'cos he's playing his guitar or reading those nudie books)." John did most of the talking and maybe stop a song, light a cigarette, and yell at some of the tie-wearing young shop clerks in on their lunch hour, "Shurrup, you with the suits on!" Paul would step in and be his charming self. As Bob Wooler later said, John was the perfect embodiment of defiant youth—no musician was ever younger or better, especially in leather. And Paul was John's perfect foil.

Just to John's right Paul played to all the girls with his big eyes and his soulful glances and his heartfelt ballads. He and John became a perfect point and counterpoint for each other. John the cheeky sod and Paul the charmer, the straight man who cleaned up after John's little excesses. Almost without exception, people who dealt with and worked for the Beatles uniformly described

Paul as the best public relations person they had ever encountered. Cynthia Powell, for example: "Paul even in those early
days could have earned a living in public relations. He would
work his backside off in potentially explosive situations in order
to keep things on an even keel, unless of course he was the
instigator, which was rare."

In the Cavern Paul would declare that so many people wanted
to hear "Over the Rainbow" that he would just sing it. That was
John's cue to laugh loudly and sneer. "Oh God, he's doing Judy
Garland." Sometimes Paul would stop and they would argue and
no one was ever completely sure whether they meant it or not.
With Stu gone, Paul and John grew ever closer. They already,
though, had begun to show signs of the big difference that
would one day drive them completely apart: Paul was relatively
happy with the success they were having and he enjoyed the
regularity of it, the playing in familiar surroundings for familiar
audiences. In many ways it was like the "job for life" that his dad
had, the security that Paul had cherished while his mother was
alive and that he missed so much after her death. John disliked
any sort of routine, disdained the familiar, and looked forward to
change and challenge.

The other Beatles enjoyed their followers too. George, as ever,
was praised for being the serious musician. With his own money,
he had bought a Gibson amp and a Gretsch guitar. George was
also singing lead on a number of songs, from "Take Good Care
of My Baby" to "The Sheik of Araby."

And then there was Pete Best. Everyone said Pete Best was the
sexiest of the Beatles and he had a huge female following. Not
something that John and Paul looked to with pride. Not with
their egos and not with the vision they shared of the future of the
Beatles. It was strictly a Lennon–McCartney vista that they saw
stretching ahead. But Pete had his fans, lots of them. After Bill
Harry's *Mersey Beat* paper started in the summer, Bob Wooler
wrote a long article attempting to analyze the Beatles' enormous
local popularity. (This was still before Brian Epstein's "discovery" of the group.) Wooler outdid his compereisms in the Cavern, declaring that the Beatles were "the stuff that screams are
made of." But seriously, folks, he did argue that the Beatles were
"the real thing." He said the Beatles were "rugged yet romantic,
appealing to both sexes. With calculated naïveté and an inge-

nious, throw-away approach to their music. Effecting [sic] indifference to audience response and yet always saying 'Thank you.' "
And, he said, they were "musically authoritative and physically magnetic, example the mean, moody magnificence of drummer Pete Best—a sort of teenage Jeff Chandler." Best got a lot of mileage out of that quote, you can be sure. Even so, Pete occupied a strange spot in the group. Just from still photographs taken throughout the two years he was a Beatle, there is a quality that clearly set him apart from the others. John, Paul, and George were of a piece, were clearly cut from the same fabric. Without knowing any background, any observer could pick the odd man out. Even before the others changed their hair and Pete kept his upswept hairstyle. When John wrote his clever little history of the Beatles for the first issue of *Mersey Beat,* he began it thusly, "Once upon a time there were three little boys called John, George and Paul, by name christened. They decided to get together because they were the getting together type." Much later in the piece, John observes that they had to "grow a drummer" for their trip to Hamburg, "so we grew one in West Derby in a club called Some Casbah and his trouble was Pete Best." Pete was, to put it politely, a temporary convenience for the Beatles. They had needed his drum kit and a body sitting behind it to get them to Hamburg and they now appreciated using his mother's Casbah as storage depot, rehearsal hall, and meetingplace. It was nice having Pete handle the bookings and his mother bring in nice-paying engagements. And Pete got them Neil to be their driver and roadie. So Pete was handy to have around. At the time, though, many people felt he was the most popular Beatle with the girls.

The group was starting to pull rival groups of girl fans: not gangs, exactly, but circles of girls who would dub themselves the Wooden Tops or the like and try to crowd in early to the Cavern to seize the fifty or thereabouts seats at the front (everyone else had to stand in the three long archways that made up the club). As a sometime afternoon diversion, John and Paul started tapping some of the choicest female talent for photographic sessions. Both of them had gotten cameras in Hamburg (inspired by Astrid), and John first got the idea to spend the odd moment after a lunchtime show in a "glamour photo session." He was never any good with machines or instruments that required any sort of delicate adjustment, but he had little trouble in persuading girls to go to their place and pose for pictures. Posing first fully clothed and then with the stray bit of clothing removed. Paul soon joined him in their afternoon glamour studies. They had to have their film developed at the neighborhood chemist's (drug-store), so all they got back were the mildest of soft pornography. The Beatles all looked forward, though, to viewing the latest batch of art pictures. And then Pete and George had the stray thrill of looking through the crowd the next day for a familiar face and try to match it with the pictures. And then wink at the girl and ask, "Still wearing black, then?" Pretty harmless stuff after Hamburg. John, who was really enthusiastic about his hobby, was always warning the others not to let Cynthia know what he was doing.

The girls who loved the Beatles decided to form the first Beatles fan club in October of 1961. To kick off the club's activities, they collected five pounds and, with that, booked a room in the David Lewis Club on Great George Place on the night of October 17. It was, obviously, an off-night for the Beatles and so they were expected to show up. They did so, to their great regret. It was a dismal evening, presided over by Paul's father, who, for some reason, showed up. About sixty girls finally showed up and the Beatles spent most of the evening just sitting and talking to them. They were expected to sing, but there was no sound system, so the Beatles delivered a few numbers and struggled away.

This was only three days after Paul and John had gotten back from their two-week holiday in Paris, where they had gone to celebrate John's twenty-first birthday—financed by a forty-pound gift from John's Aunt Elizabeth in Scotland. They went to see their Hamburg friend Jurgen Vollmer in Paris and had intended to go on to Spain, but spent all their money in the cafés of the Left Bank. They also returned with new hairdos and new shoes. Jurgen finally persuaded them to try the greaseless combed-forward "fringe" look that Astrid had championed in Hamburg and had gotten Stu and George to adopt. All the smart young people in Paris were wearing it, so Paul and John gave it a whirl.

Also, on their stopover in London, Paul and John did a bit of window shopping on Charing Cross Road. In the windows of a shoe shop named Annello and Davide they spotted some odd-looking black, narrow-toed, high-heeled boots and went in to check them out. They were very rakish, Cuban-heeled, ankle-length black flamenco boots and Paul and John decided they had to have them on the spot. They would look great, they realized, with leather trousers.

Once they got back to Liverpool and George and Pete got a look at their feet, they had to have some boots too and ordered them from Annello and Davide. Pretty soon all the Mersey groups were wearing Beatle boots.

Meanwhile the Beatles were still pretty much running in place in Liverpool and—while not giving it all that much thought—wondering when something was going to happen. They were booked almost daily, frequently playing two or three times a day. Ray McFall of the Cavern put them on riverboat cruise shows with Acker Bilk and his Paramount Jazz Band. One night—October 19—when they were sharing the bill at the Litherland Town Hall with Gerry and the Pacemakers, they decided to merge with the Pacemakers, just for the hell of it. After a break the boys from both groups came out onstage and were announced as the Beatmakers. Gerry Marsden played lead guitar and sang lead vocals, Pete Best and Freddy Marsden were sitting sidesaddle on the drums, Paul played rhythm guitar, George played lead, Les Maguire was on saxophone, and Les Chadwick on bass. John played piano. They never did anything similar again. It was born of boredom.

On another, earlier night, August 17, at St. John's Hall in Tuebrook, Paul turned over his bass to Johnny Gustafson of the Big Three, who were sharing the booking, and took the unprecedented—for the Beatles, anyway—step of singing into a hand-held mike and moving around the stage like a Frank Sinatra, the balladeer Paul was at heart.

So they continued to futz around, like all the Liverpool groups: moderately popular locally, making enough money to get by, but still ignored by the record companies, shunned as ignorant Northern hicks. And still there was no local music industry structure: no strong and experienced managers, no record companies, just hit-and-miss promoters. The one encouraging development was Bill Harry's *Mersey Beat* paper, which, when it it appeared in the summer with the first issue on July 6, was the first chance for the local bands to really find out what was happening around town on the scene. It was only after the first few issues that the Beatles finally found out that they were actually as great as they knew they were. It was no surprise that John and Paul embraced *Mersey Beat* immediately. John, of course, knew *Mersey Beat* founder and editor Bill Harry from art school, but he and Paul seemed to automatically realize the value of favorable newsprint. They both could smell good ink. And that was the reason for the success of *Mersey Beat.* The Establishment newspapers refused to acknowledge the existence of rock 'n' roll and gave it no coverage whatsoever. The Liverpool *Echo* would not even allow clubs to advertise "rock 'n' roll" groups in its pages.

John and Paul both wrote for *Mersey Beat.* John's "Beatcomber" column became the basis for his first book, *In His Own Write,* which Paul both encouraged him to do and suggested the title for. Paul's two articles did not share the flair that John brought to his journalistic hobby. Paul wrote about playing for the stripper in Liverpool and about the Beatles' first trip to Hamburg. Wrote Paul: "There was an article on the group in a German magazine. I didn't understand the article, but there was a large photograph of us in the middle page. In the same article there was a photograph of a South African negro pushing the jungle down. I still don't quite know what he has to do with us, but I suppose it has some significance."

PAUL'S father Jim was to initially oppose the notion of what he called a "Jewboy" coming on board as manager of his boy's group. Once he got to know Brian Epstein, though, Jim McCartney found himself thoroughly charmed by the smooth-talking, sincere-seeming twenty-seven-year-old record shop manager. John's Aunt Mimi had also been against Brian when she first heard what was afoot, that some poncy hairdresser or something was adopting her John's group as a trendy hobby or something, like buying some exotic pet or plant. She was right to be suspicious, as was Jim, although for the wrong reasons. Brian worked his hocus-pocus on Aunt Mimi, telling her that her John was the only important one in the group and that he, Brian, would do nothing but spend every waking moment and then some tending to John's present and future career (Jim, of course, got the same speech, with Paul's name used in place of John's). Paul himself was very skeptical of Brian. The plain fact was that Brian Samuel Epstein was the least likely candidate in all of Liverpool to manage the Beatles. And his motives for wanting to do so will probably never be known.

Brian didn't care that much about the Beatles' music. They knew that early on and he always acknowledged it. He had absolutely no experience in managing a group and the Beatles knew that. His contacts, such as they were, were with the business side of record companies. His assistant Peter Brown, his supposed friend, later wrote that he thought Brian was rather a typical closet homosexual, given to his little tantrums and drinkie spells and bitchy periods when he was just not himself. And, Brown thought, Brian took on the Beatles because he wanted to *take on* the Beatles and mainly liked the idea of cute boys dressed in snug-fitting rough denim and tight leather: in other words, that Brian was a rough-trade freak.

Brian—who, apart from Colonel Tom Parker, will be rock history's best-known manager—was born on September 19, 1934, to Harry and Queenie Epstein. Both parents were from prominent Jewish families in Liverpool. Harry's furniture credentials were I. Epstein and Sons. (The Epstein family did not originate the North End Music Stores chains, for which they became well known, but acquired the NEMS stores in the late thirties.) Queenie—born Malka Hyman—came from the fine furniture family responsible for Sheffield Cabinet, Ltd. As a child Brian bounced around from school to school. At age ten he was expelled from Liverpool College for scrawling dirty pictures. He and his mother attributed the expulsion to anti-Semitism, as they would later label the source of other problems in Brian's adolescence. He had what could only be termed a wretched experience as a schoolboy. He went from school to school like a Ping-Pong ball, accumulating a string of grievances along the way. At thirteen he failed the common entrance examination that could have gotten him into a good private school. Queenie and Harry gave a sigh of relief when, at age fourteen, he was admitted into Wrekin College in Shropshire, a school with a very good reputation. Brian wrote in his journal that he hated the idea of the school and was going only because Harry and Queenie were forcing him to.

Much later, in 1964, when he was acknowledged as the wizard behind the Beatles, Brian wrote in his autobiography that his biggest disappointment about being sent to Wrekin was that he spent the day before he began school with his mother and expected to be feted at the Grand Hotel in Sheffield, which was the grandest hotel around, but his mother didn't take him there. The fact that she didn't still riled him years later. "Now," he wrote, "on a wider, more discriminating and rather more expensive scale, I still find little pleasure in accepting less than the best and it may be this leaning towards superlative which drove me on in business and will continue to whip me into fresh activity."

After a time at Wrekin, wherein he and the school hurled their best attacks at each other, Brian wrote home to Harry and Queenie and "asked to be taken away from school so that I could become a dress designer. This caused a great deal of distress. The masters at Wrekin naturally thought it was ruinous to leave school without a single qualification and there was, to their minds, nothing less manly than dress designing." Well. Brian managed to convince everyone involved that he did not belong at Wrekin. His father—distressed, determined that his son would become anything but a dress designer—decided that Brian might become a man if he joined the family business. So Brian, at the age of fifteen, went to work in the family furniture store in Walton, Liverpool. He grew to love design and was apprenticed for six months to another store, The Times on Lord Street, where he became an expert at window dressing. He did so well there that when he decided to go back to the Epstein family store he was given a Parker pen and pencil set, which he would much later hand over to Paul to sign the Beatles' contract with Brian.

Back at the family store in Walton Brian continued with his window dressing. He argued with his grandfather Isaac over window concepts. The old man wanted the windows packed to the gunwales with—What else?—lots of furniture, so all the passersby could see what was available. Brian favored the dramatic window, with perhaps only one elegant chair. "I think," Brian said, "that if you show the public something lovely, they'll accept it."

Then his happiness was destroyed by a letter that came on December 9, 1952, informing him that he was being conscripted for national service and was going into the Army. As Brian well knew, it was the last place in the world where he should be. It turned out to be every bit as bad as he had feared. "For if I had been a poor schoolboy," said Brian, "I was surely the lousiest soldier in the world, not excepting the sad, demented creatures who blanco their trousers and eat their webbing belts in their attempts to fiddle a discharge."

After being passed over for the officer corps and undergoing basic training at Aldershot in the south, which Brian said was the most depressing place in all of Europe, he was posted to the

Regent's Park barracks in London. At least there, he could dress up at night and frequent the clubs and restaurants in London's West End. One particular night, when he was dressed to the nines in pinstripe suit, bowler hat, and umbrella, he hired a limousine to drive him back to the barracks and, at the gate, found himself being saluted by the other enlisted men. He was brought up the next day for impersonating an officer and disciplined.

After less than a year in the Army and after psychiatric tests, Brian was given a medical discharge. Although the grounds were not specified, the whispers were that the Army had determined he was unfit for military service as a homosexual and that that was how Queenie and Harry finally learned of his problems. He would subsequently keep the family attorney busy, getting him out of trouble.

At the time, though, Brian was happy to be free. "I ran like a hare for the Euston train after handing in my hideous uniform and I arrived in Liverpool prepared to return, to my parents and Clive, as a junior executive anxious to work very hard."

Queenie and Harry gave him his own store in Hoylake and for a year or so he made it prosper. Then, abruptly, at the age of twenty-two, he decided to chuck it all and become an actor. The furniture business was, it was true, full of glamour and Brian had begun hanging out with a group of actors and actresses from the Liverpool Playhouse. One of them, Brian Bedford, from the Royal Academy of Dramatic Arts in London, persuaded Brian one Saturday night in a bar called the Basnett, frequented by the actors, that Brian too could become an actor. That was all Brian needed. He was off to London to audition for the RADA's director himself, John Fernald. Brian did two readings, from *Macbeth* and from Eliot's *Confidential Clerk,* and was accepted on the spot.

He quit the Hoylake store, astounding his parents, and moved to London to begin his acting studies. He shortly discovered that he hated the world of acting as much as he had hated the military. He lasted through three terms and "discovered a distaste for the actor-type which lingers even now. The narcissism appalled me and the detachment of the actor from other people and their problems left me quite amazed."

He also, though, was arrested in the lavatory of a public park in London for "importuning." Queenie had to send the family lawyer, Rex Makin, to London to hush up the sordid affair. Brian returned to Liverpool for a rest. On the eve of his scheduled return to RADA to start a fourth term, he and his parents went to dinner at the Adelphi Hotel. Queenie pleaded with him to stay and that was all it took for him to abandon the world of acting.

It was 1957. Brian was then twenty-three. His brother Clive had returned from the military and so Harry and Queenie decided to give their two sons an entire store to run. They opened a new NEMS store on Great Charlotte Street in downtown Liverpool. Clive handled the appliance department and Brian was given the records section. He began the section with one assistant and gradually built to a staff of thirty and the music section expanded to occupy two floors. Brian worked very hard and devised his own "fool-proof system" of never running out of any particular item and thus never having to turn a customer away. He also made up his own top-twenty list of the bestselling pop records. Although he had not been a pop music fan, he educated himself quickly.

By 1959 things were going so well that the Epsteins decided to open another NEMS store in the center of the city in Whitechapel. Through his contacts with Decca Records Brian was able to get actor pop singer Anthony Newley to attend the shop's opening. Newley was a big success, quite open, without pretension, and quite friendly with Brian and his family. This, said Brian, "was how a real star should behave. In fact it is precisely the way my artistes behave, when they are permitted by press and public."

It was also about this time that Brian was involved in a very sordid affair. He was in the habit of visiting a public lavatory in West Derby, where men picked up men. One night, though, the man he approached at the urinals turned on him, beat him very badly, and took his wallet and watch. When the attacker studied Brian's identification later and recognized him as being from a prominent Liverpool family, he decided that he could blackmail him. When the phone call came, Brian turned to Queenie, who called in attorney Makin. Unfortunately, Makin told them, there was nothing he could do. Brian would have to go to the police. Humiliated beyond belief, Brian had to tell all to the detectives. Worse, they made him act as a decoy to catch the blackmailer.

The police got him, but then Brian had to go through the agony of a court trial, during which he was identified only as "Mr. X." The blackmailer went to jail, but threatened that he would get Brian when he got out.

Brian threw himself into his work, but emotionally he was a wreck. His blackmailer was due out of jail in the fall of 1961, so Queenie sent him off alone on a six-week vacation in Spain. He got back in October. Then, on Saturday, October 28, at about three in the afternoon, Brian said he had his epiphany. He claimed that a customer named Raymond Jones, wearing "jeans and a black leather jacket," walked into his Whitchapel store and said, "There's a record I want. It's 'My Bonnie' and it was made in Germany. Have you got it?"

Brian said he was stumped and asked Jones who the record was by. "You won't have heard of them" was the supposed reply. "It's by a group called the Beatles."

Brian said he wrote down on a pad: "MY BONNIE." THE BEATLES. CHECK ON MONDAY. And that on Monday before he had time to make any inquiries, two girls came in and asked for the record. So he began calling around and had no luck in finding such a record. As he later said, there "seems now no valid reason why, beyond my normal efforts to satisfy a customer, I should have gone to such lengths to trace the actual recording artistes. But I did and I wonder sometimes whether there is not something mystically magnetic about the name 'Beatle'?"

Bill Harry, friend of the Beatles and founder of *Mersey Beat,* the magazine that chronicled (and paralleled) the rise of the Mersey sound and of the Beatles, knew Brian long before the so-called Raymond Jones incident.

The first issue of his *Mersey Beat* was published on July 6, 1961. Page two of the first issue contained an article by John Lennon called "Being a Short Diversion on the Dubious Origins of Beatles, translated from the John Lennon." The first print run was for five thousand copies and Harry personally delivered most of those himself to local clubs, news dealers, record shops, and musical instrument stores. At the NEMS store on Whitechapel, Harry made an appointment to see the manager, who was of course Brian Epstein. Brian was conversant with the bands in the first issue of *Mersey Beat* and ordered a dozen copies of the magazine. The following day he called Harry and asked him to bring over another 100 copies. He told Harry he was fascinated by the local music scene and that, as manager of the shop, he had to keep up with all the groups. Brian ordered 144 copies of the second issue of *Mersey Beat,* which had a picture of the five Beatles on the cover along with the headline: BEATLE'S [sic] SIGN RECORDING CONTRACT! Brian also asked Harry if he could contribute record reviews to the magazine, which he subsequently did.

So Harry and a lot of other people in Liverpool were surprised when Brian later issued the "official" story of his "discovery" of the Beatles: That on the Monday after Jones came in, he started calling around and found, to his great amazement, that the record was by a Liverpudlian group that was at that very moment playing only a stone's throw from his store, at the Cavern Club on Mathew Street.

There are many problems with Brian Epstein's version of his discovery of the Beatles. His insistence that he had never heard of them is at variance with Bill Harry's recollections of Brian's ties with *Mersey Beat.* The very week that Brian claimed Raymond Jones came in asking for a Beatles record Brian's NEMS store was selling tickets for the first "Operation Big Beat" dance at New Brighton Tower Ballroom and the Beatles' name was at the top of the list of groups on the ticket. Sam Leach, who booked the Beatles into that dance, recalled that his assistant, Terry McCann, knew Brian and had seen him at earlier Beatles shows.

Another problem is that the Beatles' name did not even appear on the record that Raymond Jones supposedly wanted. The Beatles appeared on "My Bonnie" and on the flip side, "The Saints," as the backup group for Tony Sheridan, who sang the lead, but they were listed as the Beat Brothers on the record. It was available in England only as a German import, as Polydor number 24-673. Polydor would later issue it as a single in the United Kingdom with the Beatles credited by name, but not until January 5, 1962, as Polydor number NH 66-833. So, as of October 1961, at least, there were no Beatles on record by name in England. The group was certainly there, however. "Brian was fully aware of their activities," Harry recalled.

In his autobiography, *A Cellarful of Noise,* which John and Paul later derisively referred to as *A Cellarful of Boys,* Brian went to great lengths to create a scenario for a genteel screening of the Beatles. He carefully noted that, while he preferred Sibelius, others were free to exercise their tastes. And he claimed that he had actually seen and been offended by the Beatles' presence before he knew who they actually were: "I had been bothered a little by the frequent visits of a group of scruffy lads in leather and jeans who hung around the store in the afternoons, chatting to the girls and lounging on the counters listening to records. They were pleasant enough boys, untidy and a little wild and they needed haircuts." Just imagine what he could do for them if he got ahold of them!

So after Raymond Jones—if there ever actually was a Raymond Jones—supposedly asked Brian about "My Bonnie," which is actually a pretty bad record and certainly unidentifiable as bearing any Beatle contributions whatsoever, Brian made his inquiries, which mainly consisted of calling up Bill Harry at *Mersey Beat.* Certainly he knew the Beatles, Bill said. Their record was being plugged by Merseyside disc jockey and compere Bob Wooler, who had gotten a copy from George Harrison. He also informed Brian that the Beatles' noontime shows at the Cavern were the hottest ticket in town, which is probably how the Raymond Jonses of the world knew about the record. Actually, though, all Brian wanted was for Bill to get him into the Cavern to see the Beatles, almost as if he was crafting a careful scenario for his memoirs.

As Brian recalled it: "So I asked a girl to have a word with the Cavern, to say that I would like to pop in on November ninth at lunchtime and to ensure that I wasn't stopped at the door. I have never enjoyed scenes on doors with bouncers and people asking for 'your membership card, sir,' or that sort of thing."

So Bill Harry called the club and arranged for Brian to bypass the long line at the door and be admitted straightaway. Brian, neat as ever in pinstripe suit, attaché case under his arm, and accompanied by Alistair Taylor from his shop, thus descended down the eighteen stone steps into the teenage netherworld. He quickly regretted it, at least momentarily. The fastidious Brian was horrified by what he found: a dark dank sweaty cellar, full of the offensive odors of sweat, piss, disinfectant, and cheap tobacco and rocked by music that was far too overamplified for one of Brian's refined sensibility. Even though Brian was only twenty-seven at the time, he reacted as if he was generations removed from the largely harmless teenagers who crowded into the Cellar for a "Cavern lunch" of a Coke and a roll or a sandwich and the sounds they loved. It was also a blessed teenage escape for the shopgirls and apprentices and so on who could get away from the adult workaday world even if only for a few stolen moments at lunchtime.

Even though Brian knew that he was clearly out of his element, he lingered, fascinated by what he saw and heard. The Beatles, honed to near-perfection by playing hundreds of hours in Hamburg, were at their powerful peak. And, as Brian was careful to notice, they looked great in their leathers. After only a few minutes of playing in the unventilated basement, they were dripping with sweat. The very ceilings and walls perspired, producing a very fine rain made up of peeling paint and condensation that was called "Liverpool dandruff." It was very close and even sensual down there.

Brian was pretty impressed by what he saw and heard, even though he noted that the Beatles were "not very tidy and not very clean . . . They were rather scruffily dressed—in the nicest possible way or, I should say, in the most attractive way—black leather jackets and jeans, long hair of course . . . I had never seen anything like the Beatles on any stage. They smoked as they played and they ate and talked and pretended to hit each other. They turned their backs on the audience and shouted at them and laughed at private jokes."

Even though Brian was quite obviously staggered by the spectacle before him, he was later to observe that the Beatles "like me, were becoming bored because they could see no great progress in their lives."

That day, November 9, Brian decided to steel himself and wade through the teenage mobs to try to meet the group after their set. Bob Wooler had introduced Brian on the speaker system. Obviously, the Beatles knew vaguely who he was after hanging out in his record shop. George greeted Brian at the low bandstand, shook his hand, and said, "Hello there. What brings Mr. Epstein here?"

Brian said he was just there to inquire about their Tony Sheridan record. As Brian recalled it, George summoned the other Fabs and said, "This man would like to hear our disc." Brian recalled then that Paul "looked pleased" and went into the band room to get the record put on. Brian listened to it and "thought it was good, but nothing very special."

Nonetheless, Brian stayed around to catch the second half of the lunchtime show. "There was some indefinable charm there," he recalled. "They were extremely amusing and in a rough 'take it or leave way' very attractive. Never in my life had I thought of managing an artiste or representing one, or being in any way involved in behind-the-scenes presentation, and I will never know what made me say to this eccentric group of boys that I thought a further meeting might be helpful to them and to me."

Obviously something did. Much has since been made of Brian's hidden homosexuality and there are entire sections of Beatles books devoted to Brian's "lovesick" devotion to the Beatles, especially to John. Not to put too fine a point on it, Brian was an odd choice to choose the Beatles and to—by hit-and-miss, certainly not by genius—manage and catapult them to a position of world preeminence unforeseen by anyone else in Liverpool or anywhere else who ever had anything whatsoever to do with either Brian or the Beatles. Obviously, where superstars or their managers are concerned, none of them would ever win an election by their peers. Nonetheless, the Beatles did reach the upper limit of show business and world popularity and Brian Epstein did manage to get the Beatles there—and they did it without the support and in spite of the backbiting of their detractors and naysayers.

That said, it is still fair to observe that Brian's role in the Beatles' lives and career is not such an odd one when one considers the alternatives. The Mersey Beat was still largely ignored outside Liverpool as having no commercial potential other than for basements full of dancing teenagers. In Liverpool the candidates for managing rock 'n' roll bands had pretty much come forward and identified themselves. If the Beatles had stuck with people on the order of Allan Williams or Mo Best or Brian Kelly or Sam Leach or Ray McFall—all of whom had the group's best interests at heart somewhere—the Beatles would probably still be playing in a basement somewhere for five pounds for the entire group for the whole night. Brian was the first one who gave the

Beatles a glimpse of a world that existed outside the cellars they were playing in.

That was the first thing John and Paul recognized. The second thing, which set them apart from all the other Mersey groups, was realizing that their songwriting was their greatest strength and that it would ultimately carry them far beyond and above everyone else. In the early days of the Mersey Beat, a strong repertoire of Eddie Cochran, Chuck Berry, Buddy Holly, and Little Richard could sustain a Liverpool group. But—increasingly after the groups went off to Hamburg to become apprenticed and toughened—the local fans demanded showmanship, musicianship, and professionalism.

The Beatles had not been terrifically impressed by Brian and his little visit to the Cavern. Even though they knew who he was, the fact that he came to see them was of no great import.

Meanwhile another local man had set his cap for the Beatles. Sam Leach wanted to manage them. He had promoted many Beatles shows around town. The day after Brian's first visit to the Cavern the Beatles played Leach's biggest, most grandiose show to date. His "Operation Big Beat" at the huge Tower Ballroom in New Brighton featured the Beatles, Gerry and the Pacemakers, Rory Storm and the Hurricanes, the Remo Four, and Kingsize Taylor and the Dominoes. It drew over three thousand people (and many of those people had bought their tickets at Brian's NEMS store over the previous days, leading one to think Brian must have been aware of that). That was a busy night for the Beatles. They opened the Tower show at 8:00 P.M., then raced through the Mersey tunnel to play at Knotty Ash Village Hall, and then hurried back to the Tower to close the show at 11:30.

Leach later said that he had sold hundreds of "Operation Big Beat" tickets through NEMS. Leach also heard, in the days following that show, that Brian was interested in the Beatles. Said Leach: "A race between Eppy and I had begun, although at the time neither of us knew it. Events were moving fast, unfortunately for me, a little too fast."

Leach intended to use some of the money from "Operation Big Beat" to promote the Beatles in London and get in with the big agents there. As of yet, London was still completely ignoring the Liverpool groups. First, Leach went to see London agent

Tito Burns, who referred him to his assistant Malcolm Rose, who told Leach, "We have five thousand groups in London. Who needs the Beatles?"

So Leach decided to take the Beatles to London. Unhappily for Leach, as it turned out, he booked them more than thirty miles outside London in Aldershot (where Brian had enjoyed basic training). He booked them for two shows at the Palais Ballroom on Queens Road in Aldershot on the evening of December 9, 1961.

He and the Beatles set off from Liverpool at five o'clock that morning for the nine-hour drive south. Leach was aglow on the trip down. He had invited all the big London agents to the show and had taken out a half-page ad in the Aldershot newspaper. When they finally got there, Leach bought a newspaper and said grandly, "What about that for publicity?" The Beatles looked all through the paper and John finally asked acidly, "What bloody publicity, Sam?" Leach searched through the paper. Nothing. They went to the newspaper office, where they were told that Leach had sent them a check and they took only cash from new advertisers. So the Beatle ad was thrown out. Leach was just sick, of course, and the Beatles weren't feeling much better.

They hit every club and coffee shop they could find and started inviting everyone they saw to come to the show.

Once they got to the ballroom and set up and started playing, they looked out over the vast dance floor and counted: exactly eighteen people showed up. No top London agents. They played for almost four hours. Paul kept announcing, "There's no business like show business!"

After the show Leach bought four cases of Watney's brown ale, they started playing soccer (with bingo balls) on the dance floor, and they all got so drunk that someone called the police and they were thrown out of the ballroom. The police, in fact, ordered them to leave town. Leach and the boys decided to head for London, where they went to see an old friend, Brian Casser of Cass and the Cassanovas, who had opened a London club called the Blue Gardenia on Greek Street in Soho. It was an all-night club, so they got up onstage and jammed into the early hours. The Beatles finally had made their London debut.

Leach knew that the Beatles had talked with Brian Epstein about his managing them, but what he didn't know was that the very minute that the hungover Beatles got back to Liverpool, they held an immediate band meeting at the Casbah and decided to accept Brian's offer to become their manager. They had already agreed in principle to take Brian on, but this made it concrete.

Brian's courtship of the Beatles had been gradual. After that November 9 visit, he started going back often to the Cavern, just hovering in the background and watching. Sometimes he took Alistair Taylor along. Every time he went back to NEMS, all he could talk about was the Beatles. The operative word was "magnetic": Didn't everyone agree that the Beatles were magnetic?

He ordered two hundred import copies of "My Bonnie" and had a BEATLES sign put on the front window of his store in foot-tall letters. He acted, in a word, lovesick. Many of the girls who came to the Cavern had shoulder bags that were embroidered with inscriptions: I LOVE PAUL or I LOVE JOHN. Brian put his inscription in the NEMS store window.

A few days later he asked George to relay a request to the others for a meeting with him. Brian still had no inkling that he would try to manage the Beatles. At that point, he apparently just had a vague idea that he could work with them in some way. They finally met on December 3, at around four-thirty in the afternoon, in his office. At least the meeting was scheduled for four-thirty. First John, George, Pete, and Bob Wooler, whom they invited along as "adviser," met at the Grapes, their favorite pub near the Cavern, and had a few pints. When they got to Brian's office, they were late and there was no Paul. Half an hour later a slightly annoyed Brian asked George to phone him. George came back with a little smile that annoyed Brian even more. "Paul's just got up and he is having a bath." Brian's quick temper went off. "This is disgraceful," he stormed. "He's very late."

"And very clean," George added.

Once Paul arrived they went out for coffee and talked in general terms. Brian was nervous at first. "I used to dread you people coming in, completely disrupting the place." They liked that. He went on, "I'm the manager of this store and I think I can do something for you."

Lennon asked, "Can you buy us into the charts, Brian?" They got along after that and agreed to a second meeting on Wednesday, December 6. In the meantime Brian made inquiries about their background, about their management or lack of, and he also went to see the Epstein family lawyer, Rex Makin, and asked him what he thought of Brian perhaps managing a group. Makin dismissed him: "Oh yes, another Epstein idea. How long before you lose interest in this one?"

At the same time the Beatles were talking about Brian. They thought he was a little "antwakky" (scouse for "strange"), but he seemed successful and together and they agreed that their careers could use some kind of professional help. Besides, they said, Brian might be strange, but they could change him, loosen him up. He certainly couldn't do anything to change them. Paul was the most dubious about Brian, but he had no alternative to propose and even he had to admit they were in need of something or somebody—and after the disastrous Aldershot gig, it certainly wasn't Sam Leach.

Brian, meanwhile, continued his research. He went to see Allan Williams at Allan's Blue Angel club, which had become the chief hangout place for Liverpool's musicians. Williams said that Brian was going around town, asking everyone about the Beatles. And that he not only blushed when he talked about them, he started sweating. On this particular night he told Williams that he planned to manage them, "push them as far as I can. I believe in them. . . ."

Williams started cursing the Beatles and then he said, "They're completely unscrupulous. They're nice lads, all right, but unpredictable when it comes to contracts." He ranted on.

Brian asked, "Okay, Allan, should I take them over or not? Your honest opinion?"

"My honest opinion, Brian, is this: Don't touch them with a fucking bargepole."

When they met again on Wednesday Brian had decided that he wanted to manage them. He spelled out to them what he intended to do for the group: get them out of their recording contract with Polydor and Bert Kaempfert in Hamburg, use his record company contacts to get them with a big British record company, handle all their bookings and upgrade them in prestige, and accept no gig for less than fifteen pounds. In exchange for all of that, he would take 25 percent of the gross monies they brought in, to be computed weekly.

The Beatles were silent after Brian's little presentation. They were impressed at how businesslike his pitch was and they knew it made sense. Brian said, "Quite simply, you need a manager. Would you like me to do it?"

Silence again. Then John blurted, "Yes."

Paul nodded his assent but asked, "Will it make much difference to us? I mean, it won't make any difference to the way we play."

"Course it won't," Brian said.

No one knew what to say next. Finally John spoke up: "Right then, Brian. Manage us. Now, where's the contract? I'll sign it." There was no contract, since Brian didn't know how to draw one up. He later got a copy of a typical manager-group contract and took it with him when he met with the Beatles after they got back from Aldershot. But after scrutinizing it, Brian and the others agreed it was unfairly biased to management. So he altered it and several weeks later the Beatles, witnessed by Alistair Taylor, signed it in a little ceremony in the sitting room at Pete's house on January 24, 1962. Brian himself did not sign it and never said why. "But," he later said, "I abided by the terms and no one worried."

The others wondered. But he was right that they didn't worry. Once Brian had their verbal agreement in December, he had thrown himself into managing them with a vengeance.

First, he wanted to get them into the Liverpool *Echo*. He felt that *Mersey Beat* was all well and good but that the Beatles wouldn't be legitimate until they were in the "real" newspaper. The only problem, of course, was that the *Echo* didn't cover such music. The only pop music coverage in the *Echo* came in the form of a record review column called "Off the Record" on Saturday. It was bylined only by the name Disker. Brian wrote to Disker anyway, encouraging Disker to at least drop the name of his Beatles in the column.

Brian's reply came from Tony Barrow, a Liverpudlian living in London and working as a liner-note writer for Decca Records. He was Disker. He explained that he could only review records. Brian made a trip to London anyway, taking a rough Cavern tape of the Beatles for Barrow to hear. Barrow said he still could not help Brian, but after Brian left Barrow called around to the Decca sales office. He said that a major Decca account was pushing a certain Liverpool group and it might be politic if Decca sent a talent scout to check the group out.

Dick Rowe, Decca's head of A&R, agreed and sent his assistant, Mike Smith, to the Cavern. Smith was impressed and wanted his boss to see what he liked. So he invited the Beatles to come to London to audition for Rowe on January 1, 1962.

The audition was a stone fiasco, a disaster from the beginning. The Beatles left Liverpool on the morning of New Year's Eve, driven by Neil Aspinall in a rented van, large enough to haul all of them and all their equipment on the long trip. Neil had never driven to London before and lost his direction in the snow. The drive took around ten hours and they got to London around ten o'clock at night. They finally found their hotel, the Royal near Russell Square, and then set out to get a New Year's Eve drink and dinner. They were invited to leave the first restaurant they tried because of their appearance.

They went on to Trafalgar Square to watch the drunks congregate for the New Year and were frightened by two marijuana smokers who wanted to use their van to smoke a joint. (The Beatles had yet to be introduced to cannabis.) So they just went to bed.

Brian, meanwhile, had taken the train first-class from Liverpool and spent a comfortable night at his Aunt Freda's house.

The next morning Brian was the first to arrive at the studios, at 165 Broadhurst Gardens in West Hampstead, for their 11 A.M. appointment. Mike Smith, plagued by a New Year's hangover, was late, much to Brian's extreme annoyance. Once they got into the studio Smith—astonished at the ragged state of the Beatles' well-traveled and well-worn amps—insisted that they use studio equipment instead. They were all nervous at being in a real recording studio for the first time. Paul's voice kept cracking as he tried to finish "Red Sails in the Sunset" and "Like Dreamers Do." George strained to hit the notes on "The Sheik of Araby." John's voice was dragging on Chuck Berry's "Memphis." Brian had chosen an odd assortment of standards and ballads and everything across the menu: "Money (That's What I Want)," "Your Feet's Too Big," "To Know Her Is to Love Her," "Crying, Waiting, Hoping," "Searchin'," "Take Good Care of My Baby," "Sure to Fall (in Love with You)," "September in the Rain," "Till There Was You," Paul's "Love of the

Loved," and John's and Paul's "Hello Little Girl." Brian was quickly demonstrating that his musical judgment wasn't very sound.

Still, they got through fifteen numbers by 2 P.M. Smith rushed them because he had a second group coming in, Brian Poole and the Tremeloes from Barking. The Beatles left, thinking they had done fairly well. Smith had effusively told them he loved what they had done. The Beatles had yet to learn the language of record companies, where "fabulous" can—depending on the inflection—indicate total failure. At any rate they would not be told until March that Decca was turning them down. Even then they weren't told that the reason for their rejection was mere convenience. Rowe told Smith he could sign one of the two groups he auditioned on New Year's. He picked Brian Poole and the Tremeloes because they were local; the Beatles were two hundred miles away in Liverpool. When Rowe told Brian that his group was being turned down, he said it was because, "Not to mince words, Mr. Epstein, we don't like your boys' sound. Groups of guitarists are on the way out." In a cold fury Brian replied, "You must be out of your mind. These boys are going to explode. I am completely confident that one day they will be bigger than Elvis Presley."

When they struggled back to Liverpool the Beatles found one heartening development. In the January 4 edition of *Mersey Beat,* they found themselves on the front page as the *Mersey Beat* Readers' Poll winners. BEATLES TOP POLL! read the headline. Paul was still being identified as Paul McArtrey. The order of finish for the ten most popular Liverpool groups in the readers' poll was: Beatles, Gerry and the Pacemakers, the Remo Four, Rory Storm and the Hurricanes, Johnny Sandon and the Searchers, Kingsize Taylor and the Dominoes, the Big Three, the Strangers, Faron and the Flamingoes, and the Four Jays. The Beatles, like all the groups did, voted for themselves a number of times.

Mersey Beat didn't know about the Decca audition, since Brian only wanted to make successes public. And later, when the group members learned that Decca had turned them down, John, Paul, and George kept that news from Pete. His days as a Beatle were clearly numbered. Best later said that the news was kept from him for days: "When I did eventually learn our fate, their lame excuse was that they had all thought I would take the result extremely badly."

Disker finally mentioned the Beatles in his Liverpool *Echo* column:

> Decca disc producer Mike Smith tells me that he thinks The Beatles are great. He has a continuous tape of their audition performances which runs for over thirty minutes and he is convinced that his label will be able to put The Beatles to good use. I'll be keeping you posted.

Brian, of course, later hired Tony Barrow to do press for the Beatles.

Also in January of 1962 Brian was able to get Polydor to release "My Bonnie" as a single in England. And he was able to plant a story about that event in the South Liverpool *Weekly News*. Concluded the little article:

> The boys have always been full-time musicians ever since they left school, and are making quite a name for themselves locally. Who knows, it might not be long before they achieve nation-wide acclaim.

For someone with no experience in this line of work, Brian was making things happen in one big hurry. He was upgrading their bookings, a record contract seemed very near, he was about to get them their most lucrative Hamburg engagement yet, and he was determined to put his polish on their stage act. Paul turned out to be his unlikely ally as Brian argued that the Beatles had to get out of their scruffy leathers and into suits and ties. Lennon raged, but Paul and Brian prevailed. Making it big, after all, was the name of the game and John and Paul would do anything to that end. Brian ordered them tailored suits of gray tweed, for forty pounds each (discounted, finally, to thirty), from Beno Dorn, "The Master Tailor for Impeccable Hand-Made Clothes," in Birkenhead.

The great day came on March 24, as the Beatles were about to go onstage in the Heswall Jazz Club at the Barnston Women's Institute. Brian handed them big paper bags containing their new suits. The transformation onstage was astounding. Gone was the menace—real or implied—that they had projected. Now, with their matching suits and ties and brushed-out hair, it seemed more like Paul's group than John's. It would not surprise anyone to hear this group sing "Over the Rainbow."

Brian also drew up stage rules: no more drinking, smoking, eating, cursing, fighting, farting, or belching onstage. He also insisted on a set song lineup, to last no more than sixty minutes. Sometimes he would amend that to two thirty-minute sets, just like the big stars, such as Anthony Newley, did. He also wrote up incredibly detailed "advance sheets" or "details of engagements," which he gave to the Beatles every week. A sample portion of one such briefing paper:

> Sunday 29.7.62: REST. Monday 30.7.62: L.T. [lunchtime] Cavern. St. Johns, Bootle. Equipment to arrive not later than 7:15 p.m. and group no later than 8.0 p.m. Dave Forshaw is looking forward to this night for some time and it is, of course, for this hall a major investment. Give 'em a good night.
>
> Wednesday 1.8.62: L.T. Cavern. [Night] Cavern. Friday 3.8.62: Grafton Ballroom. This is easily the biggest night of the week and you are very much the stars of this night. I hope there will be a good crowd which will be truely a tribute to your popularity and I will expect a magnificent show.
>
> Saturday 4.8.62: Victoria Hall, Higher Bebington. I'll find out the exact location of this hall during the week. Equipment to arrive no later than 7.0 p.m. and group no later than 8.0 p.m.

Brian was also still running his store, attending to Beatle details, worrying about getting a recording contract, going to most of the Beatles' gigs and generally running around everywhere. His newly found endurance astounded those who recalled how hard he had used to work and saw that he was now working even harder. His secret was that, like some of the Beatles, he had discovered the potency of pep pills, the Musician's Best Friend. Twenty-hour days were a snap when your blood was boiling with amphetamines. Where some of the Beatles (except Pete, of course) used speed, they would take the edge off of it with beer or ale or a Brown Mix (mild and brown ale) or Black Velvet (Guinness and cider), Brian favored Scotch or brandy, so much so that "Brandyman" became his second nickname, after "Eppy." The mix of speed and hard liquor wasn't good for his nerves, but Brian was on a sort of metaphysical quest with the Beatles. It was clearly the first time in his life that he had a mission he believed in and a goal he thought was attainable and he was in a rush to get things done.

And peculiarly, given all the talk about how much Brian loved John and had taken on the band just to try to take John on, he seemed subdued around John. If anything, Paul was jealous of the attention that John got. But his homosexuality was not a big thing with the band. Brian long thought they didn't know, but it didn't take them long to figure out how things were. They had even heard talk about his "Mr. X" episode. But Brian didn't make any moves on John. There were jokes made—not in front of him—that he imagined all he had to do was to get John out of Liverpool and John would then succumb to Brian's charms. Copenhagen was the usual destination in the joke. "Going to Copenhagen, then, John?" "Shruup!" Peter Brown also said that Brian rented a secret apartment at 36 Faulkner Street in Liverpool with the hopes that someday he could lure John there. It seemed, though, more likely that it was used occasionally by Brian and his few homosexual friends. Later, after John and Cynthia had their secret wedding, he let John and Cynthia move into the flat.

John was always sensitive about the rumors, make no mistake about that. When Brian and John went on vacation together in Spain in 1963—just after Cynthia gave birth to their son Julian—he never said anything about it at the time. A few weeks later, at Paul's twenty-first birthday party at Aunt Jin's house, Bob Wooler, after a few drinks, asked John about his "Spanish honeymoon." Lennon became livid, knocked Wooler down, and kicked him so viciously that he had to be hospitalized. Lennon was later apologetic and Wooler got a two hundred pound settlement to keep things quiet. (Later that night Pete Shotton, John's lifelong friend, reported, after Wooler was taken to the hospital, John offered to swap wives with Pete.)

Shotton later said that John had told him about the "Spanish honeymoon." "What happened," John said, according to Shotton, "is that Eppy just kept on and on at me. Until one night I finally just pulled me trousers down and said to him, 'Oh, for Christ's sake, Brian, just stick it up me fucking arse then.' And he said to me, 'Actually, John, I don't do that kind of thing. That's not what I like to do.' 'Well,' I said, 'what is it you want to do then?' And he said, 'I'd really just like to touch you, John.' And so I let him toss me off. So what harm did it do, then, Pete, for fuck's sake?"

Oddly, Pete Shotton claimed that Brian tried to seduce him before the "Spanish honeymoon." He said that on his first meeting with Brian at the Blue Angel, Brian had invited him to go for a drive to "have a word with you about John." What happened then, Pete said, was that Brian invited Pete to go home with him—to his secret apartment, for Brian still lived with Harry and Queenie. Pete said he refused and Brian was very gentlemanly about it and they remained friends.

Pete Best later told almost the same story about Brian trying to seduce him. They went for a drive, which Pete did not think unusual, since Brian often consulted him about bookings and other business matters to do with the band. They were cruising in Brian's Ford Zodiac when Brian popped the question. "Pete, would you find it embarrassing if I ask you to stay in a hotel overnight? I'd like to spend the night with you."

Pete said that he would rather go home and nothing more was said about it and he, for his part, tried to forget it.

A major obstacle fell on March 7, 1962, at 8 P.M. when the Beatles recorded their first BBC radio show. Brian had gotten them an audition with the BBC on February 12 and they had, typically, charmed Peter Pilbeam, the producer of the show "Teenager's Turn (Here We Go)." On that day, after hearing John and Paul both sing, Pilbeam wrote on his audition notes: JOHN LENNON, YES. PAUL MCCARTNEY, NO. He later reconsidered his judgment.

The first show was taped before an audience at the Playhouse Theatre in Manchester and was broadcast on March 8 at 5 P.M. For the taping John sang lead on "Hello Little Girl," "Memphis," and "Please Mr. Postman" and Paul sang "Dream Baby (How Long Must I Dream?)," the Roy Orbison song that Paul had done at the audition. ("Hello Little Girl," the only Lennon-McCartney song they did, was dropped from the broadcast.)

This was the first of more than fifty BBC appearances by the Beatles. (They started calling it the Beatles Broadcasting Corporation.) Said Pilbeam: "I was very impressed with them and I booked them straightaway for another date after that first show."

It did not hurt that the audience, comprising more than three hundred young girls, broke into fervent applause.

When the Beatles came back to tape a second show on June 11, they brought along a busload of fans from the Cavern. Songs they taped this time were "Besame Mucho," "Ask Me Why," and "A Picture of You." When they tried to leave the Playhouse after the taping, they encountered another manifestation of spreading Beatlemania: They were mobbed by the girls. Pete Best, who was the last in leaving, said, "They came at us like a pack of hounds." The other three got into the van, but the girls surrounded him and he lost his tie and a handful or two of hair. Paul's father Jim had come along for the taping and later reprimanded Best.

"Why did you have to attract all the attention?" Jim asked Pete. "Why didn't you call the other lads back?" Pete tried to explain that there was nothing he could have done. Jim wasn't mollified and he snapped, "I think that was very selfish of you." Pete later asked Brian to have a word with Jim on the matter, which may not have been entirely politic on Pete's part.

In early April, on the eleventh, the Beatles were off to Hamburg again. Earlier in the year their friend Peter Eckhorn from the Top Ten had come to Liverpool to firm up his lineup of groups for the year. He had expected the Beatles to return to the Top Ten, but they referred him to their new manager. Peter was shocked when Brian demanded five hundred DM per Beatle per week. He offered four hundred and fifty, but Brian wouldn't budge. Next in town was Horst Fascher, Peter's former head bouncer. Horst had jumped to the newest thing in Hamburg, the Star-Club, which was happy to pay five hundred per man per week. So they were booked there from April 13 to May 31.

John, Paul, and Pete flew from Manchester to Hamburg on the eleventh. George had the flu and planned to leave the following day with Brian. The three were met at the airport by Astrid, alone. One look at her face and they knew there was bad news. Stu's headaches over the past few weeks had gotten worse and worse, to the point that Astrid had to restrian him from leaping from the window. The doctors could find nothing wrong with him. Then he had begun blacking out and suffering periods of blindness. The day before the Beatles arrived he had collapsed again and died in Astrid's arms in the ambulance. She was completely distraught at the airport. "Stu is dead!" was all she could whisper. As Pete Best recalled, all of them broke down, with John taking Stu's death the hardest.

Stu's mother Millie by chance was on the same plane with Brian and George the next day. The others met with Millie later. Paul, in trying to find comforting words for her, told Millie, "My mother died when I was fourteen and I'd forgotten all about her in six months."

The Beatles settled in for a joyless Hamburg stay. They later—much later—learned that extensive tests finally showed that Stu had died from a small brain tumor, next to a fairly recent depression in the skull: He was likely killed by that long-ago kick to the head he had suffered as a Beatle when a jealous ted went after him.

John and Paul, who were still actively collaborating on songs then, sat down in the first days there and came up with a song they at first called "Love, Love Me Do." They were not quite satisfied with the arrangement and John began working on a harmonica introduction to it.

And the Beatles returned to their Hamburg diet of pills, beer, and women.

For novelty they had George's "Thing." One night in their room George threw up on the floor after a bit too much to drink. He left the mess there for the cleaning lady to remove. She was tired of Beatle messes and refused. George said he wouldn't touch it either. So it became a standoff. They christened it "The Thing" and began to feed it cigarette butts and pieces of stale food and so it grew. Members of other bands came to view it. Finally George said he was almost afraid to sleep near it. He still wouldn't touch it. Horst Fascher solved the matter by arriving with a shovel. The Beatles followed him out to the Grosse Freiheit to give "The Thing" a decent burial.

This was also when John supposedly peed on the nuns walking by, although Paul denies that it ever happened and gets incensed whenever anyone brings the subject up.

While the Beatles were occupied in Hamburg for seven weeks, Brian flew back to Liverpool, desperate to get the Beatles a recording contract. The Decca rejection had been taken bitterly and they blamed Brian for it, citing his insistence of recording such a weird variety of songs. Brian was also coming under pressure from his father, who wanted him to either run the store or get on with his hoodlum beat group, but not to do both.

Brian decided to give London one last shot. He had the tapes from the Decca audition and he started knocking on doors. He heard the same thing everywhere—at Columbia, HMV, Philips, Pye, Oriole. No one was interested. Brian had heard that the large HMV record shop on Oxford Street could make a quick phonograph record from a tape, so he decided to have his tapes transferred to disc. They would be easier to play, he reasoned. It cost just a little over a pound. While the engineer, Ted Huntley, was transferring the tapes, he liked what he heard and asked Brian if this group had a song publisher yet. Brian said no and Huntley called a friend, Syd Coleman, who ran an EMI publishing subsidiary called Ardmore and Beechwood in the same building.

In a few minutes Brian was playing his new demonstration discs for Coleman, who liked the sound and offered to sign the Beatles to a publishing contract. Brian said that what he was really after first was a recording deal. Coleman decided to introduce Brian to his friend George Martin, a producer at EMI's Parlophone Records. An appointment was made for the following day, May 9, at Martin's offices at the EMI studios in Abbey Road.

Martin, thirty-six, was head of A&R for Parlophone, but had little pop music experience. He was best known for the comedy records that he had produced: solo albums by Spike Milligan and Peter Sellers of "The Goon Show."

The next day Brian was early as usual for his appointment at EMI's unobtrusive studio building on tree-lined Abbey Road in a an elegant neighborhood near Regent's Park. Martin ignored Epstein's hype and instead listened to the discs. Very favorably too. As he said later, he was willing to listen to anything and that's what he had expected. But as he listened he found himself liking the voices. "There was something tangible that made me want to hear more, meet them and see what they could do. I thought as I listened: Well, there just might be something here." He asked Brian to bring the Beatles in for what he later recalled would be a recording test. They set the date for June 6.

Excited, Brian ran out to the nearest post office, at Primrose Hill, and phoned his parents before firing off two telegrams. The first, to the Beatles in Hamburg, read: CONGRATULATIONS BOYS. EMI REQUEST RECORDING SESSION. PLEASE REHEARSE NEW MATE-RIAL. The second one went to Bill Harry at *Mersey Beat*. It said: HAVE SECURED CONTRACT FOR BEATLES TO RECORDED [sic] FOR EMI ON PARLAPHONE [sic] LABEL. 1ST RECORDING DATE SET FOR JUNE 6TH.

When the Beatles returned from Hamburg, they signed a recording contract with EMI on June 4, although Martin later thought the contract had been signed sometime in July. Brian not only thought it had been in July, he was under the impression that the Beatles were in Hamburg in July.

The Beatles traveled by their van down to London and signed their contract and two days later, on July 6, they met with Martin at Abbey Road. "It was love at first sight," he said. "My first impression was that they were all quite clean. That was obviously Brian's influence . . . But the most impressive thing was their engaging personalities. They were just great people to be with."

For their part, the Beatles were impressed by Martin, with his imposing physical presence and his competent manner, rather like a retired RAF pilot. John and George had been big fans of "The Goon Show," so Martin was a hero to them. Martin was so taken by Paul's air of self-assurance that he thought of turning Paul into the leader of the group. Only Pete Best failed to make an impression and Martin later took Brian aside to tell him, "I don't know what you intend to do with the group as such, but this drumming isn't at all what I want." That sealed Pete Best's fate.

That day at Abbey Road they recorded "Besame Mucho," Paul's favorite standard at the time, and three Lennon–McCartney songs: "Love Me Do," "P.S. I Love You," and "Ask Me Why."

Martin and his assistant Ron Richards and sound engineer Norman Smith gave the group a little talk—very fatherly—about what the recording business entailed. As he wound up, Martin asked, "Is there anything you don't like?" And George passed immediately into legend by answering, "Yeah. I don't like your tie."

All this time Paul and John, the only Beatles with steady girls, still went with Dot Rhone and Cynthia Powell. The two girls had become fast friends and had moved into adjacent furnished rooms on Garmoyle Road. Not long after the Beatles got back from Hamburg in June, Cynthia and Dot were home one night, expecting nothing but a quiet evening. Dot had washed her hair and put it up in rollers and, dressed in an old sweater and a large pair of her mother's bloomers, was in Cynthia's room, talking about nothing. Cynthia later said that Dot had showed her an engagement ring Paul had gotten Dot in Germany.

There came an insistent knock, first at Dot's door, then at Cynthia's. It was Paul, unexpected. Dot was horrified, but led Paul off to her room.

There was only the sound of muted voices for a while. Then Cynthia heard Dot's door being opened and closed, the sound of a person running down the stairs, and then the crash of the front door being slammed. Then Dot came into Cynthia's room and collapsed. She was hysterical. "Crying and moaning like a wounded animal, her face blotchy, the so-carefully-applied rollers haphazardly falling out, strands of tear-wet hair in straggles round her crumpled little pixie face, and still wearing her mother's bloomers. Poor little defenceless Dot."

It was pretty obvious what had happened. Paul had given her the brush-off. He had not been what you would call entirely faithful anyway, but Dot thought that Paul had left her because of the way she looked that night. Dot soon gave up on the independent career girl life and moved back in with her parents. Cynthia seldom saw her again. (Dot later moved to Canada, married, and reportedly met briefly with Paul after a Wings concert. In September 1984 she reportedly sold some of her Paul memorabilia at auction through Sotheby's in London.) Paul's next steady girlfriend was Iris Caldwell, who was Rory Storm's sister. Iris later married singer Shane Fenton, who was better known as Alvin Stardust.

Iris was a knockout who first caught Paul's eye at the Tower Ballroom. She was a dancer and was onstage in fishnet stockings that showed off her gorgeous legs and he was hooked. She was seventeen when they started going out together and she thought that Brian did not approve because she got the idea that he did not want his Beatles to be attached to any one girl. Bad for the image. So Paul would come to her house after his shows. Paul become very attached to Iris's mother, who of course later killed herself in what was apparently a mutual suicide pact with her son Rory Storm.

At the time, though, things were much happier. When the Beatles went back to Hamburg in November, Paul wrote to Iris often and signed his letters Paul McCoombie. She said at the time that Paul had written "Love Me Do" expressly for her and that he later wrote "Please Please Me" at the Caldwell house. "I told him I thought the words sounded terrible. I remember once my mum told him he had no feelings, so he phoned her up one night and said, 'Listen to this song I've just written,' and sang her 'Yesterday' over the phone. That was when they were appearing at the ABC, Blackpool. After he'd finished the song he said, 'There! And you say I've got no feelings!' "

She and Paul, when he could still go out like a normal person, took the bus to the movies together. Then he got his first car, a dark green Ford Cortina, and Iris was thrilled: "Wow, I'm going out with a feller who's got a car! That was a big thing because we were all broke and not many people of our age could afford cars in Liverpool."

Her fling with Paul was to end early in 1963 when he met someone more glamorous. "I'm quite sure there were many other girls around at that time, but I didn't know about any of them and I didn't actually know that he was going out with anyone else, if you see what I mean. I used to say to him, 'Why don't you go out with somebody else?', though I never thought that he did, and then when he came back from London once and said that he had met Jane Asher I didn't want to go out with him any more, though we remained good friends and kept a good relationship."

Not long after Cynthia sadly said good-bye to her friend Dot, she was in for a real shock. She discovered that she was pregnant. She was terrified. To be single and pregnant in Liverpool in 1962 was something that just was not done—or at least not acknowledged. Cynthia was alone in her little furnished room most of the time. Her mother had moved to Canada and John was always on the road. She had already applied for Social Security. Finally she told John, for she had no one else. And he did, after all, share the burden of the situation somewhat.

John turned white and temporarily lost his tongue. When he finally regained some composure, he said, "There's only one thing for it, Cyn. We'll have to get married." It was not a joyous occasion. Then John went off to tell his Aunt Mimi, who got into an awful argument with him. But he persisted in wanting to do the honorable thing. Finally John went to the only person he could turn to: Brian Epstein.

To his credit, Brian told John not to worry, that Brian would take care of setting up a wedding. The main thing, of course, was to keep it a secret. With the Beatles just on the verge of making it—and possibly making it very big—the fact that the chief Beatle not only had a girlfriend but had knocked her up and married her could not be made public. As Brian later wrote in his book, "A Beatle must not marry. It is all very well if one is married before one is a fully-grown Beatle but a fully-grown Beatle must stay single." Obviously, John would be the exception.

John and Cynthia were married on August 23, 1962, at the Mount Pleasant Register Office in Liverpool, where his mother and father had wed in 1938. Those present were Paul, George, Brian, and Cynthia's brother Tony and his wife Margery. James Paul McCartney signed his name as a witness. The short civil ceremony was rendered almost unintelligible by construction noise. The wedding reception was held at nearby Reeces Café, once the wedding party could get a table during the noontime crush. The toast was drunk with glasses of water. Then Brian, who had supplied his car to pick up Cynthia, surprised Cynthia and John by offering to let them live in his apartment at 36 Faulkner Street, near the art school, rather than having the two of them crowd into Cynthia's little room. Or trying to squeeze in with John's Aunt Mimi, who had angrily boycotted the wedding.

Obviously Brian thought it would be easier to keep the wedding a secret if he could keep the pair tucked away. He also, of course, genuinely cared for John. That evening Cynthia moved her things to Faulkner Street while John went off to play the night's gig at the Riverpark Ballroom in Chester.

Meanwhile the Beatles were caught up in the festering Pete Best business.

Back in June, not long after the session with George Martin in London, Pete had been visited by Joe Flannery, who managed the group Lee Curtis and the All-Stars and was an old friend of Brian's. During the visit Flannery asked, "When are you going to join us, Pete?" Best, taken aback, told him he must be joking. Why would Pete leave the Beatles just as they were going with

Parlophone and EMI? Flannery tried to cover his gaffe and said he had heard some rumor.

That bothered Best enough that he asked Brian about it. "There are no plans to replace you, Pete," Brian assured him.

Shortly thereafter Paul and George were overheard in the Grapes talking to Bob Wooler about sacking Pete. Once they had John's approval, they went to Brian and told him to get rid of Pete. It was not something Brian especially wanted to do, for he had gotten along decently with Pete, but it was something his group wanted done. And, initially at least, it was not a "Get Ringo, dump Pete" business. It was just that they wanted Pete out. They had needed a drummer to get to Hamburg and Pete had been convenient, but he had worn out his usefulness.

Ringo was by no means a sure thing. Brian wanted Johnny Hutchinson of the Big Three and he called Hutchinson first and offered him the job. Hutchinson, who, long ago, had drummed for the Beatles' audition for Larry Parnes, turned him down. He did not think much of the Beatles (although, ever the pro, he filled in for the Beatles for three engagements between the time Best was sacked and Ringo came aboard).

After Johnny Hutch turned down the job, Brian and then John called Ringo at the Butlin's holiday camp in Skegness, where he was appearing with Rory and the Hurricanes. They had to have him paged over the camp's public address system. Ringo agreed to John's offer to join the Beatles for a starting salary of twenty-five pounds a week. He gave Rory three days' notice and then started packing for Liverpool.

That was on August 14, a Tuesday. On Wednesday Pete Best played lunchtime and evening sessions at the Cavern as a Beatle. That night, as they packed up, they discussed the logistics for Thursday's show at the Riverpark Ballroom in Chester. Usually Neil and Pete would meet and pick up the others in the van. That evening Pete told John he would be by to get him on the morrow. "No," John said, "I've got other arrangements." Paul and George had already hurried away.

Brian was still there and asked Pete to drop by his office in the morning to discuss some business. That was not unusual, since Pete had done so much of the group's booking before. So the next morning at ten o'clock Neil and Pete drove downtown and Pete walked into Brian's office in the Whitechapel store. Brian was flustered and nervous, but finally blurted out his business: "The boys want you out and Ringo in." Pete was poleaxed into silence. Brian went on. "They don't think you're a good enough drummer, Pete. And George Martin doesn't think you're a good enough drummer."

Pete asked, "Does Ringo know about this yet?"

"He's joining on Saturday."

Pete was catatonic. It was a fait accompli. Brian went on to ask him if he would play the remaining gigs before Ringo could join the band. "Yes," Pete said unthinkingly. Then he left.

He rejoined Neil downstairs and told him the news. The two of them headed for the Grapes to drink many pints as soon as possible. Neil threatened to quit as Beatles' road manager; Pete urged him to do what was best for him.

By the time Pete got home, he was weeping. Neil had already called Mo Best, who was furious and had been trying unsuccessfully all afternoon to get Brian on the phone. Neil went off to handle equipment for the night's gig at Riverpark Ballroom. Brian asked Neil where Pete was, for hadn't he agreed to fill in till Ringo could join the band? Neil—faithful "Nell," as he was nicknamed—told Brian, "Well, what did you expect?" So Brian had to press Johnny Hutch into service.

Neil asked Paul and John about what had happened with Pete and was told, "It's got nothing to do with you. You're only the driver!"

Mo Best, meanwhile, hell on wheels, got George Martin on the phone, who denied that he had ever advocated the sacking of Pete Best or anyone else within the Beatle walls. All he had said, Martin told Mo, was that he would prefer a session drummer he was familiar with in a recording session (which he would do even after Ringo joined the group).

There was a quick reaction by Beatle fans in Liverpool, who flooded the offices of *Mersey Beat* with letters of protest. They also ruined the paint job on Brian's Ford and caused him to be afraid to visit Mathew Street for days. On the first night that Ringo joined the Beatles at the Cavern, there were several tense scuffles outside and George ended up with a black eye from a punch thrown by a Pete Best supporter.

Pete was shattered by his sacking. Undoubtedly, he was not suited to the others, but the manner of his abrupt termination after two years of apparently blemish-free service to the band was cruel. Even John later said, "We were cowards when we sacked him." Paul has not commented on the matter.

Pete, unfortunately, spent years brooding on the matter of his dismissal, obsessing over whether or not it was a matter of his hairstyle or his bass beat or what. He later, after many years of failing in music and then in business, attempted suicide. What he cannot understand is that there was no concrete reason for his being fired by the Beatles. The best explanation to date has been supplied by Pete Shotton, who himself was dumped by the Quarry Men many years earlier. What happened, Shotton said, was that "the bottom line is that the Beatles were bored with Pete Best—and that, of course, was always fatal."

Boredom was the one unforgivable sin. Ringo was, if anything, not boring. His quirky personality was perhaps the one unfilled slot in the Beatles' roster. Richard Starkey had already slipped in and out of Rory's lineup several times. Once he had decided to emigrate to Texas and become a cowboy and had corresponded with the Houston Chamber of Commerce about possible opportunities there. And Peter Eckhorn had lured him to Hamburg to work with Tony Sheridan. And he had sat in with the Beatles at the Cavern when Best was ill a time or two. But once he sat down behind John, Paul, and George, he fit in like a missing tooth. He was anything but boring. And he looked right. Although John, on Brian's orders, instructed Ringo that he had to shave his beard and brush out his hair and trim back his "sidies" (sideburns) a bit. But he could keep his rings.

Beatlemania

WITH Ringo aboard the Beatles weathered their storm, George's black eye and all. The Beatles and Pete Best never again passed another word between them, although Brian sent Pete a congratulatory telegram on his twenty-first birthday and signed the Beatles' names to it. Pete quickly became a Beatle nonperson. The week after he was sacked Pete made the mistake of letting Neil talk him into going down to the Cavern to watch the Beatles' first televised appearance on Granada TV. Pete unfortunately ran into Jim McCartney, who asked him triumphantly, "Great, isn't it? They're on TV!"

Ringo's actual first Beatle gig—the day before George got his shiner—was on August 18 at the very sedate Horticultural Society Dance at the Hulme Hall on Bolton Road in Port Sunlight, Birkenhead. And no one there cared about Pete Best.

Once the new Beatles plunged back into the Cavern, they still got their quota of fans chanting Pete's name. But they had transcended that. For relatively unsophisticated young men from the provinces, John and Paul had developed fierce enough ambitions and strong enough egos to rise above any obstacles.

Even though all their projects, now that they were under Brian's reins, had seemed to forge ahead with unstoppable energy, they still had the occasional setback. On November 23, under intense pressure from Brian, they had gone to London for an audition for BBC-TV and had been turned down cold. It was a bitter disappointment, but as Brian said and as John and Paul told each other and realized and fully believed, it had been a BBC failure, not a Beatle failure. Beatles simply did not fail. Not even after Brian's disastrous booking of the Beatles into what he thought would be a prestigious double bill, opening for the tony Frank Ifield at the Embassy Cinema in Peterborough, Northamptonshire, the night of December 2. The audience sat on its hands. The reviewer in the Peterborough *Standard,* after lamenting the "gradual decline in the standard of supporting artists," wrote:

> The exciting Beatles' rock group quite frankly failed to excite me. The drummer apparently thought his job was to lead, not to provide rhythm. He made far too much noise and in their final number, "Twist and Shout," it sounded as though everyone was trying to make more noise than the others. In a more mellow mood, their "A Taste of Honey" was much better and "Love Me Do" was tolerable.

Still, the show had achieved Brian's objective, which was to get Arthur Howes, the most prominent concert promoter in the United Kingdom, to be favorably impressed by the Beatles.

It was yet another rung up the ladder, which would be translated for Beatle fortunes into two lucrative 1963 United Kingdom tours, first with chanteuse Helen Shapiro and then with the touring American singers Tommy Roe and Chris Montez.

On September 4 the Beatles went back to Abbey Road in London for George Martin's next recording session. Although neither he nor Brian would later recall the rigors of it, Martin—after the Beatles had rehearsed most of the day with a nervous Ringo—ran them through seventeen separate takes of "Love Me Do" before he thought it might be passable. The Beatles were unhappy to start with because Martin and Brian made them record a song called "How Do You Do It" by a tunesmith named Mitch Murray. They knew the song had nothing to do with them or their style, but Martin and Brian insisted on it.

Which was one reason why the Beatles had to return to London and Abbey Road the following week, on September 11, for another session. Martin, if he was going to set his reputation behind a push for the Beatles, wanted a superlative effort on disc and he felt he didn't have it yet. So Martin brought in a session drummer, Andy White, which did not set Ringo at ease at all. Ringo played the maracas or the tambourine on "Please Please Me," "Love Me Do," and "P.S. I Love You."

On their van trips down to London the Beatles had a new road cheer. John would ask: "Where are we going, fellas?" Paul and George and Ringo would shout in unison: "To the top, Johnny, to the top!" Yelled back John: "And where is the top, fellas?" Came the shouted answer: "To the toppermost of the poppermost!"

George Martin summoned up enough clout to have Parlophone release "Love Me Do," backed with "P.S. I Love You," on October 5, 1962, as R 4949. The "Love Me Do" version that was released came from the September 4 session with Ringo drumming, although subsequent pressings were from the Andy White session on September 11. The first pressings are on a red label; the second are on black.

There was an immediate rumor floating around Liverpool that Brian had bought ten thousand copies of the single because he had heard that was how many copies needed to be sold to make the Top 20, although Brian denied it. But Paul did say once to a friend in Liverpool that the reason he was hungry that day and couldn't afford to eat was that: "Somebody had to pay for it." "Love Me Do" finally hit number seventeen on the British charts on December 27 after a seesaw ride up and down.

On October 2 Brian finally drew up an official contract and had the Beatles sign it: He had never signed the original one and it hadn't been legal anyhow, since John had been the only Beatle who was over twenty-one at the time and the others hadn't had parents or guardians sign with them.

After "Love Me Do" started showing chart action, George Martin got the thumbs-up signals from his bosses at EMI and he had the Beatles back down to Abbey Road on November 26, when they recorded "Please Please Me" and "Ask Me Why," which would eventually be released on January 11, 1963. John and Paul had obviously won their argument with George Martin and Brian Epstein over recording or not recording Lennon–McCartney original songs.

As 1962 wound down, Brian could be pretty pleased with what he had accomplished in less than a year. In addition to what he did directly for the Beatles, Brian had also formed—with his brother Clive—a separate corporation called NEMS Enterprises and had signed up other groups for NEMS to manage: Gerry and the Pacemakers, the Big Three, and Billy Kramer and the Coasters, whom he transformed into Billy J. Kramer and the Dakotas.

As a way of patting himself and his charges on the back, he took out a full-page advertisement in *Mersey Beat*'s December 13 issue. Headlined: 1962, THE BEATLES YEAR OF ACHIEVEMENT, it went on to a checklist of events in 1962:

Won "Mersey Beat" Popularity Poll (2nd Year), Voted fifth in "New Musical Express" poll for best British vocal group, E.M.I. Recording Contract, Four B.B.C. Broadcasts, Four T.V. Appearances, Two Luxembourg Broadcasts, Two Hamburg Engagements [actually three], Entered the Top Fifty within Two Days of "Love Me Do" Release, Hit No. 21 in the charts with "Love Me Do," Their first Disc, Appeared with Little Richard, Frank Ifield, Joe Brown, Jet Harris, Gene Vincent, Johnny and the Hurricanes, Craig Douglas, and many others, Appeared at Liverpool (Empire), Birmingham, Manchester, Hull, Doncaster, Crewe, Stroud, Coventry, Shrewsbury, Bedford, Peterborough, Preston, Blackpool, etc., etc.

And in 1963: "Please Please Me" released by Parlophone January 11th, Appearances in "Thank Your Lucky Stars," "Saturday Club," and B.B.C.-T.V. (January), Scottish Tour (January), Helen Shapiro Tour (February), "Love Me Do" Release America, Canada and Germany, Tommy Roe/Chris Montez Tour (March), And Who Knows!

For all intents and purposes the Beatle machine was in place and the parts were starting to function and hum efficiently. All the personnel shifting in the band was over, musically they were meshing, they were quickly building up an incredible catalog of songs, they were selling records, fan reaction was already bordering on the fanatical, and Brian was expertly divining how to exploit them commercially and how to get the press and radio and television exposure that was necessary to finally break them outside Liverpool to London and then the world. They could finally begin to feel that a bit of a reward might be coming along in return for all the struggling.

"Yeah," John said in response to a question of mine many years later, "if '62 is the time you're talking about, I guess we were locked into what we were gonna do and gonna be. I'm no good about dates and times. All that was a blur. But yeah. Right after we got Ringo—we had Brian already for a while—that's when that was. The shows started to get crazy. Paul and me were close still, we had a hundred songs at least. We still wrote together then, but not for much longer. But yeah, oh yeah, we knew we were gonna make it, be bigger than Elvis and all that shit. At least that's what we said. We could smell it. When was 'Love Me Do'? Was that in there then?

"Right, then. Just starting to make the records. But you know our best work was never recorded. When we played the dances, we were incredible. Just incredible. You never heard rock like that. But when we put on the suits, when we started to make it, there was something that was lost. It's too bad you never heard that, that people couldn't hear that. It was fucking amazing."

The Beatles ended 1962 at the Star-Club with their fifth and last Hamburg club date. On their last night, New Year's Eve, Ted Taylor of Kingsize Taylor and the Dominoes, who were also playing the Star, asked the Beatles if he could use his new German Grundig reel-to-reel tape recorder to make a recording of the Beatles onstage. They didn't mind, so Taylor and Adrian Barber, a Liverpool musician and engineer who built the Beatles' first big amps and speakers, recorded several hours, using a hand-held microphone in the midst of the drunken New Year's Eve audience roiling about in the Star-Club.

In 1963 Taylor offered the tapes for sale to Brian, who offered him twenty pounds for them (although technically they would have belonged to EMI since the Beatles were under contract), and Taylor turned him down. After all, there was no demand whatsoever for a live recording of murky sound quality of a group that was just beginning its recording career. Taylor gave the tapes to a recording engineer in Liverpool to see if he could clean up the sound. The tapes were eventually forgotten until the ubiquitous Allan Williams came across them in 1972 and tried—unsuccessfully—to sell them to George and Ringo. Five years later, through circuitous routes, the tapes were released on record, as *The Beatles Live! At the Star-Club in Hamburg, Germany, 1962,* first in Germany and then in England and the United

States. The Beatles tried and failed in the courts to have the record withdrawn.

The double album is of substandard audio quality but is fascinating as history. Hearing Paul sing "I Saw Her Standing There" for one of the first times is rewarding and this is undoubtedly the only record that will allow the listener a chance to hear Paul sing the Marlene Dietrich classic "Falling in Love Again." And the song selection is indicative of the Beatles' vanished club era: "Twist and Shout," "Hippy Hippy Shake," "Mr. Moonlight," "A Taste of Honey," "Your Feet's Too Big," "Shimmy Shimmy," "Little Queenie." And the Beatles' favorite Star-Club waiter, Horst Obber (incorrectly identified on the record as their old friend Horst Fascher), sings lead on "Be-Bop-A-Lula" and "Hallelujah, I Love Her So." But the sound is generally so bad that it's impossible to hear that magic that John was so wistfully talking about. Within months of this New Year's Eve date, Beatlemania was raging so fiercely that Brian decreed that the Beatles would never again play a club or dance hall.

The reasons for the ban on club gigs were both fiscal and physical. They couldn't afford the clubs anymore because of danger to both sectors of Beatle health. On August 3, 1963, they had to bid good-bye to their beloved Cavern in Liverpool after 274 or so performances there. They were simply too big for the Cavern—or indeed for Liverpool. Not too long after that they played their infamous Royal Command Variety Performance at the Prince of Wales Theatre on Coventry Street in London on November 4, 1963, during which John advised Queen Elizabeth the Queen Mother and all the others not sitting in the cheap seats to just "rattle your jewelry" in lieu of applause.

On New Year's Day 1963, after their last Hamburg date, the Beatles flew from Hamburg to London and after a layover there flew straight on to Aberdeen to start the first-ever Beatle tour as a Beatle tour. They were not to stop for four years. Brian worked them like drayhorses and they responded like thoroughbreds. All those hundreds of hours of basic training in Hamburg had them in superb shape for what lay ahead.

Beatlemania spread south to London, then across the whole of the United Kingdom, and then began to burst national boundaries. Whole acres of trees would be felled over the years to provide the pulp for the paper on which would be printed all the

Above: At the Cavern in Liverpool, circa 1961. They had recently washed the grease out of their hair, but Pete Best still combed his hair pompadour style. (KEYSTONE) Below: This was shortly after Brian made the Silver Beetles start wearing jackets and ties. Gone forever were the black leather outfits. (MICHAEL OCHS ARCHIVES)

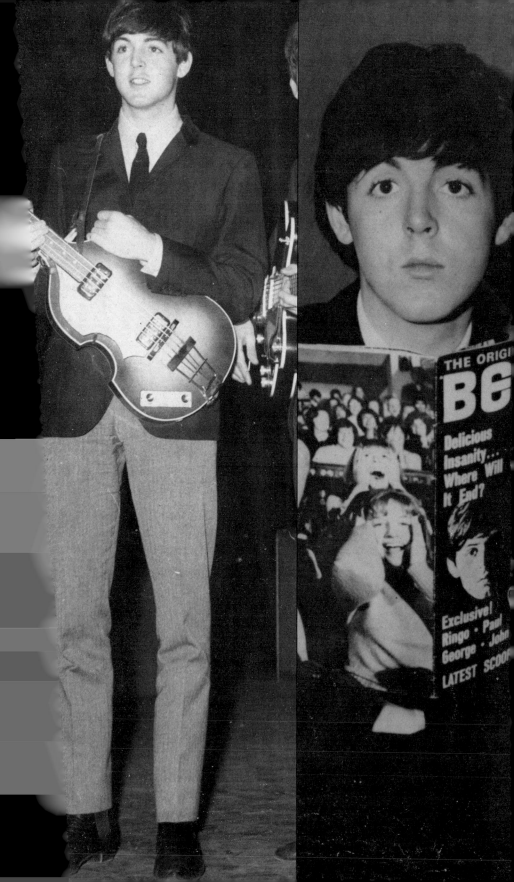

THE ORIGI
B6

Delicious
Insanity...
Where Will
It End?

Exclusive!
Ringo · Paul
George · John
LATEST SCOO

Far left: Paul got his violin-shaped Hofner bass in Hamburg after original bassist Stu Sutcliffe was forced out of the group. The clothes are still strictly pre-Beatle. (PICTORIAL PARADE)   In the first incredible rush of Beatlemania, the Fabs actually were so trapped in their hotel suites that they sat around and read and posed with Beatle fanzines such as Paul is reading here. (MICHAEL OCHS ARCHIVES)   Top right: The famous collarless Pierre Cardin suits, when the Fab Four became disgustingly wholesome and healthy-looking. (MICHAEL OCHS ARCHIVES)   Bottom right: Brian Epstein (center, in the suit and tie) with his charges when all was well with their world and Beatlemania reigned. (BETTMANN ARCHIVE)

*Above: Paul, his dad Jim, and his younger brother Mike at home in Jim's garden.
(KEYSTONE)   Top right: In 1965 Queen Elizabeth presented the Beatles with medals
and named them Members of the Order of the British Empire. Contrary to long-standing
rumor, they did not smoke a marijuana cigarette in Buckingham Palace on the occasion.
(PICTORIAL PARADE)   Bottom right: Paul's two loves of the early 1960s were actress
Jane Asher and his sheepdog Martha, for whom he wrote the song "Martha My Dear."
Jane is now married to artist Gerald Scarfe and acts and writes. Martha died of old age in
1982. (PICTORIAL PARADE)*

The Summer of Love. It was 1967 and the Beatles were proud of their Sgt. Pepper regalia. (MICHAEL OCHS ARCHIVES)   Bottom right: In 1968 the Beatles went to Rishikesh for religious studies with the Maharishi Mahesh Yogi. Paul was a dropout from the course. (PICTORIAL PARADE)

Paul married Linda Eastman on March 12, 1969, at Marylebone Register Office in a civil ceremony. Linda was pregnant at the time. None of the other Beatles attended or was invited. (PICTORIAL PARADE).   Right: Linda and Paul in London. As their marriage flowered, Paul's union with the Beatles was dissolving. (PICTORIAL PARADE)

This was the last photo session of the Beatles, held at John's Tittenhurst Park manor in 1969.
(MICHAEL OCHS ARCHIVES)

Left: A rococo scene from Paul's ATV music special, James Paul McCartney, which was part of an agreement to settle a huge lawsuit. This particular number was "Gotta Sing, Gotta Dance," which Paul had originally written for Twiggy. (MICHAEL OCHS ARCHIVES) Below: Paul donned a suitably Texanish ten-gallon hat for a Wings concert in Houston. (CHARLYN ZLOTNIK)

) TOKYO, JAN. 17 (AP)--MCCARTNEY AND POLICE--SCARF COVE
HANDS OF FORMER BEATLE PAUL MCCARTNEY LATE WEDNESDAY N
SE POLICE ESCORT HIM TO METRO POLICE HEADQUARTERS IN TO
HIS ARREST ON CHARGES INVOLVING 219 GRAMS OF MARIJUANA
LUGGAGE. MCCARTNEY AND WINGS ARRIVED TO BEGIN CONCERT

Left: Paul being led away in handcuffs after his 1980 arrest for marijuana possession in Tokyo. (AP/WIDE WORLD) Above: Paul on his farm in Scotland. (MICHAEL OCHS ARCHIVES)

This is how Paul looked recently. The chief Beatle is now gray of hair and crinkly of eye. (LONDON FEATURES INTERNATIONAL) various theories behind and analyses of Beatlemania. In the United Kingdom it was supposedly a general public that had wearied of the seamy Christine Keeler–John Profumo government scandal and was looking for something fresh and new. Several pundits actually suggested that cynical Fleet Street editors made up the whole business of Beatlemania just to sell newspapers. In the United States sociologists pondered that the recent assassination of President John F. Kennedy had caused a weary public to seek something fresh and new. Many people complained that the cynical members of the media were simply manufacturing a craze just to sell newspapers, magazines, and television time.

George Harrison later attributed Beatlemania to the phenomenon of romantic teenage girls lusting after sexy rock singers and he even pinpointed the actual date and place that Beatlemania began. And it started, he asserted, with Paul. It was at the Casbah in West Derby, Liverpool, and it happened on Valentine's Day of 1961. The Beatles were playing and Paul held up a wooden heart that had been given to the Beatles by loving fans. It was satin-covered and had their names embroidered on it. The Beatles raffled it off that night. Paul sang "Wooden Heart" and then presented the heart, along with a big kiss, to the winning girl. But as she approached the stage, George said, "the audience erupted and with wild squeals they stormed the stage, clutching at each of us. John was thrown to the floor, we were all mobbed and the curtains were hurriedly closed. The bouncers closed in to save us but there were girls everywhere. Beatlemania, as it later became known throughout the world, had begun."

Even as Brian had the Beatles crossing and crisscrossing the United Kingdom throughout all of 1963, he was already looking ahead to the United States. No British pop music performer had ever done well in the United States, so everyone told Brian to forget it. Even though the United Kingdom had fallen to the Beatles during 1963, that was to be the end of it, people told him. EMI, which was selling Beatles' records as fast as they could be pressed in the United Kingdom, had bought Capitol Records in the United States. So Brian Epstein and George Martin, for two, thought it would be an easy matter to get the Beatles under way on Capitol in the States.

It didn't happen that way, though. Capitol turned down the

Beatles three times during 1963 before finally rising to the bait. The record company didn't accede until early November, when Brian himself met with company executives and turned on the charm. He had flown to the United States in early November to show off Billy J. Kramer, his newest act. While he was in New York City, Brian sought out Ed Sullivan and talked the crusty variety show host into having the Beatles on "The Ed Sullivan Show" for two live appearances and a taped one in February.

That same week Brian learned that "I Want to Hold Your Hand" had sold over a million copies before it was even released—such was the press of advance orders. It was the first time that had ever happened in the United Kingdom, although "She Loves You" had sold half a million before its release on August 23. "She Loves You" was one of the last of the true John and Paul compositions. They sat down and wrote it together in a hotel room in Newcastle-upon-Tyne after a show at the Majestic Ballroom there on June 26 and then recorded it on July 1.

Strangely, as the Beatles broke the country open, the London press still largely ignored what was transpiring. As the Beatles barnstormed all through 1963, there were minor riots in many cities. "Beatle queues"—girls camping out on the pavement outside box offices with blankets and thermoses and hot water bottles and transistor radios for however many days and nights it took to buy their precious Beatle tickets—became a national phenomenon. Still, the London newspapers did not declare it official until they saw it happening under their own noses.

The official christening date of Beatlemania was October 13, 1963, when the Beatles performed at the London Palladium on the live broadcast of the TV show "Val Parnell's Sunday Night at the London Palladium." The newspapers the next day were full of the mayhem in the streets, the "siege of the Beatles," and screaming girls piled up in the street like so many cords of wood.

And not long after that, on October 31, the Fleet Street boys turned out en masse to witness the Beatles' return to England from a brief Swedish tour. To the press' satisfaction, there were hundreds of screaming Beatle fans waiting at London Airport when the Beatles deplaned. And, of course, only four days later was the Royal Command "rattle your jewelry" Variety Performance. The press had something truly meaty to chew on and they showed no signs of ever letting go of it. Especially after the first few Beatle interviews when the press discovered that "the lads" could not only talk, they were funny and cheeky and down-to-earth and frank and earthy and anything that you could possibly hope for in an interview.

After the success of "I Saw Her Standing There," Paul, perhaps unwisely, talked about the genesis of the song. Fortunately for him, his remarks, to a reporter for *Beat Instrumental* magazine, were largely overlooked. After discussing his early instruments and his own self-taught skills on the guitar, piano, and drums, Paul brashly went on to offer advice to budding musicians. "One thing I would like to say about learning an instrument and that is you *should steal* various bits and pieces from other guitarists and bassists. Okay, so you know they belong to other people—so what! Does it really matter? I think this is a much better way of learning than with a tutor. I never had one myself and I think you can 'feel' music much better without one. With a tutor, you are told what to play and therefore get into a rut.

"Here's one example of a bit I pinched from someone: I used the bass riff from 'Talkin' About You' by Chuck Berry in 'I Saw Her Standing There.' I played exactly the same notes as he did and it fitted our number perfectly. Even now, when I tell people about it, I find few of them believe me; therefore, I maintain that a bass riff hasn't got to be original."

By early November noises were finally being heard in the States about the Beatles and on November 16 all three U.S. television networks sent camera crews to film the Beatles as they performed at the Winter Gardens Theatre in Bournemouth. The networks aired news clips of the Beatles and on January 3, 1964, "The Jack Paar Show" on NBC ran all of "She Loves You."

Even though Capitol's earlier refusals of the Beatles had caused Brian Epstein and George Martin to license Beatle songs to other U.S. record labels, Capitol finally went all-out once the label was committed to the group. A Capitol Records sales department memo from National Merchandising Director Paul Russell to his field force on December 23, 1963, shows some level of the company's intent. The memo detailed some of the company's advertising and promotional push for the Beatles, including trade magazine ads, the distribution of thousands of BE A BEATLE BOOSTER buttons, thousands of Beatle tabloid newspapers to be distributed, record store display items, and thousands of THE BEATLES ARE COMING stickers that the Capitol sales force was instructed to blanket the country with:

> It may sound funny, but we literally want your salesmen to be plastering these stickers on any friendly surface as they walk down the street or as they call on radio or retail accounts.

Finally all the regional sales managers could expect to receive after January 1:

> bulk quantities of a Beatle hair-do wig. As soon as they arrive—and until further notice—you and each of your sales and promotion staff are to wear the wig during the business day! Next, see how many of the retail clerks in your area have a sense of humor . . . Then offer some to jocks [radio disc jockeys] and stores for promotions. Get these Beatle wigs around properly, and you'll find you're helping to start the Beatle Hair-Do Craze that should be sweeping the country soon.

The American campaign soon was operating with breathtaking precision. Even before the Beatles left for the United States, they learned that "I Want to Hold Your Hand" was number one there. By the first week in April (after the Beatles had come over and done just three live performances and three "Ed Sullivan Shows"), they had the two top-selling albums on the *Billboard* chart and—unbelievably—the top five singles on the *Billboard* Hot 100 Chart were these: "Can't Buy Me Love," "Twist and Shout," "She Loves You," "I Want to Hold Your Hand," and "Please Please Me."

The first Beatle appearances on U.S. soil induced the kind of fan hysteria that now seems so charmingly antiquated that one forgets that it was also potentially highly dangerous to the members of the group. And one also overlooks the fact that the feverish intensity of fan identification with the Beatles continued building to higher and higher levels that grew uglier and uglier until it would one day result in the only unfortunate end that it could.

Back on February 7, 1964, though, when the Beatles' Pan Am Flight 101 came into New York's John F. Kennedy Airport, there was an old-time newsreel atmosphere attached to the event. America instantly clutched the Beatles to its collective bosom. Even though on the flight coming over both Paul and George had worried about the reactions of U.S. audiences—"What do they want us for?"—at JFK they had only to look out the windows of their 707 to see the thousands of Beatle fans clustered and waiting for them. No one to this day will admit to any of the rumors that young girls were actually recruited and paid to go out to JFK and scream when the Beatles' plane hove into view, but the rumors persist nonetheless.

As the story has been told and told again, they were literally prisoners at the Plaza Hotel, which was laid siege to by mobs of young fans pressing against police barricades—and no one had paid these fans off; that was for certain. They had come purely out of love—or Beatle fanaticism—and in many teenage minds the two were eternally intertwined.

The Beatles, dodging the mobs, did their first live "Ed Sullivan Show" the evening of February 9 in Manhattan and were watched by six out of ten TV-watching Americans. They performed "All My Loving," "Till There Was You," "She Loves You," "I Saw Her Standing There," and "I Want to Hold Your Hand." Earlier that afternoon they had taped the show that would be aired on February 23. The traveling fishbowl that by then had become the Beatles and their entourage then journeyed to Washington, D.C., by train for the Beatles' first U.S. live concert on February 11 at the Washington Coliseum. Back in New York City they did two thirty-four-minute concerts on February 12 at Carnegie Hall for the grand sum of $7,000 for both shows. That evening Sid Bernstein, the promoter for the Carnegie Hall shows, took Brian out for a stroll down Seventh Avenue to point out Madison Square Garden and to offer him $25,000 for a Beatle show there. "Next time, Sid," said Brian, who as ever was worried about overexposure.

As would be brought out in numerous Beatle exposé books over the years, Brian did not always demonstrate the best business sense in the deals he made for the Beatles. Nor did some of the people he trusted to run the business and some of the people who ran businesses that fed directly off the Beatles. In fact, it would not be understating the case to say that the Beatles are undoubtedly the greatest gravy train in show business history.

There have been, over the years, people draining millions of dollars from the Beatles' earnings and potential earnings that they never even met and may only scarcely have heard of. The various business entanglements surrounding the Beatles and the many companies interwoven with them were still not sorted out almost two decades after the group officially broke up. It is a certainty that the lawsuits will continue into the next century.

After New York the Beatles went to Miami for no good reason, other than to do their third "Ed Sullivan Show" from there and to provide many photo opportunities of the Fab Four frolicking on the beach and, reluctantly, going to meet fighter Cassius Clay and going to a drive-in movie to see an Elvis flick. Doing all-American things, in other words.

The American reaction to the Beatles was beyond staggering or amazing or mind-fucking or any other inadequate adjective that one can dredge up. The Beatles managed to seduce an entire 200-million-populace, 50-state, leader-of-the-Western-world, Boston-Tea-Party-proud nation. They took back the Colonies. Despite everything Brian could do, they started overexposing quickly, although it would take a couple of years and many Beatle gaffes to complete the meltdown. For the time being, though, every printed word and every televised image and every broadcast signal seemed to carry but one message: Beatle!

And that was only reinforced after the release of the movie *A Hard Day's Night* (which the Beatles had rush-filmed in March and April) in August. Brian had done a wonderful job of selling the Beatles as the "mop-tops," as the cheeky but wholesome (and clean) and lovable (and clean) and wacky (but clean) guys everybody loves to love. It made John puke and even Paul was starting to wonder a little bit about what was happening to them. But it literally was happening so fast that all they could do was react to what was thrown at them. They had trusted Brian to manage them and to try to launch them and now, by God, he had hurled them into stellar orbit, so far beyond where anyone had been before that all the rules were broken. In fact, there were no rules at all. The Beatles were operating in uncharted hyperspace. The rest was up to them.

How to react to that? Consider. When Brian took them over, they were the hottest thing in Liverpool. Just Liverpool (and maybe Hamburg). And were still under a weird record deal with

Bert Kaempfert in Hamburg, with no records happening. Two years later they were global, selling millions of records, being quoted everywhere by everybody, being courted and desired by everyone. They were instant pop royalty. They quickly got used to the sharp intakes of breath—"Gasp! There's a Beatle!"—when they would appear anywhere. So they had to quit appearing anywhere.

Within a year or so they would be truly graven into stone when they would each be awarded England's MBE, thus being named Members of the Most Excellent Order of the British Empire—a really big deal. Paul insists that they didn't actually smoke a joint in the john at Buckingham Palace. It was just a quick cigarette and of such clouds of smoke are Beatle rumors wafted.

Back in 1964 Brian sent the Beatles off to conquer the world and they encountered few difficulties. After finishing *A Hard Day's Night* and a quick U.K. tour, the Beatles tried a two-week vacation. John and wife Cynthia and George and actress Patti Boyd went to Tahiti. Paul and actress Jane Asher and Ringo and girlfriend Maureen Cox traveled to St. Thomas in the Virgin Islands. Just the travel plans alone were secretive and paranoid: Paul's travel name was Mr. Manning, Ringo's was Mr. Stone, and their companions were Miss Ashcroft and Miss Cockcroft. John and Cynthia were Mr. and Mrs. Leslie and George and Patti became Mr. Hargreaves and Miss Bond. Brian even changed travel agents out of fear of disclosure.

When it came time to leave all eight of the vacationers had stayed the night elsewhere than in their homes, donned what they imagined were disguises (large floppy hats, sunglasses, fake mustaches), were met at dawn by small unmarked cars, and taken to "staging points." Paul and Ringo took a charter flight to Paris and switched to a commercial plane to Lisbon, where they would meet Jane and Maureen and fly to San Juan, where they would separate and rendezvous later at a yacht and then head to St. Thomas.

There were similar loopy arrangements for the others. The press, of course, figured it all out within a matter of hours and soon had photographers dispatched to the Beatle hideaways or "love nests." And this is when, incidentally, they first started coming under heavy moral and religious criticism, both at home and abroad, for alleged immoral behavior: three fourths of them traveling with an unmarried woman. Especially when most of their constituency—in fact, 99 percent of it if it could have been accurately measured at the time—was teenaged and female and seventeen and under. Numerous American sociologists and columnists and the like made much of that.

Even so, when the Beatles began their first "real" American tour on August 19 at the Cow Palace in San Francisco, it was just more of the same old audience mania. The teenage girls in the paying public didn't really care what they got, as long as it was Beatles. The Beatles had cut their concert down to twelve or so songs usually, which amounted to just over half an hour onstage, which in turn amounted to a fairly contemptuous assessment of the audiences they were milking. The Beatles couldn't hear themselves because of the audience's screams and the audience couldn't hear the Beatles because of their screams, so they all figured it was an even trade.

"We should have stopped it when it got crazy," John later told me, "but we were the almighty Beatles! Right? We were finally cashin' in, right? But it started gettin' hard, fuckin' hard, gettin' hard to do it. Nobody could hear a fuckin' thing we were playin', so who could care anyway? Sometimes we would just stop playin' and nobody could tell the fuckin' difference."

The Beatles' nonstop will to succeed—at least that will that was fairly dripping from John and Paul—led them to go along with Brian's grandiose schemes. Up to a point, that is. After their 1965 U.S. tour ended in August, Brian wanted an extensive U.K. tour and another extravagant Beatles Christmas show. All of the Beatles—even Paul—were exhausted after the touring and the recording. They had spent a month in the studio doing the *Rubber Soul* album alone. So 1965 ended on a compromise. They did a quick nine-date U.K. tour, beginning on December 3 in Glasgow and ending on December 12 in Cardiff. Along the way they performed at the Empire Theatre for the last time ever in Liverpool. Supposedly there were in excess of forty thousand applications for tickets. No one could know then, though, that it would be the last time around.

BEATLES' TOUR, 1963

Jan.	3	Elgin, Scotland
	4	Dingwall
	5	Bridge of Allan
	6	Aberdeen
	10	Liverpool
	11	Cavern
	12	Chatham
	14	Ellesmere Port
	17	(2 shows) Cavern, Birkenhead
	18	Morecambe
	19	Shropshire
	20	Cavern
	23	Cavern
	24	Flintshire
	25	Darwen
	26	(2 shows) Macclesfield, Stoke-on-Trent
	27	Manchester
	28	Newcastle-upon-Tyne
	30	Cavern
	31	(2 shows) Cavern, Birkenhead
Feb.	1	(2 shows) Tamworth, Sutton Coldfield
	2	Bradford
	3	Cavern
	4	Cavern
	5	Doncaster
	6	Bedford
	7	Wakefield
	8	Carlisle
	9	Sunderland
	11	EMI Recording Session
	12	(2 shows) Sheffield, Oldham
	13	Hull

	14	Liverpool
	15	Birmingham
	16	Oxford
	18	Widnes
	19	Cavern
	20	Doncaster
	21	Birkenhead
	22	Manchester
	23	Mansfield
	24	Coventry
	25	Leigh
	26	Taunton
	27	York
	28	Shrewsbury
Mar.	1	Southport
	2	Sheffield
	3	Hanley
	4	St. Helens
	7	Nottingham
	8	Harrogate
	9	East Ham
	10	Birmingham
	12	Bedford
	13	York
	14	Wolverhampton
	15	Bristol
	16	Sheffield
	17	Peterborough
	18	Gloucester
	19	Cambridge
	20	Romford
	21	(West) Croydon
	22	Doncaster
	23	Newcastle-upon-Tyne
	24	Liverpool
	26	Mansfield
	27	Northampton
	28	Exeter
	29	Lewisham

	30	Portsmouth
	31	Leicester
April	4	Stowe
	5	Leyton
	6	Buxton
	7	Portsmouth
	9	Kilburn
	10	Birkenhead
	11	Middleton
	12	Cavern
	15	Tenbury Wells
	17	Luton
	18	Kensington Gore
	19	Stoke-on-Trent
	20	Frodsham
	21	(2 shows) Wembley *(New Musical Express* Poll Winners' Concert)
	23	Southport
	24	Finsbury Park
	25	Croydon
	26	Shrewsbury
	27	Northwich
May	11	Nelson
	14	Sunderland
	15	Chester
	17	Norwich
	18	Slough
	19	Hanley
	20	Southampton
	22	Ipswich
	23	Nottingham
	24	Walthamstow
	25	Sheffield
	26	Liverpool
	27	Cardiff
	28	Worcester
	29	York
	30	Manchester
	31	Southend-on-Sea

June	1	Tooting
	2	Brighton
	3	Woolwich
	4	Birmingham
	5	Leeds
	7	Glasgow, Scotland
	8	Newcastle-upon-Tyne
	9	Blackburn
	10	Bath
	12	Liverpool
	13	(2 shows) Stockport, Manchester
	14	New Brighton
	15	Salisbury
	16	Romford
	21	Guildford
	22	Abergavenny
	25	Middlesbrough
	26	Newcastle-upon-Tyne
	28	Leeds
	30	Great Yarmouth
July	5	Old Hill
	6	Northwich
	7	Blackpool
	8–13	Margate
	14	Blackpool
	19, 20	Flintshire
	21	Blackpool
	22–27	Weston-super-Mare
	28	Great Yarmouth
	31	Nelson
Aug.	2	Liverpool
	3	Cavern
	4	Blackpool
	5	Urmston
	6, 7	St. Saviour
	8	St. Peter Port
	9, 10	St. Saviour
	11	Blackpool

	12–17	Llandudno
	18	Torquay
	19–24	Bournemouth
	25	Blackpool
	26–31	Southport
Sept.	4	Worcester
	5	Taunton
	6	Luton
	7	Croydon
	8	Blackpool
	13	Preston
	14	Northwich
	15	London (Royal Albert Hall)
Oct.	5	Glasgow, Scotland
	6	Sinclairtown
	7	Dundee
	11	Trentham
	13	London (Palladium Theatre)
	15	Southport
	19	Buxton
	25	Karlstad, Sweden
	26	Stockholm
	27	Göteborg
	28	Borås
	29	Eskilstuna
Nov.	1	Cheltenham
	2	Sheffield
	3	Leeds
	4	London (Royal Command Variety Performance, Prince of Wales Theatre)
	5	Slough
	6	Northampton
	7	Dublin
	8	Belfast
	9	East Ham

	10	Birmingham
	13	Plymouth
	14	Exeter
	15	Bristol
	16	Bournemouth
	17	Coventry
	19	Wolverhampton
	20	Manchester
	21	Carlisle
	22	Stockton-on-Tees
	23	Newcastle-upon-Tyne
	24	Hull
	26	Cambridge
	27	York
	28	Lincoln
	29	Huddersfield
	30	Sunderland
Dec.	1	Leicester
	2	London
	3	Portsmouth
	7	(2 shows) Liverpool
	8	Lewisham
	9	Southend-on-Sea
	10	Doncaster
	11	Scarborough •
	12	Nottingham
	13	Southampton
	14	Wimbledon
	21	Bradford
	24–31	Finsbury Park
		(Beatles Christmas Show)

BEATLES' TOUR, 1964

Jan.	1–11	Finsbury Park
		(Beatles Christmas Show)
	12	London
		(Palladium Theatre)
	15	Versailles,
		France

	16–31	Paris (Olympia Theatre)
Feb.	1–4	Paris (Olympia Theatre)
	11	Washington, D.C. (Washington Coliseum)
	12	New York City (Carnegie Hall)
April	26	Wembley
	29	Edinburgh, Scotland
	30	Glasgow
May	31	London (Prince of Wales Theatre)
June	4	Copenhagen, Denmark
	6	Blokker, The Netherlands
	9	Kowloon, Hong Kong
	12, 13	Adelaide, Australia
	15–17	Melbourne
	18–20	Sydney
	22, 23	Wellington, New Zealand
	24, 25	Auckland
	26	Dunedin
	27	Christchurch
	29, 30	Brisbane
July	12	Brighton
	19	Blackpool
	23	London (Palladium Theatre)
	26	Blackpool
	28, 29	Johanneshovs Isstadion, Sweden
Aug.	2	Bournemouth
	9	Scarborough
	16	Blackpool

19	San Francisco (Cow Palace)
20	Las Vegas (Convention Center)
21	Seattle (Coliseum)
22	Vancouver (Empire Stadium)
23	Los Angeles (Hollywood Bowl)
26	Denver (Red Rocks)
27	Cincinnati (Cincinnati Gardens)
28, 29	New York City (Forest Hills)
30	Atlantic City (Convention Hall)
Sept. 2	Philadelphia (Convention Hall)
3	(2 shows) Indianapolis (Coliseum)
4	Milwaukee (Arena)
5	Chicago (International Amphitheater)
6	(2 shows) Detroit (Olympia Stadium)
7	(2 shows) Toronto (Maple Leaf Gardens)
8	(2 shows) Montreal (Forum)
11	Jacksonville (Gator Bowl)
12	Boston (Boston Garden)
13	(2 shows) Baltimore (Civic Center)
14	Pittsburgh (Civic Arena)

	15	Cleveland (Public Auditorium)
	16	New Orleans (City Park Stadium)
	17	Kansas City (Municipal Stadium)
	18	Dallas (Memorial Auditorium)
	20	New York City (Paramount Theater)
Oct.	9	Bradford
	10	Leicester
	11	Birmingham
	13	Wigan
	14	Ardwick
	15	Stockton-on-Tees
	16	Hull
	19	Edinburgh, Scotland
	20	Dundee
	21	Glasgow
	22	Leeds
	23	Kilburn
	24	Walthamstow
	25	Brighton
	28	Exeter
	29	Plymouth
	30	Bournemouth
	31	Ipswich
Nov.	1	Finsbury Park
	2	Belfast
	4	Luton
	5	Nottingham
	6	Southampton
	7	Cardiff
	8	Liverpool
	9	Sheffield
	10	Bristol
Dec.	24–31	London (Odeon Theatre, Beatles Christmas Show)

BEATLES' TOUR, 1965

Jan.	1–16	London (Odeon Theatre, Beatles Christmas Show)
April	11	Wembley *(New Musical Express* Poll Winners' Concert)
June	20	Paris, France (Palais des Sports)
	22	Lyon (Palais d'Hiven)
	24	Milan, Italy (Velodromo)
	25	Genoa (Palazzo dello Sport)
	27, 28	(4 shows) Rome (Teatro Adriano)
	30	Nice, France (Palais des Fêtes)
July	2	Madrid, Spain (Plaza de Toros de Madrid)
	3	Barcelona (Plaza de Toros)
Aug.	1	Blackpool
	15	New York City (Shea Stadium)
	17	(2 shows) Toronto (Maple Leaf Gardens)
	18	Atlanta (Atlanta Stadium)
	19	(2 shows) Houston (Sam Houston Coliseum)
	20	(2 shows) Chicago (Comiskey Park)

	21	Minneapolis
		(Metro Stadium)
	22	(2 shows) Portland
		(Memorial Coliseum)
	28	San Diego
		(Balboa Stadium)
	29, 30	(4 shows) Los Angeles
		(Hollywood Bowl)
	31	(2 shows) San Francisco
		(Cow Palace)
Dec.	3	Glasgow,
		Scotland
	4	Newcastle-upon-Tyne
	5	Liverpool
	7	Ardwick
	8	Sheffield
	9	Birmingham
	10	London
		(Odeon Theatre)
	11	Finsbury Park
	12	Cardiff

BEATLES' TOUR, 1966

May	1	Wembley
		(New Musical Express
		Poll Winners' Concert)
June	24	(2 shows) Munich,
		West Germany
		(Circus-Krone-Bau)
	25	Essen
		(Grugahalle)
	26	(2 shows) Hamburg
		(Ernst Merck Halle)
	30	Tokyo,
		Japan
		(Budokan)
July	1, 2	(4 shows) Tokyo
		(Budokan)

	4	(2 shows) Manila, Philippines (Rizal Memorial Football Stadium)
Aug.	12	(2 shows) Chicago (International Amphitheater)
	13	(2 shows) Detroit (Olympia Stadium)
	14	Cleveland (Cleveland Stadium)
	15	Washington, D.C. (D.C. Stadium)
	16	Philadelphia (Philadelphia Stadium)
	17	(2 shows) Toronto (Maple Leaf Gardens)
	18	Boston (Suffolk Downs)
	19	(2 shows) Memphis (Mid-South Coliseum)
	21	(2 shows) afternoon—Cincinnati (Crosley Field) evening—St. Louis (Busch Stadium)
	23	New York City (Shea Stadium)
	25	(2 shows) Seattle (Coliseum)
	28	Los Angeles (Dodger Stadium)
	29	San Francisco (Candlestick Park)

Paul started to wonder about the vaunted Beatles machine when he chanced to look at the *Billboard* Hot 100 Chart and noticed that the top five were by the Beatles (albeit on four different labels, given Capitol's early disbelief in the Beatles; Swan with "She Loves You," Tollie with "Twist and Shout," and Vee Jay with "Please Please Me" were the other three, joining Capitol's "I Saw Her Standing There" and "I Want to

Hold Your Hand"). He certainly, in April of 1964 when everything was coming up Beatles, should have been feeling like a
million pounds, if not two. Top two albums in the United
States, plus all those singles, plus the touring.

Paul wanted to buy a place outside London, so he hied himself
off to see the accountants. Paul estimated that the place would
cost no more than thirty thousand pounds at the top end, which
he envisioned as no problem.

Imagine his surprise when the accountants told him, "You'll
have to get a mortgage." He was fairly incredulous, but he
learned that for reasons too incredibly complicated to go into
here he had no real money.

He got the message. Unless he got back out on the road and
kept on playing those fabulous gigs and kept coming back in and
making those great records, he would not see the bucks. Not
that he didn't get any money at all—or at least some money
sometimes—but he knew what he had to do.

So the Beatles went out for the tour that only Paul, of all of
them, wanted to do (although no one bothered to poll Ringo
about his feelings), which was the 1966 tour.

The Beatles were just beginning to educate themselves about
their money. For years all that they saw was the fifty pounds a
week apiece doled out to them by Brian. It was later increased to
one hundred pounds a week. True, all their expenses were picked
up and if John wanted a new Rolls-Royce, he had only to say the
word. Still, they were treated as "the boys" by all the "men in
suits" that they increasingly seemed to be working for, rather
than vice versa.

Paul and John—thanks to their naïveté and Brian's business
ignorance—never owned their own songs. Until they started
recording, John and Paul saw no need to try to publish all those
precious songs that had been so painstakingly written down in
Paul's notebooks in his schoolboy scrawl. They knew nothing
about song publishing anyway and there was no one they could
ask. Back in October 1962 when "Love Me Do" came out, Brian
let EMI's in-house publisher, Ardmore and Beechwood, publish
it. But Brian was not happy with the job EMI did pushing the
record. He complained about it to George Martin and said,
"When the next one comes out, I don't want to give the publishing to them."

The Beatles couldn't leave EMI because they were under contract, but that didn't mean they had to give EMI their song publishing rights. Brian wanted to sign up with the American firm of Hill and Range because "they do all the Elvis Presley stuff."

George suggested trying a British firm and recommended Dick James. He was an old-time band singer whose records George had produced. In recent years James had become a song plugger and was just starting his own firm. It was James who brought Martin the song "How Do You Do It" that the Beatles did not want to record.

Brian went to see James and this is the deal that he gratefully accepted: The Beatles would form a company called Northern Songs to be administered by Dick James Music. James would own half of Northern Songs and Brian and the Beatles would split the other half. In addition, James would get 10 percent off the top in management fees. So that meant that, of every one hundred dollars coming in, James would take the first ten dollars and then would split the remaining ninety dollars with Brian and the Beatles. The score: Dick James, 55 percent; Brian and the Beatles, 45 percent. Of that 45 percent, John and Paul each had 20 percent and Brian had 5. Since George and Ringo didn't write songs, they got nothing in writing royalties. It was a deal that would turn to ashes in Paul's and John's mouths.

For the first few years, at least, James did a good job of working the songs and preventing them from being turned into television commercials and seeing that they weren't overexposed. What did John and Paul, "the boys," know about business anyway? They shouldn't worry their cute little mop-top heads about figgers. The men would take care of that.

Dick James (who is now dead) became a very wealthy man courtesy of that little deal with Brian.

Over the years that Northern Song catalog was to come to symbolize for the Beatles everything that was wrong with what was happening to them. Not the songs—just what was happening to them. It represented the almost complete lack of control that they felt over their lives. When the Beatles were recording songs for the *Yellow Submarine* soundtrack in 1968, they were ready to pack it in late one night. The film's producer, Al Brodax, insisted that the movie was one song short. At 2 A.M., while the London Symphony Orchestra sat waiting in the cavernous Studio 1 at Abbey Road, George Harrison listened to Brodax and then told everyone to sit tight. He walked out and came back in an hour with a finished song. And he called it "Only a Northern Song."

In 1965, with the idea of fully realizing the songs' earning power, Brian and James turned Northern Songs into a public company and floated it on the Stock Exchange. It took some brilliant persuasion to convince Paul and John that it was in their best interests to now have three thousand stockholders owning a piece of their work. After the flotation John and Paul each owned 15 percent of the stock, James and a partner held 37.5 percent, NEMS controlled 7.5. Ringo and George, generously, were each given 0.8 percent.

It seemed to be a great idea. Within two years the value of the stock quintupled. "The boys" and all who sailed with them were turning a tidy profit.

But some of the stockholders began to grow nervous about the increasingly erratic behavior of "the boys." That nervousness translated itself into fluctuations of the stock, which made many of them unhappy. "The boys" were acting a little wild and crazy and that seemed to be affecting their song output. Geese and golden eggs is too obvious a metaphor, but there you are. After Paul admitted in 1967, after *Sgt. Pepper,* in interviews that he had used LSD, there was a huge public flap about that. And the Beatles paid for—at Paul's direction—and signed a petition in the *Times* calling for the legalization of marijuana. And then in 1968 John got busted for grass and then started doing odd things in public with "that woman." The stockholders had no assurances that "the boys" would continue with a smooth orderly output of commercially viable songs that would enhance the value of the stock. Just imagine what "Cold Turkey" did for nervous stockholders' ulcers. And the spectacle of John and Yoko nude on the cover of *Two Virgins* must have caused a few flutters and twinges.

But that's why "Strawberry Fields Forever" and "Penny Lane" are not on the *Sgt. Pepper* album. They were the first two songs, along with "When I'm Sixty-Four," that were recorded for the album. But it was the beginning of 1967 and the Beatles had not issued a British single since "Eleanor Rigby" and "Yellow Submarine" back on August 5, 1966. There was incredible pressure on Brian to get some product out. Pressure came from the record company as well. The Beatles had to put something out soon. So they took what they had—"When I'm Sixty-Four" was obviously not a Beatle single—and rushed into release on February 17, 1967. Of their fourteen British singles, this was the first (since "Please Please Me") not to go to number one on the charts.

Dick James had for some time resisted offers to sell his substantial holdings in Northern Songs. But his dealings with "the boys" had soured somewhat over the years and Paul and John invited him to leave when he showed up at Twickenham Studios during rehearsals for the *Let It Be* album.

James felt, obviously enough, that "the boys" would not be doing all that much writing together in the future. So he sold his majority holdings to Sir Lew Grade of ATV without telling the Beatles. They read about it in the newspapers.

But that was still in the future. Back in the halycon Beatle days when Paul was wondering where his money was, Brian had been making other questionable deals. On the eve of the American invasion, as Beatlemania in the United States was just building up to fever pitch, he had turned over all licensing of official Beatle merchandise to a consortium of men that the Beatles never met or heard of. There was already a deluge of bogus Beatle goods being peddled—from wigs to lunch boxes to wallpaper—so Brian decided, correctly, that merchandising should be controlled. The trouble was, Brian left the actual terms of the deal up to his lawyer, David Jacobs. He met with a representative of Seltaeb (spell it backward) named Nicky Byrne and gave Seltaeb the first number that Byrne asked for: 90 percent. Ninety percent to Seltaeb, that is. Ten percent for Brian and the Beatles. How much money did that involve? No one can say. (David Jacobs was found dead, hanging from a rafter in his garage, in 1969, two years after Brian's death.)

Paul and Brian had never been close and they were less close after the end of the 1966 tour. In a very telling comment that Brian never forgot, after Allen Klein became manager of the Rolling Stones in 1965, Paul said to him in front of the others, "Klein got the Stones a million and a quarter, didn't he? What about us?" Paul was increasingly skeptical of and curious about all of their business dealings. The other Beatles were beginning to share his feelings. The simple fact was that they were beginning to glom onto was a familiar Beatle syndrome: They didn't need Brian anymore. He had done what he was supposed to do for them: made them bigger than Elvis. Now there was nothing further for him to do. For the past two years they had just been doing the same things. How often could they tour America and make movies and churn out the records as well? What else could he do for them? What was to manage? They made the music without anybody's help. And where was all the money? Just how many millions of records had they sold? And what kinds of deals had been made in their names? They could figure out on their own that a 90–10 split aimed the other way was a shitty deal.

Brian was also becoming a bit of a mess. Not that the others were likely to turn up in any antidrug campaign, but Brian was not handling it well. LSD, especially, seemed to have bent his brain. There had been ugly incidents on the tour involving Brian and his liking for rough trade. On that last U.S. tour, Brian's live-in valet/lover robbed him of his drugs, over $20,000 in cash, compromising photographs and letters, and business documents. Then he blackmailed him. Back in London after the tour he was at loose ends, gambling and incurring heavy debts. He put NEMS up for sale, intending to retain only the Beatles and Cilla Black. He seldom saw the elegant NEMS offices on Chapel Street in the daylight and started shuttling back and forth to Spain to try to start managing bullfighters and to do a movie about bullfighting. He twice attempted suicide, in late 1966 and early 1967, and finally agreed to enter a private hospital to undergo detoxification.

He seemed to improve. In January he renegotiated the Beatles' contract with EMI and with Capitol in the United States, getting them a significant increase in royalty rates. Still, there was no dramatic million-pound-plus bonus like the Stones had gotten.

There was nothing else he could do for the Beatles. They were in the studio, where he didn't belong. All he had left to look forward to—or to fear—was the fact that his management contract with the Beatles would expire on October 2, 1967. According to his few friends, that was exactly what he dreaded.

FOUR and a half years after that New Year's 1963 Hamburg club date, Paul sat in his shabbily elegant Georgian manse at number 7 Cavendish Avenue in St. John's Wood—just a toss of an LP from the Abbey Road Studios—and brooded about all that had happened since then. Once the Beatles' career had started on the ascent in early 1963, it had skyrocketed. It was, in two words, fucking unbelievable. The years from 1963 to 1966 had reeled by in a blur of jet airplane engines revving up for takeoffs, of endless airport corridors packed with screaming girls and shouting reporters, of an eternity of hotel rooms that they could not leave because of the screaming girls and shouting reporters, of armored cars thrusting them past screaming girls into packed halls full of screaming girls, of packed halls where they could not even hear themselves play above the roar of screaming girls, of being the world's highest-paid dog and pony show, of a mayor's wife in the Midwest demanding that they be awakened to be displayed for her daughter, of pinched-faced redneck kids in the South burning their records and beating on the windows of their limos, of their own countrymen regarding them as freaks and snipping off bits of their hair at a diplomatic reception in Washington, of getting death threats everywhere, of a chartered plane in the United States that received a number of bullet holes in its tail section (never reported), of being openly offered the best sex and the best drugs everywhere they went as a matter of routine (as if for a visiting chief of state), of openly being gawked at as the best-known four freaks in the world. But "freaks" was the operative word.

George, who was the most against touring (and who had uttered the famous post-Candlestick Park show quote: "That's it, I'm not a Beatle anymore"), was the most critical of what had happened. They were like "monkeys in a zoo," he said. "The good thing about giving up touring," George said, "was that it forced the split, or helped to." George's attitude was one reason why Paul brooded a lot. Paul himself had mostly enjoyed the tours because he loved performing and he loved going out and being Paul McCartney and pressing the flesh, as it were, before, during, and after shows. Even so, he later admitted that he didn't remember most of what happened. "The sixties for me are a blur; 1963 is the same as 1967. It was all one big blur," he said. Even so, during those blurred years the Beatles had continued to put out their singles on schedule: "I Want to Hold Your Hand," "Can't Buy Me Love," "A Hard Day's Night," "I Feel Fine," "Ticket to Ride," "Help!", "Day Tripper," "We Can Work It Out," "Paperback Writer," and "Eleanor Rigby."

And they managed a movie a year for 1964 (*A Hard Day's Night*) and 1965 (*Help!*) and John wrote a book a year for 1964 (*In His Own Write*) and 1965 (*A Spaniard in the Works*) and they churned out the albums. The fact that they managed to put such marvelous music down on record was testimony to the amazing Lennon–McCartney catalog and that itself is thanks to Paul's compulsion, ever since he and John had started writing together back in 1957, to jot everything down in his composition books. They would never have remembered all those wonderful songs otherwise. As it was, a number of them were lost when one or more of Paul's notebooks were discarded by Jane Asher at the St. John's Wood home.

Even as the touring and the Beatlemania began to escalate, they had had to move out of Liverpool once the fans had discovered their home addresses. Paul was quietly proud that in early 1964 he was able to persuade his dad to retire from his ten pound a week job selling cotton and to move outside Liverpool into Rembrandt, a house costing 8,750 pounds. Mike was still living at home and he loved the wall-to-wall carpeting, the five bedrooms, and the three indoor bathrooms. Mike later wrote that for Jim suddenly getting the house, though, "the sudden contrast was too much. Dad, a man of action who'd been striving for something 'better' all his life, had suddenly been given it . . . on a plate. From nothing to everything like Paul and the Beatles, life was sort of over before it had started, or as Auntie Mill would say . . . 'Here we are. Where are we?' "

And on the night of the London premiere of the movie *A Hard Day's Night* at the London Pavilion on July 6, 1964, after everyone enjoyed the standing ovation for the movie, they all adjourned to the Dorchester Hotel for a little supper party. Paul had introduced his dad to Princess Margaret (it was a Royal World Premiere, hosted by the Princess and the Earl of Snowden), then Paul gave his father a present for his sixty-second birthday.

He handed Jim a painting of a horse. "Thank you, son. It's very nice," Jim said, a little addled at getting a drawing of a horse. "It's a horse," Paul said.

"I can see that, son," Jim said. "It looks lovely."

Paul finally glommed on to the confusion and told Jim, "It's not just a painting . . . it's a *horse*. I've bought you a bloody horse." As a man who always loved to put a "little flutter" on the horses, Jim was teary-eyed at being given his own nag by his own son. "You silly bugger," Jim murmured. The horse, Drake's Drum, later won over three thousand pounds at the track (over a purchase price of a thousand).

Finally, though, they had all moved to London. Paul, of course, got the best bargain when he not only started going with the beautiful actress Jane Asher but also moved into her family's house as well. Then, for forty thousand pounds, he had bought the house on Cavendish and Jane helped him decorate and furnish it. Cynthia Powell Lennon probably described the other Beatles' reactions to Jane when she observed that Jane gave "an enormous boost to Paul's ambitious ego. It was as though he was saying to us all, 'Anything you can do I can do better.' "

Jane had also encouraged Paul in looking for a retreat and he bought High Park Farm, a 183-acre farm in Scotland near Campbeltown. It is stark, hilly, rocky land, good for nothing but grazing sheep and for being left alone. Paul grew to appreciate both the sheep and the solitude there.

Paul had not been accustomed to running things, except within

his own personal orbit. But now, in 1967, Paul found himself—
maybe by default, but never mind why—running the damn
Beatles. Brian was dead, a sad victim of the same excesses to
which Paul and the others felt immune. John was fucked up and
that was something nobody talked about. It was just what John
was going through. He had done so many acid trips that he had
completely destroyed his ego and he was mostly out of commission, musically at least, for the rest of his life. Later, of course, he
and Yoko drifted off into a heroin haze before cleaning up their
lives. John had his spells of musical lucidity, but it's relatively
easy in hindsight to see that Paul took over the Beatles after they
quit touring and he held on until there was nothing else left to
hold on to.

Poor Cynthia, who was treated so shabbily by John and the
other Beatles, never uttered a truer truism than when she uttered
this one: "As far as I was concerned the rot began to set in the
moment cannabis and LSD seeped its [sic] unhealthy way into
our lives."

The Beatles lived on stimulants of one sort or another, as just
about every rock group of the era depended on stimulants.
Drugs were just part of their lives in the same way that the
weather was. John said that pills and alcohol were what they ran
on from the time they were adolescents. The movie *A Hard
Day's Night,* for example, was an amphetamine movie.

Then, courtesy of Bob Dylan, the Beatles discovered marijuana when they were at the Delmonico Hotel in New York.
When Bob had first heard the song "I Want to Hold Your
Hand," he misheard the chorus and he thought that they were
singing "I get high," a sure indication that the Beatles were
brother vipers. Imagine his surprise when he got them all stoked
up and they confessed that they were all "grass virgins." The
Beatles, veterans of every hard-edged upper that England and the
Continent had to offer, suddenly found all the rough edges being
taken off things by this funny cigarette. Paul stood up, wobbled
a bit, and grabbed Beatle publicist Derek Taylor by the arm and
said, "It's as if we're up there," pointing vaguely at the ceiling,
"up there, pointing down on us!"

The first shot is the roughest, they say, or something roughly
similar. Paul seemed to take to marijuana, given his subsequent
proximity to marijuana arrests involving himself or his wife over

the years. Paul later said that grass eased into his scene. "Remember, drug-taking in 1967 was much more in the musicians' tradition," he said. "We'd heard of Ellington and Basie and jazz guys smoking a bit of pot, and now it arrived on our music scene. It started to find its way into everything we did, really. It colored our perceptions. I think we started to realize there weren't as many frontiers as we'd thought there were. And we realized we could break barriers."

Exactly the kind of double-speaking, double-schriptzing, triple-talk sort of barrier screen that the Beatles had once announced they were against. One thing critics of the Beatles should take into consideration is the fact that, as can be scientifically proven, strong marijuana played right into their hands. Or so they would have one believe.

John was having a bad time the night of March 2, 1967. The Beatles and their producer, George Martin, were in Studio 2 at Abbey Road, as they had been for many such evenings, working on their next album, which was still untitled. It was just the next album, the one after the last one.

The last one had been *Revolver,* released on August 5, 1966. At that time the Beatles were just barely back in London between two hard swings of the 1966 tour that brought them global controversies on a scale that they could just as nicely have done without. In July they just barely got out of Manila with their skins and scalps intact and were thanking God that they were flying out of Manila at all after mobs at the airport there tried to rip them limb from limb. What had happened was that the Marcos family announced to all the Philippines that the Beatles would pay a courtesy call on them at Malacañang Palace. The details of the invitation are still vague: Either the local promoter, Ramon Ramos, informed Brian of the royal summons or he did not. And either Brian said fuck it or he did not. At any rate, by that time the Beatles were such international royalty on their own that they would not have gotten out of bed early to go and kiss the asses of some tinhorn dictator and his social-climbing wife. Well, when they didn't, the whole country went into a frenzy. Newspaper and TV news reports said that the Beatles had "snubbed" the First Family. They were physically hounded and assaulted all the way out of the country.

Anyway, this was the second night in a row that they had been working on a new song by John called "Lucy in the Sky with Diamonds." Which, despite all the LSD talk over the years, actually was based on a drawing that John's son Julian had brought home from school. It was a typical little kid's drawing, showing a Lucy, a little girl, up amidst the stars, above boxy little houses and trees. The Lucy of the same name, who was at Heath House school with Julian when she was four years old, is named Lucy O'Donnell and is now a nursery school teacher in Weybridge.

But John Lennon was all fucked up that night. He had reached for an upper in his pocket to get him blasted awake for the long night ahead. The Beatles, once they were settled in at Abbey Road, didn't leave until they were through. It was not just a matter of booking Studio 2 from ten till two; they just took it over and sent out for whatever they needed—with the emphasis on whatever; be it food, musical instruments, the London Symphony Orchestra, various forms of inspiration, just whatever it took—and stayed until they were ready to leave. They pretty much changed the complexion of the place. Recording artists no longer had to wear coats and ties and keep business hours. On their first few visits the Beatles wore the coats and ties and hewed the corporate line, but all that stopped when they started getting hits and began to test their power.

The biggest surprise the Beatles had found at Abbey Road on their first visit back in 1962 had been that even the toilet paper was corporate. Each sheet was imprinted with: EMI. One roll of toilet paper that John and Paul rejected as being "too hard" was actually later auctioned off for eighty-five pounds. The Beatles were not universally loved at Abbey Road. Staff engineers didn't especially want to work with a group that might suddenly decide to work for forty-eight hours straight. And they didn't appreciate authoritarians who might demand a glockenspiel or a Chinese fire gong at three in the morning. As Sir Joseph Lockwood, the chairman of EMI, observed: "In many ways they were a bloody nuisance. When they became famous they often came to see me when they were in trouble, particularly over things like the *Sgt. Pepper* sleeve."

But poor John that night at Abbey Road was starting to float away and merge with the wall. A straight pin that he noticed shining on the floor became a blinding silver light that started to glow and grow and to take him over and swallow his entire being and then—he started screaming. He thought. He couldn't be sure. Whom could he trust to tell him the truth, after all?

George Martin, straight as a die, sitting up in the glass-enclosed control room that overlooked the studio, thought he detected a slight problem with John. He went down and asked him if he was all right. John wasn't sure. Martin suggested they get some fresh air. They couldn't go out in front because of the ever-present Apple Scruffs who were "waiting out" until the Beatles left. So Martin took him up to the roof to take in a little London night air. They were walking around the narrow parapet, looking down at the ninety-or-so-foot drop down to the parking lot, when John finally realized that he must be tripping.

They went back downstairs and found Paul back in the studio. Paul offered to take John home and then, once they got there, decided to drop some acid and trip with him to keep him company and calm him down.

John really couldn't turn to his wife Cynthia for LSD support. Cynthia was terrified of the stuff and almost walked out of a second-story window when she tried it. To tell the truth, Cynthia and John weren't getting on all that well anyway. Ever since John and George had discovered the wonders of lysergic acid when George's dentist turned them on back in 1965, John had withdrawn more and more and was content to stay home at Kenwood in Weybridge in the "stockbroker belt." He could spend days on his comfortable settee, watching television, reading, getting high, and tinkering in the crude home studio setup he had put together. He and Paul seldom saw each other socially and had, for all practical purposes, quit writing together long ago. They would still provide the odd bridge or middle eight for each other's songs, but the days of John and Paul sitting down together to write a song were long over.

Paul, ever the cautious one in most things, had held out for a long time before trying LSD, ignoring John's ridicule. John once went on the program "Old Grey Whistle Test" and said that Paul only took it four times, while "We all took it twenty times!" Finally Paul decided to see for himself what all the fuss was about. When the dreaded "heaven and hell" drug finally did its work upon him, the result was, as they say, mind-blowing.

John and Paul stared deeply into each other's eyes for two or three centuries and kept saying, "I know, man."

This was 1966, when the Beatles gave themselves some time off for the first occasion in years by refusing an English tour earlier in the year and by deciding not to tour anymore—at least for the time being—when they got back from the United States. John had genuinely hated the tour, had felt it was completely unnecessary and a waste of time and energy. The music they had been performing on tour—as if anyone could have heard it anyway—was in no way indicative of the way the Beatles were rapidly evolving musically. During that entire last tour they performed the same exact twelve songs: "Baby's in Black," "Day Tripper," "I Feel Fine," "I Wanna Be Your Man," "If I Needed Someone," "I'm Down," "Long Tall Sally," "Nowhere Man," "Paperback Writer," "Rock and Roll Music," "She's a Woman," and "Yesterday."

John had also had to go through the whole "bigger than Jesus" scandal during the tour after an old *Evening Standard* interview he had done was reprinted in *Datebook* in the United States. His remarks that the Beatles were "more popular than Jesus now. I don't know which will go first—rock 'n' roll or Christianity." His remarks had caused no stir in Great Britain, but four months later much of the United States was howling for Beatle blood. Record burnings, death threats, screaming ten-year-old children with hate-filled eyes trying to get at them in their cars—it was fairly serious. When a firecracker went off while they were onstage in Memphis, they were all sure that one of them had been shot. John had been forced to apologize in public in Chicago at the start of the tour. Apologizing was not something he liked to do or ever had done, for that matter. But, as Brian explained to him over and over again, it had to be done. It was not bad enough that ministers, radio stations, Ku Klux Klan members, and editorial writers all over America were whipping up popular feeling against the Beatles, even the Vatican had been moved to observe that "some subjects must not be dealt with profanely, even in the world of Beatniks." The fears were too great that one or more of the Beatles would be assassinated during the tour. He broke down and cried before apologizing, over the craziness of the whole thing. "If this is what rock 'n' roll had been perverted into," John said (privately, that is), "then you can just take it and stuff it."

What should have been a crowning point of the Beatles' lives had turned into a supreme disappointment the previous summer. The Beatles, who had everybody in the world wanting to meet them, had only one name on their list of celebrities they were still in awe of: Elvis. The historic meeting finally took place in Los Angeles. It took days to set up, mainly over the matter of rock 'n' roll protocol. On whose turf would it happen? Elvis was the reigning king and all that, but the Beatles were now the hottest thing ever. Should they go to Elvis or should Elvis come to them? Finally weary of all the jawboning, Elvis's autocratic old ex-carny manager, Colonel Tom Parker, ordered Brian to bring "the boys" to meet Elvis (whom the colonel always referred to as "the boy"). So they limoed from their rented Mulholland Drive mansion to Elvis's rented Bel Air mansion. "The boys" were greatly disappointed by "the boy." Everyone was ill at ease and no one had any idea of what to talk about. Four trained bears, meet another trained bear. John later said it was like meeting Englebert Humperdinck. But anyway, rock 'n' roll for John was fast running its course out.

Right after the tour John went to Spain to act in the Richard Lester movie *How I Won the War,* a serious antiwar statement. It was a relief to him to be away, immersed in a completely different world in which his talents were appreciated. At the same time Paul was doing music for a frothy Hayley Mills comedy movie called *The Family Way.* Beatle watchers were quick to point out the rather obvious differences between the nature of the two projects. In fact, though, the two projects were indicative of the divergent paths the two chief Beatles would take. John would do what he wanted and damn the consequences. Paul, who never had the self-confidence that John once had, would do what he thought was expected of him, something that people would applaud.

While John was increasingly withdrawing from the world, Paul was very much the bon vivant and man about town. He was trying to do a cram course in culture. He and Jane Asher were well connected with the right young people socially and spent many evenings on the town, going to openings, hanging out at the chic clubs, such as the Bag O'Nails, the Ad Lib, the

Scotch of St. James, the Speakeasy, Sybilla's, and the Savile Theatre, an elegant showcase club that Brian had opened at great expense in 1965. Paul had his little bachelor pad hidden away and had all of London at his feet for the taking.

While John sat at home ingesting more and more LSD, it was Paul who was actually hanging out with London's avant-garde crowd. He joined a circle that included a man named Miles who ran Indica Books on Southampton Row. The Beatles kept a running account at the store and depended on Miles to send them whatever he thought might interest them; magazines, books, newspapers, whatever. Paul and John got their information on the hippie movement in America through the underground newspapers that Miles would send them: the *Berkeley Barb,* the *Oracle,* the L.A. *Free Press,* and the *East Village Other.* He sent them Frank Zappa's album *Freak Out* and its free-form recording techniques and tracks lasting over ten minutes impressed Paul mightily. After hearing it Paul told Miles that he wanted to make the next Beatles album something other than just a collection of singles—a "concept album," in other words.

Miles started London's first underground paper, *International Times,* with a big party at the Roundhouse in October. Paul showed up in flowing Arab robes. Music was by Pink Floyd and the Soft Machine. There was a psychedelic light show, the first that Paul had ever seen, as well as a glimpse of London's first psychedelically painted car. Paul actually helped Miles put the first few issues of *International Times* together and was happy to do so, he said, because *IT* represented a side of him and the Beatles that was not being seen, that the Beatles "had become known as the cute little headshakers and that had submerged that slightly offbeat 'arty' side of us. *IT was* the other side of us."

In interviews with Miles, Paul talked about the yearnings he felt for grasping what was unheard in music and unseen in film: "To see the potential in it all. To take a note and wreck it and see in that note whatelse there is in it, that a simple act like distorting it has caused. To take a film and to superimpose on top of it so that you can't quite tell what it is anymore, it's all trying to create magic, it's all trying to make things happen so that you don't know why they've happened. I'd like a lot more things to happen like they did when you were kids, when you didn't know how the conjuror did it, and were happy just to see it there and say, 'Well, it's magic.' I use 'magic' instead of 'spiritual' because 'spiritual' sounds as if it fits into too many of the other categories."

Then there was John Dunbar, who was married to Marianne Faithfull and who owned the enormously influential Indica Gallery in Mason's Yard. Jane's brother, Peter Asher, was an investor in the Indica Gallery as well as being half of the singing duo Peter and Gordon, for whom Paul had written the hit "A World Without Love." Through Miles and Dunbar, Paul met everybody who was anybody in the creative world.

He hung out in a flat on Montague Square with William Burroughs and Allen Ginsberg and their crowd. Paul had also met the filmmaker Michaelangelo Antonioni and started making his own experimental movies. He got one of the first video recorders and started experimenting with that. Paul screened two movies, *The Defeat of the Dog* and *The Next Spring Then,* for a writer from *Punch* magazine, who wrote:

> They were not like ordinary people's home movies. There were over-exposures, double-exposures, blinding orange lights, quick cuts from professional wrestling to a crowded car park to a close-up of a television weather map. There were long still shots of a grey cloudy sky and a wet, grey pavement, jumping Chinese ivory carvings and affectionate slow-motion studies of his sheepdog Martha and his cat. The accompanying music, on a record player and faultlessly synchronised, was by the Modern Jazz Quartet and Bach.

He would also put tape loop music to his movies and video-tapes or bits of Stockhausen or Ravi Shankar. He played some of that for John and told him he was thinking of making an album in that vein and calling it *Paul McCartney Goes Too Far.* John encouraged him in that and started doing his own tape experimentation at home.

Paul also started doing cocaine during the whole 1966–67 *Sgt. Pepper,* Flower Power, Swinging London, counterculture era. He started snorting coke, he said later, along with a lot of his trendy friends as an upper after smoking a joint or two. The other Beatles were horrified at first to see Paul blasting that white powder up his nostrils. LSD was one thing and grass was organic, you know, but toot? That was a little heavy, man. (Although it must be remembered that Paul never said he was the *only* Beatle to use coke. He just said he was the *first.*) Paul gave it up for several reasons, he later said. One was the spectacle of everybody in the record business starting to adopt cocaine as a hip ritual, starting about late 1967. Offering a toot often supplanted shaking hands as a social gesture. Another reason was the plunge: the periods of profound letdown and depression that eventually come to any cocaine user. Another reason was the choking sensation that coke causes at the back of the throat. Paul had, after all, a set of the best pipes in the business. There was no real point in ruining his voice or his throat for a quick high.

It was also in 1966 that Paul met Yoko—before John did. He said that she came to his house asking him to donate any spare manuscripts or Beatle lyrics sheets he might have lying around the house for an artistic charity affair. He refused because he says that sort of thing is very dear to him. Paul did suggest she go and see his mate, John Lennon. He gave her John's address.

John's and Yoko's "official" first meeting was November 9, 1966, at the Indica Gallery for a "private preview" for John only of Yoko's exhibition called "Unfinished Paintings and Objects." Among those objects were a "Sky machine: machine produces nothing when coin is deposited: 1,500 dollars," a "crying machine," a "disappearing machine," and so on. John, who had been up for days on acid and marijuana, was delighted at what he saw: a sense of whimsy at work that was similar to his own. Yoko came up to John and wordlessly handed him a card. He looked down at it and laughed. The card had one word on it: BREATHE.

Cynthia Lennon soon started wondering who she was, this short Oriental woman dressed in black who always seemed to be underfoot. So did the other Beatles.

The next thing John did was to warn Paul to keep his hands off of Yoko, although there was little danger of any hijinks from that quarter. Paul—and later George and Ringo—came to resent Yoko so much, especially after she practically took up residence in the studio, that it would be years before there was any real friendship involved—if ever.

John, meanwhile, told his pal Shotton to try to educate Yoko as to who the Beatles were, since she seemed to be ignorant of that. Although if there had existed a single person in the Western

Hemisphere by then who hadn't at least heard of the Fabs, then that person was Yoko.

Back at Abbey Road the trauma of John's accidental self-dosing with acid passed and the next evening they were all back at work, although on many nights it was just Paul and John and George Martin and an engineer. On other nights it might be just Paul and George Martin, as Paul poured everything he had into this album. As the Beatle most concerned with the group's image (and, by inference, with his own image), he was aware of the tremendous public interest in and anticipation of the next Beatle work. When word circulated after the 1966 tour that the Beatles would likely never tour again, there was actual weeping and wailing and gnashing of teeth by the truly devoted fans. Surely, they concluded, since all rock bands tour, if the Beatles don't tour, then they are over and done with. The notion of a recording band depending for its career on carefully crafted studio productions was just not part of the whole rock scheme. Even the Sunday *Times* of London concluded: "Beatlemania is at an end."

In the United States the whole counterculture seemed at times to hinge on the Beatles. Without them, who could they turn to? Beatle albums were totems and signposts, way stations along the road on the way on the journey to . . . where? But they were certainly significant and mattered a hell of a lot to all the righteous dudes and beautiful chicks. As the Beatles upped the ante every time with each album (and as it became immediately obvious to stoned listeners that they were listening to stoned music), as the quality of their music rose and the level of their studio experimentation escalated, they were considered the unspoken, unelected leaders of whatever one wanted to call the burgeoning movement that was characterized by opposition to the Vietnam War, liberalization of marijuana laws, self-liberation in every form, and mainly freedom to be left alone to do one's own thing. All of these were Beatle principles. The fact that they could encapsulate so many unspoken yearnings into captivating music made them their generation's unwilling voice, but that's the voice they were. And their fellow generation members wanted some new Beatle sounds.

So did—for different reasons, as Paul well knew—the three thousand stockholders in Northern Songs and the directors of

EMI and everyone else who owned some little piece of the Beatles. It was this pressure that led Brian and EMI, against Paul's and John's wishes, to pull "Strawberry Fields Forever" and "Penny Lane" off the forthcoming album and to rush-release them as a single. It was without a doubt the best two-sided rock single ever released: John's hallucinatory reverie inspired by the Strawberry Fields Orphanage back in Liverpool and Paul's sunny ode to a childhood and a childhood landmark, the actual Penny Lane, in Liverpool. It also left them two songs short; since they wanted this album to be of a piece.

That left only "When I'm Sixty-Four" as a song to start with. That, of course, had been written by Paul when he was a teenager and he had kept it in his notebooks until the right time to record it. It was not, under any circumstances, ever going to be a single release and, under the old days of recording albums of singles, it would never have been considered for a traditional Beatles album. John ridiculed it, saying, "I would never even dream of writing a song like that." Paul had come to expect this from John, this give and take, but the criticism still stung. Paul held his words back and didn't lash out at John. He just got even in the studio. This was one reason all the Beatle albums, starting with *Sgt. Pepper,* became mostly Paul's albums. He could finally assert himself, given John's emotionally weakened state and mental confusion. He was in the studio much more than the others. He also tried to learn enough about studio technique to be able to tell George Martin exactly what he wanted on a record. John, who regarded Martin as his "translator" rather than his producer, would give George a vague description of what he had in mind, say, "You can fix it, George," and then walk away, confident that Martin could produce what he wanted. That could work brilliantly, although it was tough on Martin to always come up with a solution. "Strawberry Fields Forever" was a good example. When John brought the song in (which he had written in Spain while filming *How I Won the War)* and they recorded it in November 1966 with just the four Beatles, the result was a fairly straight-ahead version. A week or so later John did something he had never done before. He went to Martin and said that they should remake the song, that it just didn't sound quite right. Always before, if something didn't work the first time out—on the first session, that is, not the first take—they would just forget it. This time, though, John could hear a different sound in his mind. He asked Martin to put a score to it, strings and brass maybe.

Martin had done that for the first time with Paul's "Yesterday" (which originally, by the way, was called "Scrambled Egg") in 1965. John, George, and Ringo had not played on "Yesterday" at all. It was just Paul and his guitar and a string quartet. And that had worked nicely. So John just left it up to Martin.

When John heard the scored version of "Strawberry Fields," it sounded good to him, but he still liked the other version. So he asked Martin to just kind of throw them together. Even though the two were recorded at different speeds and different tempos, Martin spliced together the two recordings and that is the way you hear it to this day.

Many, many years later, though, John began to complain that Paul—what with all the time Paul spent in the studio and the fact that George Martin listened more to Paul than he did to John—had been subverting John in the studio by "subconsciously" screwing with his songs. This was undoubtedly the result of a drug-induced paranoia (which was certainly no stranger to any member of the group). Several times, though, John said that he thought that "Strawberry Fields" and "Across the Universe," to name two of his songs, had been ruined either through studio tinkering or simply through neglect. By neglect he meant that he often did not receive the studio help or support from the others that he felt he needed.

Whereas Paul went to George Martin with "Penny Lane" the day after attending a concert of Bach's *Brandenburg Concerti* and telling Martin how fantastic this really high trumpet in it had been. So then, according to John, Martin ran out and got this great trumpet player from the London Symphony to come in and play piccolo trumpet on "Penny Lane." It wasn't quite that easy. Martin did listen to Paul, but it was because Paul tried to make it painstakingly clear what he wanted. This was just a fundamental difference between Paul and John.

Anyway, after both were reasonably happy with their songs, they lost them from the album due to the pressure from Brian and EMI for a new Beatle single. And "Strawberry Fields"/"Penny Lane" did not make number one because Englebert Humperdinck's "Release Me" beat them. What a kick in the head that was. One thing that the "Strawberry Fields"/"Penny Lane" release did, though, was to increasingly whet the appetites of all those who were breathlessly waiting for the next Beatles album.

After a break for Christmas they went back to working on the album. There was still no talk that this would be a concept album and the words "Sgt. Pepper" still had not been spoken. Paul and John were just intent on getting songs written and recorded. Paul wrote most of it and was the only one of the four who was there for the recording and mixing and editing of all of it. ·

All they had in the can when they went back in January was Paul's "When I'm Sixty-Four." And you couldn't build much of an album from that, as John said more than once.

The other songs started coming, though. The next one stemmed from a long Lennon session on his settee at home, just lying there and reading and smoking and thinking. He got the germ of it when he picked up the *Daily Mail* on December 19. John knew one story he would find. The previous day a good friend of the Beatles named Tara Browne had been killed when his Lotus Elan hit a truck at high speed in South Kensington. He was twenty-one years old, an heir to the Guinness fortune, and now he was dead in a car wreck. The subject stayed with John. On January 17, 1967, he settled down on his settee with the *Daily Mail* and read the following short item:

> There are 4,000 holes in the road in Blackburn, Lancashire, or one twenty-sixth of a hole per person, according to a council survey.

John started writing, combining the two items and adding a reference to his recent war movie. It was still not a complete song, so John took what he had to Paul. In what was undoubtedly the last time they would sit down and work on one song together, Paul produced his own unfinished song that he thought would fit with John's unfinished piece of the puzzle. Paul's portion was, he said, about his memories of "what it was like to run up the road to catch the bus to school, having a smoke and going into class. We decided, 'Bugger this. We're going to write a turn-on song.' " This would become "A Day in the Life."

In the studio, when they recorded a first go-round, the two sections were separated by a twenty-four-bar space, during which

Paul repeated the same note on the piano. To keep count Beatle assistant Mal Evans counted each bar. He also set an alarm clock to ring and both sounds are on the finished record. That space, though, was to be filled in later and they weren't sure with what. It was John who suggested what he later called "a musical orgasm." At the time, though, he told Paul and Martin that what he envisioned was "a tremendous buildup, from nothing up to something absolutely like the end of the world." John and Paul decided that nothing would do but a full symphony orchestra—all ninety members—and once all of them got there John and Paul would tell them what to do.

George Martin, who was not sharing in the Beatles' royalties and whom EMI was paying less than three thousand pounds a year, was not eager to put ninety more musicians on his sessions sheets, especially when the musicians would come in with no idea of what they would play. The last time he had brought in an orchestra—for Paul's "Hey Jude"—there was a small uprising when Paul asked the assembled virtuosi to sing and clap along on the song.

So for "A Day in the Life" Martin booked only half an orchestra: Forty-two players were due in on February 10. Martin, after huddling with John and "trying to get inside his mind, discover what pictures he wanted to paint," worked up a rough score for the orchestra. For the body of John's part of the song he would have cellos and violas echoing John's voice. Then the players were to start building their notes, sliding into what would be John's "musical orgasm."

For that, Martin wrote a basic score which would have each instrument, at the start of the twenty-four bars, begin at its lowest possible note. Then, over the course of the twenty-four, each player would ascend to the highest note possible. And they were to begin at *pianissimo* and build to *fortissimo*. Quiet to as loud as possible.

The night before the session Paul called George Martin and asked a small favor: He would like the forty-two musicians, as well as Martin, to attend in evening dress. Martin dared ask why. "We thought we'd have fun," Paul said. Martin asked what the group would wear. "Our usual freak-outs," Paul said.

On the big night it was almost like a formal opening. Abbey Road (the road) was jammed with cars and a bigger than usual complement of Apple Scruffs and curious onlookers. The Beatles were resplendent in their colorful silks and satins, with the matching mustaches they all had grown since the tour. They looked nothing at all like the aging mop-tops who had still been four trained bears on a tiny faraway stage, performing for the screaming masses in the stadiums.

Mick Jagger and Marianne Faithfull showed up to lend their sparkle. Members of The Fool, the psychedelic art troupe, were skipping among the orchestra members, handing them party favors and skinny cigarettes and other jolly things.

When George Martin came out of the control room, this is what he saw: The orchestra leader was wearing a fake red nose and floppy paper glasses and soloist Eric Gruenberg, formerly leader of the BBC Symphony Orchestra, was playing his violin with a huge gorilla's hand at the end of his left arm. The rest of the orchestra wore silly hats along with their evening clothes. It was a grand evening. At long last it seemed as if maybe the Beatles really could do anything they wanted to.

The rest of *Sgt. Pepper* was not as much fun. Mainly just a lot of work. Paul wrote and started laying down the track that would later be called "Sgt. Pepper's Lonely Hearts Club Band" on February 1. He was, he said, fascinated by the notion of the San Francisco bands that had been naming themselves Grateful Dead or Quicksilver Messenger Service. Suddenly, after a generation of Crickets and Hurricanes and Shadows and Beatles, there were groups with more creative names, such as the Jefferson Airplane and Moby Grape and the Electric Prunes and Lothar and the Hand People. Paul liked the idea of the Beatles stepping outside themselves and assuming another identity if they were not going to tour.

It was only after he decided that the album might work as being "by" Sgt. Pepper's Lonely Hearts Club Band that the notion of other songs filling in around that concept began to jell. Then he added Billy Shears, as Ringo, fading from the theme song into "With a Little Help from My Friends." From there it was a matter of bending songs to fit. As a literal storyboard, it did not seem to be a concept album. As it was, they recorded songs until they ran out of time and they didn't always have names for those songs yet. "With a Little Help from My Friends," for example, was referred to as "Bad Finger Boogie" when Paul, with help from John, knocked it out one afternoon in Paul's workroom on the top floor of his house on Cavendish Avenue. That was the group's rendezvous point, since it was so close to the Abbey Road Studios.

John's next contribution was a fast knockoff, inspired—as was almost everything he did then—by external stimuli. In this case, it was an old circus poster that he bought in a junk shop during the first week of February when the group went to Sevenoaks, Kent, to make a promotional film clip for "Strawberry Fields"/"Penny Lane." The poster read: PABLO FANQUE'S CIRCUS ROYAL, TOWN MEADOWS, ROCKDALE. GRANDEST NIGHT OF THE SEASON! AND POSITIVELY THE LAST NIGHT BUT THREE! BEING FOR THE BENEFIT OF MR. KITE, (LATE OF WELLS'S CIRCUS) AND MR. J. HENDERSON, THE CELEBRATED SOMERSET THROWER! WIRE DANCER, VAULTER, RIDER, ETC. ON TUESDAY EVENING, FEBRUARY 14TH, 1843. At the time John dismissed the song as a "throwaway." Years later he would come to regard it as "cosmically beautiful."

In the studio he ran through it and then told Martin that he wanted the music to "swirl up and around." He wanted a circus feel so genuine that the listener could smell the sawdust and taste the peanuts. First Martin recorded himself and John playing chromatic runs on Hammond and Wurlitzer organs, with roadie Mal Evans playing his huge bass harmonica. It still wasn't circusy enough, so Martin decided to resort to some tape trickery. On the song "Tomorrow Never Knows" on the *Revolver* album John and Paul had worked with tape loops, especially after Paul realized the "sound-saturation" effects that could be gotten by removing the erase head on his Grundig recorder. For that session John had wanted his voice to sound like the Dalai Lama coming up out of the center of the earth. That song, written by John, was also very much an LSD song, both in music and lyrics. John was talking about surrendering the ego even then and that had been recorded in April 1966.

Martin himself had worked with tape bits before when he had been producing the likes of the Goons, so for "Being for the Benefit of Mr. Kite," he turned to tape once again. He recorded snippets from a number of old records of steam calliopes and old county fair organs and so on. Then he took the various tapes, cut them up at random, and took about sixty pieces, some as long as a foot, and threw them up into the air in the studio. Then he told his engineer to pick them up and splice them together. That was what became the background of "Mr. Kite," with the organs and bass harmonica over that sound.

John's next song was another fast knockoff and, again, he was reacting to whatever stimuli were coming in. He was, as usual, home in the "stockbroker belt" and watching TV. A Kellogg's Corn Flakes commercial came on and its incessant repetition of the phrase "Good morning" led to the song of the same title. Instead of fading the song, John and Paul and George Martin decided to cover the fade with a barnyard orchestra: a regular hodge-podge of everything from hounds on the chase to chickens clucking. They had already worked out a basic song order for the album and "Good Morning" was to lead into a reprise of "Sgt. Pepper's Lonely Hearts Club Band." Martin discovered that he was very lucky when he found a chicken clucking at the end of "Good Morning, Good Morning" that melded perfectly into the first guitar-scratching notes of "Sgt. Pepper."

"Fixing a Hole" was very unusual in that this time Paul was being introspective. John loved it for that reason. He was always trying to pull Paul out of himself, which very seldom happened. Not that the words were all that deep, but it was Paul attempting to deal with himself. It was inspired, Paul said, by the fans who were always outside his Cavendish Avenue home, night and day. "Sometimes I invite them in, but it starts not to really be the point because I invited one in and the next day she was in the *Daily Mirror* with her mother saying we were going to get married."

Paul's "Lovely Rita" was, as John said later, Paul writing another pop song. It was occasioned by a traffic ticket that Paul got in early 1967 in St. John's Wood. The woman traffic warden who wrote the ticket later recalled that Paul came up just after she had slipped the ticket under his windshield wiper. He studied the ticket and asked her, "Is your name really Meta?" Mrs. Meta Davies, in her spiffy black meter maid uniform, told him it certainly was. He studied the ticket some more and said, "That would be a good idea for a song. Do you mind if I use it?" Paul later said that what he remembered about the song was that he had heard that in America female traffic wardens were called meter maids and that he built the song around the words "meter maid." No matter. When Mrs. Davies retired on September 4, 1985, she got to go on the BBC and ITV to tell her story, even going on to say that she ran into Paul several years after the ticket incident. They met in a veterinarian's reception room in St. John's Wood. She said, "We chatted about animals and he didn't recognize me out of uniform and I didn't tell him who I was."

"Getting Better" was another Paul pop song. It sprang from an expression Jimmy Nicol once used. Nicol, now one of rock's footnotes, filled in for Ringo when he was too ill to play part of the 1964 tour. Nicol's stock reply to being asked how it felt to be a temporary Beatle: "It's getting better."

Paul's "She's Leaving Home" came courtesy of a news story that he read in the *Daily Mirror* about a teenage runaway and about the enormous gap between generations and the feelings of mistrust and betrayal engendered by all that. The recording of the song itself caused a division between Paul and George Martin that took years to heal. Martin, after all, had other performers he had to tend to at EMI. The Beatles tended to be all-consuming and assumed that other people were there to serve them.

So when Paul finished writing "She's Leaving Home," he was ready to record it. He called Martin and told him he needed him tomorrow at the earliest; it was time to score and record the song. Martin begged off, saying he was booked with Cilla Black the next day. Paul insisted. Martin demurred. Nothing more was said between the two.

A day later Paul showed up at Abbey Road with a finished score and told Martin, "We can record it now."

Martin was stung to the quick. He learned that Paul had gotten Neil Aspinall to call around and find someone else to score the song immediately. Martin felt deeply hurt and betrayed. "I thought: Paul, you could have waited. . . . It was the only score that was ever done by anyone else during all my time with the Beatles." Martin had yet to learn one thing: The Beatles, meaning John and Paul, were very, very sensitive about anyone else at all— apart from Ringo and George, who were Beatles too—laying claim to being close to, or central to, or essential to the Beatles. The Beatles were the world's most exclusive boys' club since Cain and Abel. And they were proud of it, as Paul and John said with considerable venom more than once. No one else was a

Beatle: not Brian Epstein, not Neil Aspinall, not Mal Evans, not George Martin, not Yoko Ono. Only the Beatles were the Beatles. Anyone else who dared get too close: Beware!

Martin swallowed his hurt and disappointment, saying nothing, and got on with *Sgt. Pepper.* For twelve years the resentment simmered and then Martin finally spilled his emotions in his book *All You Need Is Ears.* Paul read the book and said he had felt hurt at the time at being ignored by Martin, so he spurned him. You walked around Studio 2 at Abbey Road on eggshells in those days, brother. You trod very delicately, indeed. One night when the young Pink Floyd was recording next door in Studio 3, they very much wanted to come in and say hello to the Legends. They were put off for the longest time and finally got a brief audience. When they came away no one was sure just who had met whom. Not that Pink Floyd was ignorant of acid themselves.

The only non-Lennon–McCartney song on the album was George Harrison's "Within You, Without You." It was a logical outgrowth of his interest in Indian music and culture. After the 1966 tour, George and his girlfriend Patti Boyd flew to Bombay, where they registered at the Taj Mahal Hotel as Mr. and Mrs. Sam Wells. George was studying the sitar with Ravi Shankar, as well as yoga. He wrote "Within You" one night after dinner at the home of Klaus Voorman, their old friend from Hamburg, who had moved to Hampstead, London, and joined the Manfred Mann band. Voorman had a pedal harmonium, which George had never seen, and he wrote the song on that. George later wrote that the song "was written after I had got into meditation. We had entered into the 'All You Need Is Love' consciousness after the LSD period."

As George Martin later tactfully observed, George Harrison's "rather dreary" song fit the album just about as well as all the other songs did. At the time John and Paul were not paying a lot of attention to George and didn't yet appreciate the songwriting he was capable of. Once it was recorded, though (with George playing tamboura, Neil Aspinall filling in on tamboura, some Indian musician friends of George's on dilruba, tamboura, tabla, and sword mandel, and session players on cello and violin), it was all of a piece with what *Sgt. Pepper* seemed to be all about. Which, loosely spelled out was: Anything can be anything. What the record would stand for in the eyes and ears of the millions who devoured it was a slightly cockeyed blend of fatalism and ancient wisdom and acid flashes. What the record mainly meant is that this is what happens to two intuitively smart ambitious singers and songwriters from lower-middle-class Liverpool origins who scuffle to make a few bucks in rock 'n' roll and suddenly are acclaimed geniuses before they're even twenty-five. In 1964 a crowd of three hundred thousand people filled the streets of Adelaide, Australia, just in hopes of catching a glimpse of the Fab Four.

From that kind of worldwide craziness that went on for three years, they tried to set themselves right by then dropping ass-over-teakettle into a drug that can literally deprogram the human mind. It was fortunate that they came out of it as well as they did. Especially given their own personal situations, their business situations, and the advisers they had to call on, such as they were. The fact that John and Paul could not only hold their own musically against the best that there was in rock 'n' roll, but could stretch the limits and boundaries of the music and chart new ground is breathtaking.

The climactic close to the *Sgt. Pepper* album was dubbed on to follow the freak-out by the orchestra members. For this John and Paul and George Martin decided to produce an eternal chord. To try to capture that, the four Beatles and Martin shared two upright pianos and one grand piano in the studio. Engineer Geoff Emerick in the control room waited. On the count of three, all hands in the studio hit bunched chords on the pianos. As the sound started to fade, Emerick started to turn up the faders (volume controllers) slowly from zero all the way up to maximum. It took forty-five seconds for all the sound to fade and they repeated it four times, building chord upon chord. And as those chords faded away, the faders captured every little sound until they were recording the hum of the air conditioners in the studio.

So that was that. Except for the run-out groove on the record album, which heretofore had been vacant, merely serving as a signal to automatic record changers to change the record. Paul decided to put a little secret message on those grooves, just as a joke. So the Beatles went back in the studio and—from what Martin heard from the control room—chanted some unintelligible sounds. He took some of that tape and cut it up and added it to the run-out groove. For years Beatle fanatics claimed there was a message there, but it was backward. The Beatles denied it. Finally one day, after some fans had come to his door claiming to know the true message, Paul got tired of hearing about it and just decided to set the matter straight forever. Paul put his copy of *Sgt. Pepper* on his turntable and by hand ran it backward. As he said, it was there, "sure as anything, plain as anything. 'We'll fuck you like Supermen.' I thought, Jesus, what can you do?"

As one last good-bye to the record itself, Paul told George Martin that he wanted a message to dogs put on at the very end of the run-out groove. So, Martin added a brief signal at twenty-thousand hertz, which only dogs can hear. The ultimate order of songs on the album was left to Martin with, he said, appropriate suggestions from appropriate parties. It was not that hard to figure out, though, when you considered the finished songs. " 'Sgt. Pepper' obviously had to start and 'A Little Help from My Friends' had to follow on. 'A Day in the Life' had to finish. Nothing could follow that."

Some of the others, he said, were wild tracks, alien tracks. "Within You" was placed at the beginning of side two because there was no place else it would fit. "When I'm Sixty-Four" was dropped in where there was a vacancy. Martin also, in a revolutionary move for pop or rock music, eliminated the usual bands of silence between tracks, so that the songs would segue into each other. "I did it in order to make the songs more coherent. I wanted the album to be more of a unit."

The real miracle of the album is that it was all recorded on four-track tape, which now seems unimaginable, given the effects that were achieved. The technological explanation for that is very involved and boring and even the Beatles bypassed the convoluted explanations, asking instead what could be done with four-track machines, rather than what could not be done. What it comes down to is that the Beatles were going to do what they set out to do, regardless of any mechanical limitations. They didn't think in terms of limitations or ceilings.

The run-out message on the inner groove was originally described by Paul as a mantra, which would give you "a pure buzz after a while because it's so boring it ceases to mean anything." Paul's pal Miles said that he was there when they did it and it "lasts for 1.2 seconds or something and supposedly had a secret message. That took a whole evening to do. It was just a random clip taken from twenty minutes of tape that they recorded standing around a microphone all completely stoned."

For the record jacket, for the actual packaging itself, John and Paul had decided to take total control, which was unheard of for any group of "boys." Usually, a record jacket was whatever the record company wanted to throw together as cheaply as possible. The Beatles had always tried to do what they could to control their own images, though, and for *Revolver* they had gotten Klaus Voorman to do an illustration and collage. Now they wanted something that would match the music that the package would contain. Something that would blow your mind.

The first thing that Paul had wanted was something he called a "little magical presentation." First, he wanted a foldout cover, like Zappa's *Freak Out*. He also wanted, for the first time ever on a record, all the lyrics printed out on the back cover. That was great, revolutionary. But then Paul, with his natural governor a little bit skewed, went beyond what was good and wanted wretched excess. He proposed including a bag of cheap knick-knacks and geegaws, rather more like what you find in a box of Cracker Jacks. Someone, probably Blake, vetoed that and allowed instead a sheet of cardboard cutout items. One record reviewer later earnestly suggested that listeners try chewing on the cutout mustache to see what might transpire.

The original cover drawing was by Simon Posthuma and Marijke Koger of the Dutch art group The Fool, who would later that year drape a similar psychedelic mural across the façade of the Apple Boutique on Baker Street. Artist and gallery owner Robert Fraser, who had become an adviser to the Beatles in such matters, overruled The Fool's cover.

Fraser suggested that the Beatles turn to Peter Blake, the pop artist with the hippest credentials in England. John and Paul sat down with Blake and Fraser and described to them how they thought the album would turn out. They all decided that some kind of presentation of an actual Sgt. Pepper's Lonely Hearts Club Band was in order. Along with some way to suggest or present the audience. From that, the four of them decided on an actual life-sized collage of people and things. They started writing down lists of famous people they would like to be there.

When Brian heard about all this foolishness, he said he wanted it stopped and that the *Sgt. Pepper* album should be released in a plain brown wrapper. He was duly ignored. EMI wanted a twenty-million-pound indemnity from the Beatles against being sued by all these famous people if releases couldn't be gotten from all of them. They got it.

Paul said he would like to see Stockhausen and William Burroughs on the cover. John said he would like to see Jesus, Gandhi, Poe, Lewis Carroll, Wilde, and Hitler. Blake and Fraser were given a quota of their own and they contributed a number of people. When George Harrison was later asked about his preferences, he suggested Indian gurus. Ringo said he would go along with the others. Over the weeks when the Beatles were finishing the album itself, Blake and Fraser worked on pulling together a living collage of Beatle people. Some of them were life-sized, hand-tinted photographs, cut out and glued on to boards. Some figures would be life-sized waxworks. Boxer Sonny Liston's head was delivered from Madame Tussaud's. Diana Dors was 3-D and all wax, as were the four mop-tops, the old Beatles. The new Beatles themselves had ordered tailor-made silk Sgt. Pepper outfits from Douglas Hayward Tailors.

As the cover concept came together, the Beatles tried to ignore mounting criticism. EMI was stupefied, trying to figure out what the boys were up to now. Once they had it ciphered, the heavy hand came down. "Famous people cannot be haphazardly strewn about a record sleeve," said EMI. The Beatles ignored that, to the point that Sir Joseph Lockwood, EMI's chairman, went to Paul's Cavendish Avenue home to instruct him to withdraw Gandhi. "We can't offend the Indians," he said. EMI had a large presence in India, so Gandhi went. Paul offered to trade Sir Joe two Marlon Brandos for one Gandhi. Paul promised Sir Joe that there would be no lawsuits, a very LSD thing to do. "There is no risk whatsoever," Paul assured him. Sir Joseph insisted on written approvals and the Beatles actually got a few. Mae West first refused, saying, "What would I be doing in a Lonely Hearts Club Band?" All four "boys" wrote her letters and she gave in. Elvis did not, although it's probable he never knew about the request, given Colonel Tom Parker's strict guardianship of "the boy." Only Leo Gorcey, from the long-forgotten Bowery Boys, asked to be paid. He was booted off.

Hey, this was still rock 'n' roll after all, in the control of some headstrong young men not so long removed from steamy Hamburg adolescence. They would do whatever they could get away with.

Brando stayed. Hitler went quickly, as did Jesus. But EMI surprisingly caved in and the Beatles had no releases from most of those people (or their estates) who were pictured. All of these cutouts and waxworks were painstakingly assembled in the Chelsea studio of photographer Michael Cooper. Those included in the collage, apart from gurus, were Aleister Crowley, Mae West, Lenny Bruce, Karlheinz Stockhausen, W. C. Fields, Carl Jung, Edgar Allan Poe, Fred Astaire, Richard Merkin (an artist), Binnie Barnes (an actress), Huntz Hall (of the Bowery Boys), Simon Rodia (sculptor and creator of the Watts Towers), Bob Dylan, Aubrey Beardsley, Sir Robert Peel (founder of the British police force), Aldous Huxley, Dylan Thomas, Terry Southern, Dion, Tony Curtis, Wallace Berman (an artist), Tommy Handley, Marilyn Monroe, William Burroughs, Stan Laurel, Richard Lindner (an artist), Oliver Hardy, Karl Marx, H. G. Wells, Stuart Sutcliffe, Julie Adams, Max Miller, the Petty Girl, Marlon Brando, Tom Mix, Oscar Wilde, Tyrone Power, Larry Bell, Dr. David Livingstone, Johnny Weissmuller, Stephen Crane, George Bernard Shaw, Albert Stubbins, Albert Einstein, Lewis Carroll, Sonny Liston, Marlene Dietrich, Diana Dors, Shirley Temple, Bobby Breen, and Lawrence of Arabia. (The guy holding his hand above Paul's head and thus supposedly signaling that Paul is dead is comedian Issy Bonn.)

Everyone assembled at Cooper's studio on Flood Street the afternoon of March 30 for the group picture. The flowers that filled in the little trough in front and spelled out BEATLES came from Clifton Nurseries in Camden Town and for years thereafter hippies earnestly told the story about how there were real honest-to-ganja marijuana plants on the cover of *Sgt. Pepper*. Unfortunately for the wistful storytellers, there were no marijuana plants. (The picture of the four Beatles on the back of the album was taken later, after Paul had left for the United States to visit Jane Asher. Beatle roadie Mal Evans is the stand-in for Paul, with his back to the camera.)

Some of the Beatles had also brought along some favorite personal items to pose with or to maybe put somewhere in the picture. On the ground in front of the Beatles you can see John's portable TV (his most prized possession at the time) and a hookah (water pipe) from Paul's house.

Once *Sgt. Pepper* was safely in the can, Paul flew to America to see Jane. She was on a three-month tour with the Old Vic and Paul had promised that he would join her for her twenty-first birthday on April 5. Paul and Jane were not yet officially engaged—that would come on Christmas Day when Paul proposed and presented her with a diamond and emerald engagement ring. Jane was never entirely comfortable with the role of Beatle girlfriend. It was no secret that Paul—like all the Beatles a traditionally macho Northerner—wanted a subservient wife and a traditional marriage, with wife and kids at home. But Jane's career was increasingly important to her.

Beatle women, though, had to know their place, which was basically two steps behind, bowing and scraping. Jane had told Cynthia Lennon that Paul wanted an old-fashioned wife and that she wanted a new-fashioned career and so, reaching a stalemate, they just continued on with things the way they were. Jane had seen what had happened to Cynthia, who became a virtual cipher in John's shadow. And she saw the changes that befell the glamorous model and aspiring actress Patti Boyd, who had married George Harrison in a very secret ceremony in January 1966, with Paul as witness. George forbade Patti from continuing her career because he was sure it would somehow exploit the Beatle connection. And the two of them went through some spectacular battling before she finally divorced George and married his best friend, Eric Clapton. There's a famous tale of her scaling the battlements at George's Friar Park mansion, hauling down his OM pennant—representing the wisdom of the East—and raising in its place a pirate flag with its skull and crossbones. Ringo had married Maureen Cox, his sweetheart from the Cavern days in Liverpool, when she had become pregnant and she mostly stayed home with baby Zak.

In the United States Paul had Frank Sinatra's private Learjet at his disposal, thanks to some phone calls Brian had made for him. Paul flew first to San Francisco, where he went to the Haight-Ashbury and met the Grateful Dead and Grace Slick and the Jefferson Airplane. It was Paul's first direct contact with American hippiedom and he later recalled that his initial reaction to seeing the Haight was saying to himself, "I can't see this lasting because the media are going to get here and pretty soon it will turn into Rip-off Street." It actually already was. By the time George Harrison finally visited the Haight in August, he was horrified by what he saw.

From San Francisco Paul flew on to Denver and Jane. He saw her in *Romeo and Juliet,* stayed on another day, and then took the Learjet to Los Angeles. He spent some time with the Beach Boys, whose 1966 album *Pet Sounds* he had so much admired. Paul and Brian Wilson got on well and Paul ended up producing a song, "Vegetables," for the Beach Boys before he left. Paul and Brian and former Beatles publicist Derek Taylor went on to meet John and Michelle Phillips of the Mamas and the Papas in Jeanette MacDonald's old mansion, where they smoked ganja and sang far into the night. While he was in California, Paul, as an official emissary from the London chapter of the countercultural revolution, was named to the board of directors of the upcoming Monterey Pop Festival. He told the other directors that the first thing they should do was to book Jimi Hendrix, who was still relatively unknown in his native United States but was setting the clubs on fire in London. While Paul was in California, John, back in London, was having his Rolls-Royce painted in psychedelic designs and colors. He was amazed to discover the public reactions to it. People were pretty much divided along class lines, he found. Those who could not afford a Rolls were delighted and amused by it; those who could afford a Rolls were furious at the desecration of a symbol. "Mission accomplished," John said later, laughing.

Paul came up with his idea for the next Beatle project during the long flight back to London. He later said that he had started doodling on his menu there in the first-class section. Drawing clowns and other circus figures, he eventually came up with the concept of a Magical Mystery Tour, a fanciful trip to nowhere. Just getting on a bus and heading out to see what adventures could be found. Part of the idea came from California, from Ken Kesey and his Merry Pranksters, whose psychedelic bus trips had been fueled by LSD and Beatle music. But more than that, Paul—an incurable romantic—was thinking back to childhood reveries in England. Even though he had never taken one, he had heard about the mystery tours, little bus trips from the coastal resort towns. You bought a ticket but didn't know your destination until you got there.

The *Magical Mystery Tour* would, of course be both a movie and an album. A movie made by the Beatles themselves. They no longer needed any outside direction, they knew that. Besides, the Beatles had begun to hear disquieting rumors that Brian had funneled their money made from the movie *Help!* into a corporation in the Bahamas. And that the money apparently went down a sinkhole. As soon as Paul got back to England, he recorded the title track, mostly making up the words as he went along.

Just after Paul returned to London, a new company called Beatles & Co. was formed on April 19. Their original company, Beatles, Ltd., gave the new company eight hundred thousand pounds for a share of it. Thus the Beatles were apparently able to pay themselves two hundred thousand pounds each, just for reorganizing themselves. The only one of the Beatles who has ever commented on that deal, John, said that he didn't remember signing it. According to some accounts, Brian was very ill during this time. Peter Brown, for one, said he told Paul on his return from California that he would be unable to see Brian because he was in a private clinic. Although Paul returned on April 11 and Brian didn't enter the clinic, according to Brown, until May 13.

That deal is probably the point at which the Beatles' finances and business affairs started to spin so dizzily out of control that they are still a puzzle to this day. No one understands the tangled web of Beatle monies—least of all the Beatles themselves. Not even the battalions of lawyers who have been earning a nice living off the Beatles' misfortunes for the past two decades.

Brian got out of his clinic, the Priory, on May 19. While he was there he had still been conducting negotiations with an Australian show business tycoon named Robert Stigwood who wanted to buy NEMS. The Beatles didn't know about that.

From his clinic bed Brian had planned a press party for the *Sgt. Pepper* album, to be held at his town house on Chapel Street on May 19. Peter Brown organized it for Brian. The party was of course the most prestigious event in London and members of the press jockeyed furiously for invitations. One call that Peter Brown got was from a free-lance photographer named Linda Eastman.

Brown vaguely knew her credentials. Her father was Lee Eastman, a prominent New York entertainment lawyer, who had
changed his name from Epstein to Eastman after graduating
from Harvard. Linda grew up in the best New York circles and
was graduated from Scarsdale High School, where her yearbook
entry for her senior year noted that she belonged to Advertising
Club 4, Chorus 1, 2, 3, 4, and Pep Club 3, 4. She was described
as "Strawberry Blonde" . . . Yen for men . . . Shetlandish."
After high school she briefly attended Sarah Lawrence College
(not at the same time as Yoko Ono, who went there for three
years). Her mother was killed in a plane crash when Linda was
eighteen and they had been very close. Linda married, moved to
Colorado, and had a daughter named Heather. After her marriage broke up she moved with Heather to Arizona, where she
met a wheelchair-bound photographer named Hazel Archer. They
became fast friends and Archer encouraged her to try photography.

After she moved back to her father Lee and brother John in
New York, Linda worked as a receptionist at *Town and Country*
magazine, where she one day intercepted an invitation for a
Rolling Stones press party on a yacht. She got her camera and
took herself on board. The pictures she took that day of the
Stones showed that she had a tendency to use a camera angle that
was between her subject's legs and aimed upward. She was the
only photographer on the boat that day and was able to sell her
pictures and start branching out. She enjoyed photographing and
being around musicians and soon was a regular at the Fillmore
East. She had flown to London in May and was with ex-Animal
Chas Chandler at the Bag O'Nails one night when Peter Brown
was there with Paul. They all met and Linda and Paul went on to
the Speakeasy together. The next day Linda was on the phone to
Brown and brought him pictures of the Stones as a gift. She got
her invitation to the exclusive *Sgt. Pepper* party. And she made
sure that Paul knew who she was.

At the *Sgt. Pepper* party itself, the new look the Beatles were
sporting got almost as much attention as did the music. *Melody
Maker* reported:

> Lennon won the sartorial stakes with a green flower-patterned
> shirt, red cord trousers, yellow socks, and what looked like
> cord shoes. His ensemble was completed by a sporran. With

his bushy sideboards and National Health specs he resembled an animated Victorian watchmaker. Paul McCartney, sans mustache, wore a loosely tied scarf over a shirt, a striped double-breasted jacket, and looked like someone out of a Scott Fitzgerald novel.

When *Sgt. Pepper* came out on May 26—the United Kingdom release date of June 1 was rushed five days because of the incredible press of orders—the Beatles might as well have all died and gone to heaven. They were finally canonized by virtually everyone: straight press, underground press, rock press, shorthairs, longhairs, *Time, Newsweek*. The album on which the Beatles had spent the then-record sum of twenty-five thousand pounds instantly changed the face and the future of rock. It established the album, rather than the single or even the song, as the medium through which rock bands delivered their messages. Rock finally became more than respectable, it became adult. The old notion that kids somehow graduated from rock just like they did from high school and college was thrown out. Rock could go beyond the puppy love or comic book stage.

Sgt. Pepper also established the recording studio as the new church of rock 'n' roll and made the record producer its new priest. Thanks to George Martin, there soon emerged a superrace of studio wizards who became millionaires. Before Martin, with very few exceptions, rock producers did not even get their names on the album jackets.

Album jacket design was revolutionized by the Beatles. Groups started spending as much on elaborate jackets as on what went inside them.

The underlying and immediate message of *Sgt. Pepper,* though, was that it verified and validated and celebrated the notion of a counterculture, of an alternative way of life, of thinking, of living. It was much more than a commercial for drugs—if it indeed was that. The subculture that it invested with affirmation turned out to be much more fragile and vulnerable than people thought at the time, but so did the Beatles.

As soon as the BBC banned "A Day in the Life" because it was deemed to be encouraging drug use, the Beatles should have thanked them. Nothing is better for a fledgling rebel or outlaw culture than a banned song.

Of course, as people were to learn, it's difficult to rebel against an Establishment that is rushing to co-opt you. In America alone, advance orders for the album totaled more than one million and it sold two and a half million copies in the United States in the next three months. The more liberal fringes of the adult world embraced *Sgt. Pepper* with an ardor that was almost frightening. Where once the *Times* of London praised the Beatles for their use of "Aeolian modes" (which the Beatles had never heard of), now the pointy-heads of the press likened the Beatles to T. S. Eliot, Schubert, Mozart, Harold Pinter. The word *glissando* was used a lot. The *Times Literary Supplement* said the Beatles were a "barometer of our times." *Time* magazine allowed that the Beatles' music was now "post-rock" and as such was a genuine art form. "Messengers from beyond rock 'n' roll," *Time* called them.

Paul said that the most gratifying thing to him came when he went to see Jimi Hendrix perform at the Savile Theatre only a couple of days after the album's release and saw Hendrix already doing a mind-bending version of "Sgt. Pepper." Paul was proud of that.

The effect on musicians everywhere was staggering. As one example, when Brian Wilson of the Beach Boys heard *Sgt. Pepper* for the first time, he stopped working on his "masterpiece" album, *Smile,* because he felt the Beatles had already done it all. As another example, the Rolling Stones, who were friends with the Beatles but whom John and Paul looked down on because they felt the Stones were copying them, recorded and released *Their Satanic Majesties Request.* It had a 3-D cover by Michael Cooper and it was basically their attempt at their idea of psychedelia and it didn't work.

Interestingly, the Stones had recently become the first famous rock drug casualties, when they had been busted on February 12 in a huge police raid on Keith Richards's house, Redlands, in Sussex. Keith and Mick Jagger, along with Robert Fraser, were arrested. The invading police were surprised to find Marianne Faithfull wearing nothing but a smile and a bearskin rug. George Harrison had just left the house. Many years later, in recalling that night, George said, "I was at that party and the funny thing about it was that they said in the newspapers later: 'Another internationally famous pop star and his wife escaped moments before the net closed in.' I left there about 7 A.M., so it showed me they were waiting until I had gone because they were still climbing the ladder, working their way up. They didn't want to get to the Fabs yet." George was correct in his assumption that the police did not yet want to bust a Beatle. The Beatles, with their MBEs and their international stature, were seen as a national treasure. They certainly felt and acted as if they were immune. Their use of drugs was hardly a secret. Even Sir Joseph Lockwood of EMI admitted that he "knew there was some possible connection with cannabis in the studios—'smells' were noted—but I never pursued it."

Beatles and drugs first became an issue after Paul's little slip of the tongue. In an interview with *Queen Magazine,* Paul said that he had indeed flirted around with the devil drug, LSD, had succumbed to it, and was glad that he had done so. The quotes were picked up in the United States in a *Life* magazine cover story on June 16 and the acid certainly hit the fan there. It was like John's Jesus scandal all over again. Vice President Spiro Agnew was after Paul and the Reverend Billy Graham announced that he was praying for Paul's eternal soul. Paul had defended the use of LSD, saying, "It opened my eyes. It made me a better, more honest, more tolerant member of society."

Welcome to the Summer of Love.

On Paul's twenty-fifth birthday, June 18, 1967, he opened his electronic gates to find two warring camps. On the one side was about three dozen teenage girls who were bringing birthday presents for their beloved Paul. On the other were television crews, whirring and buzzing with hostility, demanding to know more about this dope business. Paul was glad to see the girls. The TV crews wouldn't back down, though. They asked him how many times he had taken LSD. "Er, four times." They wanted to know where he got it. He wouldn't answer that one. Shouldn't he have kept his drug use private?

"Well," he answered slowly, "the thing is, you know, that I was asked a question by a newspaper and the decision was whether to tell a lie or to tell the truth, you know. I decided to tell him the truth, but I didn't really want to say anything because if I'd had my way I wouldn't have told anyone because I'm not trying to spread the word about this, but the man from the newspaper is the man from the mass medium. I'll keep it a personal thing if he does too, you know, if he keeps it quiet. But he wanted to spread it so it's his responsibility for spreading it. Not mine."

"But, Paul," they said, "you as a public figure should know that you will be quoted."

"Yes, but to say it, you know, is only to tell the truth. I'm telling the truth. I don't know what everyone is so angry about."

"Hmm. Do you think you are encouraging drug use?"

"I don't think it will make any difference, you know. I don't think my fans are going to take drugs just because I did. But the thing is that's not the point anyway. I was asked whether I had or not and from then on the whole bit about how far it's going to encourage is up to the newspapers and up to you, you know, on television. I mean you're spreading this now at this moment. This is going into all the homes in Britain and I'd rather it didn't, you know. But you're asking me the question and if you want me to be honest, I'll be honest."

"As a public figure, aren't you responsible?"

"No, it's you who've got the responsibility not to spread this now. You know I'm quite prepared to keep it as a very personal thing if you will too. If you'll shut up about it, I will."

That wasn't the end of it, though. Brian Epstein said then that "Paul rang me to say he had told the press he had taken LSD. I was very worried. I came up to London knowing I was going to be asked to comment on Paul's decision. I finally decided that I would admit I had taken LSD as well." Then John and George 'fessed up, too. And the old Mother Goose nursery school vision of the squeaky clean mop-tops was finally erased.

Apple
10

ON the day that the Beatles were at last rendered merely mortal, by virtue of one of them finally being busted for drugs (and, of course, it was John), Paul was in conference with some representatives of the J. Walter Thompson Agency. It was October 18, 1968, and Paul had been worrying about ways to promote the release, scheduled for November 22, of *The Beatles* album, better known as the *White Album*. Paul was of a mind that the company needed a new way to promote the product. They couldn't just rely on the same old hippies and the like to buy Beatles albums because the saturation level was far too low. Paul had heard a figure from within Apple—certainly a sober-sided and dependable source—that only one person out of a hundred bought Beatles records. And he reasoned that a formidable advertising machine such as JWT would know how to up that ante.

In meeting with JWT's earnest reps on two separate occasions, Paul and his entourage of five sat and listened to many proposals. JWT variously proposed: "Helicopters and low-flying aircraft over major urban areas"; "Sandwich girls. Girls in miniskirts with sandwich boards parading up and down the main shopping streets in certain large cities . . . We could get 150 girls at three pounds ten each"; "Double-decker buses [London variety] painted white with THE BEATLES BUS on the side and photographic portraits of the Beatles plus such people as Mao Tse Tung, de

Gaulle, etc., at each window. We would suggest having six of these driving around the major urban areas. You could perhaps resell them. 100 pounds per bus for six"; "Boats displaying banners parading up and down rivers running through main towns. This we rejected because not enough people would see them and they would not generate such tremendous interest as the buses would"; "Special train, rejected for same reasons." Paul said, "Hmm." One of JWT's finest said that if Paul didn't like the buses they had an idea for Paul to do a ninety-second TV commercial reading a fictitious pop critic's review of the album. Paul asked what it would cost. "Fifty-six thousand pounds." Audible gasp from Paul.

Meanwhile at 34 Montague Square, Ringo's old flat that was now a refuge for John and Yoko, the hounded lovers and adulterers, trouble was afoot. Yoko had not endeared herself to the others. First, by pretending that she had never heard of the Beatles before meeting John at her exhibition. Second, by treating the others very coldly. Third, by demanding all of John's attention and time. Fourth, by moving herself and even a cot into the Abbey Road Studios during the recording of the *White Album,* thus inhibiting that old gang. Fifth, the others began to hear whispers that John was now dabbling with the Big H: heroin.

But the biggest problem on October 18 was that John had gotten a phone call from a friend in the police drug squad, tipping him off that a raid was imminent. John's old friend Pete Shotton arrived to find John furiously vacuuming the living room. John asked him to stay and help sanitize the place, "since fucking Jimi Hendrix used to live here, Christ knows what the fuck is in these carpets!" They started searching, looking for dope that maybe even John had forgotten about. As Shotton rummaged through the living room, John went back in the bedroom, "in which Yoko had apparently locked herself the instant she'd heard me arrive." Shotton continued to turn the living room over and he couldn't help but hear shouts from the bedroom.

"I don't want him here!" Shotton said he heard Yoko scream. "Well, I fucking want him here!" John yelled. They continued arguing until Shotton volunteered to leave, taking with him the vacuum bag of lint and presumed evidence.

The police were there shortly and John and Yoko were hauled away. The police found 219 grains of cannabis resin in a film canister that John swore he had never seen before.

As the news reached Apple, Paul left his JWT conference and phoned Sir Joseph Lockwood of EMI to see if he could intercede somehow on John's behalf. Lockwood, for whatever reason, advised John to plead guilty and to later depend on EMI's lawyers. John himself said that he agreed to a guilty plea since it would spare Yoko, who was pregnant (a fact that was not public knowledge), the spectacle of a court trial. This was the bust that would chase John forever, the drug conviction that would later lead Attorney General John Mitchell and the full force of the Nixon administration on a vengeful quest to have John deported from the United States.

There are undercurrents to John's case in the United States that may never be revealed. There were pressures brought to bear from quarters unknown, unrequested information supplied to the government, tips coming in. John had apparently made more enemies than he had thought. Additionally, the Paul–John split had seriously rendered apart the Beatles' unofficial family: People all felt they had to choose sides and some of those on either side had considerable political clout, both in New York and London.

Five days before John's case was heard on November 27, Yoko miscarried. The child was buried as John Ono Lennon II.

After John's bust it was open season on Beatles. Fair-haired children no more.

Paul rejected J. Walter Thompson's proposed advertising campaign for the *White Album.*

Paul and John wrote their last song together in June 1967, when they were invited to be Britain's contribution to a worldwide satellite feed of the program "Our World." Paul and John wrote "All You Need Is Love" and sang it to the world from Abbey Road on the twenty-fifth, with such supporting friends as Mick Jagger, Marianne Faithfull, Keith Richards, Eric Clapton, and Keith Moon. Paul stayed up all night the night before, designing a shirt. "I had these pen things that you used to draw with and the ink didn't wash out. I stayed up all night doing it and the shirt was nicked the next day."

The *Times* "legalize-it" ad that Paul had paid for ran on July 24, while all of the Beatles were in Greece, looking to buy an island where they could found a little utopia. They had first gotten the idea from their newly found friend Magic Alex. Alexis Mardas was a young Greek who claimed to be a brilliant inventor and would soon have the Beatles bankrolling his various schemes. John, who was an automatic sucker for any little bright-colored gadget with bells and whistles on it, succumbed immediately to his spiel. Soon even Paul was going in to Abbey Road and lecturing George Martin about the terrific technological advances that Magic Alex was soon going to bring about. Such as an invisible "sonic screen" to replace the sound baffles they had to place around Ringo and his drums in the studio. And telephones that didn't need dialing. You had only to say, "Get me George Martin," and lo and behold it would.

Since Magic Alex said his father was a highly placed government official in Greece, he had managed to persuade John and Paul that they could establish a little Greek paradise and then pull up the drawbridge after them. Paul and John had both tried to persuade Brian to get the British government to relax the stringent laws regulating money flow out of the country. Paul said he wanted to go "somewhere no one can get at us." John said, "It will be amazing. We'll be able to just lie in the sun." It was some indication of the power the Beatles actually possessed that they were able to get a special tax dispensation from Chancellor of the Exchequer James Callaghan. They bought a little cluster of six islands in the Aegean Sea for one hundred thousand pounds. They visited it once, tired of it immediately, and the Beatle paradise was later sold. John soon afterward bought, for a whim and for twenty thousand pounds, two small uninhabited islands known together as Dornish off the northwest coast of Ireland. At considerable expense he had the colorful psychedelic horse-drawn wooden *Sgt. Pepper* wagon shipped to Dornish. It was the only standing structure on either island. John visited the islands once, traveling by helicopter to conduct a job interview with a potential manager of Apple. It was John's idea to hold the interview there. He later gave Dornish to a hippie commune.

Their next hobby was meditation and the Maharishi Mahesh Yogi. Patti had discovered him several months earlier and when the Crown Prince of Transcendental Meditation was booked into the London Hilton on August 24 Patti persuaded George to go. George talked Paul into it and then John became intrigued, although Magic Alex, their new scientific adviser, was to warn them against the influence of the Maharishi. It takes one to know one, as they say. The group was magically ushered to front row seats and after the "meditation" they were all invited to a little backstage gathering. And then to another intimate gathering the next day.

On August 25 the Beatles, along with Mick Jagger, got on to a train at Euston Station to go to Bangor, Wales, to see the Maharishi at a weekend seminar at Normal College there. They were very proud of themselves because it was the first time since Beatlemania had set in five years earlier that they had gone anywhere on their own. There was no Brian to set things up, no Neil Aspinall or Mal Evans to take care of them along the way and pay for things. They were followed by hordes of reporters and photographers—Cynthia, in tears, was left behind at the train station—and the assembled press got a scoop when Paul announced that the Beatles were renouncing drugs in favor of spiritualism. Said Paul, "We think we're finding new ways of getting there." What he actually meant, as was borne out in the Beatles' lives, was that they were going to quit talking about drugs. Which was a good idea—in principle.

While they were there, Brian Epstein was found dead. He had gone off for a country weekend at his Kingsley Hill retreat and when the young boys he had ordered from a London agency for his weekend treat didn't arrive, he tried to order more from London. When he found he couldn't get any more, he drove back to London, leaving his weekend guests, Peter Brown and Geoffrey Ellis. On the twenty-seventh, after Brian had not responded to repeated entreaties, Brian's bedroom doors at his Chapel Street flat in London were battered down and his body was found in bed. There was no note and he left no will. He was just thirty-two years old.

The autopsy found that he had probably died from a slow buildup of Carbitrol, a sleeping pill he had been taking. There were immediate rumors then, just as there are rumors now, that Brian Epstein was murdered as the end result of one or another of the many business deals that he had cut regarding the Beatles. There were so many murky deals, involving so many people and so much money, that it could even have been a deal that he failed to do that might have resulted in such rumors of vendetta and revenge. Subsequent court hearings over the years have showed that the Beatles were probably—there is no information central for this kind of data—the most underpaid superstar performers ever. Given their worldwide acclaim and the millions of records they sold, one would have imagined that they were millionaires many times over. That was hardly the case. The money they spent publicly—the psychedelic Rolls-Royce, the islands in Greece—ended up representing most of what they had. But they didn't really know that at the time. In fact, they never knew what they had and didn't have.

When Brian died they grieved for him, in their way. In Bangor, Wales, in properly somber tones reflecting the meditation they had come in search of, they said that even in death, life went on, and that sort of thing. But really, what was there to say? He had been a sometime friend who had taken them as far as he could. And when they got there, they, as ever, had looked around and said, "Well, what's next?" And, as Paul especially had started to try to dig into the Beatle business books, which they had never even thought to do during the Fab Beatlemania years, suspicions of Brian had started bubbling to the surface.

Their management contract with Brian was to expire in October 1967 and there was no doubt that the Beatles were not going to renew the deal. They were through with Brian and it was for the plain old vanilla Beatle reason: They didn't need him anymore. Not only that, this was the first case where it appeared that a person who was Beatle-used seemed to have actually screwed them. It was true that they were all so drug-addled that no one ever really kept tabs of things. But after a while everything becomes obvious.

The biggest key was the 25 percent clause that Brian had hidden from them. When he had renegotiated their royalty deal with EMI (and with Capitol in the United States), he had inserted a clause guaranteeing that 25 percent of all Beatle record royalties would continue to go to NEMS for nine years, even if the Beatles didn't renew their management contract with Brian. The Beatles had signed that contract without scrutinizing the fine print.

After Brian's death there was an awful lot of scrabbling around at NEMS to see who would be the successor. Millions and millions were at stake. And nothing was ever settled. Robert

Stigwood, whom Brian had made a codirector of NEMS in January of 1967, left with a substantial cash settlement and with the Bee Gees and Cream.

All the scratching and clawing had to do with business executives, the Beatles quickly noticed out of their evaporating acid haze. There were enormous numbers of "men in suits" on their payroll. Even John, he told me many years later, was of two minds after Brian died. "Brian betrayed us," he said, "there was no fuckin' doubt of that. He gave a fourth of us to NEMS and never told us. NEMS was bigger than the Beatles; what the fuck is that? We were nothing, right? And the men in suits owned us, right? Brian was advised by a lot of crooks. He sold us out to strangers. We were friends, I was the one who stayed friends with Brian, but when I started to wake up and look . . . look, he had us by the balls and he couldn't even fuckin' tell us because he had sold us out. Plain and simple. Money, fuckin' money . . ."

Paul called a band meeting at his house in St. John's Wood for September 1. It was the first time that the four Beatles had ever needed a serious summit meeting. They decided that, after Brian, they did not really need another manager. They could look after themselves. The "men in suits" could do the accounting and all that, but the Beatles would manage themselves. It was a beautiful dream.

Paul convinced the others that, to launch their new managerless, self-determined career, they must immediately start work on the brilliant *Magical Mystery Tour* Beatle project. It was the only way to save the Beatles. John, still acid-fried and unable to make business decisions, agreed. George and Ringo, junior partners ever, had no say in the matter.

On September 11, the Beatles and a film crew set out from London in a Magical Mystery Tour Bus. In the most obvious example of Beatle lack of purpose and direction after Brian's death, Paul forced what was day-by-day a nonproject, a nonmovie, a pain in the ass for everyone else. The movie had no script, no director, no direction, no ideas, and not much else. It was fueled mainly by Paul's desperation to keep the Beatles alive. But, without the discipline of a director, the *Magical Mystery Tour* flew apart in no time. If Brian had been there, as both Paul and John admitted, things would have been different. Brian had made the trains run on time. Good luck if you were trying anything with John or Paul. Someone had to impose some discipline on them or what they attempted just ran out of time and out of steam after weeks.

Magical Mystery Tour, with no plot, was finally filmed as a sort of poor man's *Help!* merged with *A Hard Day's Night.* Paul thought he was a film director merely by virtue of declaring that he was one, but he would learn the hard way that you can't create a film simply by pronouncing it one. Always before, the Beatles had had Brian to clean up their messes after them, to tidy up their little appearances before them. Without Brian, Paul had absolutely no perspective of how his little Beatle movie would be received by the real world.

He didn't know what to do with it in the first place. There was no Brian to give it to when he was finished with it. So it went off to the "men in suits" somewhere. The music was great: Paul's title song (and Paul had already put out his "Hello Goodbye" as the last Beatle single of 1967), Paul's "Your Mother Should Know," Paul's "The Fool on the Hill," and John's "I Am the Walrus."

Magical Mystery Tour ended up on the BBC on December 26 because nobody else would take it. The critics gave the Beatles such a drubbing as they'd never ever experienced before. Their ears were severely pinned back. Point of fact: What was starting to happen and which would not be noticed for years was that one half of Lennon–McCartney was starting to be criticized mainly for being only one half of Lennon–McCartney. The public wanted Lennon–McCartney. Neither the one, nor the other. And that came to be because what the one and the other presented separately to the public was not fully half what they had presented together before. While Paul and John had been looking at rough cuts of *Magical Mystery Tour,* Dick James bounded into the viewing room on Old Compton Street one day, barely able to contain his excitement. Paul and John stayed bent over the editing machine to keep James waiting for a while. Finally they straightened up and he blurted out, "I've got some exciting news! Barbra Streisand is making a new album and wants to do some of your songs." Well, that was fine with "the boys." Plenty of big-name singers were recording Beatle songs and it would be nice to add Streisand to the roster. "So why are you still hanging around," they asked? "Well," he finally said, "if

you could just write a few numbers for her. . . ." The icy silence
that descended on the cutting room floor was eventually broken
by John's decidedly final: "Fuck off."

As 1968 wound on and on, even as the Beatles' music became
purer and purer, the individual human components behind it and
responsible for it were more and more miserable. John, out in
the bedroom of his mock-Tudor manse, hid his postcards from
Yoko while Cynthia's regular breathing beside him reminded
him of how guilty he should feel.

London's most eligible bachelor, Paul McCartney, tossed and
turned in his luxurious bed in his home in St. John's Wood. And
it wasn't because he wanted for female company beside him
there. He tossed and he turned and he dreamed and he got
paranoid even while he was asleep. Of course, he told himself
even while he was asleep, you were supposed to be paranoid if
you used drugs in the sixties. Paul later admitted that he dreamed
about his mother. "It gave me some strength. . . . Mother Mary
comes to me. . . . I get dreams with John in and my Dad. It's
very nice because you meet them again. It's wondrous. It's like
magic."

Over the months Paul increasingly felt he had to shoulder the
burden while Apple struggled and strained to give birth to itself.
Paul, for an egomaniac, was managing fairly well, as long as he
got enough press. How would you, after all, handle a special
Apple meeting of the board that John had convened just so that
he could announce: "I am Jesus Christ come back again"? And
John meant it. You would have to say that Paul, fucked up as he
was, took pretty good care of John, twice as fucked up as he
was.

Apple Corps, Ltd., was formed in February 1968 to formally
replace The Beatles, Ltd., the Beatle umbrella organization, which
itself had been formed on April 19, 1967. (Apple as a Beatle
name first appeared when Apple Publishing, Ltd., was registered
on September 27, 1967, shortly after Brian Epstein's death.)
Apple was to run a partnership called Beatles & Co. (Eighty
percent of Beatles & Co. was owned by Apple and each Beatle
held 5 percent.) It was what seemed to be a vain, doomed
attempt by the Beatles to seize control of their own chaotic
enterprises. In the wake of Brian Epstein's death and the subse-

quent unraveling of Beatles' business affairs, Paul had been increasingly assuming the leadership role within the group. It had been Paul who had talked the others into doing the disastrous *Magical Mystery Tour*. He had also tried—and failed—to impose order on NEMS Enterprises after Brian's death. Brian's brother Clive took over day-to-day operations of NEMS and Paul disdainfully spoke of him as a "provincial furniture salesman." Meanwhile the Beatles had—without challenging or questioning the agreement—signed over 25 percent of all their record royalties to NEMS through 1976. The Beatles alternated between periods of intense paranoid scrutiny of their business affairs and bouts of empty-headed stoned disdain for the administering of the fortunes they were making and giving or pissing away.

In an attempt to impose order on the Beatles' financial activities, Apple Corps was born. The Beatles were in a 96 percent tax bracket. Their tax advisers and Clive Epstein urged them to invest in entertainment-related businesses and eventually go public with them. The Beatles had already become large stockholders in seven London investment firms named Apricot, Blackberry, Cornflower, Daffodil, Edelweiss, Foxglove, and Greengage. The extent and the outcome of those holdings has never been made public. For tax purposes, though, their new businesses had to be in fields related to their own work.

Apple Corps, the name, was Paul's idea (as he said many times), intended as a pun with a certain innocence and naïveté to it. "If the Beatles have to go into business," said Paul, "then we want to have fun with it." Even though it was a business decision, the Beatles, especially Paul, made much of Apple's stated purpose to give something back, to nurture the creative arts, to give struggling young artists a break, to be the logical extension of what the hippie revolution or counterculture was supposed to be about—rather than what capitalism and the recording business were about.

Even though Paul took a great deal of credit for Apple and was very vocal and visible in its day-to-day activities, John Lennon later told me that Apple was in reality totally a product of management. "See," John said, "one thing people never knew was that Apple was not our idea and was certainly never Paul's idea, as he has gone on about. Apple was presented to us as a reality by the Epsteins in '67 before Brian died. Brian and his furniture salesman brother Clive. And they hadn't the slightest fucking idea what they were doing. It was really just a loony tax scheme in the end. They said we had all this cash about to come in and the only way around paying the taxes was to invest in businesses. But we would have never have come up with the notion of running a clothes store. The Beatles pushing rags? Right. Right. No, it was pure and simple a tax kite. Our incomes would be hidden inside Apple. Then the money would be moved around."

Apple Corps, with many captains at the wheel, grew and multiplied and spread itself into a number of areas: electronics, films, publishing, records, and retailing. The Apple Boutique was already a disaster. There would also be, before things got completely out of hand, plans for Apple Publicity, Apple Cosmetics, Apple Limousines, Apple School, Apple Tailoring, an Apple shopping complex on Regent Street with barber shop, restaurant, sauna, cinema, and other shops. Not to mention a line of Sgt. Pepper discotheques and a chain of Apple record stores. And a boutique at Macy's in New York City. Then there was the great talent search. Paul himself wrote the following ad, which was widely circulated and printed in such counterculture publications as *Rolling Stone:*

> This man has talent. One day he sang his songs to a tape recorder (borrowed from the man next door). In his neatest handwriting he wrote an explanatory note (giving his name and address) and, remembering to enclose a picture of himself, sent the tape, letter and photograph to Apple Music, 94 Baker Street, London W.1 If you were thinking of doing the same thing yourself—do it now! This man now owns a Bentley!

The man pictured in the ad was longtime Beatle employee and Apple staffer Alistair Taylor, who would later be one of the first Apple firings when Allen Klein took over. No Beatle stood up for him or otherwise said a word in his behalf.

Apple was soon drowning in a sea of tapes, which were tossed into closets and eventually thrown out, largely unlistened to. But the Beatles—and especially Paul, whose idea the talent search had been—paid no heed to the dreams that expired with those submitted tapes.

Apple was on a runaway course of its own. The Apple Boutique provided a perfect case in point of the excesses that could be committed in the name of rich—if well-meaning—hippies. When the Beatles learned that their accountants had bought for them, for investment purposes, a four-story building at the corner of Baker and Paddington Streets in London, it became the temporary home for Apple.

For one hundred thousand pounds they were bankrolling a wandering group of psychedelic designers known as The Fool to staff and run the Apple Boutique. The Beatles first met The Fool during the filming of a TV documentary called *All My Loving.* The Fool were led by visionary Dutch artist Simon Posthuma. His wife Marijke Koger and Dutch artist Josje Leeger completed the group. Subsequently, The Fool provided psychedelic transformations to George's house and John's piano. They also had a very energetic manager and publicist, Barry Finch, who straightaway got them into the Sunday *Times.* To their credit, The Fool were undeniably creative, even if they were expensive; at one point going on a ten-day shopping expedition in Morocco for items for Apple.

In an attempt to bring order to Apple, the Beatles brought in John's boyhood friend Pete Shotton, who had been running a supermarket that John had bankrolled for him. They paid Shotton thirty-seven pounds a week. He couldn't afford a flat on that salary, so he moved in with John. When he got to Apple, he found that a long-haired mystic, I Ching diviner, and tarot card reader known simply as Caleb was authorized to approve or disapprove all Apple business decisions as he saw fit. Caleb also did daily horoscopes in-house.

Additionally, Ivan Vaughan, the man who had introduced Paul McCartney to John Lennon so many years earlier, was given ten thousand pounds to run a nonexistent Apple School.

Shotton had the Baker Street building's main floor and basement ripped out and renovated. With some difficulty, since Paul and John got into the habit of dropping by—separately—and issuing contradictory orders to the workmen about what they wanted done to the building's interior. The Fool, meanwhile, infuriated the Westminster Borough Council by covering the exterior of the building with a large—and illegal—psychedelic mural that was fairly spectacular.

The boutique was losing money hand over lace glove even before it opened with a huge party on December 7. Paul didn't bother to attend the opening. Though he did make it to a preview party two weeks later, on December 21, for *Magical Mystery Tour.* Paul and Jane Asher—just four days shy of announcing their engagement on Christmas Day—sported matching ribbon-trimmed Swiss Alp outfits. John came as his favorite character—a teddy boy—and got drunk early on. Though he was seeing Yoko, he had brought his wife Cynthia Lennon to the party and ignored her while he pursued George's wife Patti, who was gotten up fetchingly as a belly dancer.

At this time in late 1967 Paul and John were at the supreme pinnacle of rock royalty in London—if not in the world. In the wake of the reverent critical and public reception and near-canonization of *Sgt. Pepper,* there seemed no limit to what the twin geniuses of rock 'n' roll could do. They had effectively wiped out the Stones and Dylan, their only reigning competition. They were social lions and the arbiters of London's rock and hip scene. Everything they did was admired; nothing was questioned. Especially by their employees. Apple became for John and Paul—especially Paul—a personal extension of self. In the wake of Brian's death, they felt that they could seize the reins of power in their lives and careers and, more importantly, take over that power from what they called the "men in suits" who drained their money, who prevented them from doing whatever they wanted to do, and who, in short, acted as grown-up governors, as Blue Meanies—in other words, as parents. Who could say no. That was the word that was never spoken to a Beatle at Apple. "No" was an alien concept.

No matter that The Fool insisted that the labels for all Apple clothes at the boutique be handwoven of silk, thus making the cost of the label exceeding the price of the item itself. Questioning that was questioning art itself and giving in to the base bottom-line mentality of the "men in suits" who were stomping all over art and creativity. No matter that Magic Alex didn't deliver on his promise to hang an artificial sun out on Baker Street for the opening of the boutique. Magic Alex was a kindred artist and he could have the forty thousand pounds he claimed to need to pick up two computers. He could have the laboratory on

Boston Street that he required to work on his flying saucer and his invisible paint process and the like.

Apple, founded as a tax dodge, quickly evolved into a sinkhole of a countercultural experiment down which flowed countless hundreds of thousands. It was the prototype for the skewed hippie ideal of an organization that is both more and less than an organization by dint of having a noble purpose. And not being run by "men in suits." Apple was nominally turned over to trusted Beatle roadie-in-chief Neil Aspinall (not a "man in suit") as managing director and Brian's assistant, Peter Brown (a "man in suit"), as administrative director. Still, the Beatles themselves—and Paul and John specifically—ran things, after a fashion. Directors of Apple divisions ranged from the casual (Shotton at the boutique) to the nepotistic (Jane Asher's brother Peter at Apple Music, who became a music force in his own right) to the truly professional (Ron Kass from Liberty Records' European division and Dennis O'Dell, who had worked with filmmaker Richard Lester).

Yet Apple proved to be less than a precise science. A lot of "expenses" and "journal entries" and shopping trips went for enormous buys of marijuana and hashish. The finest liquors and wines and caviars were kept stocked—ostensibly for the Beatles. The staff learned quickly. There were the cordon bleu chefs. The place was literally a bird's nest on the ground. Overseen by arrogant and spoiled superstars, supposedly run by incompetents, with no real or stated purpose other than to squander money, thumb one's nose at society, and pose as the hippest of the hip, Apple was a dream of a lifetime for rip-off artists.

At the first Apple board meeting, Clive Epstein ventured the thought that he felt Apple's purpose in life was a series of greeting cards with "the boys" providing inspirational verse on each. Apple was, if anything, the perfect tabula rasa for rock 'n' roll as a true global force encountering the world of the marketplace. Each needed the other and each saw only a rosy future of its own devising in the other. The Beatles were obviously a growth industry unlike any other before or since and there was certainly no shortage of toadies on either side of the countercultural line waiting to cash in. It would be in these trenches that the battle between capitalism and the counterculture would be fought and decided (with the end result surprising few). Early on, all four Beatles would attend board meetings, with no guarantee of what emotional, mental, or other state each would be in.

After the Westminster Borough Council made the Beatles paint over the psychedelic mural on Baker Street, Apple moved on to Wigmore Street, between Baker and Regent, above Oxford, on a block of office buildings entirely lacking in any character whatsoever. Apple employees began complaining about the strait-jacket of working all hours in a nine-to-five district and being locked in or out of the building as a result at all hours, stoned or not, but it was all a major inconvenience and with a bit of a social stigma attaching. Hippies trying to get into—or, sometimes worse, out of—an office building after dark and all that. As a remedy, Neil Aspinall went office shopping and decided on number 3 Savile Row, an elegant five-story brick building in a properly snobbish neighborhood that respected money, if it didn't pay sufficient homage to new money. At least the Beatles owned the building and had the only key to the front door. This was probably the worst neighborhood they could have found, if what they sought was good vibes and easy parking and a twenty-four-hour easy entrance and exit. This was the genteel tailoring district off Mayfair. But it was prime real estate— they paid half a million pounds for it—and was a prestigious return address to go on the executives' stationery. And on the Beatles' stationery. Than the Beatles, there were few social climbers climbing any higher. And good addresses were very important to them. Paul was finally beginning to decorate the house he had bought in St. John's Wood. Despite the critical bath he'd taken with *Magical Mystery Tour,* Paul still felt that he was blessed with a cinematic eye and he wanted to make a movie of the hippie cult classic *The Lord of the Rings* by J. R. R. Tolkien. Paul wanted to be Frodo Baggins, John would be Gollum, Ringo would portray Sam, and George would be Gandalf. Nothing came of it. At one point John met with director Stanley Kubrick to discuss the possibility of doing this or another Beatle movie and the meeting went badly. John apparently was not impressed.

Apple madness set in seriously once the word was out that the Beatles had become latter-day Medici, godparents to hip schemers everywhere.

Supplicants came, hat in hand, from around the world, looking for the Cosmic Handout. Richard DiLello, who was then the "house hippie" in Apple's press office, later described the reception room at 95 Wigmore Street as resembling "the waiting room at a VD clinic in Haight-Ashbury at the height of the acid madness of '67." The only surprise in hindsight is that Charles Manson never got to make the pilgrimage.

What had really set off the long-haired hegira to Apple had been primarily Paul's naïve expectations for what the Corps could be or perhaps was supposed to be. His open letter to artists had been distributed widely as a poster in the United Kingdom, in addition to being run in numerous publications. In the United States a highly publicized appearance on May 15, 1968, on "The Tonight Show" by Paul and John announced Apple to an audience of many millions. Johnny Carson wasn't on that night, so the two Beatles were interviewed by the guest host, former baseball player Joe Garagiola, who had only a vague idea of what they were talking about. Actress Tallulah Bankhead, whom John later said was "pissed out of her head," tried to tell John and Paul how beautiful they were.

Paul repeated his line about how Apple should be a "controlled weirdness, a kind of Western communism. We want to help people, but without doing it like a charity." In announcing the Apple Foundation for the Arts, Paul, at his sincerest, told aspiring artists and con-men everywhere that, "We always had to go to the big men on our knees and touch our forelocks and say, 'Please, can we do so and so . . . ?' We're in the happy position of not needing any more money, so for the first time the bosses aren't in it for a profit. If you come to me and say, 'I've had such and such a dream,' I'll say to you, 'Go away and do it.' "

After the show he himself went off to an assignation with Linda Eastman. Earlier in the day she had reintroduced herself to Paul at a press conference for Apple and had given Paul her phone number. He called to ask her to meet him at the apartment of Nat Weiss, rather than at his hotel, the St. Regis, where they might be seen together or photographed together, lest Jane Asher hear about it. Paul spent days with Linda, meeting her six-year-old daughter Heather and even baby-sitting her. The most-sought-after man in all of rock groupiedom baby-sat while Linda went to the Fillmore East to take pictures of other rock stars.

Paul went back to Jane in London and back to Apple, where his written and televised appeals to creative artists began to bring in massive amounts of mail, visits, and deliveries. Manuscripts, tapes, assorted gifts, packages, threats, pleas, Hell's Angels, disheveled poets, boot-shod cowboy minstrels, lovesick mental patients, starry-eyed teenage groupies, hard-eyed hippie rip-off artists, and cosmic visionaries all washed up against the shores of Apple. The poems, massive stacks of them, were the most pathetic. None were ever read. They were piled up in huge stacks that eventually fell over of their own weight. Then they were thrown out. The tapes were kept longer, even if they were also ignored. Tapes are harder than paper to throw away, but eventually they too went into the dustbin.

One of the many supplicants descending on Apple during that freewheeling summer of 1968 was a young woman who had been an advertising copywriter in New York City. Francie Schwartz, then twenty-four years old, had gotten the message from Paul's and John's appearance on "The Tonight Show" that the Beatles were speaking directly to people like her and were more than ready and willing to finance any and every scheme that might come in over the transom—or however one might get it to the magic Beatles.

Schwartz had written a movie script based on the life of a young long-haired violinist she encountered when he was playing for coins on the sidewalk outside Carnegie Hall. She took him to dinner at the Russian Tea Room and all through the meal she sensed an impending involvement with the Beatles.

After intensive interview sessions with the young violinist, Schwartz typed up a ten-page film treatment. Then when the young violinist's insensitive agent (!) refused to buy the treatment, she vowed that the Beatles would ride to the rescue. If she could only get the script to Paul McCartney, she reasoned, the Beatles would take care of the rest. The Beatles were, after all, on a mission to seek out and rescue the creative downtrodden of the world.

When Schwartz was terminated from her copywriting job soon thereafter, it seemed to be providential timing. She flew to London with her severance pay, script in hand. Little did Paul McCartney know what was in store for him.

When Schwartz touched down in London she began her Apple pursuit. In what was clearly to her a sign of things to come, she ran into Paul's brother Mike (who had changed his name to McGear to avoid the appearance of cashing in on his brother's success) at the trendy Speakeasy club, where she gave him her favorite roach clip. Then Schwartz started trying to contact Paul at Apple. Naturally, the receptionists at Apple were hip but were not so goofy that they would invite every cosmic basket case to come to Apple.

So Schwartz just took herself over to Wigmore Street, marched right into Apple Corps, and—providentially again—He Himself just happened to be standing there, radiating electricity and charm from every pore and follicle. Schwartz thought: Is this it? Is this the guy that millions and millions of chicks are moaning and groaning over? Writing letters about and masturbating about and dreaming about?

Paul took one look at her and ambled over. She was not what would be called a classic beauty, but there was no doubt that Schwartz burned with a steady level of intensity and certainly was glowing with the zeal of her purpose. She handed Paul her movie treatment, a picture of herself, and a carefully worded letter. He took them and asked where she could be reached. It was that easy.

She was sharing a coldwater flat in Notting Hill Gate with a Scottish girl whom she had met on her first night in London (at the Bag O'Nails club, where she yearned for a glimpse of Himself). She surmised correctly that Notting Hill Gate was not an address that was likely to impress Paul. So the next day when she was at Sassoon, getting herself transformed into a trendy Swinging London bird, Paul sent over a letter addressed to her, c/o Sassoon. A good address and one certainly suitable for a candidate-in-waiting for the job of Beatle Chick.

Paul's note, which was signed with love, read: COME, CALL, DO SOMETHING CONSTRUCTIVE.

She called. He took the call and told her to hurry on over. At Apple he took her into an office, put his feet up on the desk, and started talking. Through the mists that surrounded her end of the conversation Schwartz began to—dimly at first and then with an alarming clarity—discern that Paul might actually be more interested in her as a warm, moving female person than he was in her treatment for a movie. She sensed that he expected a decision from her immediately as to which side of the fence she was on. She also correctly sensed what Paul wanted the answer to be. Good-bye, movie treatment.

He declared that he wanted her, in effect, to be on call twenty-four hours a day. He said he needed to know where she would be at all times. Then Paul got up and said he had a meeting with his lawyers.

Later in the afternoon Schwartz called Apple and was connected almost immediately with Paul. He was very pleasant and apologetic, saying he was tied up for the rest of the day and then would have to leave town for a while. But, he wanted to know, would she be "all right" until he returned? It seemed to be a test to see if she wanted money from him. She didn't.

She waited for him as a week went by, then two, then three, then a month. Paul was off to Scotland with Jane Asher, who was still his fiancée. Jane apparently did not know about Paul's interest in Schwartz, nor did either of them know about Linda Eastman, with whom Paul had dallied in the States. Nor did Jane know about some of Paul's other casual dates, such as folksinger Julie Felix.

Through contacts she had made at Apple Schwartz learned where Paul was and wrote frequently to the farm in Scotland while he was there with Jane. Paul later told Schwartz that he had received none of her letters. What neither Jane nor Francie knew was that Paul kept a secret little bachelor flat in Mayfair, where he took little one-night stands and where he entertained an astonishing number of young and even not-so-young women.

When he finally called it was as if he had not been gone at all. He invited her, she claimed, to the Beatle Inner Sanctum itself: the EMI Studio on Abbey Road. That evening, she claimed, she found herself transported into Beatle ecstasy. She was at Abbey Road itself, with the Beatles themselves, and she was massaging Paul's shoulders while he and the other Fabs were recording "Revolution" in a dense cloud of hash smoke and incense. She was singing along on backing vocals herself, she claimed, although Beatle recording sessions were usually closed to all outsiders. Then she was off in limo with Paul and John and Yoko. But the three of them were dropped off at Paul's house at number 7 Cavendish Avenue. Then she was taken home alone. It happened more than once that way and every time she watched the big black gates on Cavendish Avenue close and separate her from Paul she grew more and more feverish in the chase. Not enough was happening between her and Paul. She wanted to get behind those big black gates.

Schwartz sent Paul a note. It read: DEAR MR. PLUMP, I THINK I'M GOING TO HAVE TO GO HOME SOON. WHEN AM I GOING TO SEE YOU?

A few days later, when she went downstairs to bring the morning milk up to her new flat in Chelsea, there was a telegram waiting with the milk bottles. It said: MAKE IT MONDAY, MR. P. That was a Sunday.

The next morning the doorbell chimed while she was bathing. She tore downstairs in her damp pajamas. There He was at last. The Magic Moment had come. The moment every (female) Paul fan fantasized about. Up the stairs they ran. He sat down, pulled her on to his lap, and started in on her. Martha, Paul's sheepdog, had followed him in to watch.

The three of them adjourned to the bedroom, where Schwartz soon discovered that her bliss was to be far briefer than had been her fantasy of the Magic Moment. She later was to describe Paul as not being either "terribly good or terribly bad." She thought he rushed things a bit, though. She would later refer to "the ephemeral thing we substituted for lovemaking."

That evening, after a day spent running barefoot in the rain and so on, Paul took his leave and told her, "Don't take this seriously." By "this," he said he meant "this good-bye." She didn't know if or when she would see him again.

Eight days later Schwartz was roused from sleep at five in the morning by the ringing of the doorbell. It was Paul, unshaven and seemingly half-wasted. He bounded up the stairs, singing, "It's F-Day! It's F-Day!"

As they tumbled into bed, Schwartz pressed for the advantage: She asked him if he loved her. She wasn't quite sure yet of his intent or lack of it. He merely replied, "I don't know."

That night, though, he took her to the studios at ten and—at long last—to his home on Cavendish Avenue in St. John's Wood. She finally got to see those big black gates close with her on the inside. Past the ever-vigilant Apple Scruffs who faithfully stood outside.

Inside, Paul lit a fire in the fireplace, poured drinks for them, and talked about Jane. Just what Schwartz wanted to hear. He said he was anguished that Jane simply could not see her way clear to giving him what he most of all sought: total devotion all the time. A mother, in so many words. He just could not understand why Jane wanted to keep on with her acting career when there he stood, Paul McCartney, Beatle, in need of a full-time woman.

"Jane," Paul said, "is obviously confused as to her priorities and is too selfishly caught up in her own career and doesn't see the obvious need to give it all up for me. That surprised me," he said. "True love," he reasoned, "should mean total devotion."

Schwartz told him right quick that if she herself were given such a choice she would know pretty damn fast what her decision would be. Paul turned his limpid cows' eyes on her. "Do you think you could take care of me?" he asked.

She said, "I'm not sure, but I sure would like to try."

Paul led her upstairs to the Paul Bed. At last. As they settled in, he startled her by saying that he bet that Jane was with another man even as he spoke.

So Schwartz at last became part of the Paul household. She spent the first days, while Paul was in the studio, exploring the place and getting to know it and what she at first considered the cluttered coziness of it and its unkempt garden. In fact, the place was a mess and that's the way Paul liked it. Things stayed where they fell. She was still Paul's Little Secret. She became, for her, quite domestic. She prepared his tea when he awoke at eleven or so in the morning and she was there to cook for him or to make love to him when he came home ripped to the gills at three in the morning. She called up dope dealers to get his marijuana for him. She reasoned that she could be happy if she didn't demand too much of Paul. It was pretty much a one-way relationship, but Schwartz liked where she was: someplace a million other girls would kill to be. She knew their relationship, such as it was, had begun with Paul's need for someone to care for him, not on any grand burning passion on his part. He seemed incapable of that. And further, Schwartz reasoned, great sex wasn't everything in a relationship and a man didn't have to be a great performer for a union to be happy. She did start to notice Paul's hangups, though, and she did observe that he "felt sometimes that he wasn't manly enough."

Jane still telephoned the house periodically, seemingly unaware of Paul's new live-in. Jane was off on an acting tour. It was apparent to Schwartz that Paul was trying to keep both of them on the hook, something she would have known immediately if she had become friendly with the Scruffs outside. They knew everything and might have been friendly had not Schwartz felt superior to them. The Scruffs liked Jane and approved of her as someone worthy of Paul if they themselves couldn't be in her place.

Schwartz found herself wondering whatever happened to her movie treatment and that got her down, especially when she was cleaning up the dog and cat shit from the expensive Oriental rugs. There were five cats, plus Martha the sheepdog, and to Schwartz shit was still shit even if it was on a Beatle rug in a Beatle house. Paul did not believe in housebreaking the animals. Then there was the matter of the puppy. Schwartz came home one afternoon, after a rare afternoon out with a friend, to find a little puppy shut up alone in the kitchen, whimpering and scratching to get out. And shitting. She found pedigree papers for him on the mantel. His name was Eddie, she learned. When Paul came home that night she asked him what the deal with Eddie was. "Oh," he said, "I bought Eddie for Jane, but I've decided that we should keep her. And by the way," he said, "what's for dinner?"

Schwartz gritted her teeth and hung on. But the routine dragged at her. She cooked what he liked, which was Liverpool slag food along the lines of beans and toast and grilled cheese and tomato sandwiches. And lots of Scotches and Cokes. Not to mention the ubiquitous marijuana and all the little white pills—uppers—that she would find in his pockets and about which he denied any knowledge. "Fans put them there," Paul said.

She later recounted that, when he would come home drunk or stoned or both, Paul would deliver monologues about how women sometimes liked to be knocked around a little and how Jane had seemed to be turned on sexually when he struck her. And he told Schwartz about Linda Eastman, about how the two of them had "made contact" instantly on meeting. "Well," Schwartz wanted to know, "why the hell aren't the two of you strapping it on together, then?" He said he wanted to try it with Schwartz.

The next evening, after they left the club Revolution, Paul drove to a certain former girlfriend's apartment and left Schwartz waiting in the car while he went upstairs to visit for a while and become reacquainted. For a quick fifteen minutes. Schwartz was deeply humiliated. She demanded to know why he had done that, why he hadn't at least taken her home first. "I don't know," he said.

To mollify Schwartz, Paul sent her off to work in the press office with Derek Taylor at Apple. She was naturally greatly resented by most of the people at Apple. In turn, she considered most of them to be the worst sort of "ass-kissing cocksucking creeps."

Her relationship with Paul continued to follow its yo-yo course. Way up, then way down again. They would make love in a park in the rain. Then he would ignore her and try to call Jane. They would go on long drives during which she would fellate him while he drove his green Mini-Cooper at high speed.

One evening he would yell, "Knickers down!" as he pulled Schwartz down into the bathtub with him, water splashing everywhere. On another evening he would harangue her about everything. Her accent was all wrong. Her looks were not right. She didn't suit him in any way.

Then came the encounter with Jane. It was sudden. Jane returned early from her tour and let herself in the house with her key. She had, after all, helped Paul furnish and decorate the house and had persuaded him to acquire his farm in Scotland. As far as the world knew, Jane and Paul were still the ideal young couple, the perfect symbols of Swinging London. As recently as March they had been together at the Maharishi's meditation course in Rishikesh, India, and on June 8 they attended Mike McGear's wedding, where Paul was his brother's best man. On June 18 Paul passed up the opening of John's one-act play, *In His Own Write* at the National Theatre, to see Jane in another production. Then, of course, from June 20 to June 24, Paul, unbeknownst to anyone else, was sharing a bungalow at the Beverly Hills Hotel with Linda Eastman—after kicking out two other girls—one an actress, the other a high-paid black call girl—to make way for Linda.

But in July Jane let herself in the house and started up the stairs. One of the Scruffs outside, Margo Stevens, had tried to signal Paul on the intercom, a warning that went unheard.

Upstairs, out of decorum or out of a sixth sense, Jane, instead of walking into the bedroom, knocked on the closed door. Paul sat bolt upright and asked who it was, even though he knew. He picked up a bathrobe and tried to slip out without opening the door wide. Jane fled the house in short order. This was not that long after Cynthia Lennon had returned home from a holiday in Italy to find Yoko Ono filling up her bathrobe at home.

Jane's mother arrived at Cavendish Avenue that evening to box up and cart away Jane's clothes and cookbooks and pots and pans and other possessions. Mrs. Asher was quite bitter because it had been she who had invited Paul to stay at the Asher home in London, long before Paul had made the move from Liverpool. She had countenanced his staying under her roof only because he supposedly loved her daughter. This certainly blew the whistle on all that. None of the Ashers ever commented on Paul again. Schwartz claimed that she helped Mrs. Asher pack and load up everything. Then she and Paul argued and she left for her flat. Paul, she said, called her up and begged her to come back. She did so. Life went on.

On July 20 Jane announced on the BBC's "Dee Time" show that her engagement with Paul was broken and that Paul had done the breaking. The next day Paul stormed into Apple and tried to have Jane's brother Peter fired from his job with Apple Records, but Ron Kass interceded on Peter's behalf. This did not, though, help Peter's career at Apple. His first production was James Taylor's eponymous first album. That record and Taylor were quickly not given Apple's highest priorities.

Paul finally took Schwartz home to meet Dad, although the trips were fairly disastrous. Jim still had dozens of Jane's pictures all over the house and paid little attention to Schwartz. Paul, she said, was drunk much of the time. On one occasion he slipped out of a party they were attending and disappeared. Later one of Paul's cousins found her and said, "You had better fetch your fella, Clancy," Clancy being Paul's nickname for her.

Schwartz found him in a pub. Paul was quite drunk, surrounded by relatives and friends from his pre-Beatles days. He was blubbering to them. "Why won't you treat me like just plain Paul instead of like Paul the Beatle?" She led him out and he fell to the pavement. "It's just too fuckin' much!" he told her. Paul said that he was furious that he had passed around over thirty thousand pounds to relatives and friends since success had struck and that no one had offered to pay back so much as a bob. He went home sobbing and the next day remembered nothing of the episode.

Schwartz claimed that Paul had told both his father and Mrs. Asher that Schwartz was what Paul now needed: a totally different girl who would take care of him.

After the storm caused by John—a married man—going out in public with Yoko, a scandal which broke in the press on June 18 at the premiere of *In His Own Write,* John and Yoko moved in to Cavendish Avenue with Paul for a spell to try to hide out. Things were not easy between John and Paul at the time. Paul obviously resented Yoko and the wedge that he felt she had created between himself and John. He and John had, after all, created the world's most exclusive boys' club in the Beatles and now it was being threatened by a short self-styled Oriental artist. Paul was then in the habit of sending anonymous cards and notes and letters. One day one arrived at Cavendish Avenue addressed to John and Yoko. It read: YOU AND YOUR JAP TART THINK YOU'RE HOT SHIT. John placed it on Paul's mantel. When Paul walked in and saw it, he confessed to having sent it "for a lark."

John and Yoko were not amused and moved out, continuing to live out of their bags.

Schwartz remained behind on Cavendish Avenue, along with an ever-growing pile of slights and resentments and humiliations. Paul has never discussed her, nor the circumstances of her leaving. Schwartz reported that no one thing made her leave. It was, rather, the slow accumulation of many things and the realization that their relationship would never change. Paul wanted a diligent cook and an accommodating bedmate and little else.

One evening, she later wrote, Paul would be all smiles and promise to take her to the farm in Scotland. But in the morning he would read her the riot act on everything that was wrong with her, real *and* imagined. One day she wept steadily through the afternoon and called her mother in New Jersey for a comforting shoulder to cry on. Paul came in and hugged her and told her to dry her tears. "I'm a cunt," he said.

On his way out he told her to have dinner ready when he got back. Schwartz cooked his dinner, didn't say another word to him, and in the morning got up and packed, stopped at Apple to pick up plane fare home, and went to the airport. She flew coach.

Schwartz later remembered Paul as "petulant, outrageous, adolescent, a little Medici prince, powdered and laid on a satin pillow at a very early age." She also remembered this, though: "He was so pretty."

Throughout early 1968 recording continued sporadically for the album that would become *The Beatles* (the *White Album*). Paul, while assuming control of the Beatles, was gradually shouldering John aside. It was not readily apparent to the loving Beatles' public. Paul and John had long since ceased to do any significant writing or socializing together. *Sgt. Pepper* had seen the end of their serious collaboration and most of *Sgt. Pepper* had actually belonged to Paul alone.

Paul was increasingly flexing his muscles at Abbey Road. When his brother Mike McGear went into the EMI Studios with his group the Scaffold in a sort of last-ditch effort to get a hit record, it was Paul who induced George Martin to produce the session. Paul had also exerted enough muscle earlier to get the Scaffold on to EMI Records, no mean feat when one considered the fact that the Scaffold was, as a sort of topical humor pop group, very much an acquired taste. Such previous single attempts as a Batman parody called "Goodbat Nightman" sailed right by many prospective audiences without the slightest connection being made.

This last attempt by the Scaffold to achieve a salable record was inspired, if indirectly, by Paul. Mike was a devoted photography buff and Paul had given him a new Nikon camera for his birthday. When Mike called to thank him for it, Paul—as was his superstar custom—was silent on the line, leaving the burden of communicating to the calling party.

Mike began a nervous little singsong chant of "Thank you very much for the Nikon camera. Thank you very much." When he got off the phone the chant stayed in his head. He finally recorded it on his Grundig tape recorder (which he had used to tape many of the Beatles' practice sessions at the Cavern back in the prehistoric days of the Fab Four. Coincidentally, he also accidentally erased many of those early Beatles tapes using the same Grundig recorder). The title of Mike's song became "Thank You Very Much for the Aintree Iron" (after the racetrack at Aintree, where Drake's Drum, Paul's father's horse, ran).

Paul came to the Scaffold's recording session in studio 3 at Abbey Road. He said the liked the song, but he advised Mike to change the title. "It's too oblique," he said.

Mike objected, saying that the whole song was oblique. "Have it your way," was Paul's oblique reply, "if you know so much." And he washed his superstar hands of the whole affair.

It became a huge hit, needless to say. The Prime Minister himself confessed that it was his favorite song. "Thank You Very Much for the Aintree Iron" practically became a national slogan. Paul eventually rang Mike up. "You were right about the Aintree iron," he said. "I was wrong."

Paul was also, to his way of thinking, carrying the Beatles. In February when he had conducted Beatle recording sessions, he was the only Beatle present. On February 3 he had finished recording his composition "Lady Madonna" at Abbey Road. George, John, and Ringo had played on early tracks for the song, but Paul decided on his own that he wanted a different sound and went into the studio with four jazz session players—Harry Klein, Bill Jackson, Bill Povey, and Ronnie Scott, all on saxophones—at the last minute. The flip side of the single remained George's first composition of a Beatle single, "The Inner Light." George had recorded that in Bombay in January with Indian musicians. "Lady Madonna" was released in the United Kingdom on March 15 and quickly sold more than two million copies worldwide. It was to be the Beatles' last single on EMI's Parlophone label. Henceforth, everything would be released on their own Apple Records label. "Lady Madonna," dedicated to Paul's late mother Mary, soared to number one in both the United States and the United Kingdom.

On February 4 he recorded the Beatles' first version of "Across the Universe." He decided the song needed female backup singers, so he walked out of the studio and picked two of the Apple Scruffs gathered outside, Lizzie Bravo and Gayleen Pease. (That version was not released until 1969 on the album *No One's Gonna Change Our World,* a compilation album organized by Spike Milligan to benefit the World Wildlife Fund.)

On February 19 Paul and Jane left London with Ringo and Maureen to join John and George in India at the Maharishi's meditation soiree. While he was in Rishikesh, Paul wrote "Back in the USSR" with some assistance from Beach Boy Mike Love. The Beatles even recorded "Happy Birthday Mike Love" later, but the song was never released. On March 26 Paul decided he had had enough of the Maharishi and he and Jane left for London. The meditation course was scheduled to end April 27. No Beatle finished it.

The first cracks that the public glimpsed in the façade of the Magic Kingdom of Apple started to appear very soon. Over the ill-fated overheated summer of 1968 the Apple Boutique reached meltdown very quickly. Two hundred thousand pounds, at a very minimum, had been squandered. John's selection to run the place, his boyhood pal Pete Shotton, was jettisoned in January and was replaced by John Lyndon, who finally applied the financial clamps to The Fool. He threatened them with legal action if clothes continued to walk out of the boutique on their own and if large bills continued to be charged to the Beatles and if certain other such irregularities did not cease. The Beatles were being ripped off at every pass; which really didn't bother them, as long as it was their friends who were doing the ripping off. This pattern would continue as long as Apple and the Beatles remained a sugar tit. The Fool, despite John Lyndon, managed to hang on until Mercury Records succumbed to their charm and hauled them across the Atlantic to sign them to a recording contract. Much to Mercury's regret.

While Paul and John actually didn't mind being ripped off, what finally piqued them was a newspaper column ridiculing them as mere shopkeepers. That stuck in Paul's craw quite a while. That's one reason why he went down, with girlfriend Francie Schwartz, and wrote REVOLUTION and HEY JUDE on the whitewashed windows of the closed boutique. Paul was merely pushing the Beatles' first Apple single, "Hey Jude" and "Revolution." Paul later said that the reason he had done it was that the shop was empty and he felt that it should be put to some use. He also claimed that a man from a nearby Jewish delicatessen, "some feller," called Apple the next day to complain and said, in Paul's quotes, "If my sons vere vif me, I'd send von of them round to kill you. You are doing this terrible thing with the Jewish name. Wat you want, *Juden Raus* [Jew get out], you trying to start the whole Nazi thing again?"

Paul was the one who made the decision to shut down the boutique. John still defended his pal Magic Alex, who had hundreds of his Nothing Boxes (boxes that had twelve lights and did just that) gathering dust in the boutique's basement on Baker Street. Meanwhile the shelves upstairs were cluttered with elaborate Hobbit clothes that nobody wanted to buy. It was a great place to shoplift, to star gaze, and to hang out. And that was about all, as the Beatles themselves finally admitted. So Paul was the one who finally dropped the hatchet. He held a staff meeting at Apple to announce the closing and wrote the following press handout to explain or at least try to justify it:

We decided to close down our Baker Street shop yesterday and instead of putting up a sign saying BUSINESS WILL BE RESUMED AS SOON AS POSSIBLE and then auction off the goods, we decided to give them away. The shops were doing fine and making a nice profit on turnover. So far, the biggest loss is in giving the things away but we did that deliberately. We're giving them away—rather than selling them to barrow-boys because we wanted to give rather than sell. We came into shops by the tradesman's entrance but we're leaving by the front door. Originally, the shops were intended to be something else, but they just became like all the boutiques in London. They just weren't our thingy. The staff will get three weeks pay but if they wish they'll be absorbed into the rest of Apple. Everyone will be cared for. The Kings Road shop, which is known as Apple Tailoring, isn't going to be part of Apple anymore but it isn't closing down and we are leaving our investment there because we have a moral and personal obligation to our partner John Crittle who is now in sole control. All that's happened is that we've closed our shop in which we feel we shouldn't, in the first place, have been involved. Our main business is entertainment—communication. Apple is mainly concerned with fun not with frocks. We want to devote all our energies to records, films and our electronics adventures. We had to re-focus. We had to zoom in on what we really enjoy and we enjoy being alive and we enjoy being Beatles. It's 1968; already, it's 1968. Time is short. I suppose really that what we're doing is spring cleaning in mid-summer. The amazing thing is that the amazing thing is our giving things away. Well, the answer is that it was much funnier giving things away.

Apple press officer Derek Taylor added a closing paragraph:

Well. It's just that the Beatles are the Beatles are the mop tops are the mop tops are the Beatles are the mop tops . . . are whatever you see them to be, whatever you see us to be. Create and preserve the image of your choice. We are yours with love.
—John Lennon, Paul McCartney, George Harrison, and Ringo Starr.

The night before all of Apple Boutique was to be bequeathed to the real public at large as a Beatle largess, the Beatles themselves swooped down on the Baker Street shop and stripped the place of anything worth anything. Yoko Ono led the charge and unrolled bolts of expensive Apple Boutique fabrics—silk and velvet—on the floor, loaded the bolts with goodies, rolled them up like pirate's bindles, and hauled them off in John's psychedelic Rolls.

The next morning, July 31, the general public was allowed in to paw through the remains. People were lined up for many blocks for what they thought was the biggest giveaway of their time. What actually remained in the shop—estimated at only $35,000 or so—was quickly spirited away. Then people began ripping the shop itself apart. Soon nothing remained but the four walls, the ceiling, and the floor. Even that was not sacred. The staff drew the line when people began to rip up the carpet and asked everyone to leave.

Throughout 1968 Paul kept his eye—or at least his hand—on all Apple activities. He was determined to make his discoveries not only do well but excel. Apple's first releases, all Paul's projects, were to be four singles released together in a boxed set, heralded as *The First Four*. The first of those was Paul's "Hey Jude" backed with John's "Revolution." "Hey Jude," of course, was written by Paul for John's son Julian on a visit to Julian and his mother Cynthia while John was off cavorting with Yoko. The original version of the song used the name "Jules" instead of "Jude." John later helped Paul finish it at Paul's house in St. John's Wood on the afternoon of July 26. They rehearsed the song at Abbey Road the following Monday with a camera crew present. On Wednesday they moved to Trident Studios and recorded a second version with George on guitar and Ringo playing tambourine. Paul wanted a ninety-musician symphony orchestra but producer George Martin convinced him that ninety-piece symphony orchestras were not on twenty-four-hour call for the Beatles' convenience. Martin did manage to round up forty musicians for an afternoon session on August 1. They did not receive extra pay for singing the backing vocals. The second single in the boxed set was "Thingummybob" by the Black Dyke Mills Band. Paul wrote the song himself as the theme song for a television comedy and he personally visited the band in the town of Bradford. Paul amazed the hotel staff in Bradford. When he checked in with Martha, his sheepdog, he instructed the staff to give her a bath. "It's her arse," Paul explained, lifting Martha up and displaying her matted and soiled hair. The third single was by Jackie Lomax, another Paul discovery, singing George's song "Sour Milk Sea." And the fourth "find" was all Paul's. Singer Mary Hopkin was a sweet-voiced seventeen-year-old Welsh lass when Paul found her. He took the unprecedented step of writing her press release and bio himself. It read:

I heard of Mary first in Liverpool. Justin and Twiggy had come up in their new car . . . showing off again . . . you know how it is. Well, we were eating our pudding later that evening and then talked about "Opportunity Knocks" and discovery shows generally and I wondered whether anyone ever got discovered, I mean really discovered on discovery shows. Then Twiggy said she had seen a great girl singer on "Opportunity Knocks" and luckily as it turned out this was the time we were looking around for singers for Apple Records. When I got back to London next day, several other people mentioned her so it began to look as if Mary really was something. Twiggy's not soft. So I got her phone number from the television company and rang her at

home in Pontardawe, Somewhere in Wales, and this beautiful little Welsh voice came on the phone and I said: "This is
Apple Records here. Would you be interested in coming
down here to record for us?" She said, "Well, er, would
you like to speak to my mother?" and then her mother
came on the line and we had a chat and two further telephone conversations and later that week Mary and her mum
came to London. We had a nice lunch and went to Dick
James studios in Oxford Street and I thought she was great.
She sang a lot of songs on tape and I knew she was great
. . . She seemed to mean what she sang. Most impressive.
But at the same time, I thought she was very Joan Baez—a
lot of Joan's influence showed. However, Mary said she
could do other things and I agreed that there was no limit to
her possibilities. There couldn't be a limit because she was
very together. Well . . . a long time earlier, maybe a couple
of years ago I'd first heard 'Those Were the Days' when
Gene [Raskin] and Francesca, American singers, sang it in
the Blue Angel in London and I'd always remembered it. It
was the big number in their act and Gene had written it. I'd
tried to get someone to record it because it was so good. I'd
hoped the Moody Blues might do it but it didn't really
work out and later in India I played it to Donovan who
loved it but didn't get around to doing it. So it was lovely
to be able to play it to Mary and it was lovely that she liked
it. We rang Essex Music, the publishers of the song, but
they didn't know anything about it other than they owned
the song. They had no lead sheets, no demos. But David
Platz of Essex, nice man, sent to America and we got the
demo and everything. I showed Mary how I thought the
song should be done and she picked it up very easily—as if
she'd known it for years. At first, though, she was singing
it as if she didn't mean it, which was strange for Mary, very
strange.

But it was her first time in the studio and it can be
frightening. After a few tapes, I kept showing her the way
she should sing it and generally worked on it and suddenly
she got it and we just put a tambourine on it and went
home. "Turn, Turn, Turn" we got in one take. One take.

Imagine that. When she's offstage, she's offstage and when she's onstage, she's really on. That's what's great about her. She really is like that girl next door; the real thing; kind and quiet and she blushes and smiles shyly. It's like when she says, "Yes, I go out with boys, but it's just kissing." Great. It's due to her background. Normal.

Her parents are good solid Welsh parents, her father works for the local council and her mother is a very intelligent woman so we're going to look after Mary and make sure no harm comes to her. Work starts on her album soon and we are going in all kinds of directions, as she's capable of singing anything. I'd like to hear her shout. That would be good. To hear her really shout. I know she can. Everyone can.

"Those Were the Days" was a smash hit for Hopkin and for Apple. It succeeded "Hey Jude" as number one in the United Kingdom. And, at least initially, Paul took a tremendous interest in Hopkin's career, overseeing every detail. He wrote Apple press officer Derek Taylor frequently about her, as in the following note: DEAR DEGS OR DICK, PLEASE MAKE SURE MARY'S RECORD IS PERMANENTLY OBVIOUS TO THE POPULUS. WE'RE OFF FOR TWO WEEKS; JACKIE'S [Lomax] "THUMBING A RIDE" (IF IT'S A SINGLE) NEEDS THE SAME THING, DON'T WE ALL? I MENTIONED TO SOME THE IDEA OF HAVING: "APPLE PRESENTS . . . THUMBING A RIDE, JACKIE LOMAX" PHOTO COMIC STRIP THING WHICH COULD BECOME APPLE FEATURE IN, SAY, 16 [*16* magazine]. WE DO LAYOUT. ANYWAY, THINK OF SOME OF THESE KIND OF THINGS. I LEAVE IT TO YOU. LOVE, PAUL LINDA HEATHCLIFFE LIVERPOOL, AMERICA, THEN A REST. Hand-drawn hearts were scattered across the bottom of the page.

When Paul was to present Mary Hopkin to the world, he decided on a large-scale press blowout. The result was a midafternoon press reception at the Post Office Tower, a London landmark. Paul's last-minute order was to decorate the place with a large barrel full of apples. So, at considerable expense, the Apple staff scoured London looking for a large barrel. Finally a walk-in barrel was located, along with enough cases of green Granny Smith apples to fill it. There were three hundred guests

' and enough liquor flowed for thrice that many. Paul himself "gave Mary away," as several reporters characterized the event.

Linda Eastman herself "came out" at the event and the press was of course more interested in her than in young Mary. Paul gamely stayed till the end, bravely championing his little discovery. Donovan, who had three of his compositions on Mary's album, came and sang. Jimi Hendrix showed up toward the end, after four hours or so.

Although Mary sold about four million copies of "Those Were the Days," she was obviously never comfortable at Apple. As Paul's protégée, she was both resented and isolated. Paul had little time or attention for her. He dashed off a composition for her second single, "Goodbye," in a few minutes one day when she pressed him for a song. It went to number two in the United Kingdom and number thirteen in the United States. Her subsequent Apple singles—"Temma Harbour," "Knock Knock Who's There?", and "Think About Your Children"—reached number six, number two, and number nineteen in the United Kingdom in 1970 but did not chart in the United States.

When Mary named her sister Carol as her manager, Apple grew frosty toward her. Mary was also not encouraged by the fact that Paul pressed her to record the song "Que Sera Sera." She did not want to become another Doris Day and was dismayed when Paul persisted, saying the song had been a favorite of his, that he honestly loved the song. Mary voluntarily left Apple in 1972 after marrying producer Tony Visconti.

When Apple press officer Derek Taylor met Linda Eastman (or, rather, as she first encountered the whole Apple scene), he felt her displeasure almost immediately. He had, after all, created a very comfortable little bird's nest with his cozy press office and his daily scene: cigarettes and booze being charged to the Fab Four, Scotch and other drinks being served up all day, very nice long drunken lunches, and not a great deal of work ever getting done. Taylor was charitable to Linda, feeling that it was just her way of making Paul happy. The latter was directing his ire daily at Taylor and many others at Apple. As Paul saw his and John's great Apple experiment slowly self-destruct, his distress became severe. He did try to rein in the weirdness, but it was just out of control.

One morning near the end of the summer in 1968, Paul paid a surprise visit to the office. His face unshaven and grim, he was wearing a long dark overcoat and he swept in with the obvious air of a man who feels the need to kick a little ass. He called an immediate staff meeting. Everyone who happened to be there assembled in Ron Kass's sprawling office and arranged themselves in various states of repose as they waited to see what Paul had on his mind that day. Nothing too drastic, they figured.

They straightened up right quick when he gave them a severe tongue-lashing, starting out with, "Don't forget, you're not very good, any of you. You know that, don't you?" He meant it. That's what really hurt. He had—it was obvious—as little regard for the people in that room as people as he had for the lowliest parasitic worm.

Taylor felt as though he had been kicked in the stomach. He later observed: "I don't think I ever hated anyone as much as I hated Paul in the summer of 1968."

Taylor became the object of one of Paul's favorite weapons: anonymous mail. He received a stream of postcards, the postmarks reflecting wherever Paul was at the time: America, Scotland, London. Some bore nasty messages, some were merely nonsensical. Sometimes the postage stamp had been tore down the middle, then carefully pasted on the card to leave a gap between the two halves. Taylor's wife Joan got a card that read: TELL YOUR BOY TO OBEY THE SCHOOLMASTERS. It was signed: PATRON.

Paul also decided he wanted a roof garden on the Apple building on Savile Row.

He would also stroll through the building, taking careful note of what was where and of who had what. There was originally a partition in the press office. Paul, one night when he was alone, went in and wrote SHIT on it. Then the next day he complained about it. The following weekend the partition was removed. Another one was promptly installed. A door appeared in the partition. Taylor and his coworkers put up signs reading: THIS WALL IS DISGUSTING. THIS WALL MUST GO. THIS IS REVOLTING.

One morning they found that someone—and they had a good idea of who that someone was—had written underneath THIS WALL IS DISGUSTING an addition: SO ARE SOME OF THE PEOPLE IN THIS ROOM.

Taylor, to counter what he felt was a campaign of subtle terror aimed at him and his little staff and to deal with what he called the "increasing unavailability and pessimism of the Beatles," tried to make the press office a bright center of fun and jollity at Apple. The staff's greatest problems were caused by the Beatles being there when they weren't needed or vice versa. The two words that everyone most dreaded to hear upon returning from a long and satisfying lunch were "Paul phoned."

Back in 1965, Paul had purchased the handsome 140-year-old Georgian structure at number 7 Cavendish Avenue in St. John's Wood for forty thousand pounds. Paul then had it restored and, with Jane's help, decorated and furnished. He also had a home studio built in. It was a short walk from Abbey Road and the two locations soon became the favorite London haunt of the most fanatical of all the Beatle fans: the Apple Scruffs.

The Scruffs were a tiny band of teenage girls who, by accident, hit upon the idea that the ultimate in Beatle fandom—short of marriage or at least sexual congress with an actual Beatle—was a sort of act of devotion called Waiting Out. What it entailed was exactly that: waiting for the Beatles, whether it was outside the Apple Headquarters, the studio at Abbey Road, Paul's house on Cavendish Avenue, or wherever the lads might be. It also involved knowing in advance where the Fabs would be, so the Scruffs could be there to greet their idols or idol as they arrived. The Scruffs would then wait outside until the object of love and lust departed. They also brought presents: flowers, cards, drawings, and the like. And they endeavored to protect the Beatles from Mere Tourists, or "temporary fans," as they derisively referred to them. They also shielded the boys from the large numbers of homosexuals who came around to admire them and maybe more.

The girls took new names to identify themselves: thus a girl named Sue who liked John best called herself Sue–John. Paul and George had the biggest number of hyphenated girls waiting out for them, John never had more than one at a time, and Ringo never had one. These were not fair-weather fans, mind you. Some of them did this for years, Waiting Out all night and then going on to school or work. One moved over to London from Texas, another from Chicago, yet another from Virginia.

They eventually started their own monthly magazine, which was avidly read by Beatles and Apple staff alike, for the Scruffs had developed a highly organized network of informants. They also had their own jargon. For example, their words for male genitalia were "tea bags" and "shoes."

The Beatles went from an attitude of astonishment to mild irritation with the Scruffs to a sort of amused paternalism and eventually a sort of resigned affection for the girls. Paul let one of them walk his sheepdog Martha in Regent's Park. All they seemed to want—or to settle for, at least—was recognition from Her Beatle. They would Wait Out all night just for a "Goodbye" in the morning. A word, a look, a touch—that's all they required. Of course, anything more was greatly appreciated. One of the Scruffs was eventually hired by Apple as a receptionist and John paid her a clothing allowance because he liked to see her dressed all in black or all in white. Another became a tea girl at Apple.

George wrote a song about them called "Apple Scruffs" and even arranged for *Rolling Stone* to interview them. When the piece appeared, George asked them how they liked it. They didn't. "We were misquoted," one of them complained. "Now you know how it feels," George replied caustically. The Beatles befriended the Scruffs now and then. Paul took two of them to John's birthday party.

The Scruffs were almost tolerant of the Beatle women. They basically approved of Patti Boyd for George because Patti was a gorgeous model and she seemed to be right for George if they couldn't have him. They despised Francie Schwartz for having had no respect for the Scruff system and for bypassing it to move in directly with Paul. They were happy to see that one go—and knew it would happen all along. No class, that one.

Yoko was simply outside the pale. But the Scruffs basically thought that Jane Asher was okay for Paul. She was an actress, she was stunningly pretty, she dressed well, she came from a good family, and she and Paul made a good-looking couple. If Jane married Paul, as everyone expected, it could be tolerated.

What could not be was the invasion by the American photographer, as the Scruffs first referred to Linda Eastman. Ever since she had ensconsed herself at number 7 Cavendish on Halloween Day in 1968, she had been an object of open scorn and derision by the Scruffs. She didn't dress right, for one thing. Knee socks, for God's sakes! Shapeless dresses. No style at all. And those tits! Her breasts "bounce off her knees," the Scruffs would tell each other loudly when Linda was within earshot. And Linda ignored the Scruffs, pretended they didn't exist, and, since her arrival, Paul came out of the house less and less to talk to "his girls."

But the news of the wedding cut them all to the quick. He could live with the hussy if he wanted to. But marrying her shut them, the fans, out of his life forever. They no longer could dream. He was taking that away from them. Each Scruff, especially, felt that she was special to Paul and now he was denying that specialness. So, in the face of such adversity, it was no surprise that the fans pulled together to bolster each other. The "regulars" even took in the "temporaries," who gathered in London from all over England when they heard news of the marriage. The circle of weeping girls outside the high gates to Paul's house grew. The Scruffs, thanks to their spy network, knew that Linda was pregnant, but still . . . Paul tried to apologize to "his girls," telling them they knew he would get married sometime, but they weren't having any of it. Some were literally in shock and the police were called in to stand outside the gates. Paul's housekeeper Rosie told the Scruffs that the wedding would be at Marylebone Registry Office on March 12 and that there would then be a blessing at the Church in St. John's Wood, so they had plenty of time to get to both locations. They also knew that Linda had gone herself to get the license. Paul had forgotten to get a ring and finally went out and persuaded a jeweler to open his closed doors and sell him a wedding ring for twelve pounds.

After the ceremony itself—which was delayed by Mike McGear's late arrival—the press had a field day with all the crying McCartney "widows" outside. One of them, who became quite celebrated in the press, was a hairdresser named Jill Pritchard in Redditch, Worcestershire, who had been doing a woman's hair when the news came on the radio. She left, just like that, in midcurl and turned up weeping forlornly on the front pages of London's tabloids.

The Scruff who was closest to Paul and who walked Martha for him, Margo, had had to bring her baby-sitting charge with her to Wait Out at Marylebone Registry. The child's nickname was Bam Bam because that's all he could yet say. Paul knew Bam Bam from the times Margo and Bam Bam came around to collect Martha.

When Paul and Linda left the Registry Office, there was a terrific crush between reporters and photographers and "widows" and, just as Paul managed to get Linda into his car, the "widows" were crushed by a wave of pressure from the press and Bam Bam screamed. Paul turned, for he knew the child's voice, and called out, "Is he all right, Margo?"

Paul and Linda sped away and then the press turned its attention to Margo and Bam Bam: this blond girl holding up a crying child that Paul recognized. "Whose kid was it, anyway?" the press wanted to know. So Margo and Bam Bam, the mystery kid, made their appearance on the front of the tabs that day.

John and Yoko ran off to get married eight days after Paul and Linda had done so. Paul felt rather smug that John was starting to ape *him* for a change. John, later stung by even the notion that he would follow rather than lead, publicly baited Paul as being—artistically at least—two years behind John in every way.

At Christmas in 1968, the Beatles for the first time almost lacked the heart to even send out their traditional "Beatles Christmas Record" to the members of the British Beatles Fan Club.

The tradition had started in 1963 as a genuine token of the Beatles' affection for their fan club members, who were fans in the true sense of "fanatics." Surprisingly, for a band with such widespread public acclaim, the Beatles sought to stay as close to their fans as they could. There had to be a limit to public contact, of course, but the group tried to do what they could to reciprocate their fans' regard and affection. In December of 1963, for instance, the group gave special performances for fans only: for the Northern Area Fan Club on December 7 at the Liverpool Empire and for the Southern England Fan Club Convention on December 14 at the Wimbledon Palais.

That year the Beatles also recorded and mailed out, on December 6, 1963, the first "Beatles Christmas Record." It ran five minutes and ten seconds and was recorded by all four Beatles in Studio 2 at Abbey Road on October 19 after a session for "I Want to Hold Your Hand" and "This Boy." It is mostly nonsensical, very much in the early Beatle tradition. It opens with a short version of "From Me to You," which then slides into "Good King Wenceslaus." Then each of the four thanks the fans for their support and the gifts they've sent. Paul was the most serious of the four, announcing that they no longer liked jelly babies. (George had once mentioned that onstage, much to their subsequent regret when the tons of boxes began pouring in.) At the end of the record all four harmonize on "Doo-dah, the Red-Nosed Reindeer."

The 1963 Christmas record had not been planned as an annual event, but fan reaction was so great that the four decided to try it again. And again and again. By 1966 they were actually writing scripts for the Christmas records and rehearsing them and they even brought George Martin in to produce the session. Paul told the story of "Podgy the Bear and Jasper." Then Paul, John, and Ringo did a skit called "A Rare Cheese." In 1967 they even had a special guest (actor Victor Spinetti) and an elaborate cover, designed by John, Ringo, and John's son Julian. Paul did a skit with John with Paul as the interviewer and John as "a cross-section of British youth."

In 1968, though, the four of them couldn't get together long enough to record a Christmas message. Paul still wanted to do it, though. He had already designed a cover for the record, a non-Christmasy geometric design. The others finally agreed—if the recording studio would come to them. So each of the four recorded separate Christmas greetings to the fans in what amounted to field recordings, done by engineer Kenny Everett. Then Everett managed to make it sound presentable by splicing and editing and even adding sound pieces from the sessions for the *White Album*.

The 1968 Christmas record, called "Happy Christmas," ended with special guest Tiny Tim warbling "Nowhere Man."

There would be one more "Beatles Christmas Record," released in 1969, but it was even less spirited than 1968's had been. Again it was recorded separately by the four. John and Yoko appeared together at length, singing and performing little domestic skits.

For Christmas in 1970, after the Beatles had officially broken up, fan club members received an album containing all seven Christmas singles covering 1963 through 1969.

★　　★　　★

The Beatles were dead long before Paul led them—almost, it seemed, against their will—up on to the wind-swept roof of Apple that frigid January 30, 1969.

For their final public hurrah, the four Beatles finally resembled the individuals that they were growing into. At their previous Last Concert, the August 29, 1966, farewell in Candlestick Park in San Francisco, they had still been the Fab Four, object of teen dreams on an unprecedented scale, global mass hysteria, and moist underwear. Since then they had undergone LSD, *Sgt. Pepper,* worldwide cult-status, and a startling introduction to the bizarre world of global business and finances attendant to being a Social Phenomenon. At this point, Apple was *totally* out of control. Millions of dollars came and went—where to, no one knew. As Beatles, they were at once holy figures and prisoners of tawdry fame. And targets of every would-be con artist man in the world.

Small wonder that they started to grow protective shells. At the close of 1968, John was twenty-eight years old, Paul was twenty-six, George was twenty-six, and Ringo was twenty-eight. Except for Paul, they had no illusions left for Beatledom. George and Ringo had been treated as second-class session men for so long that they grew to know their place. George had quit the Beatles a couple of weeks before the rooftop show, on January 10, after a particularly demeaning dressing-down from Paul, in which Paul told him how to play guitar. George declared that he could no longer participate in something that he couldn't believe in. But he quickly crawled back. Ringo knew he was lucky to be where he was. And John—well, he was John and he would do as he damned well pleased—after checking with Yoko, that is. Yoko, who was new to the Beatle scene, was hovering on the periphery of this action. So was Linda Eastman, for that matter.

But up on the Apple roof, the Beatles were the Beatles for the last time ever in public view. They—ever so briefly—reveled in performing once again. George, with his high-top black Converse sneakers and rakish mustache, evoked the image of his black-leather delinquent adolescence. John, long-haired and dressed all in black, played his hollow-body Gibson with rare abandon. Ringo was—well, he was Ringo, which is all anyone ever asked of him. But Paul was all business. He was full-bearded then and seemed to gain confidence with the long hair and whiskers and somber suit and hiking boots he wore. As Head Beatle, he was completely oblivious to what the others felt, wanted, needed, or even perceived.

In a scene that was deleted from what would become a film of this Beatle period (*Let It Be)*, Paul discussed writing "Don't Dig No Pakistanis." He said he was trying to make a political state-ment about the Harold Wilson government and its immigration policy. John persuaded Paul to lighten up a tad on the song and it eventually became "Get Back," the first number the group per-formed for the film. This documentary movie originally had *Get Back* as a working title. By the time it was finished, things with the Beatles reached such a perilous state that none of the Fab Four even considered attending the movie's gala world premiere on May 20, 1970, at the London Pavilion. Interestingly, both John's and Paul's exes, Cynthia Lennon and Jane Asher, showed up. Apple employees who were in attendance worried with each other about what to tell any of the Four who asked about the premiere.

Initially, the *Let It Be/Get Back* project was no more loopy an idea than anything else the Beatles and their attendant Apple zanies had conceived. Paul was unarguably the most stable of the Fab Four and he had early on told Apple staffers that Apple's aim was "controlled weirdness. You are into that, aren't you?" Paul had also described Apple as a "huge commercial, creative com-plex along the lines of British Petroleum" and as "a Western form of communism."

Apple itself quickly became the logical projection of what would happen to an acid head who came into money: a wobbly, wavy nightmare except when it was a groove (which wasn't often) and oh man what the nightmares were like. Every LSD-damaged, brain-addled freak in the world, it seemed, camped out in Apple's plush waiting room, waiting for John's or Paul's healing hand or—lacking that—an Apple check for thousands of pounds to bankroll every crackpot scheme in the universe.

The whole history of what came to be *Let It Be* was, like most Beatle projects, hazy and haphazard. Paul wanted the Beatles to continue when it seemed as if the group had died. It had, effec-tively. Paul whipped the remains into doing a project. It was originally planned as a televised Beatle concert, which never materialized. It would become a movie after the Beatles realized that they still owed United Artists one more movie on their three-picture deal because the animated cartoon *Yellow Submarine* was not considered a "real" motion picture.

Let It Be began as a film/record at Twickenham Film Studios, since Ringo was appearing in *The Magic Christian* there and didn't want to go anywhere else. The place was a drafty, chilly wind tunnel, but the Beatles began to assemble an album and a documentary there on January 2. Paul had whipped the others into shape; he had been so addled on the idea of touring again that he once performed at a Bedfordshire pub totally out of it. He alone of the four felt an acute need to perform before a live audience—without that he, as a performer, was not whole. Paul at one point delivered a startling lecture to the others: "I mean we've been very negative since Mr. [Brian] Epstein passed away. That's why. We haven't been positive. That's why all of us in turn have been sick of the group, you know. There's nothing positive in it. It is a bit of a drag. It's like when you're growing up and then your daddy goes away at a certain point in your life and then you stand on your own feet. Daddy has gone away now, you know, and we are on our own little holiday camp. You know, I think we either go home or we do it. It's discipline we need. It's like everything you do, you never had discipline. Mr. Epstein, he said, sort of, 'Get suits on' and we did. And so we were always fighting that discipline a bit. But now it's silly to fight that discipline if it's our own. It's self-imposed these days, so we do as little as possible. But I think we need a bit more if we are going to get on with it."

In the face of this paternal air on Paul's part, George automatically turned into the rebellious son. Paul continued: "Would you like to do a live show, lads?"

George replied: "It's like hard work really to do it. It's a drag 'cos I don't wanta work really . . . have to get up at eight and get into my guitar . . . 'You've got to play your guitar now' . . . You dig, baby?" Paul replied, "Yeah."

"You're so full of shit, man," George said.

"What?" Paul demanded.

George: " 'Before you can pry any secrets from me, first you must find the real me. Which one will you pursue?' . . . Did you see that?"

"What?"

"The Beard."

"No."

"It's Jean Harlow and Billy the Kid in eternity. It's just the idea of two people onstage and all this audience of different people overhearing what they're saying. Jean Harlow says: 'Before you can pry any secrets from me, first you must find the real me. Which one will you pursue?' "

When the movie/record had first been mentioned as an idea, back in November 1968, Paul said the group agreed to perform a series of three live shows in London, which would be recorded for a worldwide television broadcast. He wanted the concerts to be mostly made up of songs from the *White Album,* which had been released in England on November 22. This was Paul's master plan to rejuvenate the group. A film crew was hired for the period of January 17–24, 1969, and the group booked the Roundhouse Theatre in London for the night of January 18. Concert dates had been tentatively set for London in late December 1968, but these plans went awry when Paul took an extended vacation in Algarve, Portugal, beginning on December 11, with Linda Eastman and her daughter Heather. In Portugal they stayed—as unexpected guests—with Official Beatles Biographer Hunter Davies. Paul had chartered a plane and arrived in the middle of the night, unannounced, with no Portuguese currency but with several bottles of whiskey in hand. Davies had to pay the taxi driver.

On January 2 the Beatles began filming and recording at Twickenham Studios. Paul was bubbly, enthusiastic. But John later remembered: "It was hell making the film. When it came out a lot of people complained about Yoko looking miserable in it. But even the biggest Beatle fan couldn't have sat through those six weeks of misery. It was the most miserable session on earth."

Plans still called for a TV show of sixty minutes' duration, similar to their "Hey Jude" clip, with audience participation. Paul also persuaded the Beatles to allow a documentary film to be shot of their preparations. As rehearsals went on, the group worked on eight new songs, thus getting away from the *White Album* idea, and ideas were bounced around as to where to shoot a live concert. The director, Michael Lindsay-Hogg, wanted to go to Africa. He and producer Denis O'Dell had once been to an old Roman amphitheater in Tunisia and wanted to film there. There were many discussions about where to film.

At one point Lindsay-Hogg said to the group: "Well, I think one of those things that's wrong about doing the show here is that it's too easy. Like when we are in the car looking for locations and glorified boutiques, I think that's wrong. But just doing it in the backyard. I mean it's literal. It's almost your backyard. Twickenham. There's no balls to the show at all. I mean there's no balls in any of us, I'm included, and that's why I think we are being soft about it. You are the Beatles; you aren't four jerks. You know what I mean."

Paul replied: "It bugs me when they zoom in and out. I'd like it to be like an old movie. If you want to say anything, you walk up to the camera. The only thing that doesn't need to move is the camera. It's like Oriental medicine and Western medicine. We practice for the symptoms; they are into preventing it. It's like a switch—get us to do the movement."

Ringo: "I'd like it like a country program where you have one camera, just step in and do your bit, like Flatt and Scruggs on 'The Grand Ole Opry,'; they'd all move in when their solo came around and take the center so they acted out the shots."

Paul: "Dreaming in public is the thing. You know those dreams where you go down a helter-skelter? And the scene changes? But doing that awake. The latest thing from Apple!"

Paul would later claim extensive familiarity with the world of the avant-garde; that, long before John and Yoko began their much-publicized happenings and bag-ins and whatnot, he had been showing his films to Antonioni and that he regularly hung out with William Burroughs and Marianne Faithfull and that circle, making little avant-garde tapes. And he was a regular at the UFO Club. And that he used to throw Ravi Shankar records on with his home movies, to John's great amazement and wonder. But, Paul would add tellingly, he, unlike John, never felt moved to run and tell *New Musical Express* or *Melody Maker* about all the hip things he was doing. But Paul certainly felt at home with that *Let It Be* film. After all, hadn't *Magical Mystery Tour* been his idea, a true brainstorm? His assumed familiarity with visuals is a constant throughout his career with varied results.

With *Let It Be,* though, he was not timid to issue directions: "Get very bright lights so you see everything, instead of moody lighting, that kind of thing. With everything here, it hardly needs scenery. Really, it all should be about him and his drum kit. Look at his drum kit. It really looks great, beautiful, sitting there. Then John and his guitar and his amp, sitting there, actually showing it at that minute. The scenery would be just the other things around, like the scaffolding, the other cameras. It's like in a news event, like on 'Jude' the little screams were more interesting than the postman. If you can think slow, not bang! bang! bang! Instead of getting all the pacing, a chair lift, the flow, the pace is already there. You can glide down from the roof on a one shot on to Ringo's face, float around, being careful not to miss anything. It's like Warhol's things; he goes to the other extreme, but he reckons there's a pace in 'Empire.' Even a Tunisian amphitheater can be boring. I don't dig underestimating what's here. If it's going to be scenery, we should go the whole way and get galloping horses. You should get really close up, like right into one of John's eyes. Can you do that? That direction, rather than John and the moon."

That the film took on a schizophrenic air is understandable. They continued to debate exotic settings, each more grandiose than the one before, including the famous Tunisian amphitheater, the House of Parliament, a cathedral in Liverpool—the possibilities were endless. Even an ocean liner was mentioned.

George: "You know it's going to be the same thing there as here; it's going to be a nicer place to be in, but it's going to be even more complicated trying to plug in on all the mikes and tapes and all that crap."

Michael Lindsay-Hogg: "First of all visually the thing that interests me . . . naturally . . . think of the helicopter shot over the amphitheater with the water with the lights and the water, torch-lit, two thousand Arabs. You know what I mean. Visually it's fantastic."

Paul: "But if it was a fan club show—You remember the Wembley, or the Wimbledon one where we were in a cage, and like people were filing past—it was just a different kind of thing from what we ever did. It was terrible. That's not it. But that kind of thing made that show different because it was like playing to a thing, like a fan club."

John: "I'm warming up to the idea of an asylum."

Ultimately, a sort of crazed common sense prevailed and the roof of Apple was decided upon as a location.

Lindsay-Hogg: "Shall we go on filming until we leave here?"

Paul: "What we're doing is still rehearsing and we'll get it together."

George: "We'll collect our thoughts and you collect yours about where we'll do the concert."

Lindsay-Hogg: "What about the roof tomorrow?"

Paul: "We'll do the numbers. We're the band."

George: "I'll do it if you've got us on the roof."

John: "I'd like to go on the roof. I'll record the songs when you want to do it."

George: "Anytime is paradise."

John: "Anytime at all. You suggest where: Pakistan, the moon, I'll still be there till you don't let me down. You'll be surprised at the story that will come out of this."

Ahead they forged, ultimately assembling some eight hundred hours of film (four cameras in use) over two months. Visually, it became a harried, haphazard record of the Beatles supposedly at work, but in truth going through a slow disintegration. You see revealing asides, such as Paul talking down to John: "Now look, son." And Paul going after George: "I always seem to be annoying you . . ." George snaps back: "All right, I'll play whatever you want me to play. Or I won't play at all if you don't want me to play."

Surprisingly, as chaotic as the situation was and as reluctant as John and George were to share Paul's vision of the Beatle future, much of the music recorded in these rehearsals was memorable and still stands up. By most accounts, about thirty hours of music was recorded, and most of that has never surfaced. Presumably, it is still in the Apple vaults. What would later be issued as the *Let It Be* album did not reflect the richness of what was recorded, but that was due more to the politics surrounding the group than to the inherent quality of the tapes themselves. Paul's "The Long and Winding Road," for example, was released in a sweetened version that he himself did not hear until the public did. And he was furious about it, but that was due to group politics and the Allen Klein Factor.

Apple originally announced an August 1969 release for *The*

Beatles Get Back album, with the following cuts on it: "The One After 909," "Save the Last Dance for Me," "Don't Let Me Down," "Dig a Pony," "I've Got a Feeling," "Get Back," "For You Blue," "Teddy Boy," "Two of Us on Our Way Home," "Maggie Mae," "Dig It," "Let It Be," and "The Long and Winding Road." As Apple and Beatles politics deteriorated, the album never appeared.

Too, since the *Let It Be* movie was still unresolved, the group decided to hold back the album until everything was sorted out. The tapes, which had been produced by George Martin and engineered by Glyn Johns, were given to Johns for a complete remix. Later, as we shall see, Phil Spector became part of the mix. Also, as a stopgap album measure, the Beatles went back into the studio during the difficult summer of 1969 to record "Abbey Road," which is pretty much Paul's album.

During the *Let It Be* sessions, the group recorded, as was their custom, numerous versions of rock standards as they warmed up: everything from "Thirty Days" to "Hippy Hippy Shake" to "Hitch Hike" to "High-Heel Sneakers" to "It's Only Make Believe" to "Baby I Don't Care" to "Rock Island Line" to "Good Rockin' Tonight" to "All Shook Up," just to mention a few. It was as if the music created by the Beatles still stood apart—and on a much higher plane—from the reality of the group itself. Looking at the film is one thing; hearing it is another. The eventual *Let It Be* album had twelve songs; the movie had twenty-three, as songs were repeated, including three different versions of "The Long and Winding Road," "Two of Us," and "Get Back" and two different versions of "I Got a Feeling," "Dig a Pony," "Shake, Rattle and Roll," "Lawdy, Miss Clawdy," "Maxwell's Silver Hammer," "I Me Mine," and "Across the Universe."

Michael Lindsay-Hogg, stoical during the filming, later described the reality of his experience. "It's lucky there is a movie," he said. "There was a big push all the time to get them going. Even though half of them always were behind it, the trouble was it was never the same half. It was a terribly painful, frustrating experience. It's not that I don't like them. I do. It's just that when we were trying to make the film, every day there was a different one to hate."

After a year of editing *Let It Be* was released to a chorus of critical yawns. To sample some of the British press: The *Morning Star* wrote that "For those who expected it to throw some light on the development of the Beatles phenomenon, it is disappointingly barren . . . Paul McCartney, now very much the guiding spirit of the team, comes over as a thoroughgoing professional who, one can imagine, may switch off his Beatle self out of studio hours and change into quite a different kind of person at home. George Harrison, with his strong-boned face and shut-in expression, looks as if he could fit into any tough and isolated position—as a shepherd in Bulgaria or the manager of a suburban sub-post office. John Lennon and Ringo Starr appear to be the true individualists, as far as the film allows us to glimpse their individuality, with Beatle eccentricity running through their veins." Said the *Times:* "It might be fun if it were not so grainily photographed, so incomprehensibly recorded and, at times, so earratically synchronised." The *Sunday Telegraph* observed that "It is only incidentally that one gleans anything about their real characters—the way in which music now seems to be the only unifying force to hold them together: the way Paul McCartney chatters incessantly even when, it seems, none of the others is listening." The *Evening Standard* said "Yoko passes by like Lady Macbeth sleepwalking . . . I'm told the film was made to complete the three-picture deal with United Artists . . . Let it pass." Said the *Daily Sketch:* "It's like a rehearsal for an event that has been washed out by rain." The *Daily Express* said: "It is obvious that Paul McCartney is the musical leader of the group and that Yoko Ono has no intention of being further away from John Lennon than a distance of two inches at any given moment. Apart from these trivial details, the film gave me no new information about the team." The *Daily Mirror* wrote: "Domestic touches are added by Paul McCartney's little stepdaughter frisking around the studio and by Yoko, who sits broodingly at her husband's elbow throughout, looking like an inscrutable miniature Mother Earth. This seems to inhibit John Lennon more than somewhat, especially when he and Yoko perform an ungainly waltz which will win them no Astaire–Rogers medals, and it is McCartney who comes over as the dominant figure and the musical boss."

No kudos, there, to be sure, but critical salvos somewhere down the road were the least of Paul's concerns as he wrapped "his" little movie on the roof, with stinging versions of "I've Got a Feeling," "The One After 909," "Dig a Pony," and "Get Back." That was January 30, 1969. During the next 45 days, he and Linda Eastman would marry, as would John and Yoko, and the control of Apple and the Beatles would be up for grabs as Paul pitted his in-laws, the Eastmans, against Allen Klein and the rest of the Beatles. They went up on the roof of Apple as equals and came down with some being more equal than others.

That was the beginning of the end, although the world at large didn't know it. The Beatles as a unit had actually been dead for quite some time and its individual members were just beginning to acknowledge that fact. What was unfortunate was the discovery that they were almost broke, despite their unprecedented popularity and sales of millions of records. What would or could they do to remedy that? They had different ideas about that and Paul McCartney, the most confident of the group, had the most different ideas of them all about how to proceed.

Alone

PAUL felt the weight of the world on his shoulders. He was still trying to revive the corpse that the Beatles had become. He didn't know yet that John had been planning for some time to leave the group. Paul had never had a close male friend other than John and they had grown apart as they grew up. They had almost become strangers, passing each other in the studio at Abbey Road as they came and went to record their own stuff. Paul desperately wanted the Beatles to keep on. He wanted to instill some order to Apple and get the group back on track. He was the only one of the group who had not yet done a solo album. John, with Yoko, had recorded *Unfinished Music No. 1: Two Virgins; Unfinished Music No. 2: Life with the Lions; The Wedding Album;* and *The Plastic Ono Band: Live Peace in Toronto, 1969.* George had done *Wonderwall Music* and *Electronic Sound* and Ringo had just finished *Sentimental Journey.* Paul felt defensive and vulnerable.

With Linda and her daughter Heather in the house in St. John's Wood, Paul practically pulled up the drawbridge. He aggressively pursued the domesticity that he had cherished as a child before his Mother Mary died. Since both John and Paul had lost their mothers early in their childhood and were obviously traumatized by the losses, they were—as many of their friends said— looking for mother substitutes as wives and companions. John always called Yoko "Mother" and Paul was so close to Linda that she sometimes escorted him to the men's restroom in restaurants lest any Paul fan leap onto him en route and perhaps steal his very essence away.

Paul and Linda had gotten to know each other quickly. Although her first Beatle target had been John, she shifted her attention very quickly to the Cute One. They had many common interests. Both Paul and Linda liked and worshipped Paul, they loved smoking dope together, they adored animals and children, and they both favored a life-style at home that came to be called "casual" in the London newspapers. "Casual" was a code word for what the few visitors to the house on Cavendish called "sloppy" and "a mess." The garden behind the house, with its once-beautiful glass meditation dome, was a jungle of weeds and crabgrass and dog shit. When it rained, it became a sea of mud. Paul and Linda were very tender-hearted when it came to animals and those animals were everywhere—not just Martha with her doggie door to the garden. The menagerie grew over the years to include myriad cats and dogs and chickens and guinea hens and ducks and geese and God knew what else. And they all had access to the house, with all that entailed. There was pet poop everywhere. Paul loved it. He wanted hearth and home and animals and kids and earthy smells and mud and dog shit and Linda cooking up some homemade soup on the stove. It was the perfect home that he had never had as a child, especially after Mother Mary died. The house was cozy and comfortable, like an overstuffed chair. Original Magrittes, including the apple painting that inspired the Apple Corps logo, were arranged around the high-ceilinged room like afterthoughts. A matching green easy chair and couch flanked a low coffee table covered with a madras cloth sent by one of Paul's fans. The couch had a rip in it that the kittens liked to try to hide in. There was a charcoal portrait of Paul that a fan had sent to him. A picture of John's son Julian. And a worn wooden desk stuffed with fan mail and other papers. The kitchen tucked away on the first floor still bore Jane Asher's domestic signs: the spice racks that she had once filled and the now-empty cookbook shelves that she so happily had set up. On the second floor was Paul's master bedroom, two bedrooms converted into one. The walls were white and the curtains were red velvet. The carpet was bright orange. One entire wall was taken up by a lighted dressing table and floor-to-ceiling drawers for clothes. The third floor was occupied by three smaller bedrooms and by Paul's music studio, which over-looked the front yard. He often serenaded the Apple Scruffs who were yearning away out on Cavendish. Linda didn't like that. She made him stop that and she made him stop going out to talk to the lovely little Scruffs who camped outside the high metal gates. The graffiti on the walls got uglier after Linda moved in, on the order of: MICK JAGGER HAS A BIGGER DICK THAN ALL THE BEATLES PUT TOGETHER.

The "golden prison" (George Martin's term) that the Beatles had become was just as confining as any jail cell. The Beatles were trapped inside a myth that they would never escape. The breakup was inevitable and, in retrospect, what seems really remarkable is how long they did actually stay together. Given the incredible pressures they were under and the constant scru-tiny and perpetual publicity, it is a wonder they weren't in worse shape than they actually were.

The Beatle split was a long and gradual thing and it was punctuated by many small explosive bursts, rather than by one spectacular explosion. An indication of the state that they had gotten to was the closing down in late 1969 of *Beatles Book,* the authorized Beatle fan magazine. It was independently run and the staff decided it had ceased to fulfill an important function any-more. The last issue carried a bitter attack on the Fab Four, charging them with becoming uncooperative with the magazine, with failing to come out squarely against drug use, and a general lack of a sense of humor ever since they started Apple. (The magazine's dwindling circulation may have had something to do with its demise. It had once sold 330,000 issues a month but circulation had dropped to about 26,000.)

Money and Apple were serious bones of contention. None of the Beatles was an actual millionaire, even though they had grossed an estimated fifty-five million pounds since 1963. No one was in charge anymore, it seemed. They had thirty-seven different companies under the corporate umbrella. No one actu-ally knew how much money was drained out of those companies and particularly out of Apple, which had become a bit of a public embarrassment. Paul and John, to a lesser extent, had tried to find a capable executive to take charge of Apple, but had no luck. They even approached Lord Beeching, the retired head of British

Rail, but he turned them down. The word was that Apple and the Beatles were simply unmanageable.

Paul became increasingly frustrated with the situation. He knew he couldn't handle it alone. At one point he said, "I don't find much fun in offices. I never did. I only enjoyed it as a novelty. I woke up one day and I was talking and I didn't mean anything I said. I heard myself doing business. But I didn't want it."

In late 1968 he turned to Linda's father, Lee Eastman, for advice. Lee was quite a successful man in Paul's eyes. He included in his clients' roster the artists Willem de Kooning and Robert Motherwell. He owned such music publishing copyrights as "Never on Sunday" and "Young at Heart." He was an expert on copyright law, although he was not universally liked in the legal community because of his arrogance and abrasive manner. Lee recommended his son John as the perfect candidate to straighten out Apple's mess. John, a graduate of Stanford and NYU Law School, had worked in Washington with Senator Ralph Yarborough before joining his father's practice.

John flew to London and met with the Beatles. Although John Lennon was immediately skeptical of John Eastman, he was retained as general counsel for the Beatles. His first recommendation was that the Beatles buy NEMS, thus effectively ridding themselves of the obligation of paying NEMS 25 percent of all their royalties (the deal Brian had secretly struck). NEMS had been bought by Triumph Investment Trust, a large banking concern. More "men in suits" who owned the Beatles. To finance the deal, EMI agreed to loan the Beatles one million pounds against future royalties.

Paul also bought several thousand shares of Northern Songs without telling John, who was incensed when he found out. He accused Paul of going behind his back, but Paul was unfazed. When John confronted him, Paul just said, "I had some beanies and I wanted some more."

Meanwhile John started looking around for a manager other than Paul's future brother-in-law. At Mick Jagger's urging, he agreed to meet with a New York accountant named Allen Klein, who had turned around the Rolling Stones' financial situation. Perhaps he could do the same for the Beatles. Klein was known as a sharp hustler in the music business. He had made his name by ferreting out hidden monies owed to performers by their record companies. He was also involved in around fifty lawsuits and was being investigated by the Securities and Exchange Commission for his involvement with Cameo Parkway Records. In that deal, he took over the failing record company and its stock suddenly catapulted from three dollars a share to seventy-five dollars in the wake of rumors that the company would be acquiring other larger music firms, such as Chappell. That did not happen, but Cameo Parkway did acquire Allen's accounting firm, which he named ABKCO Industries. He likes to say that ABKCO stands for either "'Allen and Betty Klein Company' or 'A Better Kind of Company'—whichever way you'd like to look at it." He had long coveted landing the Beatles and he felt he heard them calling him when he read in a newspaper story that John was complaining that at Apple's current rate of losing money the Beatles would be broke in six months. He flew to London and met secretly with John Lennon and Yoko at the Dorchester Hotel. John was taken immediately by him, especially by the fact that he knew the Beatles' music intimately, knowledge John Eastman had not demonstrated. That night John wrote a letter to Sir Joseph Lockwood of EMI, saying, "Dear Sir Joe, from now on Allen Klein handles all my stuff." And the next day at Apple John announced, "I don't give a bugger who anybody else wants, but I'm having Allen Klein for me."

At an impasse, John and Paul decided to retain both Klein and Eastman to advise Apple. Klein was opposed to the purchase of NEMS, saying he knew another way to get them rid of NEMS. Eastman pursued the purchase of NEMS and when the deal fell through, John, George, and Ringo started having serious doubts about his usefulness to them. Those three signed a management deal with Klein in May 1969, paying him 20 percent of all future monies. Paul refused to sign, but the others reminded him that under Britain's Partnership Act the majority rules. Klein took over Apple, with John Eastman remaining as counsel. Sides were chosen and the battle was on. On one side were Paul and Linda and John and Lee Eastman; on the other were Klein and the rest. Klein and the Eastmans greatly disliked each other and the wrangling was constant. Klein referred to John Eastman as a "pain in the ass." Paul started referring to Klein as a "punk."

Klein moved quickly, though. He cut a wide swath through

Apple. Ron Kass and Peter Asher departed, Peter Brown was no longer on the board of directors. Zapple, Apple's spoken word division, was shut down immediately, along with Apple Electronics.

He also, he said, earned the Beatles ten million dollars immediately in capital gains from NEMS and Northern Songs by selling them back the shares the Beatles held in those companies. That effectively ended NEMS' 25 percent deal. Paul had wanted to try to buy it after Dick James—without telling Paul or John—sold his controlling interest in Northern to ATV and Sir Lew Grade. More "men in suits." Klein was opposed to buying it, but the Beatles made an attempt, which was defeated by a consortium of institutional stockholders within Northern.

Klein also renegotiated their contract with EMI, getting their royalty rate increased by the simple expedient of threatening that there would be no more Beatle records. Their royalty rate jumped from six cents for each album sold to sixty-nine cents for their old albums and to eighty-four cents for all future albums.

Although Paul had to go along with what Klein did (with Klein later claiming that Paul endorsed his actions), his resentment simmered, especially after he and Linda were married that March and he became an honorary Eastman. Paul fought and argued with the other Beatles about Klein, but it was no use.

Another thing greatly on his mind was the ever-widening split between himself and John. It had to be repaired if the Beatles were to continue, which is what he most of all sought, but he was at a loss to determine how to do it. The whole John and Yoko thing had really thrown him. He was long-suffering (after a fashion) and he genuinely did love John in his own way. But the whispers of heroin had badly unsettled him. As did the whole business of Yoko never leaving John's side. When she moved into the studio with them, that was going over the edge. Nobody had ever been the fifth Beatle before, but there she was. A genuine threat to the Fab Four. But John wanted it and there was no question of challenging him on what he wanted.

And Paul did not approve of John's treatment of Cynthia. It was clear that John and Cynthia had grown apart but she was treated shabbily. He had already let Cynthia discover him with Yoko in Cynthia's house in Cynthia's nightgown in Cynthia's bed. When he finally decided on a divorce, he took the usual

Beatle method of sending bad news: Have someone else do it. In this case it was Magic Alex.

But as months went on and John became more erratic in Paul's eyes, he didn't know if it was the heroin or Yoko or what, but John was changing and not, in Paul's view, for the better. Uppers were one thing, as had been LSD and booze and marijuana, but heroin was a totally Other Thing. And the way Paul—and George and Ringo—saw it, Yoko had made it quite clear that she did not intend to be friends with them; that she, in fact, did not recognize the Beatles as being anything but hangers-on who were physically and psychically in her way and blocking her from John.

The big problem facing Paul and John was that they simply could no longer talk. They could only argue. Their dealings with each other became formal and stilted. They had never really discussed their private lives with each other and now, with Yoko and Linda on the scene (and not getting along terribly well with each other), that was completely out of the question. John knew that Paul disapproved of Yoko and Paul knew that John thought very little of Linda, thought that she was pushy and unattractive. So they continued to grow farther apart. John later claimed that, in his own mind at least, he had decided to leave the group right after *Sgt. Pepper*. He felt that things had simply run their course and that he was just standing still. And that there was never any doubt in his mind that it was up to him and him only to decide when the Beatles would cease to be.

"The Beatles were my fucking band," he later told me. "I put the band together and I took it apart. I had threatened once before to disband the Beatles, when Brian came to me and said he had had it, and that Grade had offered to buy the Beatles and he was ready to sell [around the time of "I Want to Hold Your Hand," Lew Grade had offered Brian one hundred thousand pounds for the Beatles] and I told him, 'If you do sell, we'll never play again. We'll disband.' And Paul told him the same thing. See, nobody could make us do anything that we didn't really want to do. The funny thing was, when it was all over, Paul wanted credit for breaking up the band. 'I'm leaving,' he kept saying. But he couldn't because I had already left."

★　　★　　★

The amazing thing about this whole drawn-out tragedy was that, as the fighting escalated and the relationships deteriorated over the years from 1967 through 1969, the music just got better and better. In fact, everything they did up until the breakup still stands up very well. The lion's share of it was done by Paul. As uneven and scattered as *Magical Mystery Tour* was as a movie, the music had been superb. The *White Album,* it is true, was virtually a series of solo numbers bound together by the fact that the soloists were Beatles. Nonetheless, it remains a remarkable musical document by the four of them, on which George Harrison was finally able to emerge from behind John's and Paul's enormous shadows. And *Abbey Road,* which was recorded over the course of that last Beatle summer, the summer of 1969, remains in many ways the purest expression of Beatle music. John didn't much like it, mainly because it was really Paul's album. John would later dismiss it as "folk songs for grannies." His own contributions, however, were minimal compared to Paul's. John was more interested in the work he was doing with Yoko. Paul, though, poured his heart into it and turned side two, most of which he wrote, into an elegant little pop symphony, each exquisite song flowing into the next jewel-like song with no break in between: "Here Comes the Sun" (which George wrote on a brilliant sunny afternoon in Eric Clapton's garden, the same Eric Clapton to whom George was best friend and "husband-in-law"), "Because" (another of John's songs about Yoko), "You Never Give Me Your Money" (Paul's lament about Allen Klein and the situation at Apple), John's "Sun King," "Mean Mr. Mustard" (by John and left over from the *White Album* sessions), "Polythene Pam" (also by John and written in India, it is about a Liverpool "scrubber"), "She Came in Through the Bathroom Window" (by Paul, about an Apple Scruff who got into his house via that method), "Golden Slumbers" (by Paul, inspired by a traditional song of the same name), and Paul finishes the album with his songs "Carry That Weight," "The End," and "Her Majesty." The album went immediately to number one on the British charts and sold four million copies worldwide in the first two months it was out.

The week that it was released in England, the last week of September 1969, Paul was arguing with John as usual at an Apple meeting when John stunned Paul with some very unexpected news. John and Yoko had just performed as the Plastic Ono Band on September 13. John had been invited to play an event known as the Rock and Roll Revival Concert in Toronto and decided to go. He called up Eric Clapton and bassist Klaus Voorman and drummer Alan White. They rehearsed a little on the flight over and took the stage in Toronto for a supercharged concert that also became an album. John and the band got side one of *Live Peace in Toronto, 1969,* and Yoko occupied all of side two.

When Paul heard about the show, though, he was pleased that John had finally gotten up on a stage again—the first time any of the Fabs had performed in concert since the 1966 Candlestick show (since the Apple rooftop recording date was not a true concert). So Paul took that as a happy sign that now John was ready to start touring again, as Paul had been unsuccessfully proposing for months. They could do little college gigs and use an assumed name, he suggested, like Ricky and the Red Stripes.

Unfortunately, Paul had assumed wrongly. John looked at him blankly and said, "I think you're daft. In fact, I wasn't gonna tell you, but I'm leaving the group. I've had enough. I want a divorce, like my divorce from Cynthia." He was very matter-of-fact about it, but also obviously very determined about it. It was probably the first time that John had ever delivered the bad news on his own. Paul was devastated. John had meant what he said and would not be talked out of it. He finally agreed to keep the news secret for the time being to protect contract negotiations that were under way with EMI.

Paul was badly shaken. He went home and withdrew to his home and to his remote farm in Scotland, High Park Farm, reachable only by four-wheel-drive vehicle or on foot, and he began work alone on what would become his first solo album. John, meanwhile, was ebulliently plunging headlong into his "new life," as the others called his involvement with the antiwar movement and the avant-garde. He went into the studio with Yoko on September 30 to record "Cold Turkey" as a single. It was a new song he had first performed at the Toronto show and it was, as the title suggests, about kicking heroin. When Paul heard about it, he refused to allow John to release it as a Beatle song. So John was the one to finally break the agreement he and Paul had had for so long—that any song they wrote would be credited to Lennon–McCartney. "Cold Turkey" appeared with songwriting credits by John Lennon only. The single was credited to the Plastic Ono Band (which in that studio incarnation consisted of John, Yoko, Clapton, Voorman, and Ringo).

Paul, meanwhile, had to face the fact that not only were the Beatles dead (although the public didn't know that), so was he dead (which the public knew all too well). The bizarre "Paul Is Dead" rumor had started with an article in the September 23 issue of *Northern Star,* the student newspaper at the University of Illinois. The article was headlined: CLUES HINT AT POSSIBLE BEATLE DEATH. Then it spread to Detroit on October 12 when disc jockey Russ Gibb of radio station WKNR-FM received an anonymous phone call. The caller told him that Paul was dead and he listed a number of "clues," in the form of songs and album covers. Chief among them, of course, was the *Abbey Road* cover, on which Paul appears barefoot (like a corpse) and out of step with the others. Paul, who is left-handed, holds his cigarette in his right hand. John is dressed as a minister, Ringo as an undertaker, and George as a gravedigger. The license plate on a Volkswagen in the background reads 28IF, the age Paul would have reached if he had lived. The rumormongers could not have known that Iain Macmillan, the photographer for the photo session (which took place at ten in the morning on August 8, 1969, at the zebra crosswalk outside the Abbey Road studio) had tried to have the Volkswagen towed away and out of the picture but couldn't get a police tow truck there in time. And the reason Paul was barefoot was that he had strolled over from his house on Cavendish wearing only sandals and had decided to doff them for the picture.

Still. . . . On the cover of *Sgt. Pepper* there is a hand held above Paul's head, supposedly a symbol of death. And so on. The "news" spread. An article by Fred LaBour in the Michigan *Daily* attracted wide attention. Radio station WMCA in New York City picked up the "story" and, astonishingly, an entire mythos was created within days. Alex Bennett of WMCA went to London to "investigate" Paul's death and interviewed Paul's barber, who said that Paul had a tiny flaw in the part in his hair and that the flaw was still there, so he was satisfied that Paul was still Paul. Even so, radio stations across the United States ran retrospectives about Paul's life and career. Bill Gavin, editor of the influential *Top Forty* newsletter that served radio stations, wrote: "The thing about this is that it's got staying power. It's all based on clues and they're all so elusive. It hangs on McCartney proving it's really him and how can he manage that?"

So far he stayed hidden. November, meanwhile, proved to be, as vice president of Capitol Records Rocco Catena said, "the biggest month in history in terms of Beatles' sales." There was no trace of irony in his voice. There was certainly never any indication that the Beatles or Apple or Capitol or EMI might have encouraged the "Paul Is Dead" movement. It picked up plenty of momentum. Dr. Henry Truby of the University of Miami's language laboratory conducted "voiceprint" experiments of Beatle recordings. He concluded that John, George, and Ringo each had a distinctive voiceprint, but that Paul had three different voiceprints. "These passages were taken from Beatle recordings dated from before and after November 1966 [when Paul "died"] and have been advertised as having been sung by Paul McCartney," he said. "I cannot conclude that the same voice appears in these early and late passages."

Such conclusions only fueled the rumor. It came to have a core of a story: Paul had been killed on November 9, 1966, after an argument with the others at the Abbey Road Studio. He left in his Aston-Martin in a fury and was involved in a car wreck in which he was decapitated. The ever-shrewd Brian Epstein could not let the Beatles die, so he found a double for Paul. After plastic surgery this Paul look-alike filled in admirably. He even sounded like Paul and was a better songwriter. That explains Paul's sudden domination of the group, beginning with *Sgt. Pepper.*

Well, that's a better yarn than the theory that the John Birchers had, which was that the Kremlin had started writing the Beatles' songs for them as part of the conspiracy to corrupt the youth of the west. There were other theories propounded: Paul's double, named William Campbell and often referred to as Billy Shears, started putting clues to Paul's death on Beatle records. The myth grew and grew, becoming more elaborate and detailed. Paul had sold his soul to the devil in exchange for the Beatles' success. And that explained how the well-known Beatle fan Charles "Helter-Skelter" Manson was programmed to murder Roman Polanski's pregnant wife, Sharon Tate, after Polanski had offended Satan with the film *Rosemary's Baby,* which took place in the Dakota apartment building in New York City and that's why John was later sent to live in the Dakota. Or: William Campbell was a CIA agent, sent to replace Paul in order to tone down the Beatles' music. Or: Paul was assassinated by the CIA in order to silence the Beatles' revolutionary music. But John Lennon refused to be cowed by the killing and brought in his friend William Campbell to replace Paul (because there had to be somebody to appeal to the females) and then started planting clues on the records in order to let the truth out. There was even a television special about "Paul Is Dead," with lawyer F. Lee Bailey weighing the evidence. There was no conclusion. Oh, it drove Paul crazy, as you might imagine. He finally was driven to call on the press. He (or someone who looked and sounded remarkably like him) appeared before journalists in London in late November to allow himself to be photographed. He said: "Reports of my death are greatly exaggerated. If I were dead, I'd be the last to know." Which is just what people would expect "him" to say, of course. "It's all a drag," this "Paul" said. "We can't control what people read into our music."

The story simply will not die. Sociologists still study it as a classic example of the spontaneous myth. No one, it seems, is immune to its appeal. In 1988, when George Harrison was making a video clip of his song "When We Was Fab," he was able to persuade Ringo, but not Paul, to appear in it. As a result, there is a left-handed bass player wearing a walrus costume in the video. Supposed to be Paul, in case you miss the punch line.

When Paul resurfaced in early 1970, he was due for a couple of rude shocks. First of all, in his absence, John and George had given the tapes from the *Let It Be* sessions to Phil Spector to let the eccentric American producer try to work his wizardry on them, something that none of the Beatles had been able to do. Spector's vaunted "wall of sound" production had worked well for such groups as the Crystals, the Ronettes, and the Righteous Brothers, but it was not necessarily well-suited to what the Beatles—read "Paul," in this case—were trying to do. Even before he heard the results, Paul was disturbed that this had been done behind his back. John thought it was fine and later called on

Spector's talents for "Imagine" and the studio sides of the *Some Time in New York City* album.

What Spector had done to the original album was to totally remove the documentary feel that Paul had wanted to capture. He replaced that with lush orchestral arrangements, female backup choirs, and rich string sections, especially on "Across the Universe," "Let It Be," "The Long and Winding Road," and "I Me Mine." Three songs were dropped altogether: "Save the Last Dance for Me," "Teddy Boy," and "Don't Let Me Down." But what really sickened Paul when he heard it was what had been done to his precious "The Long and Winding Road." It sounded like Mantovani had run amok with it. Paul dashed off an angry letter to Allen Klein at Apple, demanding that the changes to his songs be removed. Klein ignored him.

Furious, Paul gave a very self-serving interview to *Rolling Stone* in which he made a few very telling points. Of *Let It Be*, he just said that the album was looking to be "a joke." But he raked Allen Klein over the coals, saying, "I am not signed with Allen Klein because I don't like him and I don't think he is the man for me, however much the other three like him." Paul hinted broadly that the Beatles might be finished, but his hint drew no follow-up question from his interviewer, *Rolling Stone* editor Jann Wenner. Paul rather wistfully looked back in time. "In the very early days of the Beatles we sort of thought of ourselves as a democracy. But nothing ever came to a vote—the chemistry of the four of us made the decisions naturally. John dominated the group in making the decisions and John and I dominated the group musically. What's happened now is that each of us has become very strong individuals in our own right."

He also gave a broad indication of where his future lay when he said he preferred to stay at home with Linda, Heather, and their new daughter, Mary, who had been born on August 29, 1969. "I love being at home," he said, "and I love music. That is largely what interests me and I am not looking for anything else to interest me." Linda, of course, took the pictures that accompanied the article.

Paul's next move was to inform Apple that he wanted his solo album to be released in early April. He was refused because the *Let It Be* album and Ringo's album had already been scheduled and his album would conflict with those. He would just have to get in line and wait. Paul started to feel as if the world had decided to gang up against him. In protest, he telephoned Sir Joseph Lockwood at EMI to see if he could perhaps intercede in Paul's behalf. With a touch of regret in his aristocratic voice, Lockwood told Paul that he must bow to majority rule.

After a meeting John and George decided to dispatch Ringo, as a sort of neutral messenger, to go and talk to Paul about this testy matter of release dates for albums. Ringo, carrying letters from John and George, set out for St. John's Wood.

He did not tarry long in Paul's house. He said later in a court affidavit (in connection with the appointment of a receiver to handle Apple) that Paul "went completely out of control, shouting at me, prodding his fingers toward my face, saying, 'I'll finish you all now' and 'You'll pay.' He told me to get on my coat and get out. . . . While I thought Paul had behaved a bit like a spoiled child, I could see that the release date of his record had a gigantic emotional significance for him. Whether he was right or wrong to be so emotional, I felt that since he was our friend and since the date was of such immense significance to him, we should let him have his own way."

In an answering affidavit Paul said, "I really got angry when Ringo told me that Klein had told him my record was not ready and that he had a release date for the *Let It Be* album. I knew both of these alleged statements were untrue and I said, in effect, this was the last straw and if you drag me down, I'll drag you down. What I meant was anything you [the group] do to me, I will do to you."

John Eastman stepped in and took the tapes to New York, where he told Capitol Records that if they didn't put it out when Paul wanted it out, he would give the album to Columbia Records. It was a bit of a hollow threat, since Apple was obligated to let Capitol release it in the United States, but Klein and John and George backed down. Paul got his way. Ringo's *Sentimental Journey* album was moved to March 27, Paul's *McCartney* was set for April 17, and *Let It Be* was pushed back to May 8.

Paul was still furious, though, and decided he was leaving the group. And in what he has since admitted was a very rash move, he decided to use the release of his album as a vehicle to announce the breakup of the Beatles and to state his views relating to the whole Beatle state of affairs. He got Derek Taylor to help him draw up a list of questions for him to answer so that he, in effect, interviewed himself. The resulting document was sent out on April 10 (now the Official Beatle Breakup Day) to Fleet Street and to radio stations and it was included with the album through the first British pressing only.

Derek Taylor later recalled, "I drank steadily throughout the bad day of Paul's quitting." That was the day the roof fell in at Apple. In response to one reporter's question, Taylor, who identified very closely with the Beatles, said, "If the Beatles are dead, then you are dead." Later he asked, "What could I have meant? I had prepared the press statement from Paul's very dry answers to a questionnaire form I had written earlier and sent him in an effort to determine just what the future was to hold. The press, using what they could sift from my statement, expressed the break as firm but temporary." Paul would later, on April 21, tell the *Evening Standard* that the break was permanent: "The party's over, but none of us wants to admit it."

This is Paul's interview with himself that went out on April 10:

Q: Why did you decide to make a solo album?

A: Because I got a Studer four-track recording machine at home—practiced on it (playing all instruments)—liked the results and decided to make it into an album.

Q: Were you influenced by John's adventures with the Plastic Ono Band and Ringo's solo LP?

A: Sort of, but not really.

Q: Are all the songs by Paul McCartney alone?

A: Yes, sir.

Q: Will they be so credited: McCartney?

A: It's a bit daft for them to be Lennon–McCartney-credited, so McCartney it is.

Q: Did you enjoy working as a solo?

A: Very much. I only had me to ask for a decision and I agreed with me. Remember Linda's on it too, so it's really a double act.

Q: What is Linda's contribution?

A: Strictly speaking she harmonises, but of course it's more than that because she is a shoulder to lean on, a second opinion, and a photographer of renown. More than all this, she believes in me—constantly.

Q: Where was the album recorded?

A: At home, at EMI (number 2 studio), and at Morgan Studios (Willesden!).

Q: What is your home equipment—in some detail?

A: Studer four-track machine. I only had, however, one mike . . . and I worked without VU meters or a mixer, which meant that everything had to be listened to first (for distortion, etc.), then recorded. So the answer—Studer, one mike, and nerve.

Q: Why did you choose to work in the studios you chose?

A: They were available. EMI is technically very good and Morgan is cosy.

Q: The album was not known about until it was nearly completed. Was this deliberate?

A: Yes, because normally an album is old before it comes out. (Aside) Witness *Get Back [Let it Be]*.

Q: Why?

A: I've always wanted to buy a Beatles album like "people" do and be as surprised as they must be. So this was the next best thing. Linda and I are the only two who will be sick of it by the release date. We love it, really.

Q: Are you able to describe the texture or the feel of the theme of the album in a few words?

A: Home, family, love.

Q: How long did it take to complete—from when to when?

A: From just before (I think) Xmas, until now. "The Lovely Linda" was the first thing I recorded at home and was originally to test the equipment. That was around Xmas.

Q: Assuming all the songs are new to the public, how new are they to you? Are they recent?

A: One was 1959 ("Hot as Sun"), two from India ("Junk," "Teddy Boy") [which had been bumped from *Let It Be* by Spector], and the rest are pretty recent. "Valentine Day," "Momma Miss America," and "OO You" were ad-libbed on the spot.

Q: Which instruments have you played on the album?

A: Bass, drums, acoustic guitar, lead guitar, piano and organ-Mellotron, toy xylophone, bow and arrow.

Q: Have you played all these instruments on earlier recordings?

A: Yes—drums being the one that I wouldn't normally do.

Q: Why did you do all the instruments yourself?

A: I think I'm pretty good.

Q: Will Linda be heard on all future records?

A: Could be. We love singing together and have plenty of opportunity for practice.

Q: Will Paul and Linda become a John and Yoko?

A: No, they will become Paul and Linda.

Q: Are you pleased with your work?

A: Yes.

Q: Will the other Beatles receive the first copies?

A: Wait and see.

Q: What has recording alone taught you?

A: That to make your own decisions about what you do is easy and playing with yourself is difficult but satisfying.

Q: Who has done the artwork?

A: Linda has taken all the photos and she and I designed the package.

Q: Is it true that neither Allen Klein nor ABKCO have been nor will be in any way involved with the production, manufacturing, distribution, or promotion of this new album?

A: Not if I can help it.

Q: Did you miss the other Beatles and George Martin? Was there a moment when you thought: Wish Ringo was here for this break?

A: No.

Q: Assuming this is a very big hit album, will you do another?

A: Even if it isn't, I will continue to do what I want when I want to.

Q: Are you planning a new album or single with the Beatles?

A: No.

Q: Is this album a rest away from the Beatles or the start of a solo career?

A: Time will tell. Being a solo album means it's "the start of a solo career" and not being done with the Beatles means it's a rest. So it's both.

Q: Have you any plans for live appearances?

A: No.

Q: Is your break from the Beatles temporary or permanent, due to personal differences or musical ones?

A: Personal differences, business differences, musical differences, but most of all because I have a better time with my family. Temporary or permanent? I don't know.

Q: Do you foresee a time when Lennon–McCartney becomes an active songwriting partnership again?

A: No.

Q: What do you feel about John's peace effort? The Plastic Ono Band? Giving back the MBE? Yoko's influence? Yoko?

A: I love John and respect what he does—it doesn't give me any pleasure.

Q: Have you plans to produce any other artists?

A: No.

Q: Were any of the songs on the album originally written with the Beatles in mind?

A: The older ones were. "Junk" was intended for Abbey Road, but something happened. "Teddy Boy" was for *Get Back [Let It Be]*, but something happened.

Q: Were you pleased with Abbey Road? Was it musically restricting?

A: It was a good album (number one for a long time).

Q: What is your relationship with Klein?

A: It isn't. I am not in contact with him and he does not represent me in any way.

Q: What is your relationship with Apple?

A: It is the office of a company which I part-own with the other three Beatles. I don't go there because I don't like the offices or business, especially when I'm on holiday.

Q: Have you any plans to set up an independent production company?

A: McCartney Productions.

Q: What sort of music has influenced you on this album?

A: Light and loose.

Q: Are you writing more prolifically now? Or less so?

A: About the same. I have a queue waiting to be recorded.

Q: What are your plans now? A holiday? A musical? A movie? Retirement?

A: My only plan is to grow up.

Paul also added an extensive song-by-song commentary on the album, which was mostly technical. Edited highlights include:

"The Lovely Linda": On the first track was vocal and guitar, second—another acoustic guitar—then overdubbed hand slaps on a book, and finally bass. Written in Scotland, the song is a trailer to the full song, which will be recorded in the future.

"That Would Be Something": I had only one mike, as the moxer and VU meters hadn't arrived (still haven't).

"Valentine Day": Recorded at home. Made up as I went along. This one and "Momma Miss America" were ad-libbed, with more concern for testing the machine than anything else.

"Every Night": This came from the first two lines, which I've had for a few years.

"Hot as Sun": A song written in about 1958 or '59 or maybe earlier, when it was one of those songs that you play now and then.

"Glasses": Wineglasses played at random and overdubbed on top of each other—the end is a section of a song called "Suicide"—not yet completed.

"Junk": Originally written in India, at Maharishi's camp, and completed bit by bit in London.

"Man We Was Lonely": The chorus was written in bed at home, shortly before we finished recording the album. . . . Linda sings harmony on this song, which is our first duet together.

"OO You": This, like "Man We Was Lonely," was given lyrics one day after lunch.

"Momma Miss America": An instrumental recorded completely at home. Made up as I went along—first a sequence of chords, then a melody on top.

"Teddy Boy": Another song started in India and completed in Scotland and London . . . recorded for the Get Back film, but later not used. . . . Linda and I sing the backing harmonies on the chorus.

"Singalong Junk": Guitars and piano and bass were put on at home.

"Maybe I'm Amazed": Written in London, at the piano, with the second verse added slightly later, as if you cared. . . . Linda and I are the vocal backing group. . . . A movie was made, using Linda's slides, and edited to this track.

"Kreen-Akrore": There was a film on TV about the Kreen-Akrore Indians living in the Brazilian jungle, their lives, and how the white man is trying to change their way of life to his, so the next day, after lunch, I did some drumming. The idea behind it was to get the feeling of their hunt. . . . The end of the first section has Linda and I doing animal noises (speeded up) and an arrow sound (done live with bow and arrow—the bow broke), then animals stampeding across a guitar case. . . . We built a fire in the studio but didn't use it (but used the sound of the twigs breaking).

The release of this self-indulgent album, with its chatty little notes about Linda and "bed" and so on, along with the McCartney self-serving interview and the news about the breakup of the group, pretty much got Paul pilloried throughout the English-speaking world. Since no one knew about John's having left first, Paul got the blame for killing the Fab Four and there were a lot of people around the world who wanted the Beatles to last forever. Paul was suddenly very unhip for his views on family and home.

Allen Klein had his revenge on Paul. The ads in *Rolling Stone,* for both Paul's album and Ringo's, displayed prominently the words: APPLE RECORDS—AN ABKCO MANAGED COMPANY with ABKCO's New York City address. Also, Ringo's ad came before Paul's in the magazine. And Klein had instructed Capitol Records not to include Paul's interview-manifesto with the record. The Eastmans were careful to send out review copies and radio station copies with the interview included—to get Paul's message out. But on the copies they mailed out, the words AN ABKCO MANAGED COMPANY on the record jacket had been meticulously covered over with strips of black tape.

The album did not sell badly, but not as well as *Abbey Road* had done, which sold five million copies in the first three months. Paul's album in England had advance orders of nineteen thousand copies, entered the charts at number six, and rose to number two (Simon and Garfunkel's "Bridge Over Troubled Water" was above it at number one). In the United States it went onto the charts at number fourteen and rose to number one. It went on to sell two million copies worldwide.

Many Beatle fans were puzzled by the album. It was indeed "light and loose," as Paul had promised in his interview. But five instrumentals on one album? The overwhelming impression the album created was that it was simply unfinished. The songs were clearly missing that Lennon eight in the middle. But as Paul pointed out in his interview, he was no longer going to do anything he didn't want to. The breakup of the Beatles had shaken him, had knocked the confidence out of him, and once he started recovering he started to exercise the extreme control over everything he did that is still the hallmark of his post-Beatles career. What he does may not be right, but it will be done only his way or not at all.

But as many rock critics pointed out, he was suddenly becoming a musical reactionary. In turning away from the Beatles, he was making musical castles in the air with no foundation to them. Langdon Winner in *Rolling Stone* was typical when he wrote: "when compared to the best of the Beatles' previous work, the songs of McCartney are distinctly second-rate." Winner also, like most reviewers, was bothered by Paul's interview that accompanied the album, which cast a bitter pall over the record and seemed almost a part of the work. As he wrote, all of Paul's attempts on the record to convince the listener that Paul had found supreme happiness at home with Linda and the kids rang false.

McCartney was an album chock-full of desperation in many ways. It is clearly the work of a severely distracted man. It was astonishing at the time to listen to the vapidness of *McCartney* (apart from "Maybe I'm Amazed," which retains its strength even today) and to wonder at what had happened to Paul. Could this actually be the same man who was the architect of *Sgt. Pepper* and who had written the foundation, the very guts of the magnificent *Abbey Road* album only a few short months earlier? What had befallen him? What happened to the confident authority he had brought to "The End"? What had become of the easy assurance of a song like "Carry That Weight"? And now he was shooting off bows and arrows in the studio and half-apologizing for recording animal noises with Linda?

Well, John's self-indulgent stuff was no better. And they both knew it and out of pride would never admit missing each other. It is so obvious a point but nevertheless such a true one that John and Paul badly needed each other in the musical process. Not in writing, actually, because they had quit truly writing together years earlier. It was the bullshit detector that each brought to the other's work that was forever gone. Nobody had ever successfully criticized Lennon and McCartney about a Lennon–McCartney song except Lennon or McCartney. Not George Martin, not George Harrison, not Brian Epstein, not the Queen of England. John and Paul had always brought out the best in each other and discouraged the worst. Who needled Paul into creating side two of *Abbey Road*? Who dismissed so many of John's songs that he couldn't wait to get into the studio to fill up the *White Album*? Who else would dare tell Paul McCartney that he had written a piece of crap? Who would risk John Lennon's considerable ire by dumping on some little piece of junk song that he thought he could get away with? Not Linda and not Yoko, that was for sure. Those two women had married geniuses whose work became only the more brilliant once they started collaborating with their brilliant wives instead of with that surly asshole guy they had been wasting their time with. And the two brilliant geniuses believed it.

The strange thing was the sudden role reversals that the breakup brought about. John, once he got off heroin and started believing in himself again, became the confident outgoing leader he once had been. And Paul, after losing his identity with the loss of the group, became the surly recluse with no confidence in his abilities anymore. John walked away from the wreckage a new man, physically lighter, happier, freer. He even legally changed his name from John Winston Lennon to John Ono Lennon.

Paul, on the other hand, looked suddenly older and tired, despite all the talk of the happiness of hearth and home. He was literally adrift. "When the Beatles split up," he later told Hunter Davies, "I felt on the rocks. I've been accused of walking out on them, but I never did. It's something I'd never do. One day John left and that was the last straw. It was the signal for the others to leave. . . . The Beatles were a security blanket. Everything just went right ahead and we never thought of contracts or problems. Then the job folded beneath me. Suddenly I didn't have a career anymore. I wasn't earning anything and all my money was in Apple and I couldn't get it out because I'd signed it all away." That last was not quite true. After Apple funds were frozen until the partnership was formally dissolved, none of the Beatles could draw on the money. A major problem was that as the money piled up, a huge tax bill would accompany any withdrawals. All the money that Klein said he was bringing in was to lie un-touched for years. With the money frozen, of course, the Beatles had no income. And none of them was really that wealthy. Their money had never been managed well and certainly had not been invested wisely. At the time of the breakup, they owned houses and cars and Apple and Paul had the farm in Scotland.

He said he started staying up all night, drinking and chain-smoking his Senior Services, watching television, unable to con-centrate on anything else. He worried about money but obviously what he missed most was the security of the Beatles. "I had no idea what I was going to do," he said. "There seemed to be no point in joining another group. Not after all that. 'Ladies and gentlemen, follow that.' I was out of work and the ghosts from my past came back, from those early days when relations and friends said we'd never do anything anyway and we should get proper jobs."

For the time being, at least, both Paul and John entered into the business of being an ex-Beatle with a vengeance. Indeed, they would both expend years in trying to deny the reality, let alone the importance, of what they had achieved as Beatles. They started sniping at each other, first in print, later using their records to fling hateful messages back and forth (even Allen Klein got into the music act, actually claiming that he had helped write John's painfully anti-Paul song "How Do You Sleep?"). Neither at the time realized fully how much each had hurt the other: John by the tone of Paul's interview with himself and the fact that he had gone straight to the press with it, ignoring John; Paul by the treatment he had gotten from his erstwhile mates over his solo album, by what had happened to the *Let It Be* album, and by John's taking the group away from him.

After Paul's interview made headlines everywhere, John called up *Melody Maker,* the music newspaper, to inform them: "Paul hasn't left. I sacked him."

Less than two weeks after the big brouhaha occasioned by Paul's press release, John took a drastic step that he had been contemplating for some time. He flew to Los Angeles with Yoko to begin an intensive four-month-long course of primal therapy with Dr. Arthur Janov. John was always open to drastic steps. Paul later recalled the time that John had heard about trepanning, the ancient custom of drilling a hole in the skull to relieve pressure on the brain. John proposed, to Paul's horror, that they all go and try it out. "It might be good for us," he said.

Just as primal therapy was a logical move for John, Paul's next career move was nicely in step with the kind of life he was now trying to put together. He bought the film rights to Rupert Bear, the famous comic strip character that had been a staple in the *Daily Express* for many years. Paul had loved the character as a child and had rediscovered the delights of Rupert while reading the comics to Heather after she came into his life. In fact, before Apple crumbled and before the breakup, he had tried to get Apple interested in doing a Rupert Bear movie with Beatle music. He said he thought it would be a much better project than *Yellow Submarine*. "It could be lovely," he said, "if the right people are got to do it—none of that psychedelic shit." It took Paul some years, as it does with some of his projects, to finally put together a Rupert vehicle. In 1985 his video cassette of "Paul McCartney's Rupert and the Frog Song" was England's bestselling music video.

Otherwise, Paul brooded about the business wrangles, the Eastman versus Klein bitterness, and about how to resolve the whole mess. In June 1970 he started pressing to get the Beatles partnership dissolved. John Eastman started talking to tax lawyers about how to proceed with a dissolution and wrote to Klein, asking him to "put your fertile mind to work on all the aspects" of dissolving the Beatles partnership. Klein ignored it. Paul continued chafing at the bit and in August, when John was back from primal therapy, Paul wrote to him, asking for a dissolution of the partnership, to "let each other out of the trap." John replied with a photo of himself with a dialogue balloon coming out of his mouth, reading: HOW AND WHY? Paul shot back: HOW, BY SIGNING A PAPER WHICH SAYS WE HEREBY DISSOLVE THE PARTNERSHIP. WHY, BECAUSE THERE IS NO PARTNERSHIP. John sent back a postcard: GET WELL SOON. GET THE OTHER SIGNATURES AND I WILL THINK ABOUT IT.

On August 29 Paul sent a handwritten letter to *Melody Maker* for publication. It read: "In order to put out of its misery the limping dog of a news story which has been dragging itself across your pages for the past year, my answer to the question: 'Will the Beatles get together again?' is no."

And Paul wearied of London. Of the fans asking when would

the Beatles get back together. Of the press asking when would the Beatles get back together. Of the vision of his Apple being ruthlessly run by Klein, of Yoko actually working out of an office there. Of John having dispatched Neil Aspinall on an undercover sleuthing mission to New York City and Neil returning with the gleeful revelation that the Eastman family's real name had been Epstein before Lee changed it. Of the Apple Scruffs who hated Linda so much that they broke into the house and stole her photographs. Of the whole "Paul Is Dead" hoopla, which refused to go away. He finally just packed up Linda and Heather and Mary and headed for the farm in Scotland.

John Eastman came for a long visit and talked to Paul about what he should do next in the increasingly bitter Beatle fight. The whole thing with Allen Klein had really escalated into a class war pitting Paul against John Lennon. Lennon accusing Lee Eastman of calling Klein "scum of the earth." Paul making digs about the way Klein dressed. Of Eastman's insisting on having a New York business meeting with Klein at the Harvard Club to try to intimidate him. Of the intransigence of Paul and John in championing their candidates for Apple manager.

Paul had been aspiring to the good life and the Eastmans represented that for him: coolly elegant Park Avenue apartment, Picassos and Magrittes on the wall, Fifth Avenue office (actually on 54th Street between Fifth and Sixth, but close enough), summers in the Hamptons, collections of music copyrights. Klein, on the other hand, was Lennon's champion precisely because he was the exact opposite of the Eastmans. Klein was definitely not a "man in a suit." He was a foul-mouthed tough-talking street fighter who invariably wore rumpled turtlenecks to try to conceal his fleshy jowls. An office on seedy Broadway. Working-class. Down-to-earth.

Klein and Eastman were merely extensions of what John and Paul were becoming and what they wanted to be. It was no surprise when the bulk of the interviews they gave dealt with snide put-downs of Klein and the Eastmans.

This pattern followed: Paul moved to the country and adopted the horsey, tweedy, Land Rover and Wellington boots life-style. And started seriously collecting art and buying up music copyrights. You'd be surprised how quickly Linda picked up an English accent. On the other hand, John moved as soon as he

could to Greenwich Village, started sporting coarse denim over-
alls and work boots, jumped feet-first into whatever radical
projects he could find, and quick as a wink became Mr. Working-
Class Hero.

What had happened was very simple. "The boys" were finally
growing into the men that they would be. That was all. They
had finally found the women who suited them and both "boys"
were horrified by whom the other selected.

But they were finally getting to do their growing up. They
had sacrificed their formative years by being Beatles, by being
locked away in the basements and cellars of Liverpool and Hamburg. Now they were figuring out who they were and what they
wanted out of life. John was stepping back into the eye of the
hurricane. Paul wanted out of it.

Both of them would later—independently—refer to their relationship as having been like "Army buddies together." That, of
course, is a relationship that must one day end. John had welcomed that end, as he did any sort of change. Paul had been
terrified by it. He abhorred any sort of violent change and
preferred the familiar and the known.

Imagine then the depths of his anguish when he, Paul McCartney,
performed his most violent act of change to date when he finally
decided to sue the other Beatles. Up there on the farm, in the
simple and rustic isolation he was coming to favor, Paul had
been talked into it by John Eastman. He filed writs against John,
George, Ringo, and Apple Corps Ltd. on December 31, 1970, in
the Chancery Division of the High Court in London, seeking a
dissolution of the partnership known as "The Beatles Co." His suit
also sought court costs and release of monies being held by Apple
and the appointment of a receiver to administer the group's affairs.
Paul later said that he had had no choice. "I wanted to sue Klein,"
he said, "but the only recourse was to sue my former mates." He
said he had made the decision on a long walk through the Scottish
countryside with his brother-in-law and counsel, John Eastman.
"We'd been searching our souls," Paul said. "Was there any
other way?" It was a decision that made him no friends anywhere.
Pepper Land had been invaded by Blue Meanies from within.

Paul had four basic legal arguments when the case was heard in
court, beginning February 18: that the Beatles were no longer a

group, that his artistic freedom was threatened by being yoked to a no longer viable partnership, that no partnership accounts had been computed or presented since they formed their partnership in 1967, and that the other three Beatles were trying to force upon him a manager that he found unacceptable.

After days of testimony detailing and attempting to make sense of the Beatles' incredibly involved financial picture and trying to delve into Klein's dealings since becoming manager of Apple, the court agreed with Paul. Justice Stamp said, "Apple is not . . . a Frankenstein set up to control the individual partners. . . . Whatever powers may be conferred on a partner, he is bound not only to be just and faithful to his partners, but to render them full information of all things affecting the partnership. . . . However successful Mr. Klein may have been in generating income, I am satisfied, on the evidence of the accountants and the accounts to which I am referred, that the financial situation [of Apple and the Beatles] is confused, uncertain, and confusing. A receiver is, in my judgment, needed not merely to secure the assets, but so that there may be a firm hand to manage the business fairly as between the partners and to produce order. I have no doubt that a receiver and manager ought to be appointed."

So Paul won, although with appeals by the other three and legal foot-dragging, the partnership was not formally dissolved until 1975. But for now, he had succeeded in removing Klein from the picture and attempting to have some order imposed on the Beatles' situation.

A receiver was appointed on March 10. John Lennon celebrated the occasion by having his personal assistant, Anthony Fawcett, drive him in his Rolls to Paul's house on Cavendish, where John scaled the high wall, opened the big gates, returned to the Rolls, and removed two bricks from the car. He walked back through the gates and hurled the bricks through Paul's front windows. Laughing, he was driven off to Apple, where he gathered together some of the Apple Scruffs who were clustered outside the building on Savile Row. "The reporters from the court will be here soon," he said. "Can you help us with a show of strength for the vultures?"

"Yes! What is it?"

"Tape up pictures of the three of us all across the front of the building. To show we're not dead yet!"

So they all set to work putting up eight-by-ten glossies of John, George, and Ringo on the elegant façade of Apple. John soon pulled one of the Scruffs aside, the one known as Sue-John, and asked her to put up a few pictures of Yoko as well. She looked very doubtful. Her name was not Sue-Yoko, after all. "For me, please?" he asked. So they stuck up a few of Yoko too, but managed to mostly hide her.

And that was the way it all ended.

Paul entered into his brave new life with fear and trepidation. He and Linda decided to stay at the farm in Scotland, where he was moping around, taking care of the sheep, and not doing much else. Even before the Chancery trial in early 1971, when he was depressed and pessimistic about his future, Linda urged him to continue with his music. When they went to New York City in January to get ready for the court case and to visit Linda's family, he decided to do a little recording while he was there. So he and Linda went into A&R Studios, where they were backed up by three local sessions players: drummer Denny Seiwell and guitarists Dave Spinozza and Hugh McCracken. They eventually recorded twenty-one songs, with Linda cowriting and singing on a number of them. Linda's daughter Heather sang on one, "Monkberry Moon Delight." For four songs they decided to use the New York Philharmonic Orchestra, which Paul decided to conduct. The orchestra was featured on the song Paul issued as a single.

"Another Day" was the first song he and Linda had written together and was a fairly barmy little ditty of domestic bliss. When it was released in England on February 19 (with "Oh Woman Oh Why" on the B-side), it became a number one hit. But there was immediate trouble for Paul after Sir Lew Grade of ATV and Northern Songs took a look at the writing credits: BY MR. AND MRS. MCCARTNEY. Since Linda stood to get 50 percent of the royalties and since she was not part of the Northern Songs arrangement, Grade was not happy and filed a lawsuit, alleging that the credits were a sham and that Linda was not and could not be the co-composer of the song.

As Paul later told Tim White: "I had a contract with Northern Songs for me and John as writers. As I wasn't collaborating with John anymore, I looked for someone else to collaborate with. I assumed there wouldn't be any sweat. . . . They were so wonderful to me after all the successes I'd brought them with me and John—more than they ever dreamed of earning anyway—they immediately slapped a million-dollar lawsuit on us. So they were charming pals who shall be remembered ever thus. . . . If my wife is actually saying, 'Change that' or 'I like that better than that,' then I'm using her as a collaborator. I mean, John never had any input on 'The Long and Winding Road' and Yoko still collects royalties on it. . . . The joke at that time was that Linda was the only one getting paid in our household 'cause we were all held up with Apple being subject to litigation. I wasn't seeing any money."

The case actually went to court, with Linda having to get up and testify that she felt competent to cowrite a song with the Great Paul McCartney. The matter was eventually settled, with Paul agreeing to appear in a television special for ATV called *James Paul McCartney*. In exchange Linda got her royalties. (It may not have been a fair exchange. The show was televised in both the United States and the United Kingdom in 1973 and did much to reinforce Paul's new image as family man and middle-of-the-road minstrel. There were film clips of Paul and Linda on the farm and Paul sang some medleys. The centerpiece of the show was an elaborate production number done to Paul's song "Gotta Sing, Gotta Dance" (which he had originally written for Twiggy) with Paul in a white tailcoat, hoofing it with a number of chorus girls dressed as chorus girls down the right half of their bodies and dressed in men's tuxedos on the left half, giving a rather bizarre effect.

On May 21 the *Ram* album was released and credited to Paul and Linda McCartney. It was number two in the charts (under the Rolling Stones' *Sticky Fingers*) and eventually became number one for one week. Paul designed the album cover, featuring a picture by Linda of Paul holding a ram by its horns. The letters L.I.L.Y. on the cover were widely assumed to stand for LINDA, I LOVE YOU. Pictured on the back are copulating beetles, presumably Paul's statement about the treatment he had received by his mates.

Musically, it was a wildly erratic album, though not nearly as bad as some yet to come. Two songs, "Dear Boy" and "Too Many People," appeared to be direct attacks on John Lennon.

"Uncle Albert/Admiral Halsey," which Paul said was actually about his Uncle Albert with Halsey thrown in just because he liked the name, was a number one hit in the United States, although it wasn't issued in England. There, the single was the lackluster "The Back Seat of My Car," which did not do well, not even entering the *New Musical Express* record chart at all. It was another example of Paul's increasingly erratic judgment. *Ram* amply displayed the fact that Paul remained in the throes of a severe crisis of confidence. What was even worse—although the public at large did not ever hear it or really hear about it—was a dreadful promotional album that Paul and Linda threw together to publicize *Ram*. It was called *Brung to Ewe by Hal Smith* and it was sent to unsuspecting radio stations and music journalists and critics. It was made up of a number of witless little scripts featuring Paul and Linda. Paul sang scraps of "Now Hear This Song of Mine." The overriding sound was the bleating of sheep. The record mainly confounded everyone who heard it. The impression one got was that this was the sort of thing that might be concocted by two bored people sitting out on an isolated farm somewhere and, after smoking a couple of joints, getting this kind of cockeyed inspiration. But who would tell Paul that it was a bad idea?

The thing about *Ram* was not so much that some of the music was so mediocre. It was just not the sort of excellence that critics and the public had become spoiled with by the Beatles. It was that kind of comparison, though, that most critics pointed out and it made Paul furious. "How do you tell an ex-Beatle that he has made a lousy album" was a common refrain.

John was getting the same sort of Beatle backlash. On March 12, the same day that the court had appointed a receiver to take charge of the Beatles' business and the same day that John heaved the bricks through Paul's windows, John and Yoko released a single. The A-side was "Power to the People" by John Lennon and the Plastic Ono Band (John had hoped it would match the success of his 1969 anthem "Give Peace a Chance). The B-side was "Open Your Box" by Yoko Ono and the Plastic Ono Band. "Problems" that EMI had with the lyrics of the B-side had delayed the record's release. EMI managing director Philip Brodie found Yoko's lyrics "distasteful" and ordered them cleaned up a bit before he would approve the record's release. But, brave as John's new militant and avant-garde stance was, it was just as baffling to press and public as was Paul's obsession with home and family. Diehard Beatle fans did not necessarily become staunch fans of the solo efforts of their former heroes. They were also weary of the backbiting between John and Paul.

But it went on. As soon as John listened to *Ram* and heard little digs at himself and Yoko in the songs "Too Many People" and "Dear Boy" (and maybe "3 Legs" also, but he wasn't sure), he could not wait to get in the studio and fire back at Paul, as he did with the *Imagine* album later in the year. If there were more vituperative songs aimed at a former best friend than "Crippled Inside" and "How Do You Sleep?", then Paul McCartney had never heard them. He was devastated.

Paul gave an interview in November to *Melody Maker*, in which he said he thought that "How Do You Sleep?" (in which John said that "Yesterday" was the only decent song Paul ever wrote) was just plain "silly. So what if I live with straights? I like straights. I have straight babies. It doesn't affect him. He says the only thing I did was 'Yesterday.' He knows that's wrong. He knows and I know it's not true."

Furthermore, Paul said that all he wanted was for everything to be over: "I just want the four of us to get together somewhere and sign a piece of paper saying it's all over and we want to divide the money four ways. . . . That's all I want now. But John won't do it. Everybody thinks I am the aggressor. But I'm not, you know. I just want out." There were many other digs at John and Yoko, but that was his main emphasis.

As soon as John read that in New York City, to which he and Yoko had just moved (he would never see England again, although no one could have known it at the time), he rushed a long letter of reply to *Melody Maker*. John had a lot to say, most of it very sarcastic, and reading it evoked a powerful wish that he and Paul could have just had all this out in private and settled it that way. The meat of the dispute still rankled John: "If you're not the aggressor (as you claim), who the hell took us to court and shat all over us in public? As I've said before—have you ever thought that you might possibly be wrong about something? Your conceit about us and Klein is incredible. . . . You must know that we're right about Eastman. . . ."

And on and on. . . .

Strangely, there was a partial Beatle reunion in 1971, one that at one point would have reunited three of them. George Harrison had been thinking for some time about the plight of the people of Bangladesh. Musician Ravi Shankar had approached him about doing a benefit concert for the refugee children of Bangladesh, with proceeds being funneled through UNICEF. He agreed and organized what was—up to that time—the biggest rock superstar extravaganza ever. The show, at Madison Square Garden on August 1, featured George, Ringo, Bob Dylan, Eric Clapton, and the like, the cream of rock's aristocracy. George had invited all the Beatles to appear, pointing out that egos should not get in the way of a worthwhile venture such as this. John initially agreed, then angrily backed out when he learned George didn't and wouldn't include Yoko in the invitation. Paul never considered it. He still felt too injured from all the Beatle fighting. And it didn't help when he learned that Allen Klein would be involved and that Phil Spector would be producing, with George, the live album from the concert. Some of Paul's wounds would never heal.

He was also busy that week, recording with his own band. Over the summer Paul and Linda had discussed the possibility of putting a little band together to realize one of Paul's long-standing fantasies: to perform in public again (but obviously not with his ex-mates). Of the four ex-Beatles, he was the one with the real need, almost a physical yearning, to sing before an audience. He would need a band to do that, but it would obviously have to be a nonthreatening band. Paul would never again fully trust a collaborator as he had trusted John in the early days. For now, at least, Linda was his only collaborator. Otherwise he was an island, trusting only his family in matters musical, social, or legal. From the first Paul was the one who wanted Linda to be in the band. "I had a talk with Linda," he told Tim White. "She said, 'If it's gonna be kinda casual and we're not gonna sweat it, we could maybe do something together.' So we started it on that basis. . . . That was the kind of spirit we approached it all in and it was the only way we could have done it, I say. If we'd have gotten too paranoid about it, we wouldn't have even dared stay in the business."

Paul still nurtured his dream of going out unheralded and playing little club dates or college gigs, as he had tried and failed to get the Beatles to do. So Paul decided that he would do it. The first musician recruited for the still-nameless aggregation he wanted to put together was Denny Seiwell, the session drummer who had played on *Ram* in New York. Seiwell and his wife Monique flew over from New York and moved into an outbuilding on Paul's High Park Farm in Scotland. Seiwell was originally from Leighton, Pennsylvania. He was a drummer in the Army and then moved to New York, where he worked in jazz clubs and at recording sessions. He got the *Ram* job through an audition Paul held. "A lot of the boys were really put out at being asked to audition. Paul just asked me to play. He didn't have a guitar, so I just sat and played. He had a certain look in his eye. He was looking for more than a drummer. He was looking for a certain attitude too." Clearly, what Paul was looking for was a musician with a certain amount of talent and no temperament.

Next, Paul added a guitarist whom he had known for years, Denny Laine, who had long been on the London musical scene. Born Brian Hines in Birmingham, England, he had been a member of the Moody Blues and had sung lead on "Go Now," their first hit. He left the Moodies before they achieved enormous success with their album sales and Laine came to be regarded as one of those unlucky musicians who is never in the right place at the right time. He bounced around a number of bands, moved to Spain for a year to learn flamenco guitar, and was living in his manager's office in London when he got the call from Paul. He headed straightaway for the farm and Paul gave him the royal tour of the greenhouse, with its tomatoes and marijuana plants.

To round out the band, Paul told Linda that she would have to learn to play keyboards. They rehearsed over the summer in Paul's barn. Then, while George Harrison achieved the musical triumph of his life at Madison Square Garden with the Concert for Bangladesh, Paul and his still-nameless ragtag band headed to London to record an album. They did most of it in three days, doing each song in one take. Paul later said he had been inspired to do an album that quickly after reading in one of the music papers that Bob Dylan was now doing that. Paul said, "If it's good enough for Bob, that's cool." Paul would, of course, soon regret that decision after the album was heard by the public.

But the name Wings was born before the album was released. That came about in September when Linda was in Kings College

Hospital giving birth to a daughter, Stella. It was a difficult pregnancy and Paul had moved into Linda's room, sleeping on a camp bed. He and Linda discussed names for the group, as well as for the child, and one of them used the phrase "wings of an angel," from which came the name for the group.

Stella's delivery was ultimately not as painful as that of Wings, however. When the first album, called *Wild Life,* was released on December 3, 1971, it sank out of sight. This was the first album credited only to Wings and, since·Paul's name didn't appear on the cover, most people had no idea who it was. The cover picture of Paul, Linda, and the two Dennys was a murky faraway pose of the four of them on a log or something in the woods and Paul was not immediately recognizable. The whole presentation was very un-Beatley, as if Paul wanted to completely go against everything he had ever championed. It looked cheap. One thing that Beatles' records had eliminated from rock albums was the inclusion of sappy liner notes on the backs. *Wild Life* returned to that, with someone named Clint Harrigan (who was strongly suspected of being Paul himself) scribbling such embarrassing things as: IN THIS WRAPPER IS THE MUSIC THEY MADE. CAN YOU DIG IT?". Sales were so bad (the album barely charted in England, although it reached gold record status—a million dollars in sales—in the United States in January 1972) that Paul withdrew from release the planned single from the album. That was a duet by Paul and Linda on "Love Is Strange," the only song on the album that was not a Linda–Paul writing collaboration. It was also, most critics agreed, the only good song on the record. ("Love Is Strange" was written by Mickey Baker and Ethel Smith and originally recorded in 1956 by Mickey and Sylvia.)

The rest of the album was a hodgepodge of nonsense (literally, on the "song" called "Mumbo"), children's talk ("Bip Bop," from daughter Mary's gabbling), and sheer uninteresting junk. Paul would later characterize it as a "spontaneous album." One significant thing about the album, though, was the song "Dear Friend," which was written for John Lennon as a gesture of peace. Paul told Tim White that he meant it as the letter to Lennon that he couldn't bring himself to write. "With the business pressures of the Beatles breaking up, it's like a marriage. One minute you're in love, next minute you hate each other's guts. I don't think any of us really ever got to the point where we actually hated each other's guts, but the business people involved were pitting us against each other, saying, 'Paul's not much good, is he?' or 'John's not all that good. Heh, heh, heh.' It's a pity because it's very difficult to cut through all that and what can you do? You can't write a letter saying, 'Dear Pal of Mine, I love you.' It's all a bit too much. So you do what we all seemed to do, which was write it in songs."

Early on the morning of February 8, 1972, Paul's nearest neighbor in St. John's Wood, the Honorable David Astor, retired editor of the *Observer,* was treated to an extraordinary sight in front of Paul McCartney's house. It was the ex-Beatle and MBE himself helping to load up a caravan (trailer), truck, and station wagon with musical instruments, three McCartney daughters, assorted baby gear and luggage, three dogs, a couple of roadies, and four Wings, including Mrs. McCartney. Once everyone was aboard, to the accompaniment of much barking and excited talk, the little procession proceeded slowly down the street and disappeared out of sight. Wings was clandestinely going on the road.

Paul was purposely re-creating the legendary odyssey from twelve years earlier, when he and John and George and Pete and Stu had crowded into Allan Williams's little minibus in front of the Jacaranda in Liverpool and boyishly and enthusiastically set out for Hamburg and to conquer the world. Now, Paul had lost his world, so he was off on another quest. He was determined to re-create his journey to the promised land, except one thing would be radically different this time around: He, Paul, would be in total control of everything. He was steering a course north from London, heading for a series of college and university campuses to perform incognito concerts that would be the first step of his route back to the top. He had made no advance bookings anywhere. The group didn't even have any hotel reservations. They would, he said, "wing" it. But it was the only way for him to start to build back his performing confidence and to earn a new generation of fans.

Despite the failure of the *Wild Life* album, Paul was determined to start on the comeback trail and he was convinced that touring was the only way to do it.

Before setting out from London Paul had hired another musician for Wings, an Irish lead guitarist named Henry McCullough.

He was known in London as a very competent sideman whose last job had been with Joe Cocker's Grease Band. He played on Wings' first single, which was recorded on February 1, before the university tour. The single was Paul's first and only political song, "Give Ireland Back to the Irish," written in response to the Bloody Sunday Massacre in Ireland on January 3. John Lennon had also felt moved to write a song about that event. His was "Sunday Bloody Sunday," which appeared on his *Some Time in New York City* album in September of that year.

Paul's record, issued as a Wings release on February 25, was banned immediately by the BBC. He was rather proud of that—it helped put an edge on his family image and for once put him ahead of John Lennon. Paul told Tim White: "Up until that point whenever anyone had said, 'Are you into protest songs?' I'd say, 'I liked Bob Dylan but no, I'm not.' I didn't like political songs; a lot of such songs can be boring. . . . I always vowed that I'll be the one who doesn't do political songs, but what happened over here was they had this massacre when some people had been doing a peaceful demonstration. Our soldiers, my country's Army paratroopers, had gone in and killed some people. So we were against the Irish; it was like being at war with them. And I'd grown up with this thing that the Irish are great, they're our mates, our brothers. We used to joke that Liverpool was the capital of Ireland. Suddenly we were killing our buddies and I thought, Wait a minute, this is not clever and I wish to protest on behalf of us people. This action of our government was over the top!

"I did that song and was rung up by a lot of people who said, 'Please don't release this. We don't need this right now.' And I said, 'Yes we do. Gotta have it.' "

Paul's newly found resolve was buttressed by his decision to go out on the road. He quickly discovered that he had made the right decision, for once in several years. He and his motley entourage pulled into Nottingham University, where the social secretary was startled out of her shoes when asked if Paul McCartney could play a little show there with his group. They did a lunchtime concert the next day and it went very well, but there was no Beatlemania present. Paul refused to perform any Beatle songs. Just Wings material and some old Little Richard stuff.

But the show was very gratifying to Paul. He found he could still manipulate an audience at will. The people still loved him. And he was in total charge of everything. He could even collect the money for the gig in cold hard cash, which was something he had certainly never been able to do with the Fab Four. He later said he felt like "Duke Ellington divvying out the money. We walked around Nottingham with thirty pounds in copper in our pockets." His thirty pounds would soon turn into millions of pounds, but in his mind, it became obvious, the pocketful of copper was more real to him than the millions he owned on paper. His musicians, who were still in awe of Paul and probably would have played for nothing for the magical gig they had landed, were not as fortunate when it came to money. They got bare minimum scale. Denny Laine, who gradually became Paul's friend and a sort of musical sidekick, was de facto bandleader and was being paid seventy pounds a week, the salary he would remain at for five years until he began to complain loudly. Linda herself was never paid more than fifty pounds a week the whole time she performed with Wings.

The college tour was like a second childhood for Paul. As they wandered on, from York to Hull to Lancaster to Leeds to Sheffield to Sálford to Birmingham to Swansea and back to London, he responded to the audience attention as Linda had never seen him.

There was criticism of Linda being onstage with an ex-Beatle, although nothing like what the critics would later rain down upon Linda when Wings graduated from playing college campuses to the real world. Paul said, "Linda wouldn't put herself up as a great vocalist, but she's got a great style—I think, anyway. Of course the critics didn't see it like that. They said, 'What's 'e got 'er on stage for?' Why not? What's the big deal? She's just singing with me, for Christ's sake. She's not exactly taking over the lead in *La Traviata* or anything. It's just a bit of background harmonies here."

Linda said that Paul, apart from wanting her with him for support, had talked her into it by greatly romanticizing the appeal of performing. "He said to me, 'Can you imagine standing on the stage, the curtain going up, the audience all waiting?' He made it sound so glamorous that I agreed to have a go."

Paul was not above criticizing Linda's playing, although she was literally learning on the job. He once dressed her down and threatened to replace her with Billy Preston. Then he apologized. Of her performances he said, "I decided not to defend Linda [to the press]; let them find out what we were trying to do. I said nothing, just as I said nothing during all John's tirades against me. I've had enough press to last me more than a lifetime."

Once back home Paul decided to do a full-blown European tour over the summer, but to hold off doing any scheduled dates in England, primarily to avoid being scrutinized by the British press.

Then, as if to taunt the press, Paul once again exhibited the perverse side of his nature that leads one to think that trepanning might have been worth considering, after all. Or that he might consider cutting back on the smoke. After he had carefully assembled his new little band from scratch and taken it on the road and gotten nothing but rave receptions and after he had sort of made up for the new band's terrible first album with a song that got him banned by the BBC, Paul once again demonstrated his willful lack of judgment. He and Linda recorded and released, as Wings' next single, "Mary Had a Little Lamb." It was more or less beyond criticism. Paul was fortunate that John Lennon shut his eyes and his ears when "Mary Had a Little Lamb" came out and did not publicly comment on it. "Why should I?" John said later. "What could I possibly have added? The fact that he put it out was comment enough, I rather thought."

Paul and Wings set out through the Continent in early July in a gaily painted double-decker bus with an open top strewn with mattresses and cushions for sunbathing and sight-seeing. Paul was reliving his Magical Mystery Tour and trying to get it right this time. The tour opened on July 9 at the Centre Culturale in Château Vallon, France. The tour was a great success. All through France, Germany, Switzerland, Denmark, and Finland, the audiences received Paul and Wings warmly. Then, on the night of August 10, as they came off the stage at Scandinavian Hall in Göteborg, Sweden, police officers were waiting for them because Paul's dope system had slipped up. Back in Beatle days, when the Fab Four were immune from search, they used to carry their dope in what was called their "diplomatic bags," their handbags that were never searched. Now, though, things were different.

Police took Paul, Linda, Denny Seiwell, and a woman identified as Paul's secretary to police headquarters. Customs officers, who claimed they had intercepted a phone call from Linda to Paul's office in London asking for marijuana to be mailed to them in Göteborg, said they had found about seven ounces of marijuana in a letter addressed to Paul. The police said, "We told them we had found the cannabis in a letter and at first they said they knew nothing about it. But after we had questioned them for about three hours they confessed and told the truth. McCartney, his wife, and Seiwell told us they smoked hash every day. They said they were almost addicted to it. They said they had made arrangements to have drugs posted to them each day they played in different countries so they wouldn't have to take any drugs through Customs themselves."

Wings' local promoter John Morris said, "Paul, Linda, and Denny did admit to the Swedish police that they used hash. At first they denied it, but the police gave them a rough time and started threatening all sorts of things. The police said they would bar the group from leaving the country unless they confessed."

They paid a fine of one thousand pounds and were released after the public prosecutor said he was satisfied that they had planned to use the dope themselves and clearly were not trafficking in it.

Paul's caretaker at High Park Farm in Scotland, a farmer named Duncan Cairns, read about Paul's arrest in the newspapers and wrote Paul a letter of resignation. He had previously ignored local rumors about drug use at the farm (and had obviously not taken care of the greenhouse). Someone else who read about it was police constable Norman McPhee, who was based in Campbeltown near the farm and had been taking a drug identification course in Glasgow. Since Paul's farm was in his jurisdiction, he paid a visit, ostensibly to check on security while Paul was away. In checking the greenhouse, he found Paul's marijuana plants. He returned later with seven policemen for a thorough search of the farm, which turned up nothing else.

Paul was charged on three counts of growing and possessing marijuana. He pleaded guilty to the cultivation charge and was fined one hundred pounds. His lawyer's defense was that Paul had received the marijuana seeds in the mail, did not know what they were, but, being an avid gardener, had planted them to see what would come up. Even so, Paul told the press that he thought the laws should be changed on marijuana possession. "I don't think cannabis is as dangerous as drink," he said.

After Paul's summer tour ended in Germany on August 24, he went back to the farm to rest up and tend to his tomatoes. That same week John Lennon offered to get together with Paul, an invitation that remains little known. John, as part of his high visibility and activism in New York City, had offered to stage a benefit concert with reporter Geraldo Rivera in conjunction with children from the Willowbrook School in New York. John called to invite Paul to appear with him at the One to One show at Madison Square Garden on August 30, along with Stevie Wonder, Sha Na Na, and others. Paul declined and has never said why.

Instead, Paul spent the rest of 1972 at the farm and recording with Wings in London at the Morgan Studios. The only record he released during the latter part of 1972 was a single, "Hi Hi Hi," which was promptly banned by the BBC for its supposed drug and sex references. For an avowed family man, Paul was certainly making his mark as an anti-Establishment figure. Paul said the song was just his parting shot at the sixties and the days of open drug use and free sex and bellbottom jeans.

He was starting to feel confident enough about his music again, though, to take much more care with crafting his songs. His recording sessions from late 1972 yielded "My Love," one of the better McCartney singles ever. He also released it (on March 23, 1973) under the name Paul McCartney and Wings, an admission that the Wings moniker itself was not big enough to carry either his ego or enough public recognition to sell records. "My Love" sold two million copies, remarkable for a single.

The album that resulted from those same recording sessions, *Red Rose Speedway,* was also credited to Paul McCartney and Wings and songwriting credits all read just: MCCARTNEY. The album was a vast improvement over *Wild Life* and *Ram,* although it was still far short of his best work. Lenny Kaye, writing in *Rolling Stone,* observed: "Paul McCartney's music tends to crumble under prolonged examination. He is not an especially intense lyricist, preferring instead to choose his words according to sound and feel alone and his melodies—particularly on more up-tempo material—appear to be fostered through basic reliance on a rotating riff."

Paul appeared to have paid more attention to the package than the product, as he often did. The record contained a twelve-page booklet, the sort of thing Paul favored, with pictures by Linda and Joe Stevens, who had been official photographer on the European Wings tour (but who was kicked off Paul's bus after Stevens remarked how great it was "working for the Beatles"), and drawings by Eduard Paolozzi, who had been Stu Sutcliffe's teacher in Hamburg. On the back cover there was a message in braille to Stevie Wonder, reading: WE LOVE YOU. Meanwhile, two of the songs were outtakes from the old *Ram* sessions.

One thing the album did, though, was to demonstrate the growing number of fans of Paul's solo work. It went to number one in the United States and number four in the United Kingdom.

Paul had an increasing conviction that what he was doing, though it was heavily criticized, was right for him. So in 1973 he decided to finally brace himself and brave the British press. After playing a benefit for the Release drug program at London's Hard Rock Café in March, Paul and Linda and Wings set out in May for a fifteen-date British tour. By and large, Paul succeeded with the public and the press. In reviewing the May 12 concert at Oxford, *Rolling Stone* critic Paul Gambaccini made the first mention of the existence of many young Wings fans who did not really remember or identify with the Beatles. "It was a respectable concert," he wrote. "Wings don't rate raves yet, but the time for snickering is over."

Of the same concert *Melody Maker*'s Chris Charlesworth observed: "Paul has at last shaken off the post-Beatles stigma which has hampered his every move in the past three years." That show had begun with a silent curious audience and ended with a standing ovation and calls for an encore, an encore that Paul had to refuse, telling the crowd that the band had already exhausted its repertoire.

So, before the summer of 1973, Paul was feeling his oats. Not only was he re-emerging with a successful tour, he was selling records again and the critics were starting to respect him again. He had also gotten back together with George Martin, who produced Paul's song "Live and Let Die" for the James Bond film of the same title. That single, released in June 1973, became the most successful Bond theme song ever. When Paul got the writing assignment, he read the Bond book on Saturday, wrote the song the next day, and recorded it the next week with Martin. The latter took the tape to Jamaica and played it for Harry Saltzmann, one of the film's producers, who listened to it and then said, "Very nice record. Who should we get to sing it? What do you think of Thelma Houston?" Paul had George Martin to thank for finally persuading Saltzmann to take the tape as it was.

He had another reason to start feeling chipper. In June the other Beatles filed suit against Allen Klein for many alleged and various forms of mismanagement. Klein countersued them for damages amounting to $63,461,372.87 (and future earnings) and then added a $34-million (plus interest) suit against Paul, charging him with conspiring with the others against Klein. When that was all settled, Klein emerged with about $5 million from the group. But he was gone and Paul finally felt vindicated for what he had done.

He had felt so heartened by public response that he held a brief press conference after the concert in Oxford and sounded aggressive. "John's not done too much lately," he said, going on to dismiss the other Beatles as well. "I don't see any of them. I mean, it's just not on. The Beatles went the full circle and you just can't do that again. We did everything except win the FA Cup [a soccer trophy]."

A reporter said, "You don't expect Wings to be as big as the Beatles. Obviously not."

"*Crap* to that 'obviously not,' " Paul shot back. "The Beatles were guys coming down from Liverpool who wanted it a lot. Now I've got the lot. I want to play. I want to live. I want to have some fun."

"Don't kill him! It's Beatle Paul!" Linda was screaming as two men came out of the black shadows of an alleyway. One grabbed him from behind in a rough chokehold and the other held a knife to his throat and said, "Give it up!" Linda was crying and screaming. Paul couldn't move. They took his wallet and shoulder bag and then grabbed Linda's bag and ran. Paul was shaking, Linda was crying, and they were lost in the back alleys of Lagos, Nigeria, only days after their triumphant British tour ended.

They had been wandering around the city, gotten lost, and now *this*. "We were lucky we didn't get hurt or worse," Paul later said. They had gone off alone to explore the city, he said, because it was a "hippy phase we were going through, we call it our funky phase. We got to the studio the next day and the head guy there said, 'You're lucky you didn't get killed! It's only 'cause you're white you didn't. They figure you won't recognize them." As it was, the attackers had taken Linda's cameras, Paul's tape recorder, and demo tapes of songs they were working on.

The next day, after smoking a joint in the studio, Paul felt as though one of his lungs had collapsed. He went outside to try to get air and fainted dead away. A doctor brought him around and told him to cut back on his smoking.

They had decided to go to Lagos in a typically well-thought-out McCartney decision. After the British tour ended in August, Paul wanted to record again but said he was getting bored with London. And he and Linda wanted to go someplace warm, where they could combine vacation and work, lie on the beach, and have a good time. Paul had asked EMI where they had studios in warm climes. "Rio de Janerio and Lagos," he was told. "I thought Lagos sounded great! Africa, rhythms, percussionists." On the basis of that observation alone, off Paul and Linda went.

They arrived to discover that Lagos is not one of the world's great resort cities. Additionally, they got there at the tail end of the rainy season. Plus, the recording studio was being renovated. "They didn't use booths or separation barriers, so they were constructing booths just for us and the guy was saying, 'Do you want glass in them?' They were just gonna make big wooden things with holes in them!"

Wings arrived in Lagos as a trio. Just prior to departure, both guitarist Henry McCullough and drummer Denny Seiwell quit the group in separate huffs. The McCullough incident had been a carbon copy of the time George Harrison quit the Beatles after being badgered mercilessly by Paul. Said Paul of Henry: "I think Henry came to a head one day when I was asking him to play something he didn't really fancy playing. We all got a bit choked about it and he rang up later and said he was leaving. I said, 'Well, okay.' " Seiwell quit after McCullough did, just saying that he didn't want to go to Africa. Both of them later dropped broad hints that they didn't especially like working with Linda. It made for a delicate situation when the boss's wife was in the band and was not a great musician. Just being a Wing was a strange role to play. They were making very little money working for one of the most famous men in music. It was Paul's music they were playing—not Wings music. No input was expected of them. And there was a real caste system involved in working like that. They were just hired hands with no room for advancement. Denny Laine, by deferring to Paul and Linda and by being Paul's right-hand man, was useful to have around. Not essential, but useful. Other Wings would come and go in a steady procession. It was a frustrating position for a musician to be in. Of the first two to depart, Paul said, "I don't think there was anything wrong with them as musicians. They were both good, but they just didn't fit in."

As Paul began recording, he wasn't overly worried. He could make an album by himself if he had to. Besides, he knew that he had some strong material for this record. The title song, "Band on the Run," came about, Paul said, because that was the way he felt. He told Tim White: "At the time, we were ourselves a band on the run. There were a lot of ordinary musicians at the time who'd come out of ordinary suburbs in the sixties and seventies and were getting busted. Bands like the Byrds, the Eagles—the mood amongst them was one of desperadoes. We were being outlawed for pot, which was the whole matter. It put us on the wrong side of the law. And our argument on the title song was 'Don't put us on the wrong side, you'll make us into criminals. We just would rather do this than hit the booze'—which had been the traditional way to do it. We felt that this was a better move. So I just made up a story about people breaking out of prison. Structurally, that very tight little intro led to a hole being blasted in the wall and we get the big orchestra and then we're off. We escape into the sun." At the time he wrote the song Paul could not enter the United States. He was denied a visa because of his drug convictions.

He had written "Picasso's Last Words (Drink to Me)" while having dinner with the actor Dustin Hoffman the year before when he and Linda were on vacation in Jamaica, where Hoffman was filming *Papillon* with Steve McQueen. After dinner Dustin asked him, "How do you write songs?"

"They just come out of the air. I dunno," Paul replied.

"Can you write them about anything?"

"Yeah."

"Try this." He handed an issue of *Time* magazine to Paul and pointed to an obituary of Picasso and read from it Picasso's last words, which were: "Drink to me. Drink to my health. You know I can't drink anymore."

Paul said, "Well, you could probably write a song about that."

After a moment he started singing it. Hoffman jumped up, shouting, "Look, he's doing it! Goddamn it! *Holy shit!*"

There were other songs that were just as strong. Paul had written "Jet" about a black Labrador puppy that he and Linda bought one day on impulse. Jet learned to jump the wall of the house on Cavendish and one day came home pregnant and soon presented Paul with nine puppies. And the song "Let Me Roll It" was an affectionate parody of the Plastic Ono Band.

They finished the album in short order, doing some recording at Ginger Baker's ARC Studio as a courtesy to Baker, the drummer from Cream who had moved to Lagos. Paul played drums, guitar, bass, and synthesizers. Linda and Denny supplied backing vocals and Denny played guitar.

The album was released on November 30, with a cover acting out Paul's fantasies about being on the run. Paul rounded up some celebrities and had them pose like a gang of prisoners pinioned in a spotlight's glare against a prison wall. His fellow prisoners were actor James Coburn, boxer John Conteh, member of Parliament Clement Freud, television interviewer Michael Parkinson, singer Kenny Lynch, actor Christopher Lee, and of course Denny and Linda.

Paul, as was often his fashion, decided not to release any single from the album. It sold tolerably well but not exceedingly well. Then in early January 1974 a Capitol Records promotion man in Los Angeles called Paul with an idea. With typical promo man's exuberance, Al Coury begged Paul for a single. "You *gotta* let me work this record! I've got a real feeling about it!"

Said Paul: "Al released 'Jet,' which I wasn't even thinking of releasing as a single, and then 'Band on the Run' too. . . . He single-handedly turned that album around." It became the first album in American music history to regain the number one spot on the charts. It sold six million copies by the end of 1974. It also won two Grammy Awards: for best-engineered recording and best pop vocals by a group. Paul said that what really thrilled him about the album was that Keith Moon, the great drummer for the Who, said he loved Paul's drumming on it.

More importantly from Paul's point of view, the album totally redeemed him as writer, singer, and musician. The public loved him and now the critics were coming around to his music again. Jon Landau in *Rolling Stone* said that the album was "remarkably catchy—the kind of album people come back to over and over again. . . . I'll take a chance and say that *Band on the Run* is an album about the search for freedom and the flight from restrictions on his and Linda's personal happiness. It is about the pursuit of freedom from his past as a Beatle. . . ."

Significantly, Paul's severest critic said he liked the record: John Lennon told *Rolling Stone* that *"Band on the Run* is a great album. Wings is almost as conceptual a group as Plastic Ono Band is. Wings keeps changing all the time. I mean the backup men for Paul. It doesn't matter who's playing, you can call them Wings, but it's Paul McCartney music. And it's good stuff."

The prospect of a thaw in Beatle relations was there. When the others finally sued Allen Klein, Paul had begun the forgiving process. He and John had not seen each other since the breakup, but physically in 1973 they couldn't. Paul couldn't enter the United States and John couldn't leave it. Deportation proceedings against John were under way, ostensibly because of his prior drug conviction, but in fact because Richard Nixon and his henchmen feared that John planned to lead a radical mob to disrupt the 1974 Republican Convention. If John had left the United States, he would not have been allowed back in and he wanted to live there.

In the fall of 1973 John, George, and Paul had rallied to help Ringo. His solo records had not done well and, with no Beatle money coming in, he needed a cash transfusion. So the others contributed material to his planned album *Ringo*. The recording session was in Los Angeles. George and John sang and played on it. Paul and Linda wrote the song "Six O'clock," sang it, and sent the tape to Ringo for him to add a lead vocal to. The Beatle help worked: *Ringo* sold about two million copies.

★　　★　　★

After the success of *Band on the Run* gave Paul a lot of breathing room—artistically, as well as financially—he and Linda took life easy for a while. Taking it easy meant home life with the kids and animals, smoking dope, making music, and taking the odd trip. For "a great loon" one weekend they went off to Paris to record two reggae songs that Linda had written after their Jamaica vacation. "Seaside Woman" and "B Side to Seaside" were originally to have been part of a whole Linda McCartney album, but that never materialized. The songs were released as a single, under the name Suzy and the Red Stripes, in England and in the United States, but the single's lack of success effectively marked the end of Linda's solo career.

Paul also started recruiting musicians to put Wings back together. Since he could call upon virtually anyone in the world, it seemed, and was again looking for reasonably talented unknowns, one writer finally thought to ask Paul point-blank why he was doing that. Why not Eric Clapton, for instance? Paul told writer Chris Welch that it "might be a bit difficult. For one reason, I don't know him very well. I like him a lot and he's a great guitarist, but I never chummed up with him. We're just quietly looking around for a really nice guitarist and drummer. I just like to play with people and see what they are like."

The guitarist and drummer Paul chose turned out to be immediately incompatible, with each other and with the group. The guitarist was Jimmy McCulloch, who had just gone along on the Suzy and the Red Stripes trip. McCulloch was a short, baby-faced Glaswegian who played a blistering guitar, had a bottomless thirst for the grape, and possessed an uncontrollable temper. He had joined his first band at the age of thirteen and played on a number one hit, Thunderclap Newman's "Something in the Air" at the age of sixteen, went on to play with John Mayall, Stone the Crows, and the Blue. He was just twenty when Paul anointed him a Wing.

The drummer was a tall muscular karate teacher named Geoff Britton. He had played with the Wild Angels and displayed as hard-hitting and aggressive a style with the sticks as anyone around. He survived two auditions that Paul held. Among the other applicants was Mitch Mitchell, who had been Jimi Hendrix's drummer.

With his new Wings lineup and with a new American visa,

Paul moved his little entourage to Nashville, Tennessee, to rehearse and to record a little. During seven weeks there, resting on a rented farm, Paul recorded just four songs. These four would make up his next two singles, even though *Band on the Run* was still high on the charts and could have yielded a more commercial song. The first single was credited to the Country Hams and, since the public could not possibly know it was a McCartney release, it sold almost no copies. But Paul had actually done it as a present for his father. The A-side, "Walking in the Park with Eloise," had been written by Jim McCartney many decades earlier. When Paul mentioned to Chet Atkins one day that "Eloise" had been the only song his father ever wrote, Atkins said, "It'd be really nice to make a record of that for your dad." So they did, with pianist Floyd Cramer joining them. The B-side was Paul improvising on guitar, with horns dubbed over, on something he called "Bridge Over the River Suite." Paul was proud of that and likened it to "film music."

The other single—credited to Paul and Wings—was "Junior's Farm" (with "Sally G." as the B-side). It was not a rollicking commercial success. These two singles were all that Paul released during the remainder of 1974 (and the only other records put out that year were the two singles from *Band on the Run* early in the year). But he could afford to be self-indulgent and fully intended to be. He took the rest of 1974 off.

According to Paul, he met with John Lennon once that year and attempted to on a second occasion. (Certain writers, such as Beatles biographer Philip Norman, suggest that Paul reinterprets history on a regular basis.) He told *Q Magazine* of London that sometime after John and Yoko separated (which happened in October 1973), Yoko was in London and visited Paul and Linda at their home in St. John's Wood. As they chatted, it came out that John and Yoko had split up and that John was out in Los Angeles doing crazy things. Paul said that he offered to go and try to talk some sense into John if Yoko actually wanted him back. She said he would have to "work his way back." Paul asked Yoko if it would be "an intrusion if I said to him, 'Look, man, she loves you and there's a way to get back'—sounds like a Beatles song—and I said, 'Would that be okay?' She said she didn't mind and we went out to visit him in L.A. in that house where all the crazy things went on and I took him into the back room and said, 'This girl of yours, she really still loves you. Do you love her?' And he said he did but he didn't know what to do. So I said, 'You're going to have to work your little ass off, man. You have to get back to New York, you have to take a separate flat, you have to send her roses every fucking day, you have to work at it like a bitch! Then you just might get her back. And he did. I mean, if you hear it from John's point of view [Paul is undoubtedly referring to Yoko, since this interview was done in 1986 and John died in 1980], it'll just be that he spoke to Yoko on the phone and she said to him, 'Come back' [which is the way the Yoko camp depicts the circumstances of the reunion]."

The second occasion, he said, was a business meeting at the Plaza Hotel in New York, scheduled to try to finish dissolving the Beatles [the final dissolution came on January 9, 1975, so this meeting was obviously before then]. Paul said that George "came off his disastrous tour." That tour ran from November 2 to December 20, 1974. Paul said he and Ringo and George were at the Plaza and John was home at the Dakota. Which means that he had reunited with Yoko and Yoko's date for that is sometime after November 28, the night he appeared at Madison Square Garden with Elton John. So the three Beatles sat at the Plaza and waited for John. From the Dakota came a messenger from John. He delivered a balloon with a note that said: LISTEN TO THIS BALLOON. George blew up and called the Dakota, shouting: "You fucking maniac! You take your fucking dark glasses off and come and look at us, man!"

Paul later said that he himself had gone to George Harrison's Madison Square Garden show in disguise: He wore an Afro wig, sunglasses, and a big walrus mustache.

Paul said there was a regular series of meetings after that one that fell apart because of the balloon. The next one blew up when John asked for an extra million pounds. Later, Paul said, down the road when they became friendly again, he had asked John why he had demanded that extra million. "I just wanted cards to play with," John said.

Even as the Beatles' dissolution became final, Paul was drawing up his blueprints for his ultimate revenge and final vindication. He was going to out-Beatle the Beatles all by himself (well, with Wings, but that point was moot). He was planning a two-year world tour that would be the biggest in rock history. It was still months away, as he and Wings settled into New Orleans in January 1975 to work on an album and rehearse the group. Even so, he had already written his opening song for the tour, "Rockshow," a strident rock anthem with its lyrical references to rock landmarks in Paul's own history and future: Concert Gebouw in Amsterdam, which was a memorable stop on Wings' 1972 European tour; Madison Square Garden, where the Beatles never played but where Wings would star in the media capital of the world; and the Hollywood Bowl, where the Beatles performed three stirring concerts.

In New Orleans—another town for a good working vacation—Wings rehearsed and recorded at Allen Toussaint's Sea Saint Studios, a fabled home of Southern music. It was here that Paul lost another Wing. Geoff Britton had been fired once earlier when they were in Nashville. He said it was for fighting with McCulloch and he also made sure the British music press knew that he—Britton—was the only one of the whole group who was a health nut and didn't regularly plow into the drugs that can be made available to rock musicians. He said he was sacked the second time in New Orleans because Laine was out to get him. He also told the British music press that when he had joined Wings he was promised royalties, on the order of "telephone numbers" [seven figures, that is], but that all that ever appeared on top of his scale wage was session fees and bonuses.

Britton was quickly replaced by Joe English, a native of Rochester, New York, who had worked in a group known as the Jam Factory and was rehearsing with Southern singer Bonnie Bramlett when Tony Dorsey, who was putting together a horn section for the Wings tour, recommended him to Paul. English was an easygoing competent drummer, someone finally fitting Paul's mold. When English inevitably quit Wings in 1977, he complained that Linda was a hindrance to the band, that he was not a Denny Laine fan, and that he had not seen any of the royalties he said he had been promised at the time he was recruited.

In February Paul decided to shift operations to Los Angeles, where he continued recording at Wally Heider Studios. On the night of March 3, Paul was driving a rented Lincoln Continental from the studio back to their rented house in Malibu. Linda was riding shotgun and Heather, Stella, and Mary were in the backseat. Paul ran a red light on Santa Monica Boulevard and an ever-alert L.A. cop pulled him over immediately. The cop later testified that he smelled a strange odor as he approached the driver's window and that he found a smoldering marijuana cigarette on the floorboard. A search of Linda's purse turned up a plastic bag of grass containing about eighteen grams. Linda said the joint that had been found on the floor was hers also, not Paul's. Linda was held at a police station until the $500 bail was posted (Paul had only $200 on him and finally, after telephoning around town, borrowed $300 from former NEMS and Apple executive Peter Brown, who was staying at the Beverly Hills Hotel). In court in May, the judge dropped the charges against Linda when she agreed to attend six sessions with a psychiatrist. Drug counseling was not an unusual sentence in L.A. for a first offender—which is what Linda was. The judge even agreed to let her see a shrink in London, rather than L.A.

That had been a close call, but Paul's feelings that he was immune from the rules of ordinary law and life had been upheld—for the time being. He was closing off certain options, though, and shrinking his world even more. He had matter-of-factly once mentioned that in a 1974 interview when he said, "I don't think I have that many friends. No one went against me or anything. I think I isolated myself a bit. We're very romantic, the both of us, and we didn't really want to hang out with anyone else."

Paul's next single release, "Listen to What the Man Said," in May 1975, was the first record by an ex-Beatle to not appear on the Apple label. (Paul also confidently went back to crediting the records to Wings, without his name appearing.) The Beatles had been dissolved finally and Apple Records was no more. The single and the album, *Venus and Mars,* were both on Capitol Records (in the United Kingdom and the United States). The album shot to number one in England and America (where there were advance orders of a million and a half copies). Even the most critical of critics, Robert Christgau of the *Village Voice,* liked it. Said Christgau: "Superficially, which counts for a lot with McCartney, his New Orleans venture is his most appealing post-Beatles album—straight rock and roll with a few pop detours and one excursion into 'When I'm Sixty-Four' nostalgia. So clear in its melodies, mix, and basic pulse that his whimsical juxtapositions—robots on Main Street, Rudy Vallee cheek by jowl with Allen Toussaint—sound like they might make some sense. Don't get me wrong—they probably don't, because McCartney's a convinced fool. But when the music is coherent it doesn't matter so much."

Paul celebrated his success with a big party aboard the *Queen Mary* in Long Beach harbor. George Harrison and Paul embraced warmly. Guests included Dean Martin, Cher, Michael Jackson, and Bob Dylan.

Then it was back to England. That summer Paul and Linda and the kids and animals moved from St. John's Wood to a two-bedroom cottage near Rye in Sussex. They kept the London house and the big farm in Scotland. The move was primarily an attempt to raise their children completely out of the public eye and have them go to regular schools like regular children. Three years later Paul would buy the 160-acre East Gate Farm nearby for one hundred thousand pounds and build a five-bedroom house on it, with pool, stables, and a paddock, all surrounded by a high fence and watched over by a high tower. He called the estate Waterfalls.

All summer Paul and Wings rehearsed in a vacant movie house in Rye, gearing up for what he hoped would equal and surpass a Beatle tour. He had decided to finally break down and perform some Beatles songs on the tour. For one thing, he said, after clandestinely attending George's Madison Square Garden Show in costume, he concluded that it was a mistake for George—or any of them—to so militantly avoid performing any songs he was known for or to radically change the arrangements when he did sing them. The other reason, he said, was that he was mellowing out a bit, that a great deal of pressure had been lifted off him after the others had finally sued Allen Klein. And, he added, "they're great tunes. . . . I just decided in the end, this wasn't such a big deal. I'd do them."

Paul slept comfortably late in his home in St. John's Wood on October 28, 1975, the day that Wings and company were to fly off to Australia for stage two of the Wings world conquest. Stage one, the eleven British dates between September 9 and 23, had been an overwhelming success. Now it was on to down under and Japan. But Paul McCartney, ever since he decided that he would do only what he wanted to do when he wanted to (when the shock of the Beatles' demise hit him), lives and works and plays on McCartney time. Which is whatever he wants it to be. Who is to challenge him? Those who have worked for him say that he is always late—for everything.

So, on that October morning, a staff aide telephoned Qantas Airways to say that, regretfully, Mr. McCartney and party would be delayed. It is no small measure of the power and prestige that had accrued to Paul that a Qantas jumbo jet full of angry passengers was held on the runway at Heathrow for over an hour until Paul could get there. There were furious protests. The London *Sun* ran an editorial cartoon of an aircraft turning, with the caption reading: WE REGRET HAVING TO TURN BACK. MR. MCCARTNEY HAS FORGOTTEN HIS TOOTHBRUSH.

After nine shows in Australia Paul found that his concerts in Japan had to be canceled after the Japanese government decided to deny his visa because of his previous drug arrests. He made a lot of noise to the press about being singled out for "having smoked some of the deadly weed." As a "martyr for the cause," Paul had his staff send videotapes of one of the Wings shows to Japanese TV so that the country would know just what it was missing by keeping him out.

Then it was back to London to record another album before starting the European tour in March. At Abbey Road in January and February, Paul and Wings recorded what would be *Wings at the Speed of Sound* and Paul tried to make it a real Wings album. He seemed sincere about the effort to turn this version of Wings into a lasting thing. Previously, the only Wings freedom he had allowed was in letting Denny Laine sing lead on Paul's song "I Lie Around" (which was the B-side of "Live and Let Die") and letting Jimmy McCulloch sing his composition (cowritten with Colin Allen) "Medicine Jar" on *Venus and Mars.*

On *Speed of Sound,* though, anarchy virtually reigned. McCulloch sang another McCulloch dope song called "Wino Junko," Laine sang his own "Time to Hide" and Paul's song "The Note You Never Wrote," Linda got to run free with Paul's "Cook of the House," and even Joe English was given Paul's "Must Do Something About It." "Cook of the House" was Linda's first solo outing and it started with the sounds of bacon sputtering and chips frying in her very own kitchen. (Ben Fong-Torres once asked Linda about the matter of her celebrating her place in the kitchen. "My answer," Linda told him, "is always: 'Fuck off!' ".) Paul took the rest himself, with "Silly Love Songs" becoming the single release after Paul, for once, knew a hit song when he sang it. The album, as with so many of Paul's ventures, was extremely uneven. Stephen Holden wrote in *Rolling Stone* that it "seems like a mysterious, somewhat defensive oddity by a great pop producer who used to be a great pop writer."

The European tour started March 20 in Copenhagen and Paul was traveling when his father Jim died on March 18. Jim had long been suffering from severe arthritis and died in his little bungalow in Heswall, near Rembrandt, the house that Paul had bought back from him. Jim's second wife, the former Angela Williams (who had married Jim in 1964), told Paul's brother Mike that Jim had said just before dying, "I'll be with Mary soon."

Jim's funeral was held on the twenty-second with cremation following at Landican Cemetery and Paul was en route from Copenhagen to Berlin at the time. Mike McCartney later wrote: "It was no coincidence that Paul was on the Continent at the time of the funeral (as I'm sure he'll tell you). Like Dad, who'd apologise for not being able to hold our stomachs when, as kids, we were being sick, Paul would never face that sort of thing. As Dad would say, 'It's just the way you're made, son.' "

Denny Laine later claimed that, although he was probably Paul's closest male friend at the time, he had no idea that Paul's father had died until they were doing a television interview in Paris on the twenty-sixth and Paul was asked if his parents were still alive. Laine speculated that from what he knew about Paul that Paul sublimated all feelings about loss and death because otherwise he would lose all control, which was very important to him.

Paul had not been close to his stepmother Angela, who was thirty-four with a five-year-old daughter, Ruth, when she married Jim when he was sixty-two. After Jim's death he became even less close after a row about her using the McCartney name in running an entertainment agency. She later sold her story to the London *Sun,* with ghostwriter Tony Barrow (Disker from the old days in Liverpool) penning it. The three-day series was bannered as THE MEAN SIDE OF PAUL MCCARTNEY, with Angela providing voluminous details of just how penny-pinching and cold Paul and Linda were. She claimed they had had to move out of Rembrandt because they could no longer afford to keep it up and that Jim pleaded with her not to tell Paul that they needed money. Jim was badly crippled by arthritis by then and she said their cover story for selling was that he could no longer manage the stairs. (Mike McCartney refers to the end of Rembrandt in his book, writing that "like all bubbles it eventually burst, with something of a shock.") She claimed that on occasions when she and Jim visited Paul and Linda at the farm that she was horrified by the accommodations. She and Jim had to sleep on mattresses on the garage floor. Angie reported that bugs were literally dropping from the kitchen ceiling into their food and that Linda refused to let her use insect spray on them, citing the bugs' right to life. Oh, there was no love left there after a time. Angela said that Linda literally took food out of their mouths when she would raid the freezer on visits, while Angela had to make do with a housekeeping allowance of twenty pounds a week and Linda had her groceries sent up by train from Fortnum's in London.

Brian Epstein would have been proud as punch of his old adversary and sometime-friend Paul on his massive Wings Over America tour. Paul had learned his lessons well from Brian. Paul had turned WOA into a finely tuned machine, such a smoothly functioning apparatus that Paul was the last little component to be plugged in every night just as the show started. The thirty-one shows across the country had even been divided into zones, so that Paul and Linda and family and Wings stayed in a home base in New York, Chicago, Los Angeles, or Dallas and then zoomed into the target city in their luxurious BAC 1011 airplane, played the show, tipped their proverbial caps, and, before the last notes of "Soily" quit reverberating in the rafters of the hall and before all fog from the insect foggers and smoke from the smoke machines had dissipated, would be at thirty thousand feet and halfway back to all the comforts of home in a cozy rent-a-mansion in Turtle Creek or Beverly Hills.

Paul temporarily lost his voice from a case of nerves the first night, May 3 in Fort Worth, but it was his first U.S. show in ten years. Otherwise, the tour was the biggest thing since . . . the last biggest thing, which had been Paul the last time around, with his mates. But this time there was no Beatlemania. Just a few screams and many Instamatic winks lighting up the stage when Paul emerged from the shadows at the outset and ripped into "Venus and Mars/Rockshow." Otherwise it was a good-time rip-roaring evening of much Wings and selected Beatles goodies. Wings had turned into an above-average backup group that could kick in with window-rattling rock and roll with "Beware My Love" or "Band on the Run." But no matter how much Paul talked about how it was a Wings tour and no matter how many words an increasingly testy Denny Laine expounded on how and why audiences should regard the show as being by Wings rather than by Paul McCartney and some backup guys, no matter how pertly Linda rested her hands on her hips and preened while Paul sang "My Love," there was no denying or escaping the spine-chilling moment of the show, the one moment when thousands of people involuntarily gasped in unison when Paul started to sing "Yesterday." Then the Instamatic brigade really fired up and the place went blinding-white from the flashes blinking away. Talk about your shock of recognition.

WOA was expected to gross five million dollars at least, which was phenomenal for the time. But Paul indulged himself as he wanted and the tour expenses would be high. At home he might wear tattered clothes and paint the barn roof himself, but when it came to music, expenses went out the window of the chartered plane. Every show was photographed by two professionals, every show was tape-recorded, every show was videotaped, every show was sketched by a staff artist, just so Paul would have all these artifacts in his files in case he wanted to do something with them someday. In fact, he did. There was a tour book, there was a hugely successful triple live album of the tour, and there was a television film. Everything was captured but that which was missing: spontaneity. The Wings Over America shows had all the spectacular special effects that money could buy: the biggest lasers, the most blinding strobes; the smokiest smoke kegs; the sound systems were the crispest and sharpest state-of-the-art. There were even expensive "flying monitor speakers" suspended out of sight above the stage so fans had unimpeded sightlines. Every sound from the albums was re-created perfectly, Paul sang with spine-tingling familiarity, the arrangements were flawless, the musicians played the notes by rote. In short, everything was perfectly in control. There was never even the slightest possibility that something untoward might happen. All of which is the perfect definition of pop music and the antithesis of rock and roll.

It was still hugely impressive and highly enjoyable, a sort of "Father Knows Best" evening of rock and pop. The New York *Times* came, saw, and duly pronounced the show "impressively polished yet vital." Dave Marsh in *Rolling Stone* predictably slagged Linda, and praised Paul, but made the point that many critics felt. In staging a show completely devoid of drama, Paul was solidly into the stage of his career where he would reveal only what he wanted to: "You leave the hall knowing almost nothing more about McCartney, as an artist or a man." The song lineup never varied, although it was an intelligently paced collection: "Venus and Mars," "Rock Show," "Jet," "Let Me Roll It," "Spirits of Ancient Egypt," "Medicine Jar," "Maybe I'm Amazed," "Call Me Back Again," "Lady Madonna," "The Long and Winding Road," "Live and Let Die," "Picasso's Last Words (Drink to Me)," "Richard Cory," "Bluebird," "I've Just Seen a Face," "Blackbird," "Yesterday," "You Gave Me the Answer," "Magneto and Titanium Man," "Go Now," "My Love," "Listen to What the Man Said," "Let 'em In," "Time to Hide," "Silly Love Songs," "Beware My Love," "Letting Go," "Band on the Run," and two encores: "Hi Hi Hi" and "Soily."

Backstage the crew resembled a Wings army, what with all the elaborate Wings clothing they were wearing and the Wings memorabilia fairly dripping off of them: Wings jeans, Wings jackets, Wings T-shirts, Wings necklaces, Wings badges, pins, and medallions. Even the paper drinking cups sported the familiar logo. Paul and Linda wore matching Wings necklaces of carved ivory.

During the tour the reunion rumors were, of course, rampant. In New York and Los Angeles, especially, the crowds were abuzz with Beatle talk. Before the tour Paul had called John in New York to invite him to the show and he said so many people were already asking him about it that he felt he couldn't go. It would have been too big a deal. Still, the possibility was always there. Paul told Fong-Torres, "My feeling, and I think the others' feeling, in a way, is we don't want to close the door to anything in the future. We might like it someday." But not yet.

In New York Paul called John again, but he and Yoko decided to stay home. In Los Angeles the Forum crowd applauded and there were girls screaming when Ringo walked in with Harry Nilsson and took his seat. There were louder screams when he showed up onstage at the end of "Soily," gave Denny Laine a bouquet of roses, kissed Linda's hand, took Paul's bass, waved good-bye, and walked off with Paul.

The American tour concluded with three dates at the Forum, after which Paul threw an $80,000 party at the late film star Harold Lloyd's mansion in Hollywood. The pool had been drained and covered with a disco floor, the Los Angeles Ballet performed, a chamber orchestra played Beatles' music, and John Belushi performed his much-criticized spastic Joe Cocker imitation.

Guests had been asked to wear white and most did. White roses and thank-you notes from Paul and Linda were left on the dashboards of all guests' cars. Most of the usual celebrities attended and there were some surprises, such as Yul Brynner and Jack Nicholson. Paul had had a stage set up with drums, guitar, bass, and mikes, but none of the guests—among them were Ringo, Elton John, the Beach Boys, Bob Dylan, and Rod Stewart—felt moved to try a little jamming. It was a very sedate and elegant affair. Just like the tour.

What do you do after you've twice conquered the world of pop music? That was a very real question looming before Paul. Wings had long been regarded by many as just a sort of pop machine that was an ex-Beatle's hobby. Indeed, *Newsweek* magazine's analysis of the wildly successful Wings tour had been that "Paul McCartney had proved that he could make it on his own," ignoring the fact that Paul and Wings had sold more records than the Beatles did. Paul had long been proud of the fact that he had made more money in his first two years with Wings than during his whole career as a Beatle. And, as the Wings' world tour wound down with September concerts in Vienna, Zagreb, Venice (a UNESCO benefit), and Munich and three dates back home at Wembley in October, Paul had the satisfaction of knowing that he had successfully staged the biggest rock tour ever: sixty-four shows in ten countries, a live audience of over two million people, twelve and a half tons of equipment being shipped all over the world.

But the question remained: After having been a Beatle and then—commercially at least—upstaged the Beatles, what can be next? Only a letdown could follow.

Paul avoided the matter for the moment: He still had his tour tapes to edit and mix down. He spent the rest of October and November in the editing room at Abbey Road, paring down about ninety hours of tape to a triple record set. The result, *Wings Over America,* was released in December and was—naturally—an instant triumph. Number one in the States and number eight in England.

Paul had also, during the week of September 7, just before the European Wings dates, organized and held the first of what he planned as an annual "Buddy Holly Week" in London. When Wings money had finally started pouring in back in 1973, Paul had asked his father-in-law for investment advice. Lee Eastman, who himself owned many music copyrights, told Paul that was what he should start buying. And he did so, with a vengeance that would make him one of the wealthiest men in England. One of the first properties that he acquired was the Buddy Holly song catalog and he was delighted to do so, for he felt in a way he was becoming caretaker of the musical spirit of a legendary writer and singer who had had such a big influence on John and himself.

In September of 1976, for what would have been Holly's fortieth birthday, Paul had a round of Holly events. Norman Petty, who had been Holly's producer, flew over to be guest of honor at an MPL luncheon, attended by such rock luminaries as Elton John, Eric Clapton, Roger Daltrey, and members from such groups as Queen, Roxy Music, and 10 CC. Holly had also been much more respected and revered in England than in the United States, so Paul had gotten himself a very desirable trophy with the Holly catalog. Petty presented Paul with the cuff links that Holly had been wearing when he was killed in the famous airplane crash in 1959. There was a memorial dance at the Lyceum Ballroom in the Strand. Paul also produced an album by Denny Laine of Holly songs called *Holly Days.* John Swenson of *Rolling Stone* labeled the record "an insult to Holly's memory."

Paul's annual "Buddy Holly Week" became a chic London affair. Mick Jagger and many others showed up in 1977 to see the original Crickets perform. In 1978 Paul held a midnight screening of the film *The Buddy Holly Story* on September 7 and had a party and dinner beforehand at Peppermint Park, a London restaurant. It was a festive affair, made the more so by Keith Moon's happy announcement of his engagement to Annette Walter-Lax. Paul and Keith had long been friends and Paul had gotten closer to Moon after Moon had complimented Paul's drumming on *Band on the Run.* Keith and Annette sat with Paul and Linda and TV personality David Frost at the head table. During the screening, however, Moon said he felt ill and left early. He and Annette returned to the Mayfair flat Moon was renting from Harry Nilsson. Keith was being treated for alcohol abuse and had several prescriptions for sedatives and muscle relaxants. Once he got back to the flat, he put on a videotape of *The Abominable Dr. Phibes* and fell asleep while watching it. Sometime during the next few hours, he got up and cooked and ate a steak and followed it with champagne and more sedatives and drifted into a permanent sleep. About four-thirty in the afternoon Annette awoke and discovered that Keith Moon was dead.

Paul, of course, handled the news by ignoring it.

In late 1976 and early 1977, after the enormous triumphs he had scored with the WOA tour and the album, Paul slipped back into a familiar pattern: When in doubt, go into the studio and record. Acquaintances of Paul and Linda say that the only arguments between the two that they have witnessed (and that spilled over in public) were about the amount of time Paul spends in the recording studio. A man I know in London who has gotten close enough to Paul and Linda to be invited to the house in East Sussex—although he said no one really gets close to them because the McCartney family is a closed universe—said that, based on his observing Paul and Linda together at home and knowing them for years, that "all Paul cares about is music and Linda and the kids and smoke. When he was a Beatle, all he cared about was music and dope and sex. It really hasn't changed that much, has it?"

And so it went. Paul wrote songs, many of them remaining unfinished forever because of his increasing lack of discipline. He recorded for endless hours in the studio, stacking up song after song. (Many of these songs will never be finished or heard at all.) Paul's ideas come faster than his attention span, or resolve, or maybe the size of his desk can accommodate. Individual Wings came and went. He fiddled around with things. Paul decided in 1977 to start his own magazine for his fans. Even though he had always been the only Beatle to take care to learn how to deal with the press, Paul remained overly sensitive to bad reviews and articles that he considered unfavorable. The solution? Bypass the media and go straight to his people with an upbeat, happy, positive publication. Thus was born *Club Sandwich,* a slick four-color oversize magazine sent quarterly to members of the Wings Fun Club (not fan club). It's a hopelessly bright, peppy, cheerful, bubbly message from McCartney central, an extremely well-done version of the fan magazines of the fifties. It is also an outlet for Linda's photographs. As a bonus, Fun Club members also receive Linda's annual calendar, replete with the sort of static photographs of knickknacks and pink coat hangers and the like that suggest a temporary fascination with—oh wow! Look at that color!—ordinary objects.

With time on his hands in 1977, Paul also did what he periodically does. Out of perversity (or from a cloud of smoke) Paul released a record that makes absolutely no sense to anyone but himself and (presumably) Linda. The album *Thrillington* was released on April 29, 1977, to a vast yawn on the part of the listening public. The record was supposedly by one Percy "Thrills" Thrillington, pictured on the cover as a ram in evening clothes.

Paul's obsession with sheep was approaching alarming proportions. It was nice that he had his executives working day and night over their Waring blenders to feed the toothless ones. And it certainly was touching that he had written "Little Lamb Dragonfly" about a poor lamb on his farm that didn't survive. And Paul sheared his sheep by hand every year and sent the wool to the Wool Marketing Board. And, by Linda's decree, all their sheep would live out their natural lives and would also never get castrated. That was all well and good. But things started really getting out of hand the day in 1977 when Paul, at the farm, realized that through a mix-up there was no one at St. John's Wood to feed the prize chickens in the backyard, so he had them delivered by taxi from London to the farm in Scotland—a taxi bill of one hundred pounds for the 518-mile trip.

But about *Thrillington*: It was an orchestral version of the *Ram* album. It had been recorded in 1972 at Abbey Road and had been—wisely—hidden away since. Not only did Paul decide to put it out, he also released a single from it in the United States: "Uncle Albert/Admiral Halsey." Paul still insists that it's "amusing to have your own tunes from an album and take them to the middle of the road as a mischievous way to infiltrate the light TV programs and things that use such fluff."

His only other record release for 1977 (until "Mull of Kintyre" in November) was a single of "Maybe I'm Amazed," released in February. This was seven years—seven *long* years—since that song had appeared on the *McCartney* album. This was a live version from *Wings Over America* (with "Soily" as the B-side), but record buyers weren't buying it.

With his record career thus firmly taken care of for most of the year, Paul and Wings went back into the studio. They were at Abbey Road through most of February and March. Then Paul decided to head for warmer climes and had a novel idea: Put a recording studio on a yacht in the Caribbean. He gave the order and it was done. New York's Record Plant installed a twenty-four-track mobile studio on a yacht in the Virgin Islands. Paul and Linda and the kids took another yacht and Wings and families filled up two more. They had a Merrie Olde Time for the entire month of May, sailing and recording most of what would become 1978's *London Town* LP. The captain of Paul's yacht smelled marijuana smoke the first night out of port and threatened to turn Paul in to the authorities. So Paul and Linda and the kids moved onto a trimaran called the *Wanderlust* and Paul later wrote a song by that name about the experience and put it on the *Tug of War* album and in his movie *Give My Regards to Broad Street*. He said the song was "about freedom, breaking away from oppression—let's get out of here" and it meant a great deal to him.

A former MPL employee told me that one reason Paul wanted to try a floating studio was for tax reasons. Even though Paul willingly pays his 98 percent tax in England, he has an obsession about paying taxes elsewhere. And entertainers are taxed where they do their entertaining: A concert in New York City is taxed by New York City, just as an actor is taxed by the locale where he does his acting. But songwriters are taxed by the locale where the song is composed. Of course, the authorities there have to be told that that's where the song was written. That, said the MPL employee, is why Paul wanted to try writing songs in international waters and recording them there as well. That is also why, he said, Paul has never done and will never do the kind of long detailed interview about his work that John Lennon used to do—that and, of course, his natural reluctance to ever really open up about himself. That's why Paul has refused the *Playboy* interview many times. Lennon would give certain interviewers the details about his songs: where they were written and where they were recorded. Cities and states and countries have entertainment tax experts who do nothing but track what actors, singers, writers, and performers are doing and where they are doing it.

Once they left Paradise and went home, reality intruded again. Drummer Joe English quit, citing money and Linda as reasons. And guitarist Jimmy McCulloch, with whom Paul had been long-suffering, finally went over the line one too many times. (Regarding McCulloch, ex-Wings mild-mannered drummer Geoff Britton called up *Rolling Stone* along about this time to complain about being misquoted in *Melody Maker*: "They said I hate Jimmy McCulloch's guts. What I really said is that he's a nasty little cunt.") His drinking and fighting and troublemaking had been problems in the past—the Wings Over America tour was delayed after McCulloch badly hurt his hand in a barroom brawl in Paris with a teenaged American television idol and recording star. But this was apparently more serious. Although the official story was that McCulloch was quitting to work with Small Faces, a former MPL employee said that Paul had been forced to fire him. It happened after Linda had given birth on September 12, 1977, to their son, James Louis. It was a Caeserian birth and she was recovering at the farm when McCulloch, who was staying there in a nearby outbuilding, went out of his head one night and wrecked his dwelling. Paul had to get rid of him before something more serious happened. McCulloch knocked round the music business until he died two years later, at the age of twenty-six, with large amounts of morphine and alcohol in his body.

Once again Paul looked for another guitarist and drummer. (No one had the courage to tell him that Pete Best was still available.)

He and Linda resumed the life they loved: raising the kids and the animals, staying home and to themselves, with Paul in his little studio and Linda in the kitchen. Doing only what they wanted to. That's the way the McCartneys live now, spending most of their time in Sussex or on the farm.

Paul, who had nothing more to prove after Wings Over America, had no burning ambition to do anything, no "fire in the belly." Music came to him naturally, though, and that's what Paul loved to do. He would make the records he wanted to. Commerciality had nothing to do with it. If they sold—fine. If they didn't, Paul didn't much care anymore.

His next one, though, surprised even him. Back in 1976 Paul had been thinking one day on the farm about the fact that there seem to be no modern Scottish songs. It awakened the songwriter's challenge in him. Over the next year he went back to the idea now and then and wrote the germ of a song and finished it with Denny Laine. He considered it "just a throwaway," but decided to record it anyway. Next, it was a natural idea to invite the local Campbeltown bagpipers to try playing on it, for it wouldn't be Scottish otherwise. The band's leader first came to the farm to show Paul what notes a bagpipe can play, since they can't modulate or change key. So he rewrote the song for bagpipes and had the pipers into his barn to record it. "It was quite a night—and quite a noise. We had a few beers and we had a hit."

"Mull of Kintyre," named after the southern tip of the Kintyre penisula, eleven miles from Campbeltown, was released November 11, 1977, as Wings' first double-sided single, with "Girls School," a song that Paul wrote "from the porn ads, which I always have to check out" and that sounded more commercial than the eerie yet stately dirge of "Mull of Kintyre." Paul says it was his decision to push it as a double single; an executive at EMI later claimed it was his brainchild. No matter. Within weeks the song was selling a quarter of a million copies a week and quickly became the biggest-selling single in British history, surpassing "She Loves You." The Campbeltown bagpipers, who had been paid only scale for their work, complained loudly that their sound was responsible for the song's success and they had been grossly underpaid. Paul eventually sent each of them two hundred pounds.

Paul's life resumed its pre-WOA leisurely pace of recording and putting out wildly erratic records and auditioning new Wings drummers and guitarists and thinking about another tour. He had been at this quite a while, not as long as he realized until he read Robert Christgau's patronizing treatment of the 1978 album *London Town* in the *Village Voice.* After patting the album on the head for having tried very hard, Christgau slipped in the dagger: "And at the very least you have to be impressed by how steadfastly Paul has resisted supersessions—he's been loyal to his group, which has now recorded longer than the Beatles." And this was only 1978. Must be time to put another tour together, make another record.

He got two young session players, guitarist Lawrence Juber and drummer Steve Holly, and started rehearsing again. Since he had no album ready to put out in late 1978, he decided on a greatest hits album for a Christmas release. Putting some songs together was no problem. Packaging it was. Paul, who has always prided himself on his eye for the visual and reportedly is quite a good painter (although he has never shown his work), has been preoccupied—if not obsessed—with packaging and design. Early on, he designed stage suits for the Beatles and did preliminary cover sketches for all the Beatle albums. His original design for the *White Album* was striking: Mount Rushmore-like visages of John, Paul, George, and Ringo looming over a pockmarked sea, with the Beatles' logo hovering in the sky. When he finally decided on a white cover (with prodding from John), Paul met with fifteen different designers just to determine exactly where the white-on-white lettering should be placed.

People he worked with soon began to refer to Paul's "excessive packaging," but he persisted in giving the fans what he felt would be their money's worth. That has meant elaborate album covers, embossing, profuse illustrations, little booklets stuffed into the jackets, lots of little messages, pop-ups, foldouts, inserts, braille lettering, and hidden messages. You get the feeling that, if he could, Paul would hide in the album jacket and jump out and say "Boo!" when you got home from the store and opened the record up.

But Paul carried his design overkill far too far with the *Wings Greatest* album cover. Linda had bought an expensive Art Deco statuette that she decided would look good on the cover. She and Paul thought it would look good posed in the snow. To that end, they dispatched an entire production crew to take the little statuette to Switzerland to photograph it there. A team of professionals spent a week in Switzerland, hired workers to create the proper snowdrift for a background, chartered a helicopter for aerial photographs, futzed around endlessly. And all they ended up with was a snapshot of a little thrift-shop figurine that looked like somebody had dropped it in the snow. And you couldn't even tell that it was Switzerland snow.

All that money and guess what Christgau said in his review of the album? Christgau called it "Pop for potheads."

After *Wings Greatest* (which had not done all that well), Paul's contract with Capitol Records in the United States was up and he was courted by several labels. He signed with Columbia Records in what has been described by an insider as the worst deal CBS ever made. The total money package involving deferments, sweetheart deals, incentive clauses, buybacks, payouts, exclusions, schedulings, release windows, and tour support has never been made public (although it was whispered on Sixth Avenue to be in the $20-million range, which meant that it was probably no more than $15 million or so, prorated and amortized).

Basically, though, it was very obvious in the music industry that CBS president Walter Yetnikoff was bagging a trophy, which is what the record companies were big on. "He bought a Beatle," a former CBS executive told me. "It was all prestige for the company. It was too much money for an artist who was obviously past his prime. We knew we would have to really work our asses off to try to earn some of that money back. None of us who had to actually work him felt that Paul had much left to say, but how can you argue with buying a Beatle? You should have been here in Black Rock [CBS headquarters] the day Paul came in to press the flesh. It was like royalty, I've never seen anything like it. Everybody in the building came out out of their offices and were just shaking."

The deal sweetener that cinched it for Columbia was that Paul was given Frank Music, which is a jewel of exquisite proportion. That is the song publishing catalog of Frank Loesser, known for *Guys and Dolls,* among many others. Paul was catalog-hungry. Besides Buddy Holly, he also owned Whale Music and about ten thousand songs from Edwin H. Morris and Co. A few of the items he owns: "Autumn Leaves," "It's Tight Like That," "One for My Baby," "Sentimental Journey," "Stormy Weather," "Ramblin' Wreck from Georgia Tech," "Sweetheart of Sigma

Chi," "Chopsticks," "Basin Street Blues," "Bugle Call Rag," not to mention the songs from *Mame, High Society, Bye-Bye Birdie, Annie, Grease, A Chorus Line, Peter Pan, La Cage Aux Folles,* and the like. There is even a rumor that Paul owns "Happy Birthday."

Despite the fact that Paul owns the publishing rights to so many musicals, he has said more than once that neither he nor John was ever interested in writing a musical. Paul said he did not hate them as much as John did, but he confessed to a lingering distaste for anything by Andrew Lloyd Webber.

"My dream is of being a composer," he said, adding that classical music is really "just one tune, or several tunes reoccurring." He said that when he was twenty-five, he had fully intended to get into serious music before he was thirty, but somehow it had never happened. "But I'm not terribly interested in writing musicals. I don't like to do anything unless there's that fire in the belly."

All those publishing copyrights, plus his Beatles and Wings earnings, explain why McCartney is worth an estimated $600 million. Money talk always makes him angry and he always says, "My father never told my mother how much he made." And for good reason too—Mother Mary made more than Jim McCartney did.

With CBS, besides his deal sweetener, Paul got an astounding 20 percent royalty rate for every album sold. At the time, that amounted to $1.80 per album—regardless of any discounts involved, which are virtually universal. Paul was a guaranteed loss-leader for CBS. The company also got his back catalog for only as long as he remained on the label. Then everything would revert to him. No bargain again for CBS. But Paul was primarily signed for visibility and he became hard to see when he did few interviews and didn't tour. "The records he delivered to us didn't help much either," said the former CBS executive. "He came in with a fair hit single, 'Goodnight Tonight,' but he refused to put it on the album [*Back to the Egg,* his first CBS LP]. So we had nothing to work the album with." That album eventually sold platinum (one million copies), but it was not the blockbuster that the company had hoped for and needed.

CBS soured on him quickly. He was the only major artist the company never had a party for. "It was a contest of wills," said the former CBS executive. "Paul wouldn't bend. He's a Beatle. He didn't have to have us. But we really wanted him."

That didn't really matter much to Paul. Back in England he still pursued his own agenda. He recorded much of *Back to the Egg* in an exact duplicate of the famous Abbey Road Studio number 2 that he had built in the basement of his MPL office building in Soho Square. Paul ordered the Replica Studio built when he tried to get into Abbey Road and discovered that Cliff Richard had booked Studio number 2 indefinitely. Paul studied his new studio when it was finished and immediately found an imperfection. The far wall of the new Replica Studio was a mural and there was a clock in the mural. Since it was a mural, the clock did not keep time. He wanted it to, so back came the workmen, who installed a real clock in his fake mural.

Paul, who seems to have a genuine physical need to perform before live humans, started talking tour again and he went back to his old idea of playing small clubs. His tour promoter, Harvey Goldsmith, pointed out that that was impossible for Paul—the crowds would make it impossible. Paul had already toyed with the idea of making his Replica Studio into a little café and having lunchtime shows there, just like in the old days at the Cavern in Liverpool.

Goldsmith booked him a series of smaller halls and cinemas throughout England in November and December. Paul had already decided to open his little tour with a benefit concert at and for the financially troubled Royal Court Theatre in Liverpool. He had not been back there in some time. He had also gotten a call from U.N. Secretary-General Kurt Waldheim, requesting a reunion of the Beatles as soon as possible to play a benefit concert for the people of Kampuchea. Paul said that he couldn't deliver the Beatles but he would promise Wings. When he did, they helped organize the Concerts for the People of Kampuchea, held at Hammersmith Odeon from December 26 to 29, 1979. Wings played the last night there, along with Elvis Costello, Robert Plant, Rockpile, and the Rockestra—an all-star group Paul had assembled without great musical success for some of the numbers on *Back to the Egg*. Putting David Gilmour from Pink Floyd together with Pete Townshend from the Who and so on seemed like a great idea, but it did not really gel.

Paul and Linda and their four kids left for New York for a

holiday visit with Linda's family before playing a Wings tour of Japan, the nation from which Paul had long been barred because of his drug convictions. Why he suddenly had decided to play Japan, neither he nor anyone else has ever said, especially after his Japan-baiting nonsense when he was refused entry before, in 1975. And he had just recorded a song he titled "Frozen Jap" that would appear on his *McCartney II* album.

In New York he called John and Yoko. Depending on biorhythms and phases of the moon and Paul's numbers and the utterances of Yoko's various psychics, numerologists, seers, I Ching consultants and tarot card experts, Paul now and again got to see John. There was the famous story of the time he decided to drop in, unannounced, guitar in hand, at the Dakota, only to have John coldly tell him that this wasn't Liverpool anymore and people didn't just drop in. Well . . . okay, but what about this postcard that Yoko had sent Paul, telling him to:

GO ROUND THE WORLD IN A SOUTH-EASTERLY DIRECTION. IT'D BE GOOD FOR YOU. YOU'RE ALLOWED TO STOP AT FOUR PLACES.

Paul had ignored it—at his own peril. That was when Yoko was really into her "directions" mode and had John traveling at a dizzying pace here and there and up and down and back and forth to—as far as Paul could understand it—get back in sync with the earth's rotation. George Martin had gotten a similar postcard from Yoko and he had asked her if it was okay to go to Montserrat because that's where Martin's studio is and Yoko had said No. So it was a chancy thing. One never knew. On this occasion they spoke on the phone and that was all.

Paul and Linda and the kids flew off to Japan, with only carry-on bags, since everything else went with the tour equipment. At Narita Airport, a Customs agent started in on the McCartneys' bags and bingoed on the very first one, which happened to be Paul's. Right there on top, stinking to high heaven, was a plump Baggie stuffed with about half a pound of the green. Jo Jo Laine, Denny's wife, claimed: "Linda had left twenty Thai sticks in her makeup bags. Paul took the rap."

Rumors and stories abound that Paul was the victim of a revenge plot. If he was indeed set up to be arrested by someone calling Tokyo with a tip, it must be remembered that the agents didn't really need to be tipped off. Paul had long been banned from entering Japan, he had made sure in 1975 that everyone in Japan knew that Paul was banned, and he continued to make no secret of his love of cannabis. Paul was virtually taunting the authorities, just the same as driving down Santa Monica Boulevard and sucking on a joint had been taunting them.

For the past several years a former Lennon–Ono employee, fired for theft, has been trying to peddle various John and Yoko scandal stories around New York City: to newspapers, magazines, writers—in short, to anyone who might buy. He offers a hint for free, but the goods will cost you. One of his favorite stories has been repeated so many times that it's become a joke. It has become so widespread, especially now that it's reported as gospel in a book about John, that Yoko agreed to reply to my request to answer it.

First, the story: Paul and Linda stop in New York on their way to Tokyo. Paul calls John up and says, "Hey, I got some great dope. Can I come right over?" John and Yoko decline. Then in a brainstorm Yoko jumps on the phone and calls her cousin, who happens to be a Customs agent at Narita Airport, and alerts said agent to the imminent arrival of a certain ex-Beatle who is carrying pounds of dope. Yoko hangs up the phone and John removes his angle-mirror glasses (which allowed him to watch TV from a reclining position), jumps out of bed, and dances around the room, shouting, "We got Paul! We got Paul!"

Since John is dead, Yoko is the only living person who can speak with certainty about what happened or did not happen. This is what she says happened and did not happen: While Paul and Linda were in New York, they did call John and Yoko on the phone. There was no mention made of dope or dope-related materials or anything else relating to drugs. Yoko has no relatives or friends who are Customs agents in Japan. Neither Yoko nor John made any phone calls to Japanese authorities. There was no dancing around the bedroom and shouting about anything.

Paul said in 1987 that the Japan bust happened because "We got some good grass in America and no one could face putting it down the toilet. It was an absolutely crazy move. We knew we weren't going to get any in Japan. Anybody else would have given it to their roadies, but I didn't want them to take the rap. It was lying on top of the bloody suitcase. I'll never forget the guy's face as he pulled it out. He almost put it back. He just did not want the embarrassment."

But that poor agent bit the bullet and swallowed his embarrassment and sent Paul off to jail. Paul thought he would have the usual rockstar half hour in the cell before his lawyer springs him. But nothing happened for Paul. After he was locked up, he fell asleep on a tatami mat on the floor and was banged awake the next morning at six o'clock. He was still in jail, his tour was canceled, his musicians had left the country, and his wife and children were fearful. Lawyers were flying in, the promoter was suing him, and for once his Beatlehood could not save him. After he was finally permitted to phone the British Embassy, Vice-Consul Albert Marshall came around to see him. Paul stood up, smiling, relieved that he was going to be released. Marshall just shook his head and said, "Well, it could be eight years, you know."

After Paul's arrest was made public, a lunatic McCartney fan was killed in Miami. Kenneth Lambert, twenty-nine, was shot to death by police at the Miami Airport as he waved a realistic toy pistol and shouted that he was on his way to Tokyo to "free Paul."

In jail Paul studied his situation. "I was very frightened," he said. "The guards all have this wooden ritual about them and I kept thinking I was watching a war film. You had to sit crosslegged, very weird, and be inspected by twelve guys. . . . After three days I'd got my humour back and my reason and I began tapping on the cell walls, communicating with the other prisoners. . . . I suppose I was treated this way because I am Paul McCartney. And why not? It's sort of cleansing. It's not bad for you to be humiliated at times."

When Paul was released and deported after ten days in jail, he virtually bowed and scraped to the press, saying, "I have been a fool. What I did was incredibly dumb. My God, how stupid I have been. I had just come from America and I still had the American attitude that marijuana isn't too bad. I didn't appreciate how strict the Japanese are about it."

Once back home Paul sat down and wrote a twenty-thousand-word journal, which he still keeps tucked away.

★   ★   ★

That Japanese bust had cost Paul two hundred thousand pounds he had to pay the promoter, plus at least another hundred thousand pounds in legal fees. He swore earnestly to anyone who would listen that he would never smoke again. What he meant, of course, just as he'd publicly sworn off drugs when he was en route to the Maharishi years ago with the other boys, was that he was going to quit talking about drugs. No more militant stance in favor of legalization.

He and Linda were later busted in their luxury villa in Barbados on January 14, 1984. Police confiscated ten grams of marijuana from Paul and another seven grams from Linda's handbag. They were taken to police headquarters in Bridgetown, questioned, and released. They eventually pleaded guilty to simple possession and were fined seventy pounds. Paul and Linda and the kids flew back to London, where they were promptly busted again at Heathrow Airport when police found cannabis in a film canister Linda was carrying. She pleaded guilty to a charge of possession and was fined seventy-five pounds. There was a bit of a hue and a cry in the British press about how these McCartneys keep getting nicked with their snoots in the dope jar, especially in front of their children. The *Sun* quoted Linda as saying: "I don't smoke it in front of the kids." Paul was quoted as saying: "A lot of colonels and vicars think I'm trying to corrupt the world. But they will probably go home tonight and have a couple of brandies and maybe kill somebody later in their cars."

The group Wings was also a victim of the Japanese bust. Juber and Holly quit. Denny Laine, who had left Japan as soon as Paul was arrested and went to the MIDEM convention in Paris, wrote a telling song called "Japanese Tears" and recorded it with ex-Wings Henry McCullough and Denny Seiwell. Laine did not immediately leave Wings, but it turned out to be just a matter of months. And that left just Paul and Linda—for the first time since he had founded Wings in 1971. Even though Wings was really, as John Lennon had said, just a vehicle for Paul . . . still—Wings had been around longer than the Beatles had and had sold more records.

Paul was better off without Laine, it turned out, who actually left after arguments with Paul about money. Then it took a couple of years, but the man who had been Paul's steady Wing and friend for ten years sold out to the lowest common denominator: the London *Sun,* which seemed to keep a column, if not a page open, for the typical Beatle-bashing section. Laine wrote a four-day series, bannered: THE REAL PAUL MCCARTNEY: SUN EXCLUSIVE ON THE MEAN, MOODY WORLD OF SUPERSTAR PAUL. Laine wrote that he had seen Paul and Linda smuggle marijuana through Customs in their infant son's coat. Laine (no dope virgin himself) said that Paul and Linda went through a thousand pounds' worth of grass a week. He said that they were just very bored rich people who loved the thrill of being illegal with their dope and that they shoplifted for the same reason. He literally got into dirt, saying that he had been living in a trailer on the farm in Scotland and he preferred the trailer because the building Paul offered him was uninhabitable. Laine and Paul had argued over where Denny put his garbage from the trailer. Laine said that Paul was ripping him off, even though he had been getting about seventy thousand pounds a year, once Paul promoted him from his seventy-pound-a-week slave wage, and that Paul gave him ninety thousand pounds in exchange for his publishing rights for songs he had written with Wings, including "Mull of Kintyre." "Paul certainly is a complex guy," Laine concluded. "Even though I have written countless songs with him and we have been stoned together hundreds of times, I still don't feel I am very close to him. He is the best person I have met in all my life at hiding his innermost feelings. Few people are really close to him at all—not even his brother Mike. Paul treats Mike in that same patronizing way he treats most people and Mike resents that like mad."

Denny's ex-wife Jo Jo picked the *Sunday People* for her McCartney exposé. Her picture, with her nipples peeking coyly through her see-through nightie, nestled next to her tale of: LIVING LIKE PEASANTS DOWN ON MILLIONAIRE PAUL'S FARM. She deplored Linda's housekeeping habits, body odor, and stinginess. And sheep were coming in the house and shitting on the floor. In the next episode, Jo Jo had worked one entire breast out and the erect nipple was . . . but you get the picture.

The bust left Paul relatively subdued for the rest of the year. In the summer he released *McCartney II,* the album he had recorded by himself the previous summer and he had number one ranking with it in England and number three in the United States.

He divided his time between Waterfalls, the five-bedroom

round house in Sussex, and his office in the MPL building in Soho Square in London. His elegant office is a stark contrast to the clutter of his home and farm. The building resembles a neat townhouse, with the letters MPL above the door. The interior is marked by Deco curves, plush carpeting and darkwood paneling. Paul's office, resembling a big comfortable den is on the third floor overlooking the Square. A large glass and metal sculpture of the MPL juggling clown logo—suspended planets above the juggler—rests on the darkwood radiator cover by the windows. The dominant piece of furniture is a huge solid-looking six-sided darkwood desk. It is a two-person desk, with two angled seating areas and two chair wells. There is not a scrap of paper on it. Paul likes to use it for interviews. On the wall behind the desk is a de Kooning tapestry in muted citrus colors. Across the room is a large Art Deco settee built into the wall. On a shelf next to it stands the Art Deco figurine that graced the cover of *Wings Greatest*. It is signed: CHIPATUA. Opposite the windows stands a graceful 1946 Wurlitzer twenty-four-record jukebox with pulsing colored-water tubes. Some of the records: "Baby Face" by Little Richard, "Give My Regards to Broadway" by Al Jolson, "All Shook Up" by Elvis, "I'm in Love Again" by Fats Domino. Paul's bathroom has the Capitol Records logo carved in intricate detail on the door.

It was from MPL that one of the staffers called Paul at home in Sussex after John was shot and killed in New York City on December 8, 1980. Paul telephoned Yoko and then rushed off to his studio to work. A reporter caught him briefly to ask his reaction to John's death and he mumbled the first thing that came into his head: "It's a drag." He would be criticized mercilessly for the comment but, given Paul's inability to deal with death, it seems natural. He was, of course, incapable of going to New York.

The next day his statement was: "I have hidden myself in my work today. But it keeps flashing into my mind. I feel shattered, angry, and very, very sad. It's just ridiculous. He was pretty rude about me sometimes, but I secretly admired him for it and I always managed to stay in touch with him. There was no question that we weren't friends—I really loved the guy. I think that what has happened will in years to come make people realize that

John was an international statesman. He often looked a loony to many people. He made enemies, but he was fantastic. He was a warm man who cared a lot and with the record 'Give Peace a Chance' he helped stop the Vietnam War. He made a lot of sense."

Paul and John had made their peace before John was assassinated. They were not intimate again, but they really hadn't been anyway—not since the last days in Liverpool. Paul protests—and with good reason—that he was really quoted out of context after John's death. Especially by Hunter Davies, whom Paul thought was a friend, he said. He called up Davies and they had a long talk, during which Paul talked about how both he and John could be "maneuvering swine" in the past when they wanted to be. Davies rushed every word into print and the "swine" quote was flashed around the world.

Paul started getting death threats immediately after John's death and hired twenty-four-hour security guards.

George and Ringo also increased their security in the wake of John's killing. The only serious incident involving Paul occurred in 1984 when police arrested two men who had made serious plans to kidnap Linda and hold her for ten million pounds' in ransom. The chief suspect, a former guardsman named Allan Gallop, said, "I could have done it easily." He said he had spent a week spying on the house, stalking the McCartneys, and camping in the woods nearby. He had detailed plans of Paul's 160-acre estate, Lower Gate Farm at Peasmarsh, East Sussex. He said, "His security is supposed to be the best around. But I could have cracked it, no bother."

Paul released no records in 1981 and when Parlophone, in an odd move, commercially released what had been a promo album— *The McCartney Interview with Vic Garbarini*—on February 23, Paul ordered it withdrawn. It was removed from release the same day.

He turned to a staunch ally from the old days, George Martin, and started working with him, escaping to Martin's AIR Studio in Montserrat with Ringo and Stevie Wonder. Reporters, smelling some kind of Beatle reunion, tracked him down there and Paul lost his temper and rammed their car with his Jeep.

The resulting album, *Tug of War,* yielded the single "Ebony and Ivory" with Stevie Wonder. The album also contained Paul's tribute to John, "Here Today," which was scored for string quartet by Martin.

That same year Paul also recorded "The Girl Is Mine" with Michael Jackson and in a way came to regret it. Because of that session, Paul forever lost the chance to own his own songs: the 159 Lennon–McCartney jewels in the Northern Songs catalog.

Out of the blue Michael Jackson bought Northern in 1985 for $47.5 million.

What happened, Paul said, was that, after their recording session, Michael kept calling and asking for financial advice. "I took him under my wing and we'd always be in little corridors discussing this stuff. I thought it was just fine, but he used to do this little joke. He'd say, 'I'm gonna buy your publishing, ya know!' I'd go, 'Ha! Good one, kid!' Then one day I get phoned up and they said, 'He's just bought your stuff!' I thought, Oh, you are kidding. But that was it, really. He had the money to buy it; he was rolling in it after *Thriller* and he had it to burn. . . . I could have bought it, but in actual fact there were complications with Yoko which prevented me from getting it. That's a whole other story. Anyway, Michael's got it and all's fair in love, war, and business, I suppose. But it's a little galling now to find that I own less of 'Yesterday' than Michael Jackson. It's a thorn in my side. . . ."

When Jackson first licensed a Beatle song for a television commercial, John's "Revolution" for a Nike shoe ad, Paul and Yoko initially approved of it (though Jackson did not need their approval). The three surviving Beatles have subsequently filed suit over the ad. Since then, George's "Something" has turned up in a Chrysler ad. Said Paul: "The other day I saw 'Something', George's song, in a car ad and I thought, Eww, yuck! That's in bad taste."

Of course, Paul owns Buddy Holly's catalog and recently sold one of Holly's showcase tunes, "Oh Boy!" to Buick, which reworked the song as "Oh Buick!" for a TV commercial. When Timothy White asked Paul about that, he was ambivalent. "It's very difficult because I do feel differently in both cases. As far as the Beatles' stuff is concerned, in actual fact what has happened is some people have used it without the right to use it. [Selling a specific performance of a song, as opposed to selling the song itself.] People who haven't got the right have been giving away the right. So it's a different affair than with the Buddy Holly stuff, where I do have the right to let people use it because we're the publishers of that. But the most difficult question is whether you should use songs for commercials. I haven't made up my mind where I stand."

Money, he said, is not really the issue, although Paul, whose fortune is estimated in the $600 million realm, does not really need to worry. Respect for one's art, he said, is the issue at hand.

"Generally, I don't like it, particularly with the Beatles' stuff. When twenty more years have passed, maybe we'll move into the realm where it's okay to do it. That's a little bit why I feel it's not so bad with Buddy. There may be people out there who say you shouldn't do it with Buddy. I've done it once or twice with him, but I don't really like doing it, I must admit. One thing I can't do with Buddy is ask him. One thing they can do with us, since there's still three of us alive, is ask us. That'd be a good move, to say, 'Do you fancy being a car ad?' And we'd say, 'No!' Yet you get your advisers saying, 'So you're gonna turn down all that money, are you?' If I was being a purist, I'd say no one should give the songs to ads. My heart says that. But, you know, we're not always as pure as you think."

Paul is very aware now of the selling of the Beatles. He does not have all that much memorabilia himself, not even a full set of Beatle records. With the recent upsurge in auctions of rock 'n' roll artifacts, Paul has started watching carefully the sales at Sotheby's and the other auction houses. He has disputed the authenticity of some items and they were withdrawn from sale. The most prominent item was a pair of pants, supposedly having once belonged to Paul and graced the royal Beatle buns. These trousers in question had been submitted by arch-McCartney nemesis Allan Williams. The catalog entry read:

> Paul McCartney's leather trousers, of black leather (altered and worn) with letter of authenticity. The above were given, in lieu of payment for a meal, to the leader of the group Faron's Flamingos, who used to play at the Liverpool Cavern with the Beatles.

*   *   *

Paul and Yoko were never extremely close and that has not changed remarkably. One of the few times that Paul has said anything about her in recent years came in a 1986 interview. He related how Yoko had said she needed to see him and asked him to come to New York. "I said I was going through New York and so I stopped off and rang her, and she said she couldn't see me that day. I was four hundred yards away from her. I said, 'Well, I'll pop over anytime today—five minutes, ten minutes, whenever you can squeeze me in.' She said, 'It's going to be very difficult.' I said, 'Well, okay, I understand. What is the reason, by the way?' She said, 'I was up all night with Sean.' I said, 'Well, I understand that. I've got four kids, you know. But you're bound to have a minute today, sometime.' She asked me to come. I'd flown in specially to see her and she wouldn't even see me. So I felt a little humiliated, but I said, 'Okay, nine-thirty tomorrow morning. Let's make an appointment.' She rang up about nine and said, 'Could you make it tomorrow morning?' So that's the kind of thing. I'm beginning to think it wasn't all my fault."

Although Paul should have learned his lesson with *Magical Mystery Tour,* he persisted with his idea of making another movie, a real one. He had serious plans once to make a TV movie based on the adventures of a family of mice (animated mice) who traveled with Wings during the 1972 tour and moved in underneath the stage. *The Bruce McMouse Show* included Bruce, his wife Yvonne and their children Soily, Swooney, and Swat.

At one point he had put a script together with a collaborator, Willy Russell, for a movie that Paul said would be "the *Casablanca* of the seventies." One reason for eventually abandoning it was that he still had the group Wings "and they would all have had to be dragged along."

Next he talked to Gene Rodenberry of "Star Trek" about doing an "ultimate flying saucer idea." Steven Spielberg's *Close Encounters of the Third Kind* effectively canceled that project. Then Paul called on Isaac Asimov and Tom Stoppard (separately, it should be noted) for screenplays. But nothing happened.

So he turned to the only available genius at hand: himself. Paul McCartney should be able to write a screenplay, he reasoned. He felt that his bad case of writer's block had been cured by his recent jail stay in Japan, after which he wrote about twenty thousand words (which he then carefully put away). At the time he was working on the album *Tug of War* and commuting back and forth from East Sussex to London and the two-hour drive—in addition to the traffic jams—gave him lots of free time in the back seat of his limo. So he started scribbling away on whatever pieces of paper were at hand and dropping them into a Safeway shopping bag. When the bag was full he figured that was pretty near a script.

The story, he said, was basically "my life," incidents from his career, although he said he exaggerated them a little. "Long ago in the Beatles era I realised the people you meet don't like to find out you're an ordinary bloke, just like them, with a bit more bread perhaps." What he finally put together was a day in his life, slightly exaggerated, with a series of little daydreams thrown in as devices to get to the next song.

He had a secretary in his office type it up and there it was. Sort of. He showed it to director Richard Lester, whose only comment was: "Don't do it!"

Paul persisted. He talked to director David Puttnam, who recommended a young director of TV commercials, Peter Webb. Paul had seen an Ovaltine commercial that Webb had done, liked it, and hired him. They started shooting in August 1982. Plans were to show it on Channel 4. Even so, Paul wanted to shoot it in 35 mm. After Paul had poured about two million dollars into it and had all of ten minutes in the can, he finally realized the main principle of moviemaking: Use other people's money.

Lee and John Eastman took the ten minutes and some songs and persuaded 20th Century-Fox to bankroll it.

So the thing picked up steam. A very capable cast was assembled: Sir Ralph Richardson (it would be his last movie), Bryan Brown, Tracey Ullman. And starring Paul, of course. Ringo was invited in, along with his wife, actress Barbara Bach. After Linda first read the script and could not find herself in it, she was added. And little things would tilt the movie in strange directions. After Paul's son James saw an early cut of the movie and found that Linda disappeared, he was upset that his mommy had gone away and so Linda's part had to be fleshed out a bit, as it were. Paul also insisted on doing all the music live, which is very difficult and time-consuming in moviemaking.

The plot was a pretty simple one: Paul is in the backseat of his limo en route to the office to firm up the plans for the release of his new album. He dozes off and, in a dream, learns that the master tapes for the album have been lost. The rest of the movie is a vague quest to find the tapes and thwart the evil bankers who would otherwise take him over. (If this sounds like a computer game, it was shortly turned into one and put on the market.) The "my life" incidents punctuating the aimless plot are hopelessly predictable: a radio interview, business meeting, recording session, and so on. It is a very pretty movie, with a painterly feel and of course the music is terrific. But what it actually is, as critics and (sparse) audiences shortly learned, was a series of music videos almost tied together. World premieres were held in October and November 1984 in Los Angeles, New York, London, and Liverpool. Paul knocked himself out pushing the movie, giving interviews to anyone who would listen. All to no avail. The critics were merciless and the audiences stayed home in droves, from all 311 theaters where it simultaneously opened in the United States. *Variety* called it "characterless, bloodless, and pointless."

In short, a nine-million-dollar home movie. By a "man in a suit."

Paul was truly shaken by the magnitude of the failure of *Broad Street*. He had put a lot on the line and came out of it a big loser. His self-confidence had taken severe jolts before, but this time he was not bouncing back the way he had done in the past. His Japanese bust, the loss of Wings, and John's murder all coming in the space of a year had badly hurt him.

Always, in the past, tragedy and trauma had only served to spur Paul on to achieve more or to stand on his own. His mother's tragic death caused him to turn to music in the first place. The breakup of the Beatles and what he considered John's betrayal of him caused Paul—after much anguish—to form Wings and slowly get back into music. His Wings quitting on him gave him incentive to do *Band on the Run*. Back in 1970, when Paul's *McCartney* album was getting mercilessly slagged by the critics and John put out his *Plastic Ono Band* album, John predicted—correctly, it turned out—that John's album would "scare" Paul into creating something better.

But in 1984 Paul was not recovering the way he should have. For one thing, he was increasingly alone. He had only Linda to turn to, even in terms of any musician friend he could relate to. This was the first time in his career there was no one else he could look to: John had been there during all the Beatle years, at least as gadfly—if not as musical comrade. Denny Laine (quite a comedown) had filled the latter function for the decade after the Beatle breakup. But now Laine, after his personal betrayal, was just a sour sensation in Paul's stomach. He could now trust no one but Linda.

Paul tried a drastic step. In July 1985 he appeared onstage for the first time since 1979 when he performed "Let It Be" at the Live Aid benefit. It was disastrous. Paul was nervous to begin with and when his microphone malfunctioned, he faltered. It was not the Paul McCartney of old. Some people whispered that it was the dope that was doing him in, eating away at his confidence and deepening his depression.

Later that year Paul turned to an outsider for his first collaborator since Denny Laine. Guitarist Eric Stewart of the group 10 CC had played guitar on Paul's 1982 *Tug of War* album and appeared in *Broad Street*. He and Paul wrote several songs together, making up over half of Paul's 1986 *Press to Play* album. The collaboration was not an overwhelming success.

Then Paul did a very McCartneyesque thing: He "got back" again. In July 1986 he went into the studio with a group of unknown young musicians and re-created the feel of the Hamburg days. They recorded thirty-six songs in two days: quick, screaming "live" versions of "Long Tall Sally," "Twenty Flight Rock," "I Saw Her Standing There," and other gems from the past. The songs will likely never be released, but for Paul it was like clearing the cobwebs from his brain. Out of that came his next collaborator.

He was talking to some of his employees at MPL one day, lamenting the fact that John was gone. He said he missed having John edit his work and help him with spaces in the songs. Someone said he should try Elvis Costello, the quirky but brilliant writer and singer. Paul, who was obviously searching, called Costello up (or had an employee summon him, which is more likely) and found to his surprise that they hit it off well.

Paul told *New Musical Express* that Elvis reminded him of John: "We wrote one song and I thought, God, this is just like the Beatles. He was actually taking John's role. At first we were a bit worried by that, but then thought, Well, if it's gonna happen, let it." Paul said he appreciated the fact that Costello talked to him straight: "He doesn't mince his words and I like that. We're a form of discipline for each other. . . . I don't want to go on about it like it's some great partnership, because it might not last, but it's certainly worked so far." Paul hinted at comeback try number three, but only to the extent that there would be an album in 1988 and that a tour might well follow that.

Paul's first public testing since Live Aid came in early 1988. The Rock and Roll Hall of Fame held its third annual induction ceremony on January 20 in a $300-a-plate black-tie extravaganza in the Grand Ballroom of New York's Waldorf-Astoria. That year's choices for induction into the Hall of Fame were the Beatles, the Beach Boys, Bob Dylan, the Supremes, the Drifters, and Motown Records founder Berry Gordy, Jr. Invitations— tantamount to subpoenas—went out to the principals involved. Induction into the Hall of Fame has come to mean a command performance. What would Paul do?

As usual around any event involving at least one Beatle, ru- mors circulated that the three remaining Beatles would take this occasion to at long last hold a Beatle reunion of sorts. The fans outside the Grand Ballroom buzzed with speculation as the cream of rock stars streamed past: Bruce Springsteen, Mick Jagger, Little Richard, Elton John, Paul Simon, Ben E. King, and so on. Ringo and George elicited ripples of murmurs and applause as they filed into the Grand Ballroom, as did Yoko, who arrived with John's sons, Sean and Julian.

Paul's official message arrived that afternoon, in the form of a fax from MPL London to Rogers and Cowan, New York, his public relations firm. It read:

AFTER TWENTY YEARS, THE BEATLES STILL HAVE SOME BUSI-
NESS DIFFERENCES WHICH I HAD HOPED WOULD HAVE BEEN
SETTLED BY NOW. UNFORTUNATELY, THEY HAVEN'T BEEN,
SO I WOULD FEEL LIKE A COMPLETE HYPOCRITE WAVING AND
SMILING WITH THEM AT A FAKE REUNION.

Reaction was swift. Beach Boy Mike Love, who was once Paul's friend back in the Maharishi days, addressed the crowd as the Beach Boys were inducted and laced into Paul, saying, "Paul McCartney couldn't be here tonight because he's in a lawsuit with Ringo and Yoko. He sent a telegram to a high-priced attorney who's sitting out there. Now, that's a bummer because we're talking about harmony, right? And it's a shame Ms. [Diana] Ross can't make it, right? The Beach Boys did a hundred and eighty performances last year. I'd like to see the mop-tops top that!"

Jagger later presented the remaining Beatles. He recalled his early days. "When the Stones were first together, we heard there was a group from Liverpool with long hair, scruffy clothes, and a record in the charts with a bluesy harmonica riff. And the combination of all this made me sick."

George responded with obvious good humor. "I don't have too much to say because I'm the quiet Beatle. It's too bad Paul's not here because he's the one who's had the speech in his pocket." He got his laugh and turned serious to say, "We all know why John's not here; we know he'd be here. It's really hard to stand here representing the Beatles. It's what's left, I'm afraid. We all loved John very much and we love Paul very much."

Yoko, when it came her turn, sounded a mite testy. "He [John] would have been here, you know. He *would've* come," she said in an obvious swipe at Paul for his no-show.

That induction ceremony was one event where Paul clearly had no chance to exercise control and he probably did the smart thing by staying away. The whole notion of a Beatle reunion, even of the three of them, has become so emotionally charged over the years that any reality could never match the fantasy involved.

Later that night a woman from Rogers and Cowan was asked how she had been able to stand the tension that day, waiting to see if Paul would show up and then getting the disappointing fax from London instead.

"What do you mean?" she asked.

"Well, you know, biting your nails, waiting for Paul, waiting to see which flight you should meet." (It is a joke in music circles that Rogers and Cowan employees should be issued gold chauffeur's caps for all the services they render for the McCartneys, starting with picking them up at the airport.)

She laughed. "That fax was just to make it official. We brought it over here to prove to all the photographers that he wasn't coming. They were driving us nuts."

"What?"

"Oh yeah. Paul decided months ago that he wasn't coming. He was damned if he came and damned if he didn't. He couldn't win either way. Don't quote me, but Paul is not going to let himself be roped into any Beatle reunion. Especially not while Yoko is going around acting like the Fourth Beatle. No siree, Paul only does what Paul damn well wants to. He *is* the Chief Beatle, after all."

So this is what it has come down to after all these years: Paul can make more news by not going somewhere than Mick and Elton and all the rest of the leftover rock aristocrats can by showing up at the Hall of Fame dinner. Dislike as he might claim to his role as Chief Beatle, Paul seems to be settling into it even as he accepts the new wrinkles etching their way around the eyes, the modest paunch a-budding, the silver threads framing the once-angelic face. He may even accept the fact that much of what he has done—especially at first—as an ex-Beatle was reactionary in nature, an attempt to deny or even purge his Beatle-works. In many ways he was sending messages to John with those first casual recordings, just as John's crude recordings in New York City were alive with lessons meant for Paul. What they were of course saying to each other was: "Fuck you! You hurt me, but I don't need you anymore! Just listen to how great I am without you and with Yoko/Linda!"

That's the sort of attitude that starts getting readjusted with middle age, perhaps, or with any passage of years. Unhappily, John will never have the luxury of knowing life past forty. Whether or not he and Paul would have reunited as collaborating writers is now a moot point. Paul, as the only other Chief Beatle, now has the dubious and solo honor of living his life out as the most celebrated, most successful, and richest of all the rock 'n' rollers who have ever lived. With Elvis Presley's premature death, Bob Dylan's premature withdrawal from the rock 'n' roll sweepstakes, and John's murder, Paul is now left as the only genuine member of rock's royalty. One hopes that Paul is starting to truly enjoy the spoils that are rightfully his, now that he can realize he wasn't actually hated as much as he had thought he was. Knighthood soon, no doubt about it. And not just the Rock Hall of Fame kind either.

Over the years those interviewers fortunate enough to find themselves admitted to an intimate audience with Paul McCartney have inevitably come away from the encounter with a glow on, feeling that they have finally captured the ultimate interview with the Great One. It's mostly due to the almost breathtaking skill he has developed in thirty years of dealing with press and public. Paul long ago learned just how much of himself he had to give—or not give—in order to satisfy the world. And that's no little skill, considering the position he is in. (That he has achieved a comfortable acceptance of and working relationship with such an incredible degree of fame is remarkable in itself.)

His charm in a one-on-one encounter is legendary. After basking in the patented McCartney glow, the object of all that focused attention comes away often giddy from the experience. (I know a woman record company executive who still, eight years or so after the fact, replays in her mind the day that Paul kissed her.) The lucky interviewer leaves the dark wood recesses of Paul's den at MPL and all of a sudden the sun is shining in Soho Square. The interviewer is hugging the precious tapes of Paul, confident that of all the interviews Paul has ever done, this is the first truly anointed one, the one in which Paul finally broke down and unburdened himself.

It's only in the hangover that the truth comes. The interviewer starts listening to those tapes and the truth starts manifesting itself: Paul manipulated and completely controlled the interview. He revealed only what he wanted made known. Now and then he lets a morsel slip through as a headline-grabber: PAUL MCCARTNEY FAVORS PMRC! (Well, only just sort of). What Paul is really doing is selling records and that's the only reason he does those interviews, which is very smart of him. The only occasion upon which he revealed any side of himself at all was his celebrated "maneuvering swine" phone call to Hunter Davies in 1981, in what Paul thought was a personal conversation with a "friend."

"It shows what a buddy he is," Paul later said bitterly of Davies. He was probably just as angry with himself, for having lost control and exposed himself. He told Davies that he and John had basically had to "clear the decks" of each other once they met Yoko and Linda. "I don't like being the careful one," Paul said of his role in the Beatles. "I'd rather be immediate like John. He was all action. John was always the loudest in any crowd. . . . I was never out to screw him, never. He could be a maneuvering swine, which no one ever realized. Now since the death he's become Martin Luther Lennon. But that wasn't him either. He wasn't some sort of holy saint. . . . I have some juicy stuff I could tell about John. But I wouldn't. Not when Yoko's alive—or Cynthia."

If Paul reveals little of himself in interviews, he shows astonishingly less in his music. It's easier, after all, to hide behind carefully crafted music. His emotions have always been carefully disguised in his songs. When he does write from the heart upon occasion, the result can be startling, as in "Wanderlust," which becomes a heartfelt personal anthem for Paul. It's (for him) almost a scream from the soul, begging to be left alone. But such moments can be counted on the fingers of one hand and that covers a musical career of thirty years.

If he has shown that he can successfully hide in his music, one thing that Paul undoubtedly did not count upon when he decided to finally make his own movie was the revelatory nature of the big screen. When you write and star in your own movie, you had better have something to show up there. A big reason that *Give My Regards to Broad Street* was such a resounding failure was the fact that Paul tried to show himself while revealing nothing. He was writing about himself, while simultaneously reducing that character (himself) to a stock character, with stock dialogue and stock action and stock emotions. Paul obviously did not see it that way, but since he was in charge there was no one to tell him otherwise. *Broad Street,* though, ultimately reveals more of Paul than he realizes. What seemed to the critics to be just a simple plot was actually a simple plot with a great deal going on beneath the surface, in terms of Paul's real life.

Judging from Paul's almost violent reaction to the movie's failure, it's very easy to see what hurt him most about that failure (other than the blow to his ego). With that movie, he had rewritten his life story—and he discovered that nobody was interested in it.

The resemblances to his life and the flights of fancy from his life are almost pathetically transparent. The Paul McCartney in the movie lives only for his music: The plot revolves around his lost tapes. Losing the music is the worst crisis that he can imagine and once the tapes (the music) are lost, the "men in suits" come after him, but he triumphs in the end. In that sense the movie is nothing but a cartoon vision of the great struggle of his life: maintaining his music in the face of adversity.

In the mythical world that Paul created in *Broad Street,* Paul's life is nothing but music and he is very much in charge. Except, that is, for the trusted but weak employee who loses the tapes (the music). The resemblance to Denny Laine is striking. In the end, though, he is absolved of blame and all is right again in the McCartney world.

Along the way Paul is very much alone and liking it that way. Instead of being relegated to the backseats of limos, he's out on his own, tearing up the highways in a customized Ford. From the driver's seat of that hot rod, Paul is in control of his world via two telephones and an onboard computer. Girls admire him and youths envy him as he thunders past. Paul remains cool even in the midst of crises, tossing off one-liners.

There is no John Lennon in this world, not even in its past. Paul is the star and much beloved by everyone. Fans are worshipful, but discreet and mindful of his privacy. The media are simple-minded and easily manipulated. Police are bumbling and ineffectual. Anytime Paul shows up in the studio, his steady, dependable, brilliant—and silent—sidemen are waiting to play out their hearts for him. Paul's business manager is a strong and loyal and competent right arm. Linda is seen but seldom heard and eventually retreats to hearthside and literally keeps the home fires burning while Paul is out dealing with the crises. With her is trusted friend Ringo, anxiously awaiting word from Our Hero.

In the most remarkably revealing scene in the film, Paul pays a belated visit to his father, in the person of Ralph Richardson. The character is even named Jim. He is an old pub owner, living above his pub. His rooms are still furnished in 1940s style, even down to the wireless radio, just like the one Jim McCartney had rigged up to let Paul listen to in bed so many years before. The character Jim here addresses Paul as "son." Jim is only a businessman, just as Jim Mac had been, but he is also a poet, just as

Jim Mac was actually a musician. And he gives Paul fatherly advice: "You're always running around. If you didn't run around so much, you might get a better view of the world, you know. Haste makes waste. And waste not, want not." Even though there was really no reason in the film for Paul to visit the Jim character, he very clearly adores him. That was perhaps as close as the taciturn Paul could come to reaching out to his late father. (He later claimed the film character was based on Polonius.)

After revealing so much of himself (inadvertently or not) and being so ridiculed for his trouble, we can probably expect to not see any more revelations in the near future.

In the lavish book that MPL published about the making of the movie *Broad Street,* Paul took great pains to claim that the Paul depicted in the movie was nothing like him, that he was completely normal and domestic and happy being so. He enjoyed washing dishes and shoveling shit and watching virtually anything that came on television. He was living a normal life, he said, because he and Linda enjoyed it, but mainly for the sake of the kids, so that they would have a better life than he did and would be more talented than he was.

How long, you wonder, will he go on overcompensating for what Mother Mary's death did to him as a child? It's the one event, as the chief trauma in his life, that both turned him into a loner and into a devoted father. What will happen to him, you again wonder, when he gets his two wishes and his children successfully leave the nest and he is totally and completely alone, just him and Linda? Paul has no other close friends—just employees and acquaintances. And, although he and George and Ringo have started making conciliatory noises of late, he was never that close to either of them to start with. If there ever is a true Beatle reunion—either in the studio, as is more likely, or onstage—you can bet that Paul will name the group something else. He won't come out and say the word "Beatles." Remember, Paul treated George and Ringo as sidemen in the Beatles' glory days. What would be so different this time around? He never wrote songs with either of them.

In a way it was not so surprising that after all these years Paul would thumb his nose at the Rock and Roll Hall of Fame and pass up his musical knighthood because of control and over business differences with George and Ringo. He obviously feels he's worth more than they are. And, remember, Paul has been wrangling over money ever since the Quarry Men days, when he forced Ken Brown out of the group over the matter of fifteen shillings. He gradually became a "man in a suit" over the years, even while railing against the Establishment—but that was mainly over marijuana laws. He was the first one to side with Brian Epstein in favor of shedding the Beatles' funky leather outfits for nice neat suits and ties. There's certainly no confusion in Paul's mind about it. As both he and John admitted, they would do and did do whatever was necessary to Make It. As John put it, the Beatles were "the biggest bastards that ever lived. We had to be, to make it." For Paul to turn into what he supposedly detested—a "man in a suit," though a figurative suit in his case—means that he always wanted to be one or that he simply never meant what he said in the beginning.

As for Paul's claims these days that he's completely "normal," that's sheer rubbish. No one who has lived the life he has or earned the adulation (not to mention the money) that he has can ever be normal—by anybody's standards. Whether he likes it or not, the Beatle legend only grows and becomes more fabled with each passing year. The fact that there will likely never again be such a group or such an era only adds to the luster. Like it or not, Paul is the royalty of rock.

Nor can life be normal for someone who has what seems to be a biological need to make music. No matter how out of step he may seem with musical trends, he cannot be counted out. When the world of rock turned to punk, Paul came out with "Mull of Kintyre." When he was ruled out as an old fart, Paul came roaring back with *Wings Over America.*

The comeback would be harder this time, the main problem being what is becoming more and more evidently a problem with him: an erosion of his musical judgment, with an attendant decline in his musical self-confidence. A former employee says that it is apparent to him—although this is a casual appraisal— that it's mainly due to the effects of long-term marijuana use. "It's changed him," said the former employee. "No doubt about it. He could have been Cole Porter. Now he's turning into Mancini."

Again, it's obvious from his erratic musical course over the past few years that the only reason Paul would ever have dared take on a strong collaborator on the order of an Elvis Costello is simple: He needs someone. Whether it will take is another matter. His habits may be so ingrained that a musical transplant will automatically be rejected. The one McCartney–Costello song that I have heard, "Back on My Feet," is inconclusive.

Paul McCartney need never write another word for his immortality to be guaranteed. The thing is, he obviously intends to write a great many words. For his sake—and for the sake of his audience—one hopes that they are good words. Should he slide into mediocrity, the analogy that's waiting is all too predictable. And "The Fool on the Hill" is the comparison that the critics will only start with. . . .

Discography

THE BEATLES

BRITISH RELEASES

"Love Me Do"/"P.S. I Love You." Parlophone R 4949. October 5, 1962.

"Please Please Me"/"Ask Me Why." R 4983. January 11, 1963.

Please Please Me. Parlophone PCS 3042. March 22, 1963. "I Saw Her Standing There," "Misery," "Anna (Go to Him)," "Chains," "Boys," "Ask Me Why," "Please Please Me," "Love Me Do," "P.S. I Love You," "Baby It's You," "Do You Want to Know a Secret?," "A Taste of Honey," "There's a Place," "Twist and Shout."

"From Me to You"/"Thank You Girl." R 5015. April 11, 1963.

Twist and Shout. GEP 8882. July 12, 1963. "Twist and Shout," "A Taste of Honey," "Do You Want to Know a Secret?," "There's a Place."

"She Loves You"/"I'll Get You." R 5055. August 23, 1963.

The Beatles' Hits. GEP 8880. September 6, 1963. "From Me to You," "Thank You Girl," "Please Please Me," "Love Me Do."

The Beatles (No. 1). GEP 8883. November 1, 1963. "I Saw Her Standing There," "Misery," "Anna (Go to Him)," "Chains."

With the Beatles. PCS 3045. November 22, 1963. "It Won't Be Long," "All I've Got to Do," "All My Loving," "Don't Bother Me," "Little Child," "Till There Was You," "Please Mr. Postman," "Roll Over Beethoven," "Hold Me Tight," "You Really Got a Hold on Me," "I Wanna Be Your Man," "Devil in Her Heart," "Not a Second Time," "Money (That's What I Want)."

"I Want to Hold Your Hand"/"This Boy." R 5084. November 29, 1963.

All My Loving. GEP 8891. February 7, 1964. "All My Loving," "Ask Me Why," "Money (That's What I Want)," "P.S. I Love You."

"Can't Buy Me Love"/"You Can't Do That." R 5114. March 20, 1964.

Long Tall Sally. GEP 8913. June 19, 1964. "Long Tall Sally," "I Call Your Name," "Slow Down," "Matchbox."

"A Hard Day's Night"/"Things We Said Today." R 5160. July 10, 1964.

A Hard Day's Night. PCS 3058. August 10, 1964. "A Hard Day's Night," "I Should Have Known Better," "If I Fell," "I'm Happy Just to Dance with You," "And I Love Her," "Tell Me Why," "Can't Buy Me Love," "Any Time at All," "I'll Cry Instead," "Things We Said Today," "When I Get Home," "You Can't Do That," "I'll Be Back."

Extracts from the Film "A Hard Day's Night". GEP 8920. November 4, 1964. "I Should Have Known Better," "If I Fell," "Tell Me Why," "And I Love Her."

Extracts from the Album "A Hard Day's Night". GEP 8924. November 6, 1964. "Any Time at All," "I'll Cry Instead," "Things We Said Today," "When I Get Home."

"I Feel Fine"/"She's a Woman." R 5200. November 27, 1964.

Beatles for Sale. PCS 3062. December 4, 1964. "No Reply," "I'm a Loser," "Baby's in Black," "Rock and Roll Music," "I'll Follow the Sun," "Mr. Moonlight," "Kansas City/Hey Hey Hey Hey," "Eight Days a Week," "Words of Love,"

"Honey Don't," "Every Little Thing," "I Don't Want to Spoil the Party," "What You're Doing," "Everybody's Trying to Be My Baby."

Beatles for Sale. GEP 8931. April 6, 1965. "No Reply," "I'm a Loser," "Rock and Roll Music," "Eight Days a Week."

"Ticket to Ride"/"Yes It Is." R 5265. April 9, 1965.

Beatles for Sale (No. 2). GEP 8938. June 4, 1965. "I'll Follow the Sun," "Baby's in Black," "Words of Love," "I Don't Want to Spoil the Party."

"Help!"/"I'm Down." R 5305. July 23, 1965.

Help! PCS 3071. August 6, 1965. "Help!," "The Night Before," "You've Got to Hide Your Love Away," "I Need You," "Another Girl," "You're Going to Lose That Girl," "Ticket to Ride," "Act Naturally," "It's Only Love," "You Like Me Too Much," "Tell Me What You See," "I've Just Seen a Face," "Yesterday."

"Day Tripper"/"We Can Work It Out." R 5389. December 3, 1965.

Rubber Soul. PCS 3075. December 3, 1965. "Drive My Car," "Norwegian Wood (This Bird Has Flown)," "You Won't See Me," "Nowhere Man," "Think for Yourself," "The Word," "Michelle," "What Goes On," "Girl," "I'm Looking Through You," "In My Life," "Wait," "If I Needed Someone," "Run for Your Life."

The Beatles' Million Sellers. GEP 8946. December 6, 1965. "She

Loves You," "I Want to Hold Your Hand," "Can't Buy Me Love," "I Feel Fine."

Yesterday. GEP 8948. March 4, 1966. "Yesterday," "Act Naturally," "You Like Me Too Much," "It's Only Love."

"Paperback Writer"/"Rain." R 5452. June 10, 1966.

Nowhere Man. GEP 8952. July 8, 1966. "Nowhere Man," "Drive My Car," "Michelle," "You Won't See Me."

"Eleanor Rigby"/"Yellow Submarine." R 5493. August 5, 1966.

Revolver. PCS 7009. August 5, 1966. "Taxman," "Eleanor Rigby," "I'm Only Sleeping," "Love You To," "Here, There and Everywhere," "Yellow Submarine," "She Said, She Said," "Good Day Sunshine," "And Your Bird Can Sing," "For No One," "Dr. Robert," "I Want to Tell You," "Got to Get You into My Life," "Tomorrow Never Knows."

A Collection of Beatles' Oldies (But Goodies). PCS 7016. December 10, 1966. "She Loves You," "From Me to You," "We Can Work It Out," "Help!," "Michelle," "Yesterday," "I Feel Fine," "Yellow Submarine," "Can't Buy Me Love," "Bad Boy," "Day Tripper," "A Hard Day's Night," "Ticket to Ride," "Paperback Writer," "Eleanor Rigby," "I Want to Hold Your Hand."

"Penny Lane"/"Strawberry Fields Forever." R 5570. February 17, 1967.

Sgt. Pepper's Lonely Hearts Club Band. PCS 7027. May 26, 1967.

"Sgt. Pepper's Lonely Hearts Club Band," "With a Little Help from My Friends," "Lucy in the Sky with Diamonds," "Getting Better," "Fixing a Hole," "She's Leaving Home," "Being for the Benefit of Mr. Kite," "Within You, Without You," "When I'm Sixty-Four," "Lovely Rita," "Good Morning, Good Morning," "Sgt. Pepper's Lonely Hearts Club Band (Reprise)," "A Day in the Life."

"All You Need Is Love"/"Baby You're a Rich Man." R 5620. July 7, 1967.

"Hello Goodbye"/"I Am the Walrus." R 5655. November 24, 1967.

Magical Mystery Tour. SMMT ½. December 8, 1967. "Magical Mystery Tour," "Your Mother Should Know," "I Am the Walrus," "The Fool on the Hill," "Flying," "Blue Jay Way."

"Lady Madonna"/"The Inner Light." R 5675. March 15, 1968.

"Hey Jude"/"Revolution." Apple R 5722 [First Beatles release on Apple]. August 26, 1968.

The Beatles. PCS 7067–8. November 22, 1968. "Back in the U.S.S.R.," "Dear Prudence," "Glass Onion," "Ob-La-Di, Ob-La-Da," "Wild Honey," "The Continuing Story of Bungalow Bill," "While My Guitar Gently Weeps," "Happiness Is a Warm Gun," "Martha My Dear," "I'm So Tired," "Blackbird," "Piggies," "Rocky Raccoon," "Don't Pass Me By," "Why Don't We Do It in the Road?" "I Will," "Julia," "Birthday," "Yer Blues," "Mother Nature's Son," "Everybody's Got Something to Hide Except Me and My Monkey," "Sexy Sadie," "Helter Skelter," "Long, Long, Long," "Revolution 1," "Honey Pie," "Savoy Truffle," "Cry Baby Cry," "Can You Take Me Back," "Revolution 9," "Good Night."

Yellow Submarine. PCS 7070. January 17, 1969. "Yellow Submarine," "Only a Northern Song," "All Together Now," "Hey Bulldog," "It's All Too Much," "All You Need Is Love."

"Get Back"/"Don't Let Me Down." R 5777. April 11, 1969.

"The Ballad of John and Yoko"/ "Old Brown Shoe." R 5786. May 30, 1969.

Abbey Road. PCS 7088. September 26, 1969. "Come Together," "Something," "Maxwell's Silver Hammer," "Oh! Darling," "Octo-pus's Garden," "I Want You (She's So Heavy)," "Here Comes the Sun," "Because," "You Never Give Me Your Money," "Sun King," "Mean Mr. Mustard," "Polythene Pam," "She Came in Through the Bathroom Window," "Golden Slumbers," "Carry That Weight," "The End," "Her Majesty."

"Something"/"Come Together." R 5814. October 31, 1969.

"Let It Be"/"You Know My Name (Look Up the Number)." R 5833. March 6, 1970.

Let It Be. PXS 1. May 8, 1970; PCS 7096. November 6, 1970. "Two of Us," "Dig a Pony," "Across the Universe," "I Me Mine," "Dig It," "Let It Be," "Maggie Mae," "I've Got a Feeling," "The One After 909," "The Long and Winding Road," "For You Blue," "Get Back."

AMERICAN RELEASES

(All are on Capitol Records unless otherwise indicated.)

"Please Please Me"/"Ask Me Why." VJ 498 Vee Jay. February 25, 1963.

"From Me to You"/"Thank You Girl." Vee Jay 522. May 27, 1963.

Introducing the Beatles. VJLP 1062 Vee Jay. July 22, 1963. "I Saw Her Standing There," "Misery," "Anna (Go to Him)," "Chains," "Boys," "Love Me Do," "P.S. I Love You," "Baby It's You," "Do You Want to Know a Secret?," "A Taste of Honey," "There's a Place," "Twist and Shout."

"She Loves You"/"I'll Get You." Swan 4152. September 16, 1963.

"I Want to Hold Your Hand"/"I Saw Her Standing There." 5112. January 13, 1964.

Meet the Beatles. ST 2047. January 20, 1964. "I Want to Hold Your Hand," "I Saw Her Standing There," "This Boy," "It Won't Be Long," "All I've Got to Do," "All My Loving," "Don't Bother Me," "Little Child," "Till There Was You," "Hold Me Tight," "I Wanna Be Your Man," "Not a Second Time."

Introducing the Beatles. Vee Jay

LP 1062. January 27, 1964. (This is a reissue, with "Please Please Me" and "Ask Me Why" replacing "Love Me Do" and "P.S. I Love You.")

"Please Please Me"/"From Me to You." Vee Jay 581. January 30, 1964.

Jolly What! The Beatles and Frank Ifield on Stage. VJLP 1085 Vee Jay. February 26, 1964. The Beatles' portion includes "Please Please Me," "From Me to You," "Ask Me Why," "Thank You Girl."

"Twist and Shout"/"There's a Place." Tollie 9001. March 2, 1964.

"Can't Buy Me Love"/"You Can't Do That." 5150. March 16, 1964.

Souvenir of Their Visit to America (The Beatles). Vee Jay LP 1-903. March 23, 1964. "Misery," "A Taste of Honey," "Ask Me Why," "Anna (Go to Him)."

"Do You Want to Know a Secret?"/"Thank You Girl." Vee Jay 587. March 23, 1964.

The Beatles' Second Album. ST 2080. April 10, 1964. "Long Tall Sally," "I Call Your Name," "Please Mr. Postman," "I'll Get You," "She Loves You," "Roll Over Beethoven," "Thank You Girl," "You Really Got a Hold On Me," "Devil in Her Heart," "Money (That's What I Want)," "You Can't Do That."

Four by the Beatles. EAP 2121. May 11, 1964. "Roll Over Beethoven," "All My Loving," "This Boy," "Please Mr. Postman."

"Sie Liebt Dich (She Loves You)"/"I'll Get You." Swan 4182. May 21, 1964.

"Slow Down"/"Matchbox." 5255. August 24, 1964.

The Beatles vs. the Four Seasons. Vee Jay DX 30. Vee Jay. Beatle songs included: "I Saw Her Standing There," "Misery," "Anna (Go to Him)," "Chains," "Boys," "Ask Me Why."

Songs, Pictures and Stories of the Fabulous Beatles. Vee Jay 1092. October 12, 1964. A repackage of *Introducing the Beatles.*

The Beatles' Story. STBO 2222. November 23, 1964. A four-disc narrative and interview album.

"I Feel Fine"/"She's a Woman." 5327. November 23, 1964.

Beatles '65. ST 2228. December 15, 1964. "No Reply," "I'm a Loser," "Baby's in Black," "Rock and Roll Music," "I'll Follow the Sun," "Mr. Moonlight," "Honey Don't," "I'll Be Back," "She's a Woman," "I Feel Fine," "Everybody's Trying to Be My Baby."

4 by the Beatles. R5365. February 1, 1965. "Honey Don't," "I'm a Loser," "Mr. Moonlight," "Everybody's Trying to Be My Baby."

"Eight Days a Week"/"I Don't Want to Spoil the Party." 5371. February 15, 1965.

The Early Beatles. ST 2309. March 22, 1965. "Love Me Do," "Twist and Shout," "Anna (Go to Him)," "Chains," "Boys," "Ask Me Why," "Please Please Me," "P.S. I Love You," "Baby It's You," "A Taste of Honey," "Do You Want to Know a Secret?"

"Ticket to Ride"/"Yes It Is." 5407. April 14, 1965.

Beatles VI. ST 2358. June 14, 1965. "Kansas City/Hey, Hey, Hey, Hey" "Eight Days a Week," "You Like Me Too Much," "Bad Boy," "I Don't Want to Spoil the Party," "Words of Love," "What You're Doing," "Yes It Is," "Dizzy Miss Lizzy," "Tell Me What You See," "Every Little Thing."

"Help!"/"I'm Down." 5476. July 19, 1965.

Help! SMAS 2386. August 13, 1965. "Help!," "The Night Before," "You've Got to Hide Your Love Away," "I Need You," "You're Going to Lose That Girl," "Another Girl."

"Yesterday"/"Act Naturally." 5498. September 13, 1965.

"We Can Work It Out"/"Day Tripper." 5555. December 6, 1965.

Rubber Soul. ST 2442. December 6, 1965. "I've Just Seen a Face," "Norwegian Wood (This Bird Has Flown)," "You Won't See Me," "Think for Yourself," "The Word," "Michelle," "It's Only Love," "Girl," "I'm Looking Through You," "In My Life," "Wait," "Run for Your Life."

"Nowhere Man"/"What Goes On." 5587. February 21, 1966.

"Paperback Writer"/"Rain." 5651. May 30, 1966.

Yesterday and Today. ST 2553. June 20, 1966. "Drive My Car," "I'm Only Sleeping," "Nowhere Man," "Dr. Robert," "Yesterday," "Act Naturally," "And Your Bird Can Sing," "If I Needed Some-one," "We Can Work It Out," "What Goes On," "Day Tripper."

"Yellow Submarine"/"Eleanor Rigby." 5715. August 8, 1966.

Revolver. ST 2576. August 8, 1966. "Taxman," "Eleanor Rigby," "Love You To," "Here, There and Everywhere," "Yellow Submarine," "She Said, She Said," "Good Day Sunshine," "For No One," "I Want to Tell You," "Got to Get You into My Life," "Tomorrow Never Knows."

"Penny Lane"/"Strawberry Fields Forever." 5810. February 13, 1967.

Sgt. Pepper's Lonely Hearts Club Band. SMAS 2653. June 2, 1967. Tracks were identical to the British album release—for the first time.

"All You Need Is Love"/"Baby You're a Rich Man." 5964. July 17, 1967.

"Hello Goodbye"/"I Am the Walrus." 2056. November 27, 1967.

Magical Mystery Tour. SMAL 2835. November 27, 1967. "Magical Mystery Tour," "The Fool on the Hill," "Flying," "Blue Jay Way," "Your Mother Should Know," "I Am the Walrus," "Hello Goodbye," "Strawberry Fields Forever," "Penny Lane," "Baby You're a Rich Man," "All You Need Is Love."

"Lady Madonna"/"The Inner Light." 2138. March 18, 1968.

"Hey Jude"/"Revolution." 2276 Apple. August 26, 1968.

The Beatles. SWBO 101. November 25, 1968. Identical to the British release.

Yellow Submarine. SW 153. January 13, 1969. "Yellow Submarine," "Only a Northern Song," "Hey Bulldog," "It's All Too Much," "All You Need Is Love." Side B consists of orchestration from the film by George Martin and his orchestra.

"Get Back"/"Don't Let Me Down." 2490 Apple. May 5, 1969.

"The Ballad of John and Yoko"/"Old Brown Shoe." 2531 Apple. June 4, 1969.

Abbey Road. SO 383. October 1, 1969. Identical to the British release.

"Something"/"Come Together." 2654 Apple. October 6, 1969.

Hey Jude. SW 385/SO 385. February 26, 1970. "Can't Buy Me Love," "I Should Have Known Better," "Paperback Writer," "Rain," "Lady Madonna," "Revolution," "Hey Jude," "Old Brown Shoe," "Don't Let Me Down," "The Ballad of John and Yoko."

"Let It Be"/"You Know My Name (Look Up the Number)." 2764 Apple. March 11, 1970.

"The Long and Winding Road"/"For You Blue." 2832 Apple. May 11, 1970.

Let It Be. AR 34001. May 18, 1970. "Two of Us," "Dig a Pony," "Across the Universe," "I Me Mine," "Dig It," "Let It Be," "Maggie Mae," "I've Got a Feeling," "The One After 909," "The Long and Winding Road," "For You Blue," "Get Back."

PAUL McCARTNEY AFTER THE BEATLES

British release information is listed first. United States information follows in brackets.

McCartney by Paul McCartney. Apple PCS 7102. April 17, 1970. "The Lovely Linda," "That Would Be Something," "Valentine Day," "Every Night," "Hot as Sun," "Glasses," "Junk," "Man We Was Lonely," "Oo You," "Momma Miss America," "Teddy Boy," "Singalong Junk," "Maybe I'm Amazed," "Kreen-Akrore." [Apple STAO 3363. April 20, 1970]

"Another Day"/"Oh Woman Oh Why" by Paul McCartney. Apple R 5889. February 19, 1971. [Apple 1829. February 22, 1971]

Ram by Paul and Linda McCartney. Apple PAS 10003. May 21, 1971. "Too Many People," "3 Legs," "Ram On," "Dear Boy," "Uncle Albert/Admiral Halsey," "Smile Away," "Heart of the Country," "Monkberry Moon Delight," "Eat at Home," "Long-Haired Lady," "Ram On," "The Back Seat of My Car." [Apple SMAS 3375. May 17, 1971]

"The Back Seat of My Car"/"Heart of the Country" by Paul and Linda McCartney. Apple R 5914. August 13, 1971. [Not released in the United States. The American single release was "Uncle Albert/Admiral Halsey"/"Too Many People." Apple 1837. August 2, 1971]

Wild Life by Wings. Apple PCS 7142. December 3, 1971. "Mumbo," "Bip Bop," "Love Is Strange," "Wild Life," "Some People Never Know," "I Am Your Singer," "Tomorrow," "Dear Friend." [Apple SW 3386. December 7, 1971]

"Give Ireland Back to the Irish"/ "Give Ireland Back to the Irish (Instrumental)" by Wings. Apple R 5936. February 25, 1972 [Apple 1847. February 28, 1972].

"Mary Had a Little Lamb"/"Little Woman Love" by Wings. Apple R5949. May 5, 1972. [Apple 1851, May 29, 1972]

"Hi, Hi, Hi"/"C Moon" by Wings. Apple R5973. December 1, 1972. [Apple 1857. December 4, 1972]

"My Love"/"The Mess" by Paul McCartney and Wings. Apple R 5985. March 23, 1973. [Apple 1861. April 9, 1973]

Red Rose Speedway by Paul McCartney and Wings. Apple PCTC 251. May 3, 1973. "Big Barn Bed," "My Love," "Get on the Right Thing," "One More Kiss," "Little Lamb Dragonfly," "Single Pigeon," "When the Night," "Loup (1st Indian on the Moon)," Medley: "Hold Me Tight," "Lazy Dynamite," "Hands of Love," "Power Cut." [Apple SMAL 3409. April 30, 1973]

"Live and Let Die"/"I Lie Around" by Wings. Apple R 5987. June 1, 1973. [Apple 1863. June 18, 1973]

"Helen Wheels"/"Country Dreamer" by Paul McCartney and Wings. Apple R 5993. October 26, 1973. [Apple 1869. November 12, 1973]

Band on the Run by Paul McCartney and Wings. Apple PAS 10007. November 30, 1973. "Band on the Run," "Jet," "Bluebird," "Mrs. Vanderbilt," "Let Me Roll It," "Mamunia," "No Words," "Picasso's Last Words (Drink to Me)," "Nineteen Hundred and Eighty Five." [Apple SO 3415. December 5, 1973. The United States album added one song, "Helen Wheels"]

"Jet"/"Let Me Roll It" by Paul McCartney and Wings. Apple R 5996. February 18, 1974. [Apple 1871. January 28, 1974. The United States release originally had "Mamunia" on the B-side; "Let Me Roll It" replaced it in February]

"Band on the Run"/"Zoo Gang" by Paul McCartney and Wings. Apple R 5997. June 28, 1974. [Apple 1873. April 8, 1974. The B-side of the United States release was "Nineteen Hundred and Eighty Five"]

"Walking in the Park with Eloise"/"Bridge Over the River Suite" by the Country Hams [Wings, joined by Chet Atkins and Floyd Cramer]. EMI 2220. October 18, 1974. [EMI 3977. December 2, 1974]

"Junior's Farm"/"Sally G." by Paul McCartney and Wings. Apple R 5999. October 25, 1974. (Reissued as the same number on February 7, 1975, with A- and B-sides reversed) [Apple 1875. November 4, 1974]

"Listen to What the Man Said"/ "Love in Song" by Wings. Capitol R 6006. May 16, 1975. [Capitol 4091. May 23, 1975]

Venus and Mars by Wings. Capitol PCTC 254. May 30, 1975. "Venus and Mars," "Rock Show," "Love in Song," "You Gave Me the Answer," "Magneto and Titanium Man," "Letting Go," "Venus and Mars Reprise," "Spirits of Ancient Egypt," "Medicine Jar," "Call Me Back Again," "Listen to What the Man Said," "Treat Her Gently," "Lonely Old People," "Crossroads Theme." [Capitol SMAS 11419. May 27, 1975]

"Letting Go"/"You Gave Me the Answer" by Wings. Capitol R 6008. September 5, 1975. [Capitol 4145. September 29, 1975]

"Venus and Mars"/"Rock Show"/"Magneto and Titanium Man" by Wings. Capitol R 6010, November 28, 1975. [Capitol 4175. October 27, 1975]

Wings at the Speed of Sound by Wings. Parlophone PAS 10010. March 26, 1976. "Let 'em In," "The Note You Never Wrote," "She's My Baby," "Beware My Love," "Wino Junko," "Silly Love Songs," "Cook of the House," "Time to Hide," "Must Do Something About It," "San Ferry Anne," "Warm and Beautiful." [Capitol SW 11525. March 25, 1976]

"Silly Love Songs"/"Cook of the House" by Wings. Parlophone R 6014. April 30, 1976. [Capitol 4256. April 1, 1976]

"Let 'em In"/"Beware My Love" by Wings. Parlophone R 6015. July 23, 1976. [Capitol 4293. June 28, 1976]

Wings Over America by Wings. Parlophone PCSP 720. December 10, 1976. "Venus and Mars," "Rock Show," "Jet," "Let Me Roll It," "Spirits of Ancient Egypt," "Medicine Jar," "Maybe I'm Amazed," "Call Me Back Again," "Lady Madonna," "The Long and Winding Road," "Live and Let Die," "Picasso's Last Words," "Richard Cory," "Bluebird," "I've Just Seen a Face," "Blackbird," "Yesterday," "You Gave Me the Answer," "Magneto and Titanium Man," "Go Now," "My Love," "Listen to What the Man Said," "Let 'em In," "Time to Hide," "Silly Love Songs," "Beware My Love," "Letting Go," "Band on the Run," "Hi, Hi, Hi," "Soily." [Capitol SWCO 11593. December 11, 1976]

"Maybe I'm Amazed"/"Soily" by Wings. Parlophone R 6017. February 4, 1977. [Capitol 4385. February 7, 1977]

"Uncle Albert/Admiral Halsey"/"Eat at Home" by Percy "Thrills" Thrillington [a McCartney persona]. Regal Zonophone EMI 2594. April 22, 1977. [No United States release]

Thrillington by Percy "Thrills" Thrillington. Regal Zonophone EMC 3175. April 29, 1977. "Too Many People," "3 Legs," "Ram On," "Dear Boy," "Uncle Albert/ Admiral Halsey," "Smile Away," "Heart of the Country," "Monkberry Moon Delight," "Eat at Home," "Long-Haired Lady," "The Back Seat of My Car." [No United States release]

"Mull of Kintyre"/"Girls School" by Wings. Capitol R 6018.

November 11, 1977. [Capitol 4504. November 14, 1977]

"With a Little Luck"/"Backwards Traveller/Cuff Link" by Wings. Parlophone R 6019. March 23, 1978. [Capitol 4559. March 20, 1978]

London Town by Wings. Parlophone PAS 10012. March 31, 1978. "London Town," "Café on the Left Bank," "I'm Carrying," "Backwards Traveller/Cuff Link," "Children Children," "Girlfriend," "I've Had Enough," "With a Little Luck," "Famous Groupies," "Deliver Your Children," "Name and Address," "Don't Let It Bring You Down," "Mouse Moose and the Grey Goose." [Capitol SW 11777. March 31, 1978]

"I've Had Enough"/"Deliver Your Children" by Wings. Parlophone R 6020. June 16, 1978. [Capitol 4594. June 12, 1978]

"London Town"/"I'm Carrying" by Wings. Parlophone R 6021. September 15, 1978. [Capitol 4625. August 21, 1978]

Wings Greatest by Wings. Parlophone PCTC 256. December 1, 1978. "Another Day," "Silly Love Songs," "Live and Let Die," "Junior's Farm," "With a Little Luck," "Band on the Run," "Uncle Albert/Admiral Halsey," "Hi, Hi, Hi," "Let 'em In," "My Love," "Jet," "Mull of Kintyre." [Capitol SOO 11905. November 22, 1978]

"Goodnight Tonight"/"Daytime Nightime Suffering" by Wings. Parlophone 12Y R 6023. March 23, 1979. [Columbia 3-10939. March 15, 1979]

"Old Siam Sir"/"Spin It On" by Wings. Parlophone R 6026. June 1, 1979. [United States release had "Arrow Through Me" as the A-side, "Old Siam Sir" as the B-side. Columbia 1-11070. August 14, 1979]

Back to the Egg by Wings. Parlophone PCTC 257. June 8, 1979. "Reception," "Getting Closer," "We're Open Tonight," "Spin It On," "Again and Again and Again," "Old Siam Sir," "Arrow Through Me," "Rockestra Theme," "To You," "After the Ball," "Million Miles," "Winter Rose," "Love Awake," "The Broadcast," "So Glad to See You Here," "Baby's Request." [Columbia FC-36057. May 24, 1979]

"Getting Closer"/"Baby's Request" by Wings. Parlophone R 6027. August 10, 1979. [United States release had "Spin It On" as the B-side. Columbia 3-11020. June 5, 1979]

"Seaside Woman"/"B Side to Seaside" by Suzy and the Red Stripes [Linda McCartney and Wings]. A&M AASP 7461. August 10, 1979. [Released two years earlier in the United States. Epic 8-50403. May 31, 1977]

"Wonderful Christmastime"/"Rudolph the Red-Nosed Reggae" by Paul McCartney. Parlophone R 6029. November 16, 1979. [Columbia 1-11162. November 20, 1979]

"Coming Up"/"Coming Up (Live at Glasgow)"/"Lunchbox/Odd Sox." A-Side by Paul McCartney. B-Side by Paul McCartney and Wings. Parlophone R 6035. April 11, 1980. [Columbia 1-11263. April 15, 1980]

McCartney II by Paul McCartney.

Parlophone PCTC 258. May 16, 1980. "Coming Up," "Temporary Secretary," "On the Way," "Waterfalls," "Nobody Knows," "Front Parlour," "Summers Day Song," "Frozen Jap," "Bogey Music," "Darkroom," "One of These Days." [Columbia FC-36511. May 21, 1980. One day later Columbia reissued the following albums: *McCartney, Ram, Wild Life, Red Rose Speedway,* and *Band On the Run*]

"Waterfalls"/"Check My Machine" by Paul McCartney. Parlophone R 6037. June 14, 1980. [Columbia 1-11335. July 22, 1980]

"Seaside Woman"/"B Side to Seaside" by Linda McCartney, alias Suzy and the Red Stripes. A&M AMS 7458. July 18, 1980.

"Temporary Secretary"/"Secret Friend" by Paul McCartney. [Limited edition twelve-inch single]. Parlophone 12 R 6039. September 15, 1980. [No United States release]

The McCartney Interview by Paul McCartney and Vic Garbarini. Parlophone CHAT 1. February 23, 1981. (Done as an interview for *Musician* magazine, this album was in commercial release for only one day) [Columbia PC-36987. December 4, 1980]

"Ebony and Ivory"/"Rainclouds." A-side by Paul McCartney with additional vocals by Stevie Wonder; B-side by Paul McCartney. Parlophone R 6054. March 29, 1982. [Columbia 18-02860. April 2, 1982]

Tug of War by Paul McCartney. Parlophone PCTC 259. April 26, 1982. "Tug of War," "Take It Away," "Somebody Who Cares," "What's That You're Doing," "Here Today," "Ballroom Dancing," "The Pound Is Sinking," "Wanderlust," "Get It," "Be What You See (Link)," "Dress Me Up as a Robber," "Ebony and Ivory." [Columbia TC 37462. April 26, 1982. Also issued as a twelve-inch single, Columbia 44-02878 on April 16, with Paul's solo version of "Ebony and Ivory" added to B-side]

"Take It Away"/"I'll Give You a Ring" by Paul McCartney. Parlophone R 6056. June 21, 1982. (Also released as a twelve-inch single with "Dress Me Up as a Robber" added to B-side, same serial number) [Columbia 18-03018. June 29, 1982]

"Tug of War"/"Get It." A-side by Paul McCartney; B-side by Paul McCartney and Carl Perkins. Parlophone R 6057. September 20, 1982. [Columbia 38-03235. September 14, 1982]

"The Girl Is Mine"/"Can't Get Out of the Rain." A-side by Michael Jackson and Paul McCartney; B-side by Michael Jackson. Epic EPC A2729. November 29, 1982. [Epic 34-03288. October 3, 1982]

"Say Say Say"/"Ode to a Koala Bear" by Paul McCartney and Michael Jackson. Parlophone R 60620. October 3, 1983.

Pipes of Peace by Paul McCartney. Parlophone PCTC 1652301. October 31, 1983. "Pipes of Peace," "Say Say Say," "The Other Me," "Keep Under Cover," "So Bad," "The Man," "Sweetest Little Show," "Average Person," "Hey

Hey," "Tug of Peace," "Through Our Love."

"Pipes of Peace"/"So Bad" by Paul McCartney. Parlophone R 60640. December 5, 1983.

"Spies Like Us"/"My Carnival" by Paul McCartney and Wings. Parlophone R 6118. October 31, 1985. [Capitol V-15212.]

Give My Regards to Broad Street by Paul McCartney. Parlophone PCTC2. October 22, 1984. "No More Lonely Nights," "Good Day Sunshine," "Corridor Music," "Yesterday," "Here, There and Everywhere," "Wanderlust," "Ballroom Dancing," "Silly Love Songs," "Not Such a Bad Boy," "No Values," "For No One," "Eleanor Rigby/Eleanor's Dream," "The Long and Winding Road," "No More Lonely Nights (playout)."

Press to Play. EMI CDP7 46269-2(id). 1986. "Stranglehold," "Good Times Coming," "Feel the Sun," "Talk More Talk," "Footprints," "Only Love Remains," "Press," "Pretty Little Head," "Move Over Busker," "Angry," "However Absurd," "Write Away," "It's Not True," "Tough on a Tightrope." [Capitol CDP7 462692]

All the Best. Parlophone PMTV1. 1988. "Jet," "Band on the Run," "Coming Up," "Ebony and Ivory," "Listen to What the Man Said," "No More Lonely Nights," "Silly Love Songs," "Let 'em In," "C Moon," "Pipes of Peace," "Live and Let Die," "Another Day," "Maybe I'm Amazed," "Goodnight Tonight," "Once Upon a Long Ago," "Say, Say, Say," "With a Little Luck," "My Love," "We All Stand Together," "Mull of Kintyre" [Capitol CLW 48287. 1988. "Band on the Run," "Jet," "Ebony and Ivory," "Listen to What the Man Said," "No More Lonely Nights," "Silly Love Songs," "Let 'em In," "Say, Say, Say," "Live and Let Die," "Another Day," "C Moon," "Junior's Farm," "Uncle Albert/Admiral Halsey," "Coming Up," "Goodnight Tonight," "With a Little Luck," "My Love"].

Bibliography

Aldridge, Alan, ed. *The Beatles' Illustrated Lyrics*. New York: Delacorte Press, 1969.

Aldridge, Alan, ed. *The Beatles' Illustrated Lyrics 2*. New York: Delacorte Press, 1971.

BBC. *The Lennon Tapes: John Lennon and Yoko Ono in Conversation with Andy Peebles: 6 December 1980*. London: BBC, 1981.

Bacon, David, and Norman Maslov. *The Beatles' England*. London: Columbus Books, 1982.

Barrow, Tony. *P.S. We Love You*. London: Mirror Books, 1982.

Bedford, Carol. *Waiting for the Beatles: An Apple Scruff's Story*. London: Blandford Press, 1984.

Best, Pete, and Patrick Doncaster. *Beatle! The Pete Best Story*. New York: Dell, 1985.

Blake, John. *All You Needed Was Love: The Beatles After the Beatles*. New York: Perigee, 1981.

Braun, Michael. *Love Me Do: The Beatles' Progress*. London: Penguin, 1964.

Campbell, Colin, and Allan Murphy. *Things We Said Today*. Ann Arbor, Michigan: Pierian Press, 1980.

Brown, Peter, and Steven Gaines. *The Love You Make: An Insider's Story of the Beatles*. New York: McGraw-Hill, 1983.

Carr, Roy, and Tony Tyler. *The Beatles: An Illustrated Record*. New York: Harmony, 1978.

Castleman, Harry, and Walter J. Podrazik. *All Together Now: The First Complete Beatles Discography, 1961–1975*. Ann Arbor, Michigan: Pierian Press, 1976.

Castleman, Harry, and Walter J. Podrazik. *The Beatles Again?* Ann Arbor, Michigan: Pierian Press, 1977.

Cepican, Bob, and Waleed Ali. *Yesterday Came Suddenly: The Definitive History of the Beatles*. New York: Arbor House, 1985.

Coleman, Ray. *John Winston Lennon*. New York: McGraw-Hill, 1984.

Connolly, Ray. *John Lennon: 1940–1980*. London: Pavilion Books, 1981.

Connolly, Ray. *Stardust Memories*. London: Pavilion Books, 1983.

Davies, Hunter. *The Beatles*. London: Heinemann, 1968.

DiFranco, Philip, ed. *A Hard Day's Night*. London: Chelsea House, 1977.

DiLello, Richard. *The Longest Cocktail Party*. New York: Playboy Press, 1972.

Doney, Malcolm. *Lennon and McCartney*. London: Midas Books, 1981.

Elson, Howard. *McCartney: Songwriter*. London: Comet Books, 1986.

Epstein, Brian. *A Cellarful of Noise*. London: New English Library, 1981.

Evans, Mike, and Ron Jones. *In the Footsteps of the Beatles*. Liverpool: Merseyside County Council, 1981.

Fast, Julius. *The Beatles: The Real Story*. New York: Putnam, 1968.

Fenick, Barb. *Collecting the Beatles*. Ann Arbor, Michigan: Pierian Press, 1982.

Fong-Torres, Ben, ed. *The Rolling Stone Rock 'n' Roll Reader*. New York: Bantam, 1974.

Fong-Torres, Ben, ed. *What's That Sound? The Contemporary Music Scene from the Pages of Rolling Stone*. Garden City, New York: Anchor/Doubleday, 1976.

Friede, Goldie, and Robin Titone and Sue Weiner. *The Beatles A to Z*. New York: Methuen, 1980.

Friedman, Rick, ed. *The Beatles: Words Without Music*. New York: Grosset and Dunlap, 1968.

Fulpen, H. V. *The Beatles: An Illustrated Diary*. London: Plexus, 1983.

Gambaccini, Paul. *Paul McCartney in his Own Words*. London: Omnibus Press, 1976.

Garbarini, Vic, and Brian Cullman. *Strawberry Fields Forever: John Lennon Remembered*. New York: Bantam, 1980.

Gelly, Dave. *The Facts About a Pop Group Featuring Wings*. London: Andre Deutsch, 1977.

Goodgold, Edwin, and Dan Carlinsky. *The Complete Beatles Quiz Book*. New York: Bell, 1975.

Grove, Martin A. *Beatle Madness*. New York: Manor Books, 1978.

Hamilton, Alan. *Paul McCartney*. London: Hamish Hamilton, 1983.

Harrison, George. *I Me Mine*. London: Genesis Publications, 1980.

Harry, Bill. *The Beatles. Beatlemania, Volume 4: The History of the Beatles on Film*. New York: Avon Books, 1984.

Harry, Bill. *Beatles for Sale: The Beatles Memorabilia Guide*. London: Virgin Books, 1985.

Harry, Bill. *The Beatles. Paperback Writers, Volume 3: The History of the Beatles in Print*. New York: Avon Books, 1984.

Harry, Bill. *The Beatles Who's Who*. London: Aurum Press, 1982.

Harry, Bill. *The Book of Lennon*. New York: Delilah Communications, 1984.

Harry, Bill. *The McCartney File*. London: Virgin Books, 1986.

Harry, Bill, ed. *Mersey Beat: The Beginnings of the Beatles*. London: Omnibus Press, 1977.

Hipgnosis. *Hands Across the Water: Wings Tour U.S.A.* London: Paper Tiger, 1978.

Hoffman, Dezo. *With the Beatles: The Historic Photographs of Dezo Hoffman*. London: Omnibus Press, 1982.

Jasper, Tony. *Paul McCartney & Wings*. London: Octopus Books, 1977.

Howlett, Kevin. *The Beatles at the Beeb*. London: BBC Publications, 1982.

Kaufman, Murray. *Murray the K Tells It Like It Is, Baby*. New York: Holt, Rinehart and Winson, 1966.

Leach, Sam. *Follow the Merseybeat Road*. Liverpool: Eden Publications, 1983.

Lennon, Cynthia. *A Twist of Lennon*. London: Star Books, 1978.

Lewisohn, Mark. *The Beatles Live! The Ultimate Reference Book.* London: Pavilion Books, 1986.

Martin, George. *All You Need Is Ears.* London: Macmillan, 1979.

McCabe, Peter, and Robert D. Schonfeld. *Apple to the Core.* London: Sphere, 1972.

McCabe, Peter, and Robert D. Schonfeld. *John Lennon: For the Record.* New York: Bantam, 1984.

McCartney, Linda. *Linda McCartney's Plates for '78 Diary.* London: MPL Communications Limited, 1977.

McCartney, Linda. *Linda's Pictures.* New York: Ballantine, 1976.

McCartney, Linda. *Photographs.* London: MPL Communications, 1982.

McCartney, Mike. *Thank U Very Much: Mike McCartney's Family Album.* London: Sidgwick and Jackson, 1981.

McCartney, Paul. *Give My Regards to Broad Street.* London: Pavilion Books, 1984.

McCartney, Paul. *Paul McCartney: Composer/Artist.* London: Pavilion Books, 1981.

McWhirter, Norris, ed. *Guinness Book of World Records.* New York: Bantam, 1986.

Mellers, Wilfred. *Twilight of the Gods: The Music of the Beatles.* New York: Schirmer Books, 1973.

Mendelsohn, John. *Paul McCartney: A Biography in Words and Pictures.* New York: Sire-Chappell, 1977.

Miles. *John Lennon in His Own Words.* London: Omnibus Press, 1981.

Norman, Philip. *Shout! The True Story of the Beatles.* New York: Simon and Schuster, 1980.

Ocean, Humphrey. *The Ocean View.* London: MPL Communications/Plexus Books, 1983.

Palmer, Tony. *All You Need Is Love: The Story of Popular Music.* London: Weidenfeld and Nicholson, 1976.

Pang, May, and Henry Edwards. *Loving John: The Untold Story.* New York: Warner Books, 1983.

Pascall, Jeremy. *Paul McCartney and Wings.* London: Hamlyn, 1977.

Reinhart, Charles. *You Can't Do That: Beatles Bootlegs & Novelty Discs.* Ann Arbor: Pierian Press, 1981.

Rolling Stone. *The Rolling Stone Interviews.* New York: Paperback Library, 1971.

Rolling Stone. *The Beatles.* Introduction by Leonard Bernstein. New York: Rolling Stone Press/Times Books, 1980.

Rolling Stone, eds of. *The Ballad of John and Yoko.* Garden City, New York: Doubleday/Dolphin, 1982.

Russell, J. P. *The Beatles on Record.* New York: Charles Scribner's Sons, 1982.

Salewicz, Chris. *McCartney.* New York: St. Martin's Press, 1986.

Scaduto, Anthony. *The Beatles.* New York: Signet, 1968.

Schaffner, Nicholas. *The Beatles Forever.* London: McGraw-Hill, 1978.

Schaffner, Nicholas. *The Boys from Liverpool: John, Paul, George, Ringo.* London: Methuen, 1980.

Schaumburg, Ron. *Growing Up with the Beatles.* New York: Pyramid Books, 1976.

Schultheiss, Tom. *The Beatles: A Day in the Life.* Ann Arbor, Michigan: Pierian Press, 1980.

Schwartz, Francie. *Body Count.* San Francisco: Straight Arrow Books, 1972.

Sheff, David, and G. Barry Golson. *The Playboy Interviews with John Lennon and Yoko Ono.* New York: Playboy Press, 1982.

Shotton, Pete, and Nicholas Schaffner. *John Lennon: In My Life.* New York: Stein & Day, 1983.

Southall, Brian. *Abbey Road.* London: Patrick Stephens Ltd., 1982.

Spence, Helen. *The Beatles Forever.* London: Colour Library Books, 1982.

Stannard, Neville. *The Beatles. A History of the Beatles on Record: The Long and Winding Road, Volume I.* London: Virgin Books, 1982.

Stannard, Neville. *The Beatles. A History of the Beatles on Record: Working Class Heroes, Volume II.* London: Virgin Books, 1983.

Taylor, Derek. *As Time Goes By.* London: Sphere Books, 1974.

Taylor, Derek. *Fifty Years Adrift.* London: Genesis Publications, 1984.

Taylor, Derek. *It Was Twenty Years Ago Today.* New York: Fireside Books, 1987.

Tremlett, George. *The Paul McCartney Story*. London: Future, 1975.

Wallgren, Mark. *The Beatles on Record*. New York: Simon and Schuster, 1982.

Welch, Chris. *Paul McCartney: The Definitive Biography*. London: Proteus Books, 1984.

Wenner, Jann. *Lennon Remembers*. San Francisco: Straight Arrow Books, 1971.

White, Timothy. *Rock Stars*. New York: Stewart, Tabori, and Chang, Inc., 1984.

Wiener, Jon. *Come Together: John Lennon in His Time*. New York: Random House, 1984.

Williams, Allan, and William Marshall. *The Man Who Gave the Beatles Away*. London: Coronet, 1975.

Woffinden, Bob. *The Beatles Apart*. London: Proteus Books, 1981.

Index of Names

(excluding Paul McCartney, John Lennon, George Harrison, and Ringo Starr, who are mentioned throughout this book)